To meli:
Ông ngoại

# Voices from Colorado

## Perspectives of Asian Pacific Americans

By

**Nestor J. Mercado**

**Elnora Minoza-Mercado**

and

**Alok Sarwal, Ph.D.**

**Denver, Colorado**
**Mercado Information & Business Services**

**2008**

**Cover Design:** Cover designed by Andrew Harris, of Quench Creative, and Alok Sarwal. At Right: The calligraphy symbol for "Hope" is provided by Harrison Tu; Bottom Left: Professional Thai dancers, instructor Pornnapa Boontha, and Rachun Charoenkaensai, at a performance for Colorado Asian Health Education and Promotion's cultural sharing event held in March 2008; Middle Left: boat race at the July 2007 Colorado Dragon Boat Festival, photograph taken by Kit Williams; Top Left: Asian children representing our true "Hope" for the future.



Library of Congress Control Number: 2008904981

ISBN: 978-0-615-20213-6
Record Number: 112776

*Printed in the United States of America*

Mercado Information & Business Services (MIBS)
1701 Orchard Dr.
Denver, CO 80221
303-635-6925
303-683-2509

voicesfromcolorado@gmail.com

Turkey
Georgia
Armenia
Azerbaijan
Kazakhstan
Uzbekistan
Mongolia
North Korea
Sea of Japan
Japan
Iraq
Turkmenistan
Kyrgyzstan
South Korea
Iran
Tajikistan
Afghanistan
East China Sea
UAE
Saudi Arabia
Pakistan
China
Nepal
Taiwan
Bhutan
Oman
India
Bangladesh
Philippine Sea
Myanmar
Arabian Sea
Laos
South China Sea
Thailand
Philippines
Bay of Bengal
Cambodia
Vietnam
Andaman Sea
Sri Lanka
Brunei
Maldives
Malaysia
Singapore
Indian Ocean
Indonesia

Map of Asia

# Table of Contents

# FOREWORD

As a sociologist and university faculty member, I have had the privilege of being in the field of Asian American studies since 1970, just after it came into existence, and of helping to develop courses and programs in this field, first at the University of Washington, then beginning in 1973 at the University of Colorado at Boulder, and for the past seventeen years at the University of Colorado Denver. Like others in this field, one of my basic goals has been to disseminate information about Americans of Asian and Pacific Islander background/descent through teaching, research, writing, and as an advocate in a variety of settings. When I write, I am motivated to give Asian Pacific Americans more visibility, enhance existing knowledge of these diverse peoples, and correct misunderstandings about the real complexities of Asian Pacific American lives, accomplishments, social and economic issues, resistance to injustice, and cultural and community adaptation and persistence. The authors of this book are motivated by this same desire.

The pages of *Voices from Colorado: Perspectives of Asian Pacific Americans* provide an abundance of factual material. However, the true core of this book are the words--the stories, observations, opinions, and advice--of individual Asian Pacific Americans (APAs) as they talk or write about their lives and families; values and beliefs; work experiences and achievements; community activities and leadership; cultural heritage and ethnic identity; prejudice and discrimination; and APA concerns and needs. These words are woven into the book's chapters on APA economic, organizational, educational, and social/health service endeavors and other topics such as community social and cultural leaders, festivals, media and the creative arts, the Japanese American internment, and current issues. Presenting the words of individuals is extremely important since it allows Colorado's Asian Pacific Americans themselves, and not others, to define who and what they are. The result is an intricate portrait of this vital part of Asian Pacific America. In addition, Colorado's APAs are an ever-changing population, and their suggestions and hopes for the future, especially regarding greater political empowerment, are a window on what might lie ahead. Readers will be struck by the wealth of APA skills and talents and by the dedication and sense of commitment of individuals the authors correctly characterize as "catalysts of change." Their words will resonate with other Asian Pacific Americans as well as those of different backgrounds.

From a broader perspective, *Voices from Colorado* is noteworthy for several reasons. It gives attention to many Asian Pacific American groups, and it has a strong contemporary focus. The few previously published books on Colorado's APAs examine specific groups, and most of them concentrate on past history. Also, the contents of this book challenge longstanding misconceptions, for example that APAs are "all alike;" that they are only proficient in scientific and technical occupations and not in other areas; that they are passive followers, never dynamic leaders; that APAs are a "model minority" and don't face any problems; and that they are "perpetual foreigners" who are "outsiders" and not an integral part of America's past, present, and future. More generally, *Voices from Colorado* serves as a reminder of the ethnic and racial heterogeneity of Colorado and that there are vibrant Asian Pacific American communities all across the United States, not just in urban areas of the West and Northeast.

I am honored that Nora and Nestor Mercado have asked me to write this foreword. They are well-known, longtime APA community leaders, and adjectives like "dedicated" and "committed" only begin to describe them. I first met the Mercados in the mid-1970s just after writing a successful state grant proposal to fund the first Japanese American community pilgrimage to Amache, a World War II concentration camp in Colorado. They approached me about getting a grant for a community-based Tagalog language and Filipino American history/culture class for youth. My first impression of the Mercados was that they were very proactive educators. While I now appreciate many more things about them, this impression of the Mercados is certainly strengthened by *Voices from Colorado* and also by their earlier publications work. For ten years, the Mercados edited the *Asian Pacific American Times*. They used this pan-Asian newspaper as a vehicle to introduce a broad audience to Asian Pacific Americans and to improve the flow of information within local APA communities. In 1991 and 2002, the Mercados coauthored and coedited respectively two publications that preserve much the organizational history of the Colorado Filipino American community so that it can be passed on future generations. Like the Mercados, *Voices from Colorado* coauthor Alok Sarwal is a prominent and respected Asian Pacific American community leader. He is an engineer and is best known for his work on

APA health issues, particularly as the executive director of Colorado Asian Health Education and Promotion and with many other state-wide public health organizations and programs, including the Interagency Health Disparity Leadership Council and Governor's Health Information Technology Council. It is through the tireless efforts of the Mercados, Alok Sarwal, and other community activists that Asian Pacific Americans will indeed become more visible.

Even with my extensive career as an Asian Americanist, I gained a deeper understanding of the diverse Asian Pacific American population in Colorado from reading this book. I am certain others will as well if they listen carefully to the voices on these pages.

Russell Endo
Boulder, Colorado
May 2008

# ACKNOWLEDGMENTS

Our grateful thanks and acknowledgment are given to Joseph "Noli" Lopez, CEO/Publisher and Concepcion Lopez, Chief Financial Officer of "Asian Pacific American Times," who provided us with the rare opportunity to serve as editors of the paper, opening the doors for us to meet the wonderful APAs who contributed to this book. We also recognize el-Dani Aguila, cartoonist, Rawley G. Soberano, Ph.D. and Maria Concepcion Panlilio for allowing us to reprint some of their columns in this book.

We especially thank Frankie Anderson, Aurora Asian/Pacific Community Partnership, faithful friend and honest critic, for her major role in the final review of this book.

We also acknowledge William Wei, Ph.D. and Daryl Maeda, Ph.D., both from the University of Colorado, Boulder, who advised and provided us with a selection of materials for our research on the history of Asian settlers in Colorado.

Grateful thanks to John Chin, former Academic Officer of Front Range Community College, Westminster, Colorado, for reviewing important portions of the manuscript and for offering valuable advise to improve the contents of the book.

We especially acknowledge the suggestions of Joseph "Joe" Nguyen, editor-in-chief of AsiaXpress.com who helped edit the first chapters of this book; Patricia Eskoz, retired librarian and good friend; and Miflora M. Gatchalian, Ph.D. and Jose C. Gatchalian, Ph.D. former professors of the University of the Philippines, who reviewed and edited several chapters and offered valuable suggestions to improve the overall contents of the book.

We want to thank our families for enduring long hours spent by us in this project: particularly for the Sarwal family: Anjali, Rahul and Ashwin and their grandparents living in India. The authors have known each other for over eight years and worked together in developing newspaper articles and collaborated on numerous social and cultural projects. This has been an inspirational experience.

Last but not least, we thank all the interviewees and all those who made the publication of this book possible.

# PREFACE

Helen Zia, a prominent activist and book author states, "I've been struck time and again by how little is really known about us and the America we are part of; how the rich textures of who we are, why we are here and what we bring to America remain absent from the picture. But a community as large, diverse, and dynamic as the Asian American and Pacific Islander peoples cannot stay on the edge of obscurity, frustrated by images that have rendered us invisible and voiceless, while other American communities wonder why we are at the center of key issues of the day."

This was written eight years ago, yet Asian Pacific Americans (APAs), particularly in Colorado, remain invisible and voiceless in many aspects of American political, cultural and social life.

Two of the book's authors, Nestor and Nora Mercado, were editors of the *Asian Pacific American Times* for ten years (1996–2006). They wanted to do something about this invisibility of APAs not only in Colorado but also in the nation. They tried to reach out to the general public during their tenure by writing and publishing not only about APA activities in Colorado but also on critical issues and concerns affecting them. They celebrated APA contributions on many occasions and announced their achievements as they occurred. Through the newspaper, they created and maintained communications among APA individuals and organizations and discovered their eagerness to be known and recognized as Americans. The co-author, Alok Sarwal, in his role as community leader, has also developed many positive relationships with APA immigrants. His involvement in APA cultural issues, but more significantly, in understanding and supporting their health and human service needs, provided him a deeper understanding of the challenges of living as an APA in Colorado. They all believe that APAs would like to share their culture and continue to contribute to American society.

All three of this book's authors feel that there is a need for concerted APA efforts to increase the quality and volume of their message so that they can be heard and appreciated. The visibility of APAs can be effectively enhanced through education and participation in civic, political and humanitarian activities, which will benefit not only APAs but also everyone else.

When people ask, "Where do you come from?" or "Do you speak English?" they see APAs as foreigners and they only look at the color of their skin or the shape of their eyes. Moreover, they really don't know much about APA history and how some APA groups have been here for centuries. In many instances, APAs may see such inquiries as caused by a lack of information, perhaps due to an educational system that often continues not to include material on APAs. On some occasions, APAs may even regard this as some form of discrimination or indifference, that learning about APAs is not a high priority. The authors respectfully disagree with the latter and now attempt to improve the situation. The distinct, rich, and long history of APAs merits more than a casual review. Today, APAs from over 40 countries and their descendents now live in the United States and have become a productive population that continues to grow at a very rapid pace. Thus, a book such as this is very necessary. While it attempts to describe the past and the present, it also projects the future. The book attempts to clearly cover all relevant aspects of the APA experience in Colorado.

APAs need not remain invisible in American society. They can be a potent force in the political arena and in decision-making bodies of the government. APAs play a significant role in the U.S. economy and continue to be leaders for positive change through teaching, research, business development, and public affairs. As part of the nation, APAs continue to enrich and strengthen the cultural fabric of American society. They subscribe to the principles of freedom and equality and believe in Martin Luther King, Jr's famous statement that America is a "nation where men will not be judged by the color of their skin but by the content of their character."

Who are Asian Pacific Americans? Where do they come from? Why did or do they come to the U.S.? These questions need to be answered in order to develop a clearer picture. There already is information about APAs in libraries throughout the country. However, this book should make it more accessible and hopefully will encourage the public school systems and universities to include more about APAs in their curricula.

The three authors arrived on America's shores as immigrants and have personal knowledge of the experiences described in this book. They joined the ranks of APAs who came before us and have a deep respect for the opportunities they have created. APAs came to America for a better life and a strong future for their children. They understand the importance of the strong democratic forces that have existed here for the past 230 years. APAs from China, the Philippines and Japan, began coming to the U.S. over 150 years ago and created distinct paths of social and economic development in the U.S. Other APAs came later but also continue to contribute to the development of America.

Through the years, they have been privileged to get acquainted with APA community leaders and public officials in Colorado. They are featuring some of them in this book. They hope this book will inspire and encourage APA youth to become better informed and respect their core values and cultural roots in order to develop as future leaders. They especially envision youth preparing for future civic and humanitarian activities, which will benefit the welfare and well being of all Coloradans. They also hope to encourage APAs to develop opinions and not be shy about voicing them. APAs must share their views and engage in dialogue with others in a constructive manner, for only through communication--- spoken and written --- can everyone become fully informed and well connected. At the same time, they hope those in the corporate world who have supported APA goals in the past will continue to sponsor their activities and causes, for example scholarships for youth and educational programs for the greater community. They hope this book will inspire greater philanthropy for causes that bring to fruition the dreams of immigrants as they embrace visions of America in a manner similar to those of earlier migrants.

APAs, through their contributions, have given back to a nation that has provided them with opportunities to enjoy a better life. They hope the subsequent chapters of this book will present information to fulfill every reader's quest for knowledge about Asian and Pacific Americans. This journey or inquiry can take some effort but prove to be very rewarding. They also hope that this book will engage readers so they will want to continue learning more about APAs in the future.

Through this book, they hope they have captured and conveyed the America of Colorado's APAs, and that it will help fellow Americans better understand Asian and Pacific Americans.

# Introduction

Asian Pacific Americans (APAs) have been one of the fastest growing groups in the United States since 1970. However, much information is still lacking about their true socioeconomic and sociocultural status. According to a 2008 Census Bureau report, there are 14.9 million APAs in the U.S. and they comprise five percent of the total U.S. population; it is projected that by 2050 there will be 33.4 million APAs and they will make up eight percent of the population. At this time, Colorado has about 160,400 APAs and they comprise 3.3% of the total Colorado population. The Asian-Pacific census category is diverse as it includes people who trace their backgrounds to 30 Asian nations and 25 Pacific Island nations that speak more than 50 languages and dialects. Colorado APAs reflect this cultural and linguistic diversity. Therefore, an understanding of the experiences of this population requires more than a casual review and suggests the need for a study of the complexity associated with the peoples who migrated from some of the oldest and richest cultures in the world.

Asian and Pacific American economic contributions to Colorado and America may not be fully appreciated, but certainly APAs have and will continue to make a significant impact in the years ahead. APAs represent a significant portion of the educated workforce in Colorado and the U.S. In Colorado, Asian Pacific Americans still lack the political power and collective clout to have substantial influence at most policy-making levels of local and state government. However, Colorado's APAs also possess strong family values, rich cultures, and inner strengths and convictions that can be appreciated by everyone as long as their voices are heard and their contributions to society are recognized.

The cultural and historical background of APAs are explored initially in this book, including how Asian cultures have evolved and the role of two great civilizations, China and India, as well as European colonization. The diversity of APA communities due to the differences in religions, languages, customs and traditions is also discussed. This book presents brief historical background material on APAs and demographic information regarding APAs in Colorado based on the 2000 census and projections.

The highlights of this book are the interviews conducted with APAs in Colorado. Originally, the first two authors based these interviews on the APAs they met during their tenure as editors of the *Asian Pacific American Times*. The third author, who provided additional interviewees, enhanced their efforts. Most of the interviewees are community leaders and volunteers. In the process of updating their information, the authors received many referrals to other APAs. The interviewees are a cross-section of APAs in Colorado, but because of time and financial constraints, they are only a small sampling of the people who could be included in this book. However all of these individuals serve as catalysts of change because their achievements and community service greatly enhance the visibility of APAs in Colorado. Many are outstanding figures in fields such as business, sociocultural affairs, agriculture, technology and architecture, health and medicine, and humanitarian services.

In answers to specific questions, interviewees gave their views on what it is like to be APAs in the U.S and described their lives and experiences. While many are first generation immigrants to the U.S., others are second or later generation American-born APAs. The interviewees are mostly adults, but some youth were interviewed to get perspectives on their lives in America and views of the future. This multi-generational approach allows the authors to weave a coherent picture of APAs and provide insights into their acculturation through the years in the U.S. The readers will read about the experiences of these interviewees and notice that they are dramatically different from those of the first Asian immigrants who came to Colorado in the late 1880's and early 1900's.

An important objective of the book is to bring out Asian Pacific American issues and concerns, including racial profiling, prejudice and discrimination. A useful article on diversity training is included to clarify some misconceptions about APAs. A Yankelovich survey in 2001, commissioned by the Committee of 100, provides insights into the nature of attitudes toward APAs. This survey reveals that a lack of education is one of the most probable explanations for prejudicial views. It also states that a majority of non-APAs cannot make meaningful distinctions between Asian Pacific Americans of different backgrounds.

Asian Pacific American community organizations, as well as health, educational, civic and religious groups, are important to each APA group for support and preservation of culture. In this book, they present community activities such as festivals and celebrations of ethnic holidays. The Colorado Dragon Boat Festival is a special feature, which is described in the chapter on pan-Asian community organizations. A chapter on education highlights outstanding educators and provides insights on the development and adjustments of younger APAs through the interviews with two directors of university Asian American student service programs regarding their experiences with APA students. A special section on APA creative arts is also featured in this book. The

Japanese American Day of Remembrance is covered in a special chapter, which includes the words of those who experienced first-hand this unfortunate part of U.S. history. Another feature of this book is interviews with three APA television news anchor/reporters in the chapter on media.

Material from the *Asian Pacific American Times* newspaper has been reprinted in this book. These include articles and columns from guest writers such as John Yee and Gil Asakawa as well as opinions and commentaries on APA communities, photos and an editorial cartoon related to topics in the book.

As a conclusion, we present a summary and analysis of the interviewees' comments and their recommendations for the future. The appendix of this book also includes an article on how Frankie Anderson, a non-APA, successfully worked with APAs to provide cultural services to the Aurora and metropolitan Denver communities. Articles on the song "God Bless America," the Bataan Death March, and Filipino veterans' unsettled issues are included to remind readers of the close relationship between the Philippines and the United States. They also added information on two Asian national heroes and an article by John Yee, "China's Contributions to the World". A table of statistics on census counts and estimates to accompany Chapter 3, a representative list of Asian Pacific American media in Colorado and a bibliography are also provided. The end of the appendix contains a checklist of contact information to organizations listed in the book as well as a simplified index to interviewees and organizations.

# Chapter 1

# ASIAN PACIFIC AMERICANS: AN INTRODUCTION

Asian Pacific Americans are from, or descendents of individuals originally from, Asia and the Pacific islands. The first part of this chapter gives some background on Asia and the Pacific islands and on Asian culture. The chapter then covers some values shared by many Asian Pacific Americans.

Asia, the largest continent in the world, is subdivided into three major areas. The Pacific islands constitute a fourth area in the Asia/Pacific region.

East Asia includes major economic powers: China, Japan, Rep. of Korea and Taiwan, with Japan considered the second largest economy in the world. China, with an average annual economic growth of 9-10%, is predicted to be the dominant economic leader in Asia in the near future. Taiwan and South Korea are democratic and highly developed countries. The prevailing religion in East Asia is Buddhism.

South Asia is primarily composed of India, Pakistan, Bangladesh and Sri Lanka (formerly Ceylon). India, in recent years, has experienced tremendous economic growth. It has become a hub of high-technology industry. Bangalore, a southern Indian city with its technology economy is well known for its burgeoning middle class. Kolkata (formerly Calcutta) has one of the most vibrant cultural scenes in India, as literature, dance, modern art and music are all thriving there. India is the largest democratic nation in the world with a population of more than 1 billion. A majority of Indians are Hindus. Pakistan and Bangladesh are predominantly Muslim countries. Pakistan is a developing country, while Bangladesh is economically less developed.

Southeast Asia includes the Philippines, Malaysia (used to be a British colony), Indonesia, Thailand, Singapore, Vietnam, Laos, Cambodia and Myanmar (formerly Burma). Southeast Asia is more diverse with countries experiencing different stages of economic development. Philippines is the only predominantly Christian country in Asia. Around 87% of Filipinos are Christian (mostly Catholic, 7% are Muslim, mainly residing on Mindanao). It has a democratic form of government and is still considered a developing economy.

Malaysia is a country with several ethnic groups such as Malays, Chinese and Muslims. Malaysia has a stable, developing economy.

Indonesia is the largest Muslim country in the world. Although a developing economy, Indonesia has rich natural resources. Like most other Southeast Asian countries, the Indonesian economy is dominated by an ethnic Chinese business population.

Thailand is a Buddhist country and the only Asian nation, which has never been a European or American colony. Its royal family is highly respected. Like Malaysia, it is a developing country with better prospect for future economic growth than many other Asian nations. Thailand has attracted more tourists from all over the world than any other Southeast Asian country.

Singapore is the only highly developed country in Southeast Asia, with a high per capita income, close to that of the United States. Its population is predominantly of Chinese background.

Vietnam is a communist country but has opened its economy to foreign investments. It is a developing economy and has a relatively large population of Chinese background. Basically a Buddhist country, other religions, such as Christianity (introduced by the Portuguese and French) and Taoism now exist side-by-side.

Laos, Cambodia and Myanmar are Buddhist countries, although animism is still practiced, especially in Laos. They are economically less-developed countries with agrarian economies.

Smaller areas in Asia include Brunei, oil-rich Sikkim, Bhutan, the Maldive Islands and Nepal.

The Pacific Islands include Guam, Samoa, Fiji, Papua New Guinea, Solomon, Vanuatu and Kiribati. Guam is a territory of the United States. Fiji is a republic and Samoa's official name is the Independent State of Samoa.

The entire region of Asia has a total area of 8 million square miles and holds 61% of the world's population. China and India each have populations of more than one billion. Asian Pacific Americans come from Asian backgrounds and, in fact, Asian-born residents in the United States comprise one-fourth of the total foreign-born population. The major countries of origin include Vietnam, Korea, American Samoa, India, Thailand, the Philippines and China. However, Asian Pacific Americans also include large numbers of American-born descendents of migrants originally from Asia.

## Asian Cultures

Culture is determined by several variables, including religion, language, philosophy and levels of economic and social development, foreign influences, and geographic location. More recently, the United Nations Educational, Scientific and Cultural Organization (UNESCO) described culture as follows: "culture should be regarded as the set of distinctive spiritual, material, intellectual and emotional features of society or a social group, and it encompasses, in addition to art and literature, lifestyles, ways of living together, value systems, traditions and beliefs."

Religion or faith, such as Buddhism, Islam, Christianity, Hinduism and Taoism dominates Asia. There are a great number of different and distinct Asian languages. Confucian philosophy from China has greatly shaped the behavior of the peoples of Asia through the years, for instance influencing the social organization of families and governments. In addition, centuries of European colonization have influenced the cultures of various Asian countries.

Each Asian country has its own distinct culture. The discussion here will focus on three major factors that have influenced Asian cultures: the civilizations of China and India, interregional trade, and the influence of Western cultures.

**Two great ancient civilizations,** Chinese and Indian are the roots of most Asian cultures. The root culture for almost the entire region of East and Southeast Asia is Chinese. The cultures of Japan, Korea and Vietnam are offshoots of Chinese culture. China's remarkable material accomplishments and inventions gave her culture an aura of superiority, which contributed to its spread in this part of the world. Confucian tradition and philosophy place a high value on education and literacy and emphasize the importance of the family and moral and ethical behavior.

India, another country with an ancient civilization, has had a great influence on Asia. Buddhism started in India and spread to China, Japan, and Southeast Asia. Filipinos absorbed some of the elements of Indian culture through the Hinduized Malays who came to the Philippines to settle permanently starting in the 15$^{th}$ century before the coming of the Europeans.

**Interregional trade** has existed for a long time. Centuries before the advent of European colonization in Asia, there already were brisk interregional trading activities among peoples of Asia, including the Chinese, Indians, Japanese, and even Persians and Arabs. These peoples exchanged not only goods but also their cultures. Arabs introduced the Muslim religion to Indonesia, and through Indonesia and Brunei, this religion was spread to the southern Philippines.

From the tenth through fourteenth centuries, relationships between the Philippines and India were established through trade in Southeast Asia. Rajeet Mitter, Indian Ambassador to the Philippines, in his speech celebrating India's 58$^{th}$ anniversary of independence, stated,

"Philippines-India relation has a long history. Our friendship goes back into the distant past, when immigrants and traders from Indonesia and Malacca Peninsula brought Indian influence over the Malacca waters and overland with Indo-China. Both of our nations shared a similar struggle against colonialism. Indian independence in 1947 closely followed the independence of the Philippines in 1946."

Japanese traders started coming as early as the 15th century to the Philippines. Sixteen Japanese ships a year were calling at Manila up to the end of the sixteenth century. The Malay Peninsula and islands of Southeast Asia have served as transit points for Eastern and Western merchandise. Arabs, Persians, Indians and Chinese traders met here by the hundreds and large number of them settled with the native populations of Asia.

It is reasonable to assume that early Filipinos migrated from South China down the coast of southeastern Asia and the Malay Peninsula. From the ninth to the 15th centuries Arabs and other Muslim merchants and sailors dominated the Southeast Asian trade.

To summarize, the Indians were the first to see the commercial possibilities in interregional trade, and by the ninth century Asians were taking advantage of these possibilities. Interregional trade established close relationships among Asian peoples. Even in Southeast Asia, music, arts and folk dances show regional similarities.

**The influence of Western cultures** and the rise of European powers in the 15th century --- especially, Spain, Great Britain, France, Portugal and Holland --- started an age of exploration and conquest of Asian countries. Later in the 19th century, the United States acquired the Philippines from Spain by virtue of the 1898 Treaty of Paris. Christianity was introduced by Spain to the Philippines. Americans introduced the democratic form of government, established an educational system with English as the medium of instruction, and spread their culture in the Philippines. America relinquished control of the Philippines on July 4, 1946. Because of the occupation of the Philippines by Spain for more than 300 years and the United States for 46 years, the Philippines has become the most Westernized country in Asia. The so-called "colonial mentality" of Filipinos is a carry-over of such a long occupation, implanting in their minds the superiority of Western culture. This even had an effect on Filipino American identity.

In the 19th century, China was fragmented by foreign powers that competed for control of trade with this country. Great Britain acquired Hong Kong and Macau became a Portuguese colony. The French occupied Southeast Asia and introduced French culture, food and language and Christianity to what are now the countries of Vietnam,

Laos and Cambodia. The Vietnam War later brought American influences to these areas. The Dutch colonized Indonesia though their cultural influence was probably lessened by their primary interest in trade and commerce. The British had an important cultural impact on what are now the countries of India, Malaysia, Pakistan, and Bangladesh. Their influences can still be seen, for example, in the areas of government, the physical infrastructure, education and in the widespread use of the English language.

After World War II, almost all the Asian colonies of Western powers gained their independence: the Philippines from the United States; Vietnam, Laos and Cambodia from France; India, Myanmar, Pakistan, Bangladesh, Malaysia and Sri Lanka from Great Britain; Indonesia from Holland; Macau from Portugal. Hong Kong was reacquired by China from Great Britain.

## Shared Values of Asian and Pacific Americans

In spite of the diversities of their cultures, Asians have some shared values. These values were brought to America by Asian immigrants.

In this section, we will discuss a few shared values of Asian Pacific Americans (APAs). While the APA population is diverse, some common values need to be taken into consideration to better understand them. It should also be pointed out that while these values are widespread, adaptation to life in America has changed the ways they are expressed and diluted the influence of some values over time. This is especially the case for second-generation American-born children of Asian immigrants and for subsequent APA generations.

In many Asian countries, the family is sacred. In the Philippines, for instance, the 1973 and 1987 Constitutions declare, "The State recognizes the sanctity of family life and shall protect and strengthen the family as a basic social institution." Thus, the family is the basic institution from which all other institutions draw their strength. It is the place where the child first encounters his faith and learns the meaning of parental authority and filial piety, of love, generosity, service and sacrifice. In Korea, the family also is the foundation of all aspects of life. The family is more important than the individual. Children in a traditional Korean home are trained to respect their parents and older persons. Asian parents often sacrifice their own personal comfort for their children's well being. In fact, even the poorest Asians may sell their only piece of land or beast of burden or the clothes on their back if necessary to be able to send their children to school. As a common practice, the oldest child is also expected to sacrifice for his younger brothers and sisters in the same way his parents have done for him or her.

Extended families are common among APAs, especially those who are recent immigrants. Aside from parents and their children, aunts, uncles, grandparents and cousins may also live in the same household. The extended families ensured that no person would live alone in complete isolation. Asian immigrants have carried over this custom to the U.S. Often, individuals who have just arrived in the U.S. from Asia are welcomed to live temporarily with their U.S. relatives until they can fend for themselves.

Respect for elders is a family-related value among Asian Pacific Americans. Elders are traditionally looked upon as a source of wisdom from whom young people could seek advice and comfort. In many APA families, especially those of recent immigrants, parents still exercise considerable authority over their children. Children, in return, respect the advice of their parents. Young children are taught never to talk back to their parents and to their older siblings. Even when they become adults, APA children might consult their parents before they decide on important matters.

In the Philippines, the word "po" is a sign of respect for older people, whether related (older brothers and sisters, uncles and aunts) or not and for those in authority. Furthermore, in the Philippines, younger members of the family call their older sisters, Ate (Ah-tee), older brothers, Kuya, or the aunts and uncles Tita or Tito respectively and it is considered disrespectful or impolite to call them by their first names.

A unique sign of respect for elders in the Philippines is called "amen" where the younger children press the extended hand of the parent or older member of the family on the forehead. This is a beautiful custom also called "mano po." Most Filipino parents and elders have preserved this custom in the U.S. Unfortunately, in the U.S. the importance of this value has tended to diminish somewhat over time.

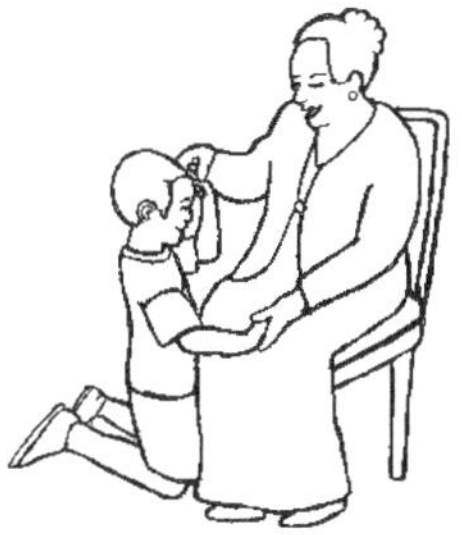

Collective responsibility is another family-related value in Asia that is important to Asian Pacific Americans, especially recent immigrants. This value refers to relationships among family members in which support and assistance are provided because of a strong sense of duty to the family. Every family member, for instance, has specific obligations they must fulfill to ensure the family's welfare. Often, family members are expected to suppress individual desires if these impair the whole family's well being.

In addition, the behaviors of each family member affect the reputation of the entire family. What this means is that the achievements of individual members enhance the reputation of the entire family while negative activities bring dishonor and shame.

The importance of maintaining harmony in interpersonal relationships is a key Asian value that is expressed in the behavior of Asian Pacific Americans. For example, it is common for Asian immigrants, especially in the workplace, to avoid conflict. An individual who has a major disagreement with his or her boss might appear to be indifferent or passively agreeable in order to avoid an undesirable confrontation. Another manifestation of this value is to withhold the open expression of feelings. Such behaviors often are misunderstood by non-Asians as timidity or even lack of honesty.

An important value in Asia that has been retained by Asian Pacific Americans is the importance of education for future success. This value can be seen in the high percentage of APA youth who aspire to a college or graduate/professional school education and the support provided by APA parents for their children's education.

One discussion of customs and values is provided by Mr. Thong D. Nguyen who wrote of his experiences when he came to America in late 1970s. In this article, he shares his thoughts as he compares values in Vietnam with contemporary American life.

According to Thong D. Nguyen, in his article "Viewpoint of an old Vietnamese man on life in America," most old Vietnamese men living in old Vietnam, if given a chance, would be very happy to come to the U.S. America is a civilized and rich country with freedom and democracy, which is especially important to Vietnamese people given the restrictive nature of the socialist system in Vietnam.

An old Vietnamese man comes to the U.S. with the belief that life will be a paradise in America. As the days pass, however, the old man begins to feel very lonely, because here, all his children either go to work or to school. The language barrier is very difficult and inconvenient to all elderly Vietnamese people. Some can speak English, but most don't. Because of this, the elderly rarely answer the phone when their family is not at home. In Vietnam, when a man leaves the house, he meets his acquaintances. They can converse together and are able to establish fellowship. In the U.S. because of the language barrier, the man can't even share news about his neighborhood with his next-door neighbors. This situation brings about loneliness to the old man.

Most Vietnamese old people are influenced by the doctrine of Confucius, Asia's great teacher. According to his teaching, old men are highly respected and are assisted in society when they reach elderly status. In America, nobody pays any attention or respect to the elderly people. They are not respected in public; there is little consideration given to the elderly population.

Confucius also teaches about sex. His teaching tells us about the subject of sex. It warns about seeing it or even talking about it. In the U.S., sexually explicit scenes are advertised in many places such as parking lots, buses, streets, movies, magazines, and too many other places to mention. This material is especially propagated through the TV, a place where children have the most access. These sexual depictions give bad examples and influences to children and young people. Particularly, programs like "The Jerry Springer Show" promote destructive sexual practices to young people. Old Vietnamese men believe that repeated exposure to these scenes numbs young people's senses of caring and could bring young men to crime in the future.

Life in America has two faces like a coin. On one face, there's opportunity for good education, access to basic necessities of life, and the freedom to choose your destiny. We have plenty of freedom here, to the extent that many take it for granted. On the other face, there are the bad influences such as greed, promiscuity and disrespect for people in general. Magazines, TV shows and other media that promote these vices can drain a person's spirituality. This is especially true for the young people and children of America. For the old Vietnamese man, life is both better and worse here. A very interesting life - maybe that's the reason for the appeal of American life.

Mr. Nguyen's experiences are similar to those of many older immigrant APAs who can often relate to sad but sometimes funny incidents, as they try to adjust to American life. The second and later generations of APAs have culturally adjusted to the American way of life, and many have successfully blended this with their Asian heritage. Among Asian immigrants, Filipinos and Asian Indians have perhaps adapted to America more easily than those from other countries because of their English-language fluency.

In an article by Ashton O. Do, "What is it like to be a Vietnamese born in the U.S." he complains that people ask much from you. "Do you speak Chinese?" "Are you from China?" when you are just an Asian kid born in the U.S. He wrote this when he was 12 years old. I'm Vietnamese and I live a life like any other kid around here. I was born in the U.S., and I still keep the Vietnamese tradition running in my life. It's not too much, but the only differences that I have with American kids are that I speak three languages, English, Vietnamese and (enough to have conversation) Spanish. I also have a large immediate family that gathers to socialize on holidays, (and birthdays) where most Americans keep individual and rarely gather with their immediate family. The next to last difference is that I live with a different culture where we celebrate different holidays, shop at very different stores, and do different arts and crafts (cooking, games), and we most of the time eat Vietnamese food. The last difference is that I have really strict parents with very strict rules (not like: "You must have correct posture!" Or silly things,) and punishments (which isn't fair once I learned what American kids go through,) - where American kids just get grounded. Other than that, I still dress, eat, read, write, sing, etc. like any other kid, only I occasionally get pestered about the "Are you Chinese?" thing. I love being Asian because I am different from Americans and get more family activities, AND getting a guest is just so cool because you get to do all this stuff for him/her that you usually don't do. I'm also proud to be Asian because I am, its just one of those things that you are happy about.

An example of how much sacrifice and hard work parents undergo for the sake of their children is demonstrated by the story of Katie Wong, one of the oldest Chinese Americans in Colorado. As a matter of fact, she sounds just like one of the early Asian settlers in America described in Chapter 2.

# Katie Wong

Katie Wong, 82, probably one of the oldest Chinese immigrants in Colorado, arrived in San Francisco, in 1948, 8 days before her oldest son, Stanley, was born. She married Albert Wong the year before in an arranged marriage, as was the custom in China. Her memory of that boat trip was very vivid. Their room was in the lowest section in the boat. Being pregnant and having no fresh air down there, she felt very sick. Her husband, solicitous of her condition, decided to do something about it. A WWII Army veteran, he decided to wear his Army uniform, went to see the captain and demanded that their living quarters be reassigned to the upper level. Sure enough, they were given rooms in the higher level. There she felt better until they arrived at their destination.

Born in Canton, China, Katie entered college at 14 and graduated in four years and immediately started teaching at 19. That was her experience back home, but when she arrived in America, she worked two jobs doing everything from cleaning to washing dishes in a restaurant. Her husband wanted a big family, because he grew up very lonely as an only child. His mother was in China; his father worked in the farm in California.

So Katie described her life working hard and having a family of seven children – five sons and two daughters. She is very proud of them and she loves all of them. She taught them well. They grew up disciplined, obedient and loving children.

Proudly, she rattles off the accomplishments of her children. Stanley is now a financial planner of a big company; Steven is a psychotherapist; Sandy is a restaurant manager, also teaches volleyball and is an opera singer (Oh, he recently sang to the Pope in the Vatican); Scott is a comptroller, Shirley is a dental hygienist; Susie, is a payroll manager, and Katie is proudest of her youngest son, Spencer, who is now an archaeologist, knows Spanish well and has been to Mexico 17 times because of his career.

Why is she so proud of Spencer? When he was 3 years old, he already knew arithmetic. He did not need a calculator. At 5, he was already the cashier at their family restaurant (Songhay Restaurant at

Colfax and Cherry), which the family owned and managed from 1975-1990. When customers paid, they would ask where his father or mother would be and he would answer, "They're around," as he handed them their receipt or change. Katie continues to talk about Spencer, who once took her to a restaurant one Mother's Day. He said, "Mama, order whatever you want." When she asked if he had money, he proudly answered, "I have $1.25." How she loves that boy!

When she came to America, she did not know any English. She learned from "her man," from her children, from work and from watching TV. Her children probably inherited her brains and her resourcefulness, because they all went to college on scholarship grants. But she disciplined them, army-style. From school, she assigned two of her sons to work at the restaurant on Mondays and Wednesdays, and the other two on Tuesdays and Thursdays. Each son would receive $5 each a day, whether they worked at home or at the restaurant. Those at home were required to eat, clean up and do their homework and all would obey Mama. They were good kids.

When Katie was asked, "What do you like most about America?" she immediately answered, "Freedom and opportunity. "Obey the law and work hard. There is a lot of opportunity to do whatever you like. You can go to school, start your own business and be good citizens."

Standing L-R: Spencer, Scott, Stanley, Sandy, Steven
Seated L-R: Shirley, Albert and Katie Wong, Susie

Her leadership in Colorado is quiet and unnoticed, but her influence is far and wide, especially among the older Chinese families in Colorado. In 1997, she received the first Mother of the Year Award from the Denver Chinese Cultural Center. When she was asked to give a speech, she felt scared at first, but she went on to thank the Center for giving her the award, then she welcomed all the guests, and she gave advice to the children. "Always love your mother and father." To the mothers, she said, "Always love your husband. Pray to God and learn to forgive. That is the only way. Teach love. Avoid the bad and forget bad things." To everyone, she said, "Be generous. The more you give, the more you have."

When someone asked her once, "Which is better -- America or China?" Her response was an indication of her wisdom. "America is only over 200 years old, while China is 4,700 years old." In other words, there's no comparison. It's like comparing a little boy to an old man.

Katie's husband, Albert Wong died recently but her love for him is still there. When they celebrated their 50th wedding anniversary, he gave her a necklace with 21 gold hearts. She said she needs only one heart for him. During our interview with her, she brought pictures of her family and when Albert received an award from the Organization of Chinese Americans for his military service. That was another proud moment of her life.

# Chapter 2

# ASIAN SETTLERS IN AMERICA AND COLORADO

## Background

A review of the literature on Asians in America shows that as early as 1565, Filipinos were the first to cross the Pacific Ocean to North America, landing in Mexico during the period of the Manila Galleon trade. In 1587, Filipino crewmembers of Nuestra Senora de Esperanza, a Spanish galleon captained by Unamuno, landed in Morro Bay, California. Later, in 1763, Filipinos began settling in southeastern Louisiana. However, the Chinese were the first Asians to come in large numbers to the U.S. Their migration began in 1848 to California. That was the year gold was discovered, leading many Chinese to go overseas to find their fortune. Chinese later worked as laborers, for instance building railroads and in the factories of San Francisco. Oftentimes, they faced a hostile environment and were exploited by unscrupulous whites. In 1882, the Chinese Exclusion Act was passed to end the entry to the U.S. of Chinese laborers.

The Chinese were followed by the Japanese, who entered the United States mainly from 1890 to 1924. Japanese migrants initially worked as laborers on the West Coast and on Hawaiian sugar plantations. Like their Chinese predecessors, they faced considerable anti-Asian agitation and discrimination and were known as the "Yellow Peril." In the early 1900s, President Theodore Roosevelt was afraid that discrimination against the Japanese in America would escalate into an international incident. In order to appease Japan and pressures at home from the anti-Japanese groups, the Gentlemen's Agreement was signed by the U.S and Japan in 1908. This agreement prohibited Japanese from issuing passports to Japanese laborers bound for the U.S. and thus ending Japanese labor immigration. All Japanese and Asian immigration to the U.S. was terminated by the 1924 Immigration Act.

In the early 1900s, Filipinos started coming to the U.S. as students (government- sponsored pensionados) since the Philippines was then a colony of the U.S. In the 1920s, Filipino laborers were recruited, particularly from the northern part of Luzon and later from the Visayan region. From 1909 to 1934 thousands of Filipinos were recruited by the Hawaiian Sugar Planters Association to work on sugar and pineapple plantations. Unmarried men were the only ones accepted, so many

Filipinos lied about their marital status. At about the same time, other Filipino laborers set their sights on the U.S. mainland. They worked in agriculture, as domestic servants, and as hotel and restaurant workers. In Alaska, they worked in the salmon canneries.

Although the Filipino migrants were considered American nationals, they were not entitled to citizenship, even though they deserved this as members of a U.S. "possession."

In Hawaii and on the U.S. mainland, Filipinos did backbreaking work. Those who were agricultural laborers had especially difficult experiences. Conditions were cruel and the pay was dreadfully low. Filipinos who unloaded, cleaned, cut and packed salmon in the canneries of Alaska were victimized by ruthless employers. When Filipinos tried to spend the little they earned at stores and restaurants, they often encountered inflammatory signs like: "No dogs or Filipinos allowed." Leaders of Filipino labor movements were persecuted and oftentimes tortured. However, despite these circumstances, Filipinos persevered to earn money and to support their families back home.

Filipino migration to the U.S. became a contentious issue. The steady influx of Filipino laborers to Pacific Coast states, primarily California, led the American Federation of Labor (AFL) and other organizations to propose that Filipinos be prohibited from entering the U.S. just like other Asians. These organizations, concerned with labor competition, justified Filipino exclusion on the grounds that Filipinos were undesirable additions to the racial composition of the American population. The 1934 Tydings-McDuffe Act effectively ended Filipino immigration.

As will be discussed below, small numbers of migrants from Korea and India also came to the U.S. prior to World War II. After the war, Asians from a variety of countries and people from the Pacific islands came to America in large numbers, especially after the passage of a liberal immigration act in 1965.

## Asian Settlers in Colorado

This section provides a brief history of Asian settlement in Colorado for background purposes. The available historical sources on this topic deal mostly with the early Japanese and Chinese in this state. Much less is known about other Asian groups.

### Chinese

Chin Lin Sou was recorded as one of the first Chinese to arrive in Colorado in 1850. He came to this state as a railroad laborer. In 1873, a daughter, Lilly Chin was born to his family. She is considered to be the first person of Chinese background to be born in Colorado. Sou got involved in mining. The Cameron Brothers of Clear Creek were one of Sou's employers. They hired him to oversee the Chinese who worked in the Cameron Placer Mines.

After the completion of the Central Pacific Railroad in 1869, more Chinese entered Colorado and eventually created a sizeable Chinese community in Denver. Other Chinese worked in mining towns such as Central City and Black Hawk and in the cities of Trinidad, Pueblo, Colorado Springs, Golden, Boulder, Loveland and Greeley.

During the latter part of the 1880s, the demand for cheap labor to meet the needs of Colorado's growing economy encouraged the hiring of Chinese laborers by various businesses, industries, and others. Chinese laborers were preferred because they were paid lower wages and because they were considered docile, apolitical, hardworking and uncomplaining. However, they faced resistance from European immigrants and other Euro-Americans. The Chinese were considered an economic threat and they faced discrimination and antiChinese violence. Because of their race and cultural characteristics, the Chinese were considered as aliens to the predominantly American society. Politicians, the media, and ordinary citizens referred to the Chinese by derogatory names such as chinks, Chinamen, coolies and heathens.

Despite the bitterness toward the Chinese, Patricia K. Ourada observed: "America has come to accept the fact that the dreams of our empire builders were realized in part through the effort of the Chinese coolie." Much of the early railroad system and other infrastructure of Colorado and the western United States were built with Chinese labor.

In 1880, it was estimated that there were at least 400 Chinese living in Denver's Chinatown on Wazee Street, a place whites called "Hop Alley." The Chinese were used as economic and political scapegoats by politicians and the media. This led to a riot on October 31, 1880. The Chinese community was destroyed, 300 were injured and one was killed. The Chinese population steadily declined after reaching a peak in 1890. Few Chinese entered Colorado over the next fifty years. By 1940, only three Chinese families – the Fongs, Looks and Chins remained in downtown Denver.

In 1943, the Magnuson Act ended an immigration policy that discriminated against the Chinese. The liberal policies of the Immigration Act of 1965 resulted in a dramatic increase in Chinese, as well as other Asian, immigration to the U.S and to Colorado. Today in the U.S., the Chinese are the largest Asian population followed by Filipinos.

## Japanese

The first Japanese to arrive in Colorado in 1879 was Matsudaira Tadaatsu. He left Japan in 1872 to work for the Union Pacific Railroad and was later appointed as assistant to the Colorado Chief Inspector of Mines in 1886. He received an engineering degree from Rutgers University.

The Japanese had a great impact on the early development of Colorado. When a Japanese visitor once asked, "What have the Japanese done in the century they have been in Colorado to make it a better state and a better place?" the late Bill Hosakawa, a respected and well-loved journalist, responded: "Much." This response, however, does not mean to overlook the contributions made by other Asians. Over the years, Japanese contributions to Colorado have been made in such fields as agriculture, business, technology, education, medicine, science, engineering, media, music, entertainment, government services and others.

Japanese began to arrive in Colorado in significant numbers in the early 1900s. By 1909, according to a government study, Colorado had a population of 6,000 Japanese. They first came as laborers to work on railroads and in coal mines. Later many were employed as laborers and then farmers in the agricultural regions of the Platte and Arkansas River valleys and the San Luis Valley. The Japanese were literate and ambitious individuals. Early Japanese farmers raised sugar beets and other crops and vegetables. Their legacy, which includes the well-known Sakata farms, still remains

In Denver as well as in other towns, Japanese business flourished. They provided needed goods and services. The largest concentration of these businesses developed along Denver's Larimer Street. There were grocery stores, restaurants, dry goods stores, supply outfits and hotels. Japanese businessmen often lived above or behind their establishments. The remnants of this community can be found in present-day Sakura Square, which includes the Tamai Towers apartment complex, the Buddhist Temple and other businesses.

The Pacific Mercantile Company, an Asian market, was opened in 1944. The founder, George Inai, came to America from Japan in 1915. With the help of his children, Susie, Sam and Robert, the store flourished and succeeded. Still located at 19$^{th}$ and Lawrence Streets in downtown Denver, the store continues to be family-owned and is now under the management of George's grandchildren, Kyle, Jolie and Kibo.

**Jolie Noguchi, granddaughter of George Inai. Jolie owns and manages Pacific Mercantile Company with Kyle and Kibo.**

## Filipinos

The first Filipino, recorded in Colorado, was Isidro Canlas. He was listed in the 1908 Denver telephone directory as a student living in Larimer St. The early Filipino settlers in Colorado came by way of Hawaii and California. The population remained small until the passage of the 1965 Immigration Act. Almost overnight, Filipinos became one of the largest Asian groups in the United States and in Colorado. While early Filipinos immigrants were primarily laborers, the majority of the later Filipinos were white-collar professionals. The most recent Filipino immigrants are, on the whole, well educated and economically successful. The National Federation of Filipino American Associations is the national organization serving as the voice for Filipinos and Filipino Americans.

## Asian Indians

Asian Indian migration to the United States has occurred in two waves. The first wave covered 1907 to 1924 and the second wave began in 1965 as a result of the new immigration law. The first wave consisted of Sikhs and Muslims from Punjab. Early arrivals settled in the Pacific Northwest and worked as laborers in the railroad and lumber industries. Just like other Asians, they were perceived as an economic threat and subjected to anti-Asian agitation. Many moved to California to work as agricultural laborers and some became farmers. A landmark opinion by the U.S. Supreme Court on February 19, 1923, in the case of Bhagal Singh Thind affected the naturalization of Indian nationals. Although Asian Indians were previously classified as Caucasian, the naturalization Law of 1790 limited the privilege for naturalization to only "free white persons," and Indians became ineligible for naturalization. Due to this fact, people who were naturalized earlier lost their citizenship, except for a few who went to court and won.

The second wave of Asian Indians, which started in 1965 dramatically, increased their numbers. By 1990, nearly 1 million Asian Indians, who were largely professionals, had entered the US. There is no official record of when Asian Indians first entered Colorado, but the Asian Indian population of Colorado has increased substantially since 1965.

## Koreans

The first Koreans who visited the U.S. came on a goodwill mission led by Min Yong on September 2, 1883, but the first official Korean immigrant to the U.S. in 1901 was Peter Ryu. In December 1902, 121 Koreans left for Hawaii, twenty years after the Korean-U.S. Treaty of Amity and Commerce. They worked on the sugar plantations. During the next three years, a total of 7,226 Koreans in 65 groups left Inchon for Hawaii. Drawn by American missionaries' glowing accounts of the new land of opportunity, they came from various classes of society. The political and economic strife ravaging Korea was an added inducement.

The first Koreans in Colorado came in the early 1900s to work in the coal mines, but the Korean population in this state remained very small until after World War II. A new wave of immigrants began arriving following the 1965 immigration law and has created major concentrations of Korean businesses in the Denver area.

## Southeast Asians and Other Asian and Pacific Americans

Since the end of the Vietnam War, many Southeast Asians have come to the United States, at first as refugees and later as immigrants. The first wave of refugees was mostly Vietnamese who fled in 1975, after the fall of Saigon, from what was then South Vietnam. A later, larger wave of refugees began to flee Southeast Asia shortly thereafter. These refugees consisted of Vietnamese, Cambodians and Laotians as well as other groups such as Hmong and Chinese-Vietnamese. Changes in U.S. policies beginning in the 1980s resulted in the migration to America of additional Southeast Asians as immigrants.

Southeast Asian refugees made dangerous and perilous journeys to leave their homelands and had significant initial problems adjusting to American society because their sudden departures left them with few resources. Refugees also were hampered by economic and social discrimination in the U.S. Over time, the Southeast Asian population has grown, dispersed geographically, and made substantial economic progress. The first influx of Southeast Asians to Colorado occurred during and just after 1975, and today this state has a large Vietnamese community. There is a major concentration of Vietnamese and Chinese-Vietnamese businesses in Denver.

Because of the 1965 Immigration Act, substantial numbers of other APAs have made their way to Colorado. Examples of these include individuals and families from Thailand, Myanmar (Burma), Malaysia, Singapore, Indonesia, Pakistan, Sri Lanka, Bangladesh, Nepal, Tibet, Mongolia, Samoa, and Guam.

The Denver metropolitan area is also home to important communities of Hmong, Laotians, Cambodians and lately, the Burmese as described in the next paragraph.

Myanmar (Burma), a Southeast Asian nation, has been under repressive military rule since 1962, and a civil war has caused the country much instability. After a 1988 democracy uprising in Burma, many political activists and ethnic minorities were forced to flee to neighboring countries --- Thailand, India and Bangladesh --- as refugees. Since 1990, Burmese refugees have come to the U.S. in search of a new life and to resettle. Colorado has been one of their destinations. In recent years, the U.S. government has welcomed many Burmese refugees into various states. Therefore, more than 350 refugees have relocated to Colorado, most in 2007 and 2008. These have included members of ethnic groups such as the Karen, Mon, Chin, and Myanmar Muslims. The refugees represent different religions, mainly Buddhism, Christianity and Islam. Burmese community leaders in Colorado are working diligently to form an official representative organization for their community in order to effectively help their people.

In this section of the history of Asians in Colorado, we now include two stories of the struggles and sacrifices of the Vietnamese and the Lao-Hmong refugees as they fled from their war-torn countries to the United States and how they worked hard to adjust in their new environment.

# Sum Nguyen

The fall of Saigon, then the capital of South Vietnam in the spring of 1975, brings out memories of survival and heroism associated with the "boat people." The experience of Sum Cong Nguyen and his family as refugees is a story that needs to be told.

Sum was born in central Vietnam, Quang Tri province. He came from a rich farming family. He and his wife, Anh Lam, have six grown children. The youngest son, however, died in a tragic car accident in Colorado in 1989.

Sum enlisted in the armed forces of the Republic of Vietnam in 1955 with the rank of army corporal and was later promoted to sergeant. In 1958, he enrolled in the Officer Reserve Academy and graduated in 1960 as a warrant officer of the transportation branch. In 1963, he was promoted to first lieutenant, after which, he was selected to receive training in the United States where he attended the Army Transportation School at Fort Eustis, Virginia. Upon his return to Vietnam, he was promoted to army captain and was assigned to the 401st Boat Group, located in Can Tho Delta, as deputy commander. There he worked closely with U.S. advisers to train Vietnamese soldiers to operate Landing Craft Mechanized #8 (LCM8). He successfully led his group to transport military cargo and equipment along the Mekong River. At the end of 1969, the Vietnam transportation branch commander and U.S. adviser appointed Sum to establish and take command of the new boat unit in Nha Trang, near the U.S base at Cam Ran Bay in central Vietnam. His last position in the Vietnam War was as chief of the division of transportation headquarters of the 3rd Army Corp.

On April 30, 1975, Sum and his family fled communist Vietnam to save their lives and look for freedom elsewhere. Their search brought them to the United States. There was chaos as thousands of South Vietnamese tried to escape by air and by sea. As a freedom-loving army officer in the South Vietnamese army, his family's only means of escape was on a rickety boat, which was overloaded with other refugees. The boat brought them to Singapore after seven and one-half days. From there, they sailed into the Pacific Ocean to Subic Bay, Philippines.

"It was a horrible experience," Sum said. They ran out of food and water to drink and they almost died. Furthermore, there were neither sanitary facilities nor a roof or cover over their heads to protect them from the elements like rain and wind. They had no binoculars, map or compass to guide them to their destination. From Subic Bay, they sailed to Guam where they stayed for some time. In July 31, 1975, Sum and his family reached American soil at the Camp Pendleton Marine base in California. They stayed there while waiting for relocation and someone to sponsor them.

In September 1975, under the sponsorship of the Denver Lutheran Church, Sum and his family came to Denver where they settled as refugees. A samaritan, by the name of "Teddy," under the auspices of the church, offered him a job as carpenter/helper in Denver. He accepted the job although he had no experience in carpentry. Since he had no means of transportation, he went to his job on a bicycle, which had no brakes. He could not afford to buy even a used car. It took him six months to buy one. The Lutheran Church helped them resettle, paying for their house rent for one and one-half months.

Adjusting to their new life was extremely difficult for Sum and his family. The first problem was language. Although he had been to the U.S. before, his family did not speak any English. It was scary for them. Luckily, his children easily picked up English in school. Still, they had English tutors, including Ba Vovan from the Denver Public Schools, who was a great help to them. In 1976, Sum decided to go to school in Denver. In Vietnam, he earned a baccalaureate #2, which is considered higher than a high school diploma. He was also taking correspondence classes in the field of law. He later enrolled in the Community College of Denver where he earned an associate's degree in electronic technology. In 1986, he graduated from the Metropolitan State College of Denver with a B.S. in electronic engineering. Through sheer determination, Sum succeeded in studying and working at the same time. His education, he says, has enhanced his career as an electronic engineer.

Sum is an indefatigable APA community leader and very visible, as shown by his participation in many APA activities and events. He is passionate in serving diverse APA communities and has an in-depth understanding of the issues and problems confronting the Vietnamese and other communities. Sum is not only generous with his time but also with his expertise and money. Sum, however, goes beyond community service. He is active in the local, city and state affairs. He volunteers in assisting law-enforcement and in enhancing the general welfare of the community such as supporting education, health and youth development. To show his gratitude to the United States for welcoming his family as refugees, Sum has contributed by serving in various capacities in community organizations including: Executive Director, Vietnamese Elderly Association of Colorado, Logistics Committee Chair, Asian Pacific American Relay of Colorado; Adviser, *Asian Pacific American Times* and *Asian Avenue Magazine*; President, Unified Vietnamese American Council of Colorado and co-chair of the Aurora Asian Pacific Community Partnership,

Being involved in community organizations, according to Sum, is not enough. The only way to show how grateful he is to America is to serve in an elective position. So he ran for an at-large position on the Aurora City Council in 2003 and 2005. Although he did not win, the number of votes he received in both elections satisfied him. At least, he has blazed the trail for other APAs to follow.

The following narrative by Yang Chee, a Hmong freedom fighter during the Vietnam War, tells of his tremendous efforts to gain recognition for the heroic support and assistance provided by the special guerilla units for American troops. He also talks of the adjustments made by his family and other Laotian and Hmong families upon their arrival in America.

## Yang Chee

Yang Chee is a freedom fighter, and founder, principal adviser and consultant to the Lao-Hmong American Coalition, a national organization. His outstanding services to the United States during the Vietnam War, to his people, the Lao-Hmong in Colorado and across the nation, needs to be told.

Yang Chee was born in Xiengkhouang province, Laos, on January 3, 1952, in a village known as Phou Houa Xang or Elephant Head Mountain. During the Vietnam War, Xiengkhouang was the most bombed region and suffered incredible devastation.

During the Vietnam War, the Hmong were the United States' most loyal allies. They valiantly fought to both defend their homeland and to support the U.S. interests in Southeast Asia. Embracing America's most covert war in Laos against the communist Pathet Lao and North Vietnamese Army regulars, the Lao-Hmong special guerrilla units (SGU) courageously served and were involved in guerrilla, conventional and air combat. They provided critical intelligence information, guarded U.S. radar installations and conducted strategic search and rescue missions to save the lives of American service men. As a result, more than 35,000 Hmong special guerrilla unit soldiers and air force pilots, including Yang Chee's three brothers, lost their lives defending freedom.

The most difficult time of his life was from 1966 to 1975. He had a hard time locating his family during his school summer breaks because they were constantly moving due to the war.

In 1966, Yang Chee was one of the only two Hmong from his province who passed the English examination for a government scholarship to attend the University of Dong Dok in Vientiane. Yang Chee received a Bachelor's degree in education from the University of Dong Dok in 1974 and subsequently attended the Master/graduate level classes in education at the same university in 1975. Yang Chee is fluent in Hmong, Lao, Thai, English and (medium) French.

In 1974, Yang Chee was a college professor of English, social science and Asian history at the College of Vang Vieng in Vientiane Province. As a professor, he was able to comprehend the causes and effects of the U.S. "secret" war in Laos that affected thousands of Hmong.

During the summers of 1972-1975, he taught English to the young Hmong in his home village as a community service. He also served as an intelligence officer, interpreter and translator for Central Intelligence Agency (CIA) working with case officer Jerry (Hog) Daniels.

On May 14, 1975, Long Chieng fell to the communist Pathet Lao. The U.S. totally withdrew its military advisors and Hmong Major General Vang Pao fled to Thailand, leaving tens of thousands of faithful Lao-Hmong SGU and their families behind. Life in Military Region 2 (MR2) was in chaotic turmoil and the unfortunate Hmong were persecuted and tortured inhumanely by their archenemies.

In Vientiane, Yang Chee felt the increasing threats to his life and the uncertainty of the future of his people. On May 27, 1975, he escaped from Laos and crossed the Mekong River to the Nong Khai refugee camp in Thailand. He witnessed many cases where ferryboat owners robbed and murdered the helpless Hmong in mid-stream. Many people died as a result of drowning and others were gunned down by communist river patrols. Then, Yang Chee was contacted by Jerry Daniels from the CIA headquarters in Udorn, Thailand. He was asked to work for the U.S. IndoChinese Refugee Program under Ambassador Charles Whitehouse to help screen and process Lao-Hmong to come to America. He helped lay the groundwork and processed over 9,600 Lao-Hmong eligible to immigrate to America before leaving Thailand for Denver, Colorado on June 16, 1976.

In 1977, Yang Chee was employed by International Business Machines (IBM). To further his studies, Yang Chee obtained his Bachelor's degree in education in 1983 at the University of Antioch, Ohio. In 1986, he went back to pursue his graduate studies at the University of Denver, where he received his Master's degree in communications in 1989. From 1976-2007, he served as a consultant on refugee issues for various agencies, including the Governor's Task Force, Colorado State Refugees Coordinators, the Refugees Volunteer Agencies, adult and vocational schools, churches, schools and health care agencies, and other institutions dealing with resettlement, education, as well as social and employment issues. He was occasionally invited to be a guest speaker in Colorado and other states.

With noble support from the late Congressman Daniel Schaefer, Yang Chee, as chair, along with a group of patriotic Americans, called the "American Tribute Committee" (ATC), was responsible for coordinating the first U.S. official "Lao-Hmong Recognition Day". This was in honor of the Lao-Hmong SGU veterans and their families for their contributions to America during the Vietnam War. This first-ever public acknowledgement event took place in Golden, Colorado on July 22, 1995. Two months later, on September 16, 1995, Yang Chee founded the Lao-Hmong American Coalition (LHAC) to represent and serve the interests of the Lao-Hmong Special Guerilla Units (SGU) veterans, their families and widows of deceased SGUs.

Yang Chee's tangible achievements at the national level include the Welfare Reform Act of 1996-1997, the Hmong Veterans' Naturalization Act of 2000, the Hmong SGU Memorial in Florida, the July 22 "National Lao-Hmong Recognition Day" each calendar year, and the "Hmong and American Air War over Laos" exhibit at the U.S. Air Force Base Museum in Colorado.

Yang Chee has a long record of accomplishments and awards that are too numerous to list here. His exemplary work with the Lao-Hmong people and his tireless efforts to help Americans understand the Lao-Hmong culture, the heroic sacrifices they made during the Vietnam War deserve commendation, recognition and appreciation.

Yang Chee is married to Pazua Yang. He has six children, two sons and one daughter from a previous marriage and one son and two stepdaughters from his current marriage. All their children hold degrees in their areas of specialization.

Yang's biggest challenges as President Emeritus of the Lao-Hmong American Coalition are helping Lao-Hmong communities make positive life changes in a new land. These changes include overcoming public fears, correcting misunderstandings/wrong perceptions, language difficulties, employment challenges, conflict with family, adapting to diverse cultures, social and religious changes, and becoming a role-model for the youth. Dealing with all these challenges requires tremendous effort, compromises, acceptance and respect for all individuals.

# Chapter 3

# THE GROWING ASIAN PACIFIC AMERICAN POPULATION IN COLORADO

The 2000 Census revealed the dramatic growth of Asian Pacific Americans (APA) in Colorado from 59,862 in 1990 to more than 134,858 in 2000 – a 125.3 percent increase. In 2000, APAs in Colorado constituted 3.1 percent of the total population, up from 1.8 percent in 1990. Although APAs made up only 4.7 percent of the U.S. population, high concentrations could be found on the West and East Coasts, in Hawaii, and in the coastal states.

What does this growth in the Colorado APA population mean? APAs are going to be increasingly more visible. More APAs will be making contributions to the social, cultural, economic, and political affairs of this state and region. More APA community organizations will be formed, and those already in existence will grow and increase the scope of their activities. More and more the voices of APAs are going to be heard throughout all facets of life in Colorado.

Richard Lin, Ph.D. of the Colorado Division of Local Government contributed the following article on APA demographic data.

Dr. Lin was one of the founding members of the Colorado Alliance of Pacific Asian Americans established in 1978 to organize resources and talents to better serve Colorado APA communities. He was a member of the Governor's Asian Pacific American Advisory Council (GAPAAC).

Richard was born in Taiwan and got his B.Ed. and M.Ed from the National Taiwan Normal University, a Master's degree in educational psychology (measurement and statistics) from the University of Oregon, and a Ph.D. in research and statistical methodology (with sub-major in psychology, counseling and Guidance) from the University of Northern Colorado.

Richard Lin is a long-time community volunteer who also is a demographer for the State of Colorado. Over the years, he has provided invaluable information on the socioeconomic status of the state's APA communities. The following sections present a succint and important set of data about APAs, compiled by Richard Lin. We should also recognize that such data is dynamic and as such needs to be updated on a regular basis.

## Asian Pacific Americans by the Numbers

### Description of Asian Pacific American (APA) Immigrants

Some Asian immigrants, especially Chinese and Japanese, had settled in Colorado long before Colorado established its statehood in 1876. But the exclusion of many Asian immigrants from the United States by the immigration act of 1924 had a great negative impact on Asian Americans in the United States. It was not until the Korean War in the 1950s and the Vietnam War in the 1960-70s that the United States was obligated to open its doors to more Asian immigrants. With growing international trade in the Pacific Rim in the 1980s and with the immigration law and policy changes since 1965, it has spurred a great influx of Asian immigrants into the United States and Colorado. The numbers of Asian-Pacific Americans in Colorado increased from 34,257 in 1980 to 59,862 in 1990 by 74.7%. Among them, the Asian Americans increased from 32,733 in 1980 to 57,122 in 1990 also by 74.5%.

### The Asian American (AA) Immigrants

In Colorado, the Asian American community traditionally includes all members with origins from Asia and the Pacific Islands. However, Native Hawaiian and Pacific Islanders had a successful signature petition to the OMB (Office of Management and Budgeting) mandating the Census Bureau to differentiate them from Asian category and form a separate tabulation category based on special needs. Since their numbers are small ranging from 4,540 (Alone) to 10,419 (All with Mix) in 2000 census counts, the only focus is on Asians rather than separating out Native Hawaiian and Pacific Islanders for lack of data and information.

## Population Growth of Immigrants in the USA

### Asian Pacific Americans (APA)

Based on the "All Mix 2000" of the Census 2000 counts for the United States, Chinese (excluding Taiwanese) is the largest Asian sub-group with 2,734,841 persons, followed by Filipino (2,364,815), Asian Indian

(1,899,599), Korean (1,228,427), Vietnamese (1,223,736), and Japanese (1,148,932).

Using the U.S. total population of 248,709,873 in 1990 and 281,421,906 in 2000 as a basis for comparison, the Asian American population of 6,908,638 in 1990 was only 2.8% of the U.S. population, while in 2000 its population of 12,275,972 accounted for 4.4% of the total U.S. population. It increased by 5.37 million or 77.7% growth.

By comparison, the Asian population of 57,122 in 1990 was only 1.7% of the Colorado population, while in 2000 the Asian population of 124,439 accounted for 2.9% of the Colorado population, using Colorado total population base of 3,294,394 in 1990 and 4,301,261 in 2000. Asians in Colorado are underrepresented by the nation's standard (4.4%) in 2000. Between 1990 and 2000, the increase was some 67,000 persons, which is equivalent to a 117.9% growth.

### Asian Americans as "All Mix-immigrant"

The greatest proportion of Asian American population growth is attributed to new immigrants. From 2000 to 2006, the Department of Home Security (DHS) has documented 7,016,178 legal immigrants to the United States and allocated 79,045 immigrants to Colorado. Within the Asian groups, the numbers are 2,355,545 to U.S. and 22,227 to Colorado. Nationwide, the leading Asian sub-group in legal immigration during 2000-2006 is from India (449,895), followed by China (412,395), Philippines (385,368), Vietnam (212,965) and Korea (140,689). It is noted that both Hmong and Laotian are from Laos.

The first ACS (American Community Survey) estimates with detailed Asian sub-groups is from 2005. Since the 2006 ACS has increased in sample sizes, the 2006 ACS estimates, theoretically, ought to be much more accurate than that from the 2005 estimates of the Asian sub-groups. There are many places where one can find the timely estimates of Asian Americans by Asian sub-groups other than from the ACS estimates. Although the ACS estimates are subject to sampling and non-sampling errors, it is still the best data source we can depend on.

Table 3-1-08 showing census counts, estimates and projections of Asian American population in the U.S. and Colorado covering the years 1980 to 2007 is presented in the Appendix.

### The Unique Taiwanese Situation

Taiwanese is a unique Asian sub-group. Since 1970, the Taiwanese communities in the United States have tried very hard to promote Taiwanese identity by differentiating from Chinese. However, it had changed very little until recently after China had blocked Taiwan from joining the WHO (World Health Organization) when the SARS epidemic occurred in 2003. After the Carter Administration normalized diplomatic relationships with China in 1979 and ceased its relationship with ROC (Republic of China) in Taiwan, the United States passed Taiwan Relations Act (TRA) in 1981 and separated China's immigration quotas in 1982 into two countries, China and Taiwan. The TRA and its immigration requirements had forced the Taiwanese government to re-issue personal identification and household registration from origin of ancestry (China's provinces) to place of birth (Taiwan). However, many of the native-born Taiwanese still habitually identify themselves as culturally "Chinese" (confused by "Chinese" nationality).

The evidence has indicated that there were some 80,000 Taiwanese in the United States by race, 192,173 Taiwanese by ancestry, and 244,102 Taiwanese by birth place (Taiwan) according to the 1990 census. In Colorado, there were 487 Taiwanese by race, 1,062 Taiwanese by ancestry and 1,343 Taiwanese by birth place ((Taiwan) in 1990. In 2000, Colorado had 760 (Alone) Taiwanese Americans, 986 (All) Taiwanese and 2,301 Taiwanese Americans born in Taiwan. The numbers can be confusing between 760 and 2,301. Therefore, the numbers of Taiwanese Americans in Colorado have changed from 227 in 1980 to 487 in 1990 and between 760 and 2,301 in 2000. Taiwanese Americans in Colorado are estimated at 1,086 (2005 ACS) and 2,619 (2006 ACS).

## Population Growth of Immigrants in Colorado

### Asian Americans as "All Mix-immigrants"

By Asian sub-groups, the fastest percent growth (from 1990 to 2000) at the state level was Asian Indian with 260.0% (from 3,836 to 13,809) followed by Filipino 171.2% (from 5,426 to 14,716), Vietnamese 137.3% (from 7,210 to 17,108), Chinese 135.0% (from 8,208 to 19,292), and Korean 79.1% (from 11,339 to 20,304). It is no surprise that Japanese American had only increased 63.8% (from 11,402 to 18,676) because there were not many new immigrants from Japan to Colorado.

### Asian Americans as Pure (based on country of origin)

The largest group in Colorado of Asian Americans with strong Asian sub-group (Alone) identity in 2000 is Korean (16,395) followed by Vietnamese (15,457), Chinese (14,898), Asian Indian (11,720), Japanese (11,571), and Filipino (8,941).

According to 2000 census, the largest groups in Colorado of Asian Americans, including members of interracial marriage (mixed with all races), are Korean (20,304) followed by Chinese (19,292), Japanese (18,676), Vietnamese (17,108), Filipino (14,716) and Asian Indian (13,809). However, the estimates derived from the 2006 ACS and the U.S. Census Bureau's annual states estimates by characteristics (age, sex, and race) may show the Chinese American (35,033) taking the lead in Colorado followed by Korean (33,748), Vietnamese (26,514), Asian Indian (21,110), Japanese (18,182), and Filipino (17,400).

## Potentials for Significant Social Influences in Colorado

It is my sincere hope that the census counts and the estimates presented in this "Asian Americans in Colorado by the Numbers" are valuable resources for decision making to benefit the Asian communities in program planning and business operations.

With the considerable increases in Asian immigrants in Colorado in the last ten years or so, it can be expected that some significant social interactions will take place. Furthermore, as their numbers increase, there will be more opportunities for Asian leadership in many social gatherings and directions. Note for example the already identified leaders in various fields particularly those that pertain to development of socio-cultural affairs. It is also highly probable that many more business leaders will emerge in the years to come.

## Sources of Data

US Census Bureau: Census Counts (1980, 1990, and 2000);
Annual National and States Population Estimates-- Characteristics (Age, Sex, Race, and Hispanic Origin), 2000-2007 (5-1-2008)
Projected Population of the United States and States, by Race and Hispanic Origin: 2000 to 2050 (3/8/2004)
Notes: APA-- Asian and Pacific Americans; 1980 Census (Alone); 1990 Census (Alone); 2000 Census (Alone or combination of interracial claims); AA-- Asian American (not including Native Hawaiian and Pacific Islanders); Chinese (excluding Taiwanese);
7-1-2006 Colorado Asian Subgroups Estimates are based proportionally on 2006 ACS estimates (Upper Bound) allocations using US Census Bureau's 7-1-2006 Colorado AA estimate as control total.
G:\Demog\Census2000\ASIAN\Chapt 3-Rev1-Population-08.xls (5/28/2008) Colorado Division of Local Government; Richard Lin (303) 866-4989

# Chapter 4

# ASIAN PACIFIC AMERICANS IN BUSINESS

Within the American economy, a very large proportion of Asian Pacific Americans, and especially Asian immigrants, are in business. The most visible evidence of this is APA businesses located in urban ethnic neighborhoods clustered together in various locations of a large city. Most of these businesses are relatively small and include restaurants, food stores, gift shops, beauty parlors, jewelry stores, and other similar establishments. In the Denver area, for example, there are several clusters of such businesses along both sides of Federal Blvd. south of Alameda and along Alameda east of Federal. Many of these are owned and operated by Vietnamese and ethnic Chinese from Vietnam. In Aurora along and around South Havana and Parker Road, there are several clusters of Korean businesses. Small clusters of APA businesses also can be found in other parts of the Denver metropolitan area, and individual APA establishments, such as restaurants, are scattered throughout the Denver metropolitan area and in other cities and towns in Colorado. Scholars have taken note of this small business activity and have advanced several theories to explain the high level of APA involvement. One theory is that Asian immigrants, when they first arrive in America, face difficulties obtaining jobs because of their limited English-language abilities or because their educational credentials and job experiences from Asia are not recognized by American companies. Also, some immigrants experience discrimination when applying for jobs. Finally, many APA businesses are fairly easy to start, especially if capital and business assistance are provided by other APAs. Many APA small businesses, particularly those in APA ethnic neighborhoods, have a built-in customer base.

Not all APAs in business work in such establishments. Highly skilled and educated APA professionals go into business in such areas as financial services, real estate, insurance, law, medicine, computer technology, engineering, and architecture. This is an increasing trend and one that is very evident in Colorado. Some of these professionals are American-born second or later generation APAs. Others are Asian immigrants who first came to the U.S. as students and later decided to stay after finishing their education or are immigrants who come to the

U.S. already having the necessary education, skills and experience to become successful in business.

This chapter features some of the many successful APA businessmen and businesswomen in Colorado. Their stories focus on the ingredients they used to reach their goals and achieve success. These individuals include John Sie, an outstanding Chinese American businessman, Ding Wen Hsu, co-owner and board chair of Pacific Western Technology, Mercedes del Rosario Huang, owner of Rocky Mountain Food Factory, Narender Kumar, founder of Kumar and Associates, Tini Malik, owner of Golden Triangle Wine and Spirits, Eric Wang and Paul Lee, both executives at Premier Bank, Sam Kumar, president and CEO of Microtech-Tel, Japanese American attorney Kerry Hada and Shiou Yun Wang Jefferson, owner of Twin Dragon Restaurant.

## John Sie

**John Sie stands in front of a poster "Retirement of the King", that was created for him when he retired from Starz Encore Group in 2004.**

John Sie, the legend that built the Starz Encore Group, has retired from his numerous businesses to devote more time to his family, but he continues his passion for the charitable activities of the Anna and John J. Sie Foundation.

Much has been written and published about the phenomenal success of John Sie, particularly in the technology and video businesses, cable and digital television industry, and satellite programming networks to name a few. This article will feature the little known story of his early life.

John Sie came to the United States in 1950 from Shanghai via Taiwan. His family landed in Manhattan, New York. His father had to return to Taiwan, leaving his wife and three sons in America. To help support themselves, John, then 14, and his brother, Charlie, 16, moved to live in a Catholic orphanage, called the Mission of Immaculate Conception on Staten Island, New York. He feels that living the hard life in the orphanage actually prepared him well for life. He learned to be tough, not to be bullied, while at the same time he absorbed the Catholic teachings of right and wrong and morality, which guided him throughout his undertakings.

While at the orphanage, John and Charlie went to three external high schools -- first to Tottenville High School, Staten Island, N.Y. as sophomores, to St. Mary's High School in Perth Amboy, New Jersey as juniors and then graduating from St. Peter's High School, Staten Island, New York in 1953. The two brothers did not know any English when they first went to school, but they succeeded. John says their grades were "C+s" in their sophomore year, "B+s" in their junior year and "A+s" in their senior year.

John had wanted to study art in college, but his father persuaded him to take up engineering as a more practical choice. Why not? He was always fascinated by electric trains, which he used to play with in the orphanage. Both brothers then received scholarships to attend Manhattan College in the Bronx, New York. Both graduated in 1957, with a B.S. in electrical engineering.

One very strong impression we got from John Sie is his positive outlook. He never considered his childhood in the orphanage, his high school years, and his college life as a hard life. For him, success always followed hard work and dedication. He also learned from his early years as a young boy in China that one must work hard and never whine. "If you are always complaining, you will never work doubly hard to overcome obstacles. It gives you a rationalization and an excuse to not achieve," he says. When he experienced discrimination or unjust treatment at work, he always spoke up; but never slacked-off while waiting for a positive outcome. Wisely he says, "Little things that go wrong are the things that shape you." He remembers well the advice of his uncle back in China: "Better not lose face in America." John Sie, with his inner ability, talents, a positive attitude and strong will power, surely has succeeded.

Look at his record of rapid rise from an immigrant young Chinese boy to become a legend in various technological, movie and television industries and a multi-awarded philantropist. In 1958, after receiving his Master's degree in electrophysics from the then Polytechnic Institute of Brooklyn, John became a senior member of the technical staff with RCA's Defense Electronics Division. In 1960, he was one of the founders and later president of Micro State Electronics, an aerospace start-up which was subsequently acquired by the Raytheon Company. In 1972, he became the general manager of the CATV Division of the General Instruments' Jerrold Electronics Corporation. In 1977, he switched to the cable and satellite programming business as Senior Vice President of Sales and Planning at Showtime/The Movie Channel, Inc.

In 1984, Denver was blessed when Tele-Communications Incorporated's John Malone persuaded John to move his family to Denver and become Senior Vice President of Strategic Planning/Programming Technology. His many positions at TCI included founding Chairman of PrimeStar Partners, founding Chairman of International Channel Networks and Encore International, and Founder and Chief Executive Officer of Starz Encore Group LLC (1991) until his retirement in 2004. He retains his title as Founder and Chairman of Starz Entertainment Group, LLC and Encore International, LLC.

Aside from being regularly consulted by both consumer and trade media for insights into programming, marketing and technology issues, John has been invited through the years as a keynote speaker on countless panels or symposia.

John is also involved with the Committee of 100, which conducted a landmark survey in the U.S. and China on American and Chinese attitudes toward each other. The results were quite revealing. Through his media background, the press briefing on the survey in December was covered live on C-Span and there was an in-depth discussion afterwards on C-Span's Washington Journal. The survey was also covered by the official China Central Television, CCTV.

John met his wife, Anna Maglione, in New Jersey and they married in 1966. They have five successful children. Susan lives in upstate New York, and graduated from Penn State University with a degree in architecture. She designed the Sie's mansion in Cherry Hills Village. Debbie, a naturopathic doctor, graduated from the Southwest College of Naturopathic Medicine and Health Sciences in Scottsdale, Arizona and practices in Santa Fe, New Mexico. Jimmy, the only son, a writer and actor, graduated from Northwest University in Chicago, and lives in Los Angeles. Michelle, who graduated from Tufts University and then earned a Master's degree in Asian studies at Harvard, is Executive Director of the Anna and John J. Sie Foundation and is the only one of their children who lives in Colorado. Allison, their youngest daughter who is an actress and producer in Los Angeles, attended the University of Colorado, Boulder.

John wants to devote all his time to the programs of the Anna and John J. Sie Foundation, with particular emphasis on Down Syndrome (DS) and China-U.S. cooperation in the areas of energy, water, and the environment. His granddaughter, Sophia, the daughter of Michelle and Tom Whitten, was born with DS. His unprecedented and very ambitious goal is to completely eradicate the ill effects of Down Syndrome by 2017.

John notes that the National Institute of Health has a yearly budget of $26 billion, but only $12 million is allocated for DS research. He and Michelle are making the rounds in Washington DC to change that shortcoming. But the Foundation is building a private/public model in this endeavor. In 2006, the Anna and John J. Sie Foundation, in conjunction with the University of Colorado, awarded $1 million to 13 grant recipients to stimulate new scientific research focusing on his defined goal. This partnership between the Foundation and the University of Colorado is the first of its kind in the world and has attracted the best research scientists into the field of Down Syndrome.

Downs Syndrome research is just one of the programs of the Anna and John J. Sie Foundation. Another major thrust for the Foundation is in setting up the Institute for Sino-American International Dialogue (ISAID) at the University of Denver's Graduate School of International Studies. The goal of ISAID is to engage the top leaders of the U.S. and China in promulgating new laws, regulations, and enterprises in the areas of energy, water, and environment for a sustainable planet.

Another program is the Film Education Program which has provided K-12 students on the Colorado Front Range with the opportunity to engage in a curriculum-based study of and cultivate a lasting appreciation for the art of film. Teachers in Denver-area schools work directly with the Denver Film Society and with Howie Movshovitz, Colorado Public Radio film critic, to bring students into the Starz FilmCenter.

The Anna and John J. Sie Foundation also recently gave a $1.5 million gift to the University of Denver to establish the Anna Maglione-Sie Endowed Chair in Italian Culture. The generous gift will increase the number of study abroad opportunities for DU students in Italy, improve the Italian language program and expand the cultural ties between the United States and Italy. The chair will honor contributions Anna Maglione-Sie has made to DU, the Italian culture and the local community.

John Sie is not only a successful businessman and a philanthropist; he is a role model for our youth to emulate. He notes that everywhere in the world, there are many bad things happening: violence, crime, broken families and drugs, but it is the individual's own responsibility to remain good and contribute to the betterment of society. "It is a matter of wanting to be good. There should be no excuses."

## Ding Wen Hsu

Ding Wen Hsu has achieved what she wants to do. She is one of those responsible for bringing the Dragon Boat Festival (CDBF) to Colorado. Ding is co-founder and chairperson of the operating committee that began this annual event, which has become the most successful pan-Asian mega water sport in Colorado. The metro-Denver area has embraced the Dragon Boat Festival as one of its major summer attractions. The seventh annual CDBF in July 2007 attracted an estimated crowd of more than 100,000 at Sloan's Lake. Her strong organizational and managerial skills in running a big sports and cultural event are evident in the success of the operation.

Ding needs an introduction before we go ahead to her other contributions to Asian Pacific American communities and to society at large.

Ding was born in China and at the age of four months, her family moved to Taiwan where she grew up and received her education. She completed a B.A. degree from Providence College in Taiwan. Later moving to Colorado with her husband, Dr. Tai-Dan Hsu in the mid 70s, she received an executive MBA from the University of Colorado.

Ding feels she is fortunate to have lived in Taiwan before immigrating to the U.S. She says she has the best of two worlds – the fusion of two cultures of the East and the West, which she says has been beneficial to her, particularly in conducting business in her adopted country. In Colorado, Ding and Tai-Dan were able to find jobs and move into their neighborhood without any objections from anybody. Since her two children grew up in the U.S., they consider themselves "American." Though they do not speak much Chinese, they look Chinese and still are considered "foreigners." They are even told, " You speak very good English!" This confirms the key findings of the Committee of 100, in their report entitled *American Attitudes Toward Chinese Americans and Asian American* that "Too many Americans see them (referring to Chinese and other Asian Americans) as foreigners or as permanent aliens." There have been instances when APAs were told to go home to their own country. When Ding, at one time, was told this, she asked, "What country? Where will I go? This is my country. I am an American!" What they don't know is that Ding is a well-known leader in Colorado, specifically in the Asian Pacific American community.

Ding is the co-owner and chair of the board of the Pacific Western Technology, Ltd (PWT), an engineering consulting company based in Denver, Colorado, with offices in Tennessee, New Mexico and California. PWT specializes in information technology, program management and environmental/facility management services. Since its beginnings in 1987, PWT has grown to include three locations with over 150 employees through focused vision, teamwork, attention to detail, hard work and trusted employees.

Ding not only has the education (executive MBA) and training, she also has the managerial skills and ability to "find the right people, identify their strengths and weaknesses and work to support them." In addition, her empowering experience as a National Fellow of the Asian Pacific American Women's Leadership Institute has developed and strengthened her natural ability to lead. These make her an outstanding and exceptional leader, not only in business but also in the community.

Her husband, Dr. Tai-Dan Hsu, Ph.D. has been the co-owner/President/CEO and a major stockholder of PWT since it was incorporated in 1987. PWT was ranked fourth among minority-owned Colorado companies in 2003. In 2001 and 2002, it was ranked among the 25 top women-owned businesses by the *Denver Business Journal.*

Another of Ding's passions is the International Multi-cultural Institute operated and funded by her family foundation for both charitable and educational purposes. Its goal is to promote harmony, eliminate prejudice and discrimination, combat community deterioration, defend human and civil rights, contribute to organizations that promote cultural diversity, fund research projects, sponsor educational seminars and establish multicultural community centers for various neighborhood activities and programs.

Perhaps, Ding's greatest community volunteer service is her involvement with the Colorado Dragon Boat Festival. Designed to build bridges among the Asian Pacific American communities and the broader society, the CDBF was co-founded by Ding together with John Chin and Howard Solow. Ding feels it is important to establish an Asian festival in Colorado. "It serves as a building block for us, the first generation immigrants and our children. It provides an opportunity for us to feel we can contribute to the overall good of society." She has found a venue for Asian Pacific Americans to share their cultural values with everyone around them.

The Dragon Boat Festival includes Explore Asia and the Cultural Unity Stage with educational and cultural presentations and colorful demonstrations of cultural diversity. There is also a display of unique merchandise and ethnic delicacies. The *Rocky Mountain News* has named the CDBF as the "Top Annual Festival."

Community activities of Ding have been focused on integrating Asian immigrants into mainstream American society. These include helping new immigrants build self-confidence and overcome prejudice they may encounter.

As chair of the Board of Directors of the Chinese-American Council of Colorado, member of the Board of Directors, Shaolin Hung-mei Kung Fu Association, member of the Board of Directors of the Colorado Chinese Language School and as teacher and former principal of the Colorado Chinese Language School, Ding is passionate about educating Asian Americans to be truly a part of the American community and not to behave and feel like foreigners. "In essence," she continues, "we are Americans living in America, our country." Without forgetting our own beautiful traditions and values, she emphasizes that we must learn to be part of America in all its aspects, including active participation in the political process. She looks forward to the time when more Asian Americans will have a more active voice in local, state and national governments.

The following are just a few of the awards Ding has received. On January 19, 2004, Red Rocks Community College gave the Community Leader award to Ding during its Martin Luther King, Jr. celebration. She was the March 2005 winner of a Channel 9 Who Cares award. Sarah Kohn, one of the speakers at this event, said. "So many people talk about the idealistic goal of making our society a better place and respecting cultures and ending prejudice and don't really do anything about it, but Ding does." On November 14, 2006, Ding received the Vision in America award from the International Channel to celebrate citizenship. *Denver Magazine Online* recognized Ding as one of the 25 most successful business women in August 2005.

Dr. Tai-Dan and Ding Wen Hsu have two very successful children. Jon, their son, was born in 1975 in Taipei, Taiwan, and Ellen, their daughter, was born in 1980 in Denver, Colorado. Jon graduated with a B.S, in mathematics, electronic engineering and computer science from Rice University in Houston. He is currently working on his Ph.D. in mechanical engineering at the University of California-Davis. He is very concerned about our environment. After working in the computer software industry for seven years he went back to school to study fuel cell technology. He wants to develop sources of alternative energy to create a cleaner environment. Ellen has a B.A. degree in computer arts from the University of California-San Diego in 2002 and is currently working for Nike in Portland, Oregon as the producer of their intra-net, a website for company internal communication. She is artistically creative. Both are focused in making a difference in places where they work.

As a parent, Ding says, "My biggest challenge was to raise our children in America. We come from a more conservative, more homogenous society, different from what is here in America. We should not force our children to be the same as we are. We need to be open-minded and sensitive to what is going on around us and help our children to choose the best assets and values from both worlds. However, our children do not have to be raised without any rules. Setting boundaries and establishing rules are good for them. It creates a safe environment for them."

"Regardless of what ability we are endowed with," Ding says, "we should all get involved. We should participate in mainstream activities and be good ambassadors for our community. We need to demonstrate our ability and contributions. We need to have one voice."

Lastly, she says, "I love to work with young people. They are our future. Maybe, we should start a program for our younger generation to prepare them to lead."

## Mercedes del Rosario Huang

Mercedes Huang's story when she entered the United States is inspirational and worthy of emulation.

"I came with two suitcases, a college graduate from Manila, with a strong will to succeed. The idea of success for me at that time, in 1972, was to get a good job and live comfortably. But since then, I have been given many opportunities to succeed beyond my expectations." Mercedes, with courage and tenacity, took the challenge. Now, Mercedes is the owner and president of a multi-million dollar business enterprise in Englewood, Colorado, the Rocky Mountain Food Factory (RMFF). She has proven beyond any doubt, that a Filipino, and a woman at that, can succeed in the U.S. under a free enterprise and competitive system.

Success, however, for Mercedes did not come that easy. Let us to go back to the Philippines where her career started. After graduation from high school in the Philippines, Mercedes still had not decided on the degree program to pursue in college. Her father advised her to get a Bachelor's degree in food technology since this was a relatively new field at that time. Furthermore, he thought that the program would be good for her, because, upon graduation, she could easily find a job or she could even work for his brother who owned a canning plant. Taking her father's advice, she enrolled in the food technology program at the Philippine Women's University (PWU) in Manila and. at the age of 19, graduated with a B.S. in food technology.

During her student days at PWU, she was active in student organizations and took the lead in organizing the Society of Food Technologists at the University (PWU-SOFT), succeeding where others before her had failed. She was able to convince practically all junior and senior food technology students and those in related sciences at PWU to become active members of PWU-SOFT. This was later acknowledged by the mother organization, the Philippine Association of Food Technologists, Inc.

Her first experience in the field of food technology was a job in a small cannery owned by her uncle in her hometown in Central Luzon. As she worked in the factory, she felt the need for further growth and development in her field. Thus, to broaden her knowledge and to advance in her career, she enrolled at the University of Massachusetts, Amherst, on a scholarship grant and graduated with an M.S. in food science and technology. After that, she worked as a research assistant in flavor chemistry and food analysis at the university. All these experiences played a critical role in providing her with the knowledge and expertise that would soon shape her career.

In 1975, she met her husband, Whittak Huang, who was also a student at the University of Massachusetts. Whittak, a Taiwanese, is now a successful aerospace engineer/rocket-scientist at the Lockheed Martin Corporation. He is one of the 120 engineers, out of the more than 200,000, selected to be a Fellow, a title bestowed on someone with proven performance by independent defense contractors in the aerospace business.

After five years as a full-time housewife and mother of two daughters, she began working in the food industry as a food technologist in the area of quality control and product development. However, she soon realized the many opportunities in the food manufacturing industry. Her first venture as an entrepreneur was her wholesale and retail bakeshop, the Food Master's Bakery in Lakewood, Colorado.

In October 1985 Mercedes opened the Rocky Mountain Food Factory. Starting with $22,000 from a second mortgage on her house, she secured a $40,000 loan the following year from the Small Business Administration. Both loans, she proudly declares, were repaid within two years. From 1985, the company grew steadily taking product samples to different companies for trial use. After six months, the plant went on full production. Soon, distributors in the area started to carry her product line.

Today, housed in two buildings, the Rocky Mountain Food Factory is a USDA-approved plant and is also certified as an organic processing plant by Quality Assurance International. The company received excellent (Gold) ratings the past two years from Sillier Laboratories, an international food expert in quality and food safety systems. The company supplies fresh and frozen convenience foods to more than 300 businesses, restaurants and retail stores, including Costco, Safeway, Albertson's, Wild Oats and Whole Foods. It also does packing and manufacturing for very large companies. The company's website is: www.rockymtnfoodfactory.com

Mercedes developed recipes along with food experts in the field for all the company's different products. For the toll-packing business, she worked with the chefs of client companies to develop the recipes into a marketable product. She combines her knowledge in food science with the art of making food. What is most amazing is her capability to overcome obstacles in this highly competitive business such that today the company is one of the top suppliers of Mexican foods in the area.

Mercedes, for her professional achievements, was recognized and given an award in 1994 by the Asian Pacific Women's Network of Colorado. In 1996, she was featured in a book, *Profile in Excellence Filipino Achievers in the USA and Canada* by Isabel T. Crisostomo . In 2004, she was one of the 96 Asians featured in *Distinguished Asian American Business Leaders* by Naomi Hirahara. She was selected by the Department of Commerce to be among the 100 U.S. representatives to the Western Hemisphere Trade and Commerce Forum in 1995. In 2001, the U.S. Food Service, a national food distributor, gave her the Top Growth award. In 2002, the Small Business Administration selected her to represent successful small area businesses featured by TV Fox News.

For community service, Mercedes served on the board of directors of the Small Business Corporation, a non-profit organization that helps small businesses secure financing. In addition, RMFF has been donating to soup kitchens, schools, non-profit and other civic and community organizations including Filipino and Asian Pacific American groups.

Her advice to other businesses is worthy of consideration because it is based on her actual experience as a Filipino and a woman. "Put aside ethnicity, language and culture when doing business. Do not dwell on the differences. Just do business professionally. Keep in mind the client and after a while, they will see you as the person they like to do business with, not because of your accent, color, etc. They forget about that."

The three major challenges she encountered in her business were: learning to do business with big distributors, producing the right food that gives satisfaction to customers and being competitive in pricing. She learned that it is important to know more about American culture besides Mastering the basic business operations such as financing, management, marketing and procurement of supplies and raw materials. Furthermore, she said, clients consider things such as quality, reliability, ability and capability to deliver on time, what was promised.

From the Western perspective, Asian culture is relatively conservative, in spite of the intrusion of modern ways, as reflected in Hollywood movies. She always made it a point to be at home when her two daughters returned from school. Respect for parents and elders and persons in authority, family unity and education rank high in her hierarchy of values. This is reflected in their two successful, loving and caring daughters, Marina Sophie and Gemma Mei.

To enhance the visibility of Asian Pacific Americans in Colorado, she suggests participation in politics and being active in civic and non-profit organizations. Mercedes dreams of building and operating a medical clinic in the Philippines when she retires. She believes in sharing her successes as a way of giving back to her country of origin.

In spite of their success both in business and professionally, Mercedes and Whittak are humble and down-to-earth. Maria Concepcion Panlilio, a fiction and non-fiction writer, wrote in the *Asian Pacific American Times* (February 2004), "Mercedes del Rosario Huang's life is many woman's fantasy that only a few can experience in life and it could not have happened to a nicer and more deserving person." We now know where the contents of the two suitcases she carried with her from the Philippines, and a lot of hard work, has eventually led her.

# Narender Kumar

Narender Kumar was born and raised in Himachal Pradesh, India. He obtained his Bachelor's degree in civil engineering from Punjab Engineering College, Chandigarh. He immigrated to the U.S. in 1969 and obtained his Master's degree in civil engineering in 1971 from the University of Utah. He worked in Chicago from 1971-1979 and then moved to Denver in 1980 and worked at Chen and Associates. He then founded Kumar & Associates, Inc. (K+A) in 1989.

K+A has been involved in thousands of projects across Colorado and its surrounding states providing professional services in the areas of geotechnical engineering, environmental sciences, engineering geology, construction observation and materials testing. At this time, K+A has five locations employing more than 80 people in Denver, Fort Collins, Colorado Springs, Pueblo and Winter Park/Fraser.

As a community leader and business visionary he notes, "America is a great melting pot, however, Americans expect you to prove yourself in each and every occasion and nothing is a given. This is a land of opportunity and you have to take advantage of the skills you have. Some of us who immigrated in early 1970s faced challenges, which have been dealt with and mitigated. Asian Indians now have a very good reputation." He feels that while there is some discrimination in the U.S., Asian people experience discrimination in their native countries as well. "We are exposed to more attitudes and discrimination in India; look at our caste system." The point he makes very effectively is that we should not let the thoughts of discrimination and perceived bias hold us back and have it become a psychological burden for good performance. To be a successful businessman, he notes that we should take advantage of the opportunities and never be afraid to take risks. To be a community leader he feels we should lead by example. "Nobody has time to listen to someone who talks about what he can do; they follow someone who does what he or she says." As recent immigrants, they should learn the customs and start working with the American system. Too many Indian/Asians stay within their community and do not reach out to other cultures as much as they should. We bring our inhibitions and regional biases as people from one country to society in Colorado.

He feels that this attitude has a particularly difficult and adverse impact on our children.

"The kids who are born or have grown up here are more used to the American lifestyle. In order for them to succeed and enjoy their lives, they should have the freedom to make choices. They may want to eat food they prefer, participate in social rituals of the American society and even marry partners of their choice. We have to trust them and let them flourish and learn from their own mistakes. In other words; it is the older generation who has to grow up and let go." Mr. Kumar has three children who are studying to be an engineer, a doctor and a writer. He is also on the board of the Hindu Temple in Colorado and is working very hard to raise funds for building a new Hindu Temple in the Denver metro area. It is surely a project that will benefit many generations of Asian Indians in Colorado with strong emphasis for culture and religion.

## Eric Wang

Eric Wang came to the United States in 1989 as a businessman. He was already in business in Taiwan, dealing with various products such as porcelain ware, advertising, entertainment and real estate. Although he graduated from college with a degree in physics, he felt being an entrepreneur was his life's dream.

He started with in real estate, buying property and building a house in Boulder. In 1996, Premier Bank, the first Asian bank was established, with Eric Wang as one of the founders. He felt the need to help people, especially the APAs who need assistance in financial and business dealings. Early on, he found out that in America, one has to establish credit first before one can apply for a credit card. That means one has to borrow first and pay loans in a timely manner before one qualifies for a loan or a credit card.

Now, as Chairman and CEO of Premier Bank, Eric Wang has the satisfaction that he is helping APA and other communities. The bank is a full-service commercial bank and offers international banking, commercial lending, and commercial and consumer deposit banking. Premier Bank has earned the distinction of being a Small Business Administration (SBA) Preferred Lender, which allows expedited processing of small business customers' financing needs. Premier Bank also has the capability to offer investment products, home mortgages, and insurance services through non-affiliated third parties. Eric Wang is proud to confirm that after 13 years, Premier Bank is now located in four locations: two in Denver and in Aurora and Colorado Springs. They have helped the Colorado economy by employing a total of 48 employees in these four branches, all offering superior customer service and state-of-the-art technology, giving customers the conveniences of a larger bank with the friendly, personal attention expected from a community bank. In addition, Eric says, many of their employees have extensive experience in banking.

Eric, and his family - wife, one son and two daughters, love Colorado. They love the space, the beauty of the mountains and the weather. They are bilingual and speak Chinese and English. The family knows all about working hard, respecting parents and elders, but as can be expected, sometimes, there are conflicts. In rearing their children, he feels the need to balance out the Western and Asian values. "The world is changing and we have to accommodate the changes in our lives. There is no right or wrong. Sometimes, we need to compromise."

"But wherever you are," Eric says, "It is how you train yourself that becomes very important. You must have passion for your work and you must work hard. There is no way to be successful without putting strong effort in whatever you do."

## Paul Lee

Paul Lee is Executive Vice President and Director of the Premier Bank in Colorado. The bank is unique in the sense that it is the only Asian bank in Colorado (ownership is 80 percent Asian). "The bank has made impressive growth, since its establishment," he says.

Paul originally came from Seoul, the capital of South Korea. He graduated with a B.S. in geology from Yonsei University, which is considered to be one of the best universities in the country. Later, he took accounting courses from the University of Maryland on the U.S. military base in Korea. He had a perfect command of Korean, English, Japanese, German and Spanish, but he is now comfortable with Korean and English, after a hiatus from the other languages.

He has talents in sports and music. He has been exercising his entire life as a body builder during high school, an amateur wrestler during college and an avid swimmer today. He lifts weights and swims daily. He sings as a soloist at his church, the St. Lawrence Korean Catholic Church.

Prior to coming to the United States, he worked for Bank of America for four years and American Express for 12 years.

He immigrated to the United States with the goal of establishing a bank. To gain experience in banking, he worked for Center Bank (previously California Center Bank) for three years as and a vice president and an international trade officer. Then he worked at Wilshire State Bank in Los Angeles for three years, as Vice President and Trade Finance Manager.

He came to Colorado and joined Premier Bank on April 15, 1997 as a top executive and stockholder. Premier Bank started operations in Denver in December 1995.

Paul is married to Theresa. They have a son and a daughter, both well established in their professions. His son, Gene, graduated from the University of Colorado at Boulder with a degree in finance and now works at Wells Fargo Bank in San Francisco as a business banking specialist. His daughter, Yulie, graduated from Haas Business School, University of California-Berkeley. She works at the Los Angeles Office of Deloitte & Touche as a tax accountant. Both children are bilingual and they are confident in the importance of maintaining the Korean culture in their heart and coping with American culture. Paul and his family have been enjoying and living in a bicultural environment.

His family still maintains the Korean culture and enjoys eating Korean food. Respect for elders is high on their hierarchy of values. He emphasizes courtesy and good behavior. He believes in close family ties and expects younger members to be responsible for older members and to take care of them in their old age. Paul wants to help APAs and supports a great number of APA organizations such as the Asian Roundtable of Colorado, the Asian Pacific Development Center and the Aurora Asian Pacific Community Partnership. Also, he has been supporting St. Anna's Home, an Assisted Living Home for Korean American Elders in Colorado, as the chairman of the construction committee and fundraising committee.

As a corporate executive, he is involved with 30 organizations and has annually supported 60 events, including aid for the Ethiopian, Korean, Vietnamese and Chinese communities. He is proud of supporting ethnic communities in their businesses, events, and their growth in the U.S. He has also been enjoying life in Colorado, together with all ethnic communities and their cultures.

## Satish (Sam) Kumar

Sam Kumar is the founder, president and CEO of Microtech-Tel. Microtech-Tel (MT) has been a Denver-based managed services provider since 1988, providing voice and data solutions to small and medium sized businesses. Some of its customers are the State of Colorado, Coors Brewing Co., Children's Hospital, Tristate Generation, PacifiCare and others. MT maintains more than 15,000 voice and data ports in the Denver area. Kumar has been profiled in the Denver Post, Denver Business Journal, Washingtonian Magazine, and quoted in Forbes and Washington Post. Kumar was also the finalist for the Entrepreneur of the Year award given by Ernst and Young.

In 1988, Sam Kumar was director of marketing of Telecom Equipment Corporation. Before that, he was a member of the Technical Staff of GTE/Siemens. Mr. Kumar has a M.S. degree in electrical engineering from Arizona State University.

On the issue of how APA immigrants cope with the social and cultural challenges he notes, one needs to be quite determined to overcome all the odds in order to succeed. There is no substitute for hard work along with the use of common sense in making decisions. Making educated decisions based on market research and intelligence also leads one to success. The competition in USA is very stiff and one has to go above and beyond the call of duty. Part of a man's responsibility is to give back to the community in many different ways like giving monetary donations, volunteering and providing leadership for the youth.

He feels that as immigrants we need to unite, work together, help each other, build a solid community and also participate in the political process. Also, we need to put our children in cultural organizations in Colorado such as in the local chapter of BalVihar in order to preserve our ethnic values. Both the father and mother should provide the necessary environment for their children to succeed, such as: providing them with adequate discipline, sending them to appropriate institutions of higher learning, encouraging them to participate in music, sports and leadership activities. He feels that there is no substitute for hard work.

# Tini Malik

Tini Malik, a successful businessman from Pakistan, came to the United States in 1971 and enrolled at Sacramento State College in California then went on to graduate from Metropolitan State College, Denver, with a B.S. degree in accounting in 1975. Soon after that, applying the principle of free enterprise, Tini started a series of businesses with the help of capital from his father in Pakistan. The first business was Mi-T-Mart, located at 22nd and Oneida. Today, this grocery store has been expanded into an 80,000 sq. foot shopping center. Family-owned restaurants in the Denver International Airport are thriving and a liquor store, Golden Triangle, Wine and Sprits, which he established 15 years ago, is doing extremely well. In 2006, he acquired his latest venture, a 96-unit apartment building.

Tini Malik's secret of his success is: "Family -- everyone works hard to keep our businesses going and everybody helps each other." In addition, Tini believes in blending the best of American culture with the best of Asian culture. He also attributes his success to the merger of these two cultures and his family's cultural assimilation in their adopted country. Tini continues to be humble, friendly and accommodating and never arrogant nor proud of his status. He said, "I have had no personal problem due to racial discrimination. I have kept my Asian identity and I am respected for it"

A close-knit family, Tini is married to Humaria and they have two girls, Tara and Farah, both studying in Cornell University, Ithaca, N.Y. Tara is majoring in political science and government, a good sign that she may be a future representative or a senator, and Farah is a freshman. They keep their Pakistani culture in the Muslim tradition. Together with 300 other families, they attend an Islamic Center in Parker, Colorado.

Tini's advice to the younger Asian generation: "Hold on to your culture, respect your elders, work hard and there is no limit to your success. Think big and have courage and you will find out that there is no obstacle that you cannot overcome."

# Kerry Steven Hada

Kerry Steven Hada has successfully established his own company, the Law Offices of Kerry S. Hada, P.C. in Englewood, Colorado. Born and raised in Denver, Kerry graduated from the University of Colorado, Boulder, with a Bachelor of science degree in marketing (1971), from Colorado State University Graduate School of Business with a Master of science degree in management (1976) and from the University of Denver, College of Law with a degree of Juris Doctor (1988). Throughout his college and graduate school years, Kerry was an honor student, on the President's Honor Roll and Dean's List, while doing graduate research and teaching.

While in college, he enjoyed sports, excelled in ski-racing and was nationally ranked. He was president of the C.U. Ski Racing Club and a coach at the Bill Marolt Ski Racing School and the Winter Park Racing Club. In addition, Kerry still had time to do volunteer work with Easter Seal handicapped people and less-fortunate children.

Where did this amazing man find the time and the energy to be a top military history student? He was president of Scabbard and Blade, tri-service military honorary, graduating first in his Army ROTC class and went on to be Cadet Battalion Commander. He was also the top military graduate at CU and was commissioned as a United States Regular Army infantry officer.

After college, he joined the U.S. Army (1971-74), again excelling in whatever he did - from Airborne Ranger infantry officer to platoon leader to company commander and special operations team leader. His training included infantry officer basic, airborne, Ranger, special operations, nuclear, biological, chemical warfare and air transportability. He obtained the highest scores on Army physical training tests. He earned an expert infantry badge and numerous medals, commendations and awards.

After his Army life, he worked as a personnel counselor and later in sales management for CF&I Steel Corporation in Pueblo and Denver. He was a law clerk at Manville Corporation and also served in the management offices of Merck Corporation.

Since 1989, Kerry began his own private practice in his Law Offices of Kerry S. Hada, P.C. with an emphasis on federal and state criminal defense, civil litigation, plaintiff personal injury, divorce and family law. He was admitted to the bar in Colorado and Hawaii and to practice before the Colorado Supreme Court, the Hawaii Supreme Court, the U.S. District Court of Colorado, the Tenth Circuit Court of Appeals and the U.S. Supreme Court.

Kerry's response to the question about enhancing APA visibility was: "Society's views about Asian Pacific Americans have changed dramatically since World War II. Through their positions as educators, politicians, judges, attorneys, doctors, and corporate officers (among many others) Asian Pacific Americans can continue to increase their visibility. However, increased visibility is not limited to only those with leadership positions. Asian Pacific Americans can increase their visibility in society through community service. Community service may be one of the few universally admired traits."

Kerry's involvement in associations related to his law career and his participation in community services would fill pages. To mention a few, he continues the volunteer services with less fortunate children, which he started while he was in college in 1970-present; he is the founder, past president, judiciary co-chair and member of the board of directors of the Asian Pacific American Bar Association of Colorado, 1990-present; he is a member of the Japanese American Citizens League, Japanese Association of Colorado (1998-present), and Asian Chamber of Commerce, 1998-present. He is coauthor of an article on Minoru Yasui published in the *Colorado Lawyer* (July 1998); he is a judge in the natural resources appellate competition, Denver University College of Law, 2003-present; Denver Kids supporter, 2005-present; advisor to the Dragon Boat Festival, 2007-present and on the board of governors of the Japanese American National Museum, 2008. He has received the Colorado Supreme Court award for pro bono commitment achievement in 2006.

# Shiou Yun Wang Jefferson

Shiou Yun Wang Jefferson has a fascinating story to tell. She was born in China, moved to South Korea where her family immigrated, studied at the Normal University, Taipei, Taiwan, lived in Japan for four years, and then studied English at the University of Denver in 1977. She married Richard Jefferson in 1978 and had a son, Joseph, in 1979. In all those years of moving and traveling, she learned to speak Korean, Japanese, Mandarin, Chinese and English, which has helped her much in her restaurant business. "I worked hard throughout my life," Shiou says. "America is fair. You have all the opportunities. If you work hard, you will succeed in whatever you do." Shiou said she started working in the Twin Dragon Restaurant as an employee, learning all the tricks of the trade from a patient and kind owner. She was treated like a daughter. Seeing her persistence and hard work, the owner decided to sell the restaurant to her when he retired. He knew Twin Dragon would prosper under her. While she found out that in America, one is evaluated by production and results, her Chinese upbringing were more relationship-oriented,

In order to run her business, Shiou needed capital. Shiou smiles as she recalls how good people were. They all trusted her. She did not have much, but the owner gave her liberal terms on a loan while friends and family offered her private loans. Bravely, she bought Twin Dragon and later moved the restaurant from across the street to the present location at Broadway and Dartmouth in 1982. From its original 10 tables, the restaurant expanded its floor area and seating capacity amidst beautiful surroundings and Chinese atmosphere. Shiou has also added another business next to her restaurant, the Twin Dragon Trading Company, a gift shop of collectibles.

She acquired all her delicious Chinese recipes when she worked on her family farm in Korea. What fond memories she had of her childhood! Although they all worked hard on their family farm in Korea, she recalls how she learned to cook with her six sisters, serving two tables every day as they always had relatives coming and going from China. "All the recipes served in Twin Dragon are her own," Shiou proudly says.

Since accomplishing her dream of owning a restaurant, she leaves another legacy for her family to remember. She built a small village in Sandong in China, where her father was buried. In this village, 75 houses were constructed for the old people in the town in honor of her father. She remembered that her old father and other seniors in the community did not have any place to meet during their leisure hours except in an open space. Now they have a center where they can play mahjong or other games. She also sends a yearly donation for its upkeep.

But her greatest achievement, which she calls her "second dream," is her son, Joseph. She wants him to be successful and that would be her happiness. Someday, she wants to go back to China with Joe and show him the village. And someday, she wants to be behind her son when he presents her to the public (perhaps acknowledging a reward or after winning an election) and says "This is my mother."

# Chapter 5

# ASIAN PACIFIC AMERICANS IN AGRICULTURE, TECHNOLOGY AND ARCHITECTURE

Agriculture is one of the leading economic sectors in Colorado. Productive farms in northeast Colorado along the South Platte River, in southern Colorado along the Arkansas River, and in the San Luis Valley, and the orchards in the western part of the state guarantee Colorado's position as one of the important food-producing regions in America. Agriculture has a long history in Colorado and Asian Pacific Americans have been an integral part of this --- from the early Chinese laborers who worked on irrigation projects and the early Japanese farm laborers and farmers right up to the present. This chapter features Bob Sakata and his son Robert, the owners and operators of the famous Sakata Farms in Brighton.

For the past few decades, Colorado has also become one of the technology centers of the nation. Prominent Asian Pacific Americans in technology are more usually associated with California's Silicon Valley computer industry or other areas along the East Coast. However, Colorado APAs have also made important contributions. This chapter features two prominent Asian Indians, Vinod Tewary and Prabhakara Rao.

In the field of architecture, we feature a well-known Japanese American architect, Ron Abo, who has excelled in this field. He discusses his struggles growing up in America.

## Robert Yosharo Sakata

Robert Yosharo Sakata, or Bob Sakata, owner of Sakata Family Farms in Brighton, Colorado, overcame numerous challenges to eventually receive many awards as a farmer and leader in the Japanese American community and Colorado. The Sakata Farms brochure proudly proclaims, “Since his modest beginning, founder Bob Sakata has held firm to some simple beliefs: grow the finest produce, build strong business relationships based on honesty and integrity, and support the community in which his family calls home. This quest for excellence has made Sakata Family Farms the nation’s agricultural leader in product innovation, industry advancement and community stewardship.”

The fields of Sakata Family Farms are monitored daily to determine the exact moment in time when crops will be at their peak for harvesting. Operations are carefully geared to eliminate bruising. Crops are packed immediately and cooled in specially-designed cold storage facilities to preserve their natural taste and nutrition.

Sakata Family Farms produce extra sweet, crisp fresh cabbage and deep green broccoli. They grow the best onions, which are skillfully harvested and gently stored in their climatically controlled atmosphere to insure freshness and quality throughout the storage season.

The Sakata Family Farms stretch for 30 miles in the Platte River Valley. Their brochure states, "Blessed with summer sunshine and clean water from the Rocky Mountains, the farm also takes advantage of the cold Colorado winters to help reduce pests. Using state-of-the-art planting, harvesting and processing procedures, more than 3,000 acres are professionally managed to produce delicious, nutritious, food for consumers nationwide."

**Bob Sakata and son Robert Sakata pose in front his office wall lined with plaques and awards**

Bob's father, Montaro Sakata, came to the U.S. from Japan in 1905 and worked in the rice fields in Stockton, California. But the San Francisco earthquake of 1906 interrupted his work. He had to help rebuild San Francisco after the terrible earthquake and fire which devastated the city. Instead of returning to Stockton, he later worked for Emmanuel George on his large orchards of apricots and cherries in Alameda, California. Montaro was a very good gardener and Emmanuel, impressed with Montaro's gardening skills, allowed him, as a sharecropper, to rent a 10-acre farm in what is now called Fremont. In 1920, Bob's mother came to the U.S. as a picture bride and Montaro's family grew. First, Harry, his older brother was born, followed by twin sisters Mitsuko and Fusako. Bob, the youngest child, was born in 1926. His mother died when he was six and he remembers how kind, loving and caring she was. Their family was close-knit, always helping one another. They all worked on the farm where they planted all kinds of vegetables – beans, cucumbers, tomatoes, and celery. His father was called a truck farmer.

The Sakatas were all doing very well economically until World War II began and that changed their lives. In 1942, President Roosevelt signed Executive Order 9066 and the entire Sakata family was relocated to the Topaz internment camp in Utah. Bob was 15 then but he remembers how obedient and law-abiding his father was. They left everything behind on their thriving farm. His father always reminded them to have faith in the U.S. He would say, "Behave and be good citizens." Still, Bob recalls how they were supposed to be protected, but in his mind he questioned why the sentrys' guns were pointed towards the camp. He knew something was wrong, but he kept this inside him. In the meantime, he did everything legally to leave camp. On December 1942, he was allowed to go to Colorado, leaving his family behind.

In 1943, a new life began for Bob Sakata. Bob began working for a farmer in Brighton, Colorado. He walked to Brighton High School where he graduated in 1943. He wanted to go on to Colorado State University but instead took extension classes on agronomy and horticulture, which helped him as a farmer. At 17, Bob was already a mature adult. In 1944, he decided to move his family from California to Brighton. There, they all worked on the farm. Unfortunately, his brother Harry died of cancer at age 34, so all of the responsibilities fell on Bob's shoulders. But he didn't complain. He continued working on the farm. Another challenge was when he had an accident. An oxygen fuel tank blew up and 65% of his body was burned. He was hospitalized for more than a year. But this didn't discourage him. He was more determined to work harder on the farm.

Not all of Bob's luck was bad. In 1955, at age 29, he was nominated and chosen as one of the outstanding young farmers of

America by the U.S. Chamber of Commerce. In 1956, he married Joanna and they had three children, Robert, Vicky and Lani.

Today, son Robert Thomas Sakata is involved in farming. He has a degree in microbiology and chemistry from the University of Colorado at Boulder. He was appointed by Governor Roy Romer to be a member of the board of the State Water Commission and later became its chair. Because of his excellent performance, he is very well respected in the Colorado legislature.

But it all began when he acquired 3,000 acres of farmland in Brighton and the Platte Valley. Starting with only $1,200, he rented his first 40 acres, which he later bought. He began hiring a few workers to grow vegetables.

Bob Sakata has loyal families of three generations working for him. In the summer, he hires 247 workers and 66 in the winter. These are full-time employees. His corporation furnishes housing with no rent and offers health insurance and workman's compensation if workers are hurt on the job. Bob's philosophy is simple. "We may not be able to offer all the fringe benefits as large corporations do, but as long as the workers know that we care for them, they remain dedicated in what they are doing." Sakata Farms is always trying to do anything possible to make the workers' lives easier and interesting because then their productivity goes up. For example, when harvesting and packing broccoli, instead of having workers wallow in the mud, Sakata Farms builds shaded platforms in the fields to shield workers from the sun. They also provide machines to harvest onions, which is backbreaking work if done by hand.

For their efforts, Bob and Joanna Sakata are recognized all over Colorado, the nation and the world. The Sakatas were hosts to Prince Hitachi, Crown Prince Naruhito, Emperor Akihito and Empress Michiko of Japan at their farm and home in Brighton. In 2000, the Emperor of Japan awarded Bob Sakata the Order of Sacred Treasure, Gold Rays with Rosette. Bob and Joanna are also recipients of the Pioneer award given by Japan America Society of Colorado on November 10, 2007 "for their substantial contribution to the Colorado community. Sakata Family Farms is a manifestation of the American dream despite numerous challenges and made possible by the Sakata's pioneering spirit and the support of their family and employees." Another honor is a Lifetime Achievement award for outstanding support of Colorado agriculture, given by Governor Bill Owens in 2005.

Both Bob and Joanna have been giving back to the community as they served as members on various boards and committees in schools, hospitals and churches. Bob served as president of the Brighton School

Board for years. Forty years ago they donated generously to the Brighton Community Hospital (now renamed the Platte Valley Medical Center).

Fortunately, Bob says, he hardly experienced any serious racial stereotyping or discrimination. He did mention a particular discriminatory bill which was once introduced in Colorado legislature due to pressure by three Brighton farmers. This bill would have kept Japanese farmers from California from buying farms in Colorado. Then Governor Carr declared it unconstitutional and promised to veto it should it come to his desk. The bill never passed.

Bob feels very blessed with much wisdom from his family and his heritage. He did not feel anger or bitterness against the three farmers. "Bitterness does not get you anywhere," he wisely says. Thirty years later, when these same farmers passed on, the members of their family asked Bob to be one of the pallbearers, and he accepted without any hesitation. He learned to forgive.

As an advice for the younger generation, he quotes Henry Ford's words of wisdom, "In this free nation, nothing is impossible. If you work harder than others, opportunities are endless." He concludes with advice from his father, "If you start getting ahead, build people up with you." That explains why he has loyal employees. He builds them up with him.

## Vinod Tewary

Dr Vinod Tewary is a physicist working on nanomaterials at the National Institute of Standards and Technology in Boulder, Colorado. He was born in Hardoi, India. He attained his Bachelor's and Master's degrees from Lucknow University and a Ph.D. from Delhi University. Before coming to the U.S. in 1985, he was a professor and dean at the Birla Institute of Technology and Science in Pilani.

Tewary is the author of a book and more than 100 research papers. He is recognized as a pioneer in the development of lattice green's functions for the mathematical modeling of solids. For his research work, he has been awarded the Bochasanwasi Swaminarayan Pride of India award, a U.S. government bronze medal, a Boulder County Multicultural award, and the Eric Reissner medal of the International Conference on Computational Engineering and Sciences. He is editor-in-chief of a leading technical journal *Computers, Materials, and Continua.* He is also a Hindi poet. His poems have been published in reputed magazines and the popular website, Kaavyaalaya, and included in a commercially released CD. He has written, produced and directed several Hindi plays staged by the India Association of Colorado.

Dr. Tewary's wife, Sharad, teaches computer technology at a Boulder school. She has been producing cultural events in Colorado for several years. They have two daughters. Kanupriya, the older daughter, is a Pilani graduate, and has a Master's degree in computer science from Clemson University, South Carolina. Anuranjita, the younger one, went to Fairview School in Boulder. She was on the honor roll and a National Merit scholar. She is an MIT graduate and has a Ph.D. in physics from Stanford. According to Tewary, American society, particularly in Colorado, is quite open and the racist attitudes are minimal. It is indeed a land of opportunities for the right person, but an Asian immigrant has to prove and keep proving that he/she is the "right person." Dr. Tewary's advice to parents is to actively communicate with their children and ensure that they get the best possible education and opportunities. His advice to youth consists of three "e"s: education, ethics and excellence. Have pride in your cultural heritage but get assimilated into American society. Derive strength from the cultural past but move forward into the technological future.

Anuranjita's experience growing up as an Indian immigrant was unique, as each immigrant's experience is in its own way. She says, "I was fortunate that my parents instilled in me a strong sense of cultural pride and the confidence to forge my own identity. I learned one of the most important lessons when I was in university. There were many children of Indian immigrants whose cultural background was similar to mine. It was easier for me to interact with these children. However, doing so was a disservice to the diversity of cultures and experiences that must exist in academic institutions. Overcoming the desire to fraternize only with people of similar cultural backgrounds was difficult but ultimately rewarding. It was a challenge I encourage others to undertake, and ask them to assume leadership in interacting with the society at large."

## Prabhakara Rao

Prabhakara Rao describes his background as follows: "I was born in a small village where agriculture was the main occupation. My parents and my father's two elder brother's families all lived together. Our family was well respected in the village. It was challenging growing up in a large family, where the needs of children were not always met. The family followed all the Hindu traditions and festivals. These religious traditions provided a rich cultural background for me while growing up, which remained with our family throughout our life."

"I came to this country when I was 26 years old and studied aerospace engineering at the University of Minnesota. I had a good educational background before I came here. After completing my Ph.D. in aerospace engineering, I got a job at Martin Marietta in Denver, Colorado. I went back to India to marry my wife, who is also from a well-respected Hindu traditional family in a small village. Upon our return, we kept our traditions at home and participated in outside events whenever possible. This helped us blend with the dominant society without much trouble."

"Aerospace engineering was in its infant stage when I came to this country. Because advances in space and rocket technology were rapidly taking place in the 60s and 70s in the U.S., I worked hard to establish myself in this growing field. I took evening and outside courses to excel in this competitive field. My greatest challenge was to keep my job in an environment where employment in the aerospace field was going through rapid changes. It was also very hard to compete with other Americans because of my Indian accent and social and cultural differences."

"To be successful in this country, Asian Pacific Americans should take the good qualities of Asian cultures and blend them with the good qualities of American culture. America is already embracing yoga, meditation and ayurveda (alternate medicine). At home, Indian Americans teach their children their native Indian language and various Indian dances such as Bharata Natyam and Garba. Our children, like many other Indian children, participate in Indian cultural programs, as well as American cultural programs in school and outside. Our children respect and appreciate Indian/Asian culture, including food, dress, dance, festivals, language and mythological stories. Asian/Indian cultural heritage can be preserved by our children and future generations by frequent visits to Asian countries."

To enhance Asian Pacific American visibility in Colorado, Rao says, "Asian Pacific Americans are doing well individually in education, business, entrepreneurship and professional jobs. They should participate more in the political system, in social events, and work with government organizations and volunteer groups. Asian Pacific American groups should work together to exchange ideas, communicate and cooperate in achieving common goals."

"Asians Indians who came to this country nearly 35 to 40 years ago as immigrants spent most of their time establishing themselves as professionals working for reputable companies. Slowly and steadily they started getting into the business world by owning companies, hiring others or getting relatives from India to help. In the process, they stayed away from politics in this country. Also, they stayed within their own Asian Indian group without participating in social and community services. Given the opportunity, Asian Indians should participate more in social, economic and political arenas in the early stages of their life in this country."

"The people from Southeast Asian countries and other Asian Pacific Americans are intelligent, hard working, have a rich cultural heritage and traditions and have similar religious backgrounds. Many of them immigrated to America to improve themselves and to provide a better life for themselves and their children. They have a strong commitment to education and family values. They should continue to instill their cultural and family values in their children. APA families always stress the importance of education to their children. Asian Pacific Americans are usually loyal to their company and willing to work extra hours."

Prabhakara Rao has retired from Lockheed Martin after 32 years of service. He does volunteer work helping Colorado Kannada Koota, the Hindu Temple and Colorado Asian Health Education and Promotion (CAHEP). Revathi Rao, his wife, is still working as an accountant at Time Warner Cable Company.

They have three children, two girls and a boy. Both girls, Jyothi and Arathi, after graduating from Columbine High School, went to India to study medicine at Kasturba Medical College in Mangalore, Karnataka State, India. They are now married and settled in the U.S. Their son, Ravi, completed his architecture studies at Iowa State University and is currently working in San Francisco.

# Ron Abo

Building community through architecture is Ron Abo's passion. For more than 30 years, Ron has dedicated himself to Denver's architectural needs on a very personal level. By 1972, Ron was the director of the Visionary Community Design Center where he gained extensive experience in consensus-building within community action committees. He has won awards for his intelligent, responsible work in Denver, including the Martin Luther King Business Social Responsibility Award in 1998. He has been listed in *Who's Who in American Businesses* since 1980.

Ron graduated from the University of Colorado at Boulder, (1969) with a Bachelor's degree in architecture, cum laude. He also took graduate courses in urban sociology and community development at the University of Colorado Denver

Committed to providing a high level of service and to fully understand an owner's needs, Ron realizes the full potential of each project and is committed to exploring design to create excellence. As Principal-in-Charge, Ron is involved with projects from inception through completion, orchestrating a multi-disciplinary team of architects, engineers and specialty consultants.

Some of his outstanding projects include: the National Park Service – Florissant Fossil Beds National Monument, Visitors' Center, Florissant, Colorado.; National Park Service – Grand Teton National Park, Moose Maintenance Center, Jackson, Wyoming; National Park Service – Mesa Verde; Denver International Airport concourses A, B and C; Cross Community Family Resource Center, Denver; Bruce Randolph "Green" Town Homes, Denver.

Ron has been recognized and honored with numerous awards among them: Colorado Holiday Commission; Wilcox Building, Douglas County Schools Administration Building, Castle Rock--First Place Commercial Category, NARI 1990; American School and University 1990; Highland Square, Denver - Citation Award, Colorado Society, American Institute of Architects.

Ron is currently the principal of the Abo Group, Inc., was an Associate of the Barker, Rinker, Seacat Architects and the ABR

Partnership; is a member of the American Institute of Architects, Denver Chapter (1980-present), of which he was president in 1991; Colorado Chapter (1980-present).

Ron talks about his pride in his Japanese heritage and culture. "First and foremost, I am most proud of my Japanese heritage. There was a time that I was not. I was born shortly after WWII ended and the sentiment against Japanese Americans was very high, visible and aimed directly at me. Parents would not allow their children to play with my sister or me. I endured taunts at school. I grew to be ashamed to have a Japanese face and hid from all that was familiar to me (food, customs, dress, language). During college in the 1960s, the civil rights movement was in full swing. Cultural identity was the key to self-realization and to rid me of the shame of my own heritage. I returned to my roots and embraced all my culture as an American of Japanese ancestry. I think it is important for anyone who has been made to feel that their racial, ethnic or cultural heritage is somehow inferior should embrace these and choose for themselves what aspects to hang onto or let go. It is the freedom of the individual to choose who they are and not be defined by anyone else."

"As a Japanese American, I think culture is very important. I think it is wonderful that in Colorado we have a rich representation of many Asian Pacific cultures. Twenty, 30 years ago, there were only a handful of APA communities. Now Asian Pacific American communities are extremely diverse and each APA community brings its own rich identity and customs to the broader community. "

To help strengthen the cultural ties and cooperation among Asian Pacific Americans, Ron is a board member of the Asian Chamber of Commerce, chair of Denver Asian Pacific American Commission and a member of the Advisory Board of the Agency for Human Rights and Community Relations of the City and County of Denver.

To enhance APA's visibility in Colorado, Ron wants more leaders in government positions to advocate for the APA community. These leaders need to be appointed, elected or volunteered to positions within all levels of government, private enterprise and civic organizations. The recent defamatory article written by University of Colorado student editor Max Karson, "If It's War Asians Want ... It's War They'll Get," created uproar in the APA communities. Ron says, "I was especially proud to see that the younger generation of APA students and professionals voice their opposition to this article. I think we should all support and encourage the young people of the APA community to become more involved in issues that concern APAs in Colorado."

# Chapter 6

# ASIAN PACIFIC AMERICANS IN SOCIAL AND CULTURAL AFFAIRS

Community members in prominent social and cultural positions can bring about positive changes and are in fact one of the greatest assets of a society. They take it upon themselves to lead, guide and support better outcomes for their brethren in formal and informal roles. Within Colorado's Asian Pacific American population, such leaders are important pillars of APA communities. They have a vision of what needs to be done and support the basic needs of their communities. They also strive to have APA communities reach greater heights through cultural sharing and the development of astute organizational skills. These community leaders wield power and influence in decision making, policy development, and the implementation of programs that utilize the collective skills of APAs. Such work can be challenging, but good leaders find the ways and means to make things happen.

Colorado has an impressive group of APA leaders in social and cultural affairs who are worthy of mention. In this chapter, we include some who have contributed selflessly to APA communities and have received recognition from their peers. These individuals have demonstrated a broad APA focus and have worked on projects which benefit numerous APA groups. Such people have committed their time, talent and even their own personal resources to lead APAs. Over the years, these dedicated individuals have contributed much to the development of Asian Pacific American communities and American society.

This chapter features Lily Shen, George Yoshida, Donna LaVigne, Van Simsiman, Gloria Williams, Tom Migaki, Chris Wanifuchi, Kit Williams, Eed Cefkin and Patty Coutts. Other chapters include individuals with exceptional talent in business, education, agriculture, technology and architecture along with the above qualities of social and cultural leadership.

# Lily Shen

Lily was born in Kaohsiung, Taiwan. After her husband, Richard Shen finished a large construction project in Guam for his civil engineering company in the late 70s, they decided to take a break and travel to the U.S. mainland. They visited many cities but they were most impressed by what they saw in Colorado – the great environment for their children's educational and professional development. They then decided to move their entire family to the U.S., settling in Littleton. Since coming to Colorado, the family successfully owned and operated the Littleton Heating and Air Conditioning Company until 2005.

With boundless enthusiasm, Lily is involved in several organizations. Her work keeps her connected to her heritage while also increasing her cultural awareness in the Metro Denver community. As a committed and generous leader, she does not decline any nominations to leadership positions in Asian organizations, oftentimes serving simultaneously. These positions include the following:

President of the Asian Roundtable of Colorado; Board Member, Asian Chamber of Commerce; Chair, Colorado Asian Pacific Spring Festival, Chinese New Year Celebration; Honorary Chair, American Cancer Society, Asian Pacific American Relay for Life; Adviser, Asian Pacific American Times, Board Member, Asian Performing Arts of Colorado; Steering Committee Member, Aurora Asian Pacific Community Partnership; President, Colorado Chinese Evergreen Society; Member, Colorado U.S. Senate Asian Pacific American Advisory Council; Ambassador for Peace, Inter-religious International Federation for World Peace, President, Summit Choir; Board Member, Wells Fargo, West, N.A. Community Forum. She has unselfishly donated her time, expertise and financial assistance to hundreds of worthy causes, and in 2006, was chosen by the Girl Scouts Mile High as a women of distinction. She has also been involved in the immediate past as officer or member of the following organizations: Asian Chamber of Commerce (Board Chair 2007); Asian Pacific Development Center; Chinese American Council of Colorado (President 1999 and 2000); Colorado Chinese Club; Chinese Youth Foundation of Colorado; Norwest Bank,

Littleton, Colorado; Denver Chinese Culture Center; Denver Museum of Natural History and Denver Performing Arts Complex. In 2001, she and her husband received the Parents of the Year given by the American Family Coalition of Colorado, Inc. for their outstanding parenting of their children and their fine example of leadership and service to the community. In the same year, they were awarded the Million Family March Family Award for their outstanding example of parental guidance and support in the family as well as service to the community. 2005 Outstanding Leadership and Dedicated Service, from Taipei Economic and Cultural Office in Kansas City; 2004 Nobel/Women, Colorado Pioneer Women's Award from The National Organization of Black Elected Legislative Women; 2004 Outstanding commitment and effort in supporting human services, from the Asian Pacific Development Center; 2004 Outstanding Contribution Award, from Colorado Asian Pacific Cultural Festival 2004 Chinese New Year's Celebration; 2003 Ambassadors for Peace Excellence in Leadership Award from Inter-religious and International Federation for World Peace. These days she also organizes health fairs in partnership with Colorado Asian Health Education and Promotion to support health and human services for the vulnerable seniors at Sakura Square residential towers, and bring about change for an improved quality of life of such seniors.

She overflows with happiness as she mentions the achievements of her family, "My oldest son, David, has a BS (in electrical engineering) from Cornell University and an MBA from the Wharton School of Finance, University of Pennsylvania. After working with Goldman, Sachs & Co. in New York and Hong Kong, he is now a partner with Olympus Capital Holdings Asia, a private equity group that focuses on direct investments in the Asia Pacific region. He and his wife, Eileen, now live in Tokyo, Japan, with their three children, Dylan, Emily and Corey.

Her second son, Peter, has a BS (in aerospace engineering) and MS (in accounting and MIS) from University of Colorado in Boulder. He started his career with Hewlett Packard and is now a Finance Director with Celestica, one of the major global EMS (electronic manufacturing services) company. He currently lives in San Jose, California.

Her daughter, Jen, received a BA (in speech communications) from Northwestern University and is now working as an independent graphics designer. She and her husband, Ben Chang, M.D., a clinical instructor in Anesthesiology Fellow, Cardiothoracic Anesthesia at Washington University School of Medicine in St. Louis, MO, have one child, Hailey.

Her perception of the U.S. before she came was different. "Because of all the Hollywood movies and TV shows we had seen in Taiwan, we thought the U.S. was one huge metropolis consisting of mega cities like New York and Los Angeles with an urban life style centered on high-rise apartments, traffic congestions, public transportation, ever-present crowds, etc. That notion had provided an ironic sense of comfort as it was similar to what were used to in Taipei. We actually had a bit of a "culture" shock adjusting to the more sprawling (and leisurely) suburban life style of Colorado, after settling in Littleton.

The biggest cultural difference that I have come to understand and accept but am not sure if I can ever make the full adjustment is modesty. Modesty is highly revered in Chinese culture. Chinese believe that a person, no matter how accomplished, should be unassuming and not feel the need to be validated externally as only unsolicited praises are considered appropriate. Even from an early age, Chinese children are always taught to remain quiet and low key rather than showing off their knowledge or ability of accomplishments.

On the contrary, in the U.S. and other western cultures, it is not only considered acceptable but often necessary for a person to more aggressively promote himself/herself. Modesty is often misunderstood as a sign of meekness or lack of confidence. In an American environment, this is where I, like many other Chinese in the U.S., have had to constantly fight against my own deeply ingrained modest instinct to speak up more and be more assertive.

"My husband and I have always tried to instill some of the traditional Chinese values in our children so that they may take the best of what the Eastern and Western culture have to offer. As a result, I think they have all grown up with a distinctive bi-cultural Chinese American identity whereby they are equally comfortable in an American as well as Chinese environment. While they have all well-assimilated into the American culture, I am pleased that they view their Chinese heritage with a sense of pride and understanding. I hope our children and grandchildren would preserve and pass on to their future generations some of the same Chinese values that my husband and I have tried to instill in our children, including work ethics, filial piety, humility, loyalty, emphasis on family and education, and, of course, love and appreciation for Chinese food and cooking."

"Asian Americans under-representation to date in political institutions at both local and national level has led to a lack of general awareness and protection of their issues and concerns. This could eventually threaten the socioeconomic success that had been hard earned by generations of Asian Americans through hard work and sacrifice.

I would therefore strongly urge members of the Asian American community to actively participate in the political process in order to have their voices heard. Furthermore, Asian Americans must cultivate and elect representatives and leaders who would focus on and represent interests of the community in order to secure our socioeconomic status in the U.S. in the long term.

To enhance Asian American visibility in Colorado, Asian Americans must be prepared to take on not only causes that are dear to their heart but also those that matter to the entire Colorado community. While we need to do a better job of communicating our own issues to the general public, we should also take an active interest in the general community. We must demonstrate to all members of the Colorado society that Asian Americans are very much a part of the community and, as such, can be counted on in supporting important issues and causes that contribute to the general welfare of Colorado. In that connection, I would urge all Asian Americans to participate and get involved in their local communities."

# George Yoshida

George Yoshida is a community leader with the "Aloha spirit." The "Aloha Spirit" is the coordination of one's mind and heart ... it is within the individual—it brings you down to yourself. You must think and emote good feelings to others." No wonder, George evokes good feelings to others. When asked why, he answers, "Because you have to live it every day of your life."

Retirement after 35 years as a clinical social worker at Denver's National Jewish Hospital and Research Center has not stopped him from his voluntary community services to the public, particularly to the Asian Pacific American community. Volunteer work dedicated to educational, cultural enrichment and social services activities, building bridges of understanding and goodwill among Asian Pacific ethnic groups and people East and West. Vicky Lubthisophon and Nancy Webster McKinney, past co-chairs of the Aurora Asian/Pacific Community Partnership, best described him. "George sets an example for what retirement is about – using free time to help others, to make the communities in which we live a notch better. He lends his vision, wisdom, insight and good sense of humor to lead people and organizations upward to new heights."

George was born in Honolulu, Hawaii, the paradise island. George prides himself as a Hawaiian of Japanese ancestry. He still has a vivid memory of when the Japanese attacked Pearl Harbor on Dec. 7, 1941. "When I was an 8-year-old boy," he said, "I climbed up a mango tree and watched the Japanese Zero fighter planes, with their insignia of the rising sun, fire live machine gun bullets from their planes. What a realistic scene! They were real live bullets!" Another vivid memory was that early morning the FBI took his father for interrogation. His father never uttered a word about this incident and he took it to his grave.

George graduated from McKinley High School and Palama Gakuen Japanese School in Hawaii. He was drafted into the army and stationed in the Scofield Barracks Training Center in Wahiawa, Oahu. While undergoing basic training, the movie, "From Here to Eternity" was filmed, featuring Frank Sinatra and Burt Lancaster. At that time, his training company was part of the scene that was filmed. The scene was a reenactment of the Japanese Zero fighter planes flying over Kole Kole Pass and flying over Scofield Barracks. "When the planes opened fired, our training company was filmed with all of us scattering for cover." The Japanese Zero fighter planes completed their mission flying over Scofield Barracks and attacking the radar and radio installation beyond the barracks in the mountain area, then returning to their carriers.

During this period, George remembers a significant incident of his life, which centers on a Buddhist card. "I was drafted in the U.S. Army and I was sworn in but before basic training, my mother took me to the Buddhist Temple for a blessing. The priest gave my mother a Buddhist card (an amulet similar to St. Christopher's medal). My mother, in turn, gave that Buddhist card to me, to protect me and to keep me safe. Both my mother and father urged me to serve my country like our 442$^{nd}$ Regimental combat team (Second World War) did. The Korean conflict ended a few weeks later and his company was deployed elsewhere. "I still have the card," George said. "It has a sentimental meaning to me," as he remembers his mother who was dear and close to him while he was growing up. He still values her life teaching in his work as a social worker and as an individual.

He met and courted Helen, who later became his wife. They have five children, four sons and a daughter. Except for one son who lives in California, the rest reside in Colorado. Kaci, their eldest granddaughter, is their first grandchild who is very active in the APA community, performing Hawaiian dances. Since coming to Colorado, Helen and George have continued to love Hawaii and the music of Hawaii. They have encouraged Kaci to learn the Hula dance and this has taken on a new meaning for them. She continues hula dancing and the expression of her dancing has been a source of pride for Helen and George.

Following his Army tour of duty in 1956, he moved to Colorado in 1956 and enrolled at the University of Colorado, Boulder, using his G.I. Bill of rights. Helen got a job at the law school and helped support him through college. George graduated in 1960, with a B.A. in Sociology. At graduation, Helen was also honored with a "PHT Degree" (Putting Hubby Through Degree) an honor to all the wives who supported their husband through college. To further his education, he enrolled at the University of Denver, earning a Master's Degree in Social Work (MSW).

While George was attending University of Denver Graduate School of Social Work, he and Helen were hired as cottage parents to troubled youths at the Clayton College for Boys/Residential Treatment Center located at the corner of Colorado Boulevard and Martin Luther

King, Jr. Boulevard. The Clayton Estate owns the property as well as the Park Hill Golf Course and the estate are administered by the Denver Court system. The work experience coincided with the book learning at the Graduate School of Social Work, as the 10 boys were the textbook examples walking right in front of them. Helen and George continued this role as cottage parents when he was employed at the National Jewish Hospital for several more years until they finally gave it up.

After graduation from Denver University, George was employed by the National Jewish Hospital and Research Center as a clinical social worker and therapist, a position he held for 35 years. He retired in 1997.

In the matter of faith in his family, George says there is some kind of openness. He and his parents were Buddhist, later converted, baptized and confirmed as Episcopalians. His brother is an ordained Episcopalian minister. His parents also converted and were baptized by his brother.

George is a fulfilled community leader. His retirement has given him a chance to give more of his time, talent and other resources under his disposal. He exudes sincerity, trust and confidence driven by his desire to help not only the Asian Pacific Americans in Colorado but also mainstream society. George can be seen attending all the sponsored APA activities, not only as a participant, but also assisting in whatever capacity he can serve, such as in the CAHEP, Cancer Relay Program, and the Project C.U.R.E. programs.

It was not hard for Asian Pacific American Times to invite him to be a volunteer community reporter. He covered events and APA activities, whenever and wherever he could attend. He always worked with a smile. George has really made a difference in the lives of Coloradoans, particularly the Asian Pacific American community, and is still going on. He is an avid student of APA cultures, always looking for occasions to learn and serve the different diverse groups.

He has also been active in the Denver Center for the Performing Arts Kindred Spirits Program, participated or attended various New Year celebrations; Japanese, Korean, Chinese, Hmong, Jewish, as well as, Native American, Filipino, Hispanic and Indian cultural activities. Likewise, George is always present during the annual Asian Pacific Heritage Month celebrations. His desire to learn more deeply about other cultures has led him to attend church events including Catholic, Lutheran, Episcopalian, Methodist, Baptist and Buddhist. He has also served on the Board of Directors of the Asian Pacific Development Center for six years (two three-year terms). During that period, Helen also volunteered at the Elmira Office in Aurora as well as in the York office in Denver. He also continues serving as Consultant of the Asian

Youth Mentor Program, headed by Ge Thao (Youth Mentor Program Director) as well as being a volunteer for the APDC outreach medical program.

George has received honors and recognition including: Mile-Hi JACL Pacesetter Award, 2007; Minoru Yasui Volunteer Community Award, 2006; Asian Pacific American Times Certificate of Appreciation, 2006; Colorado Dragon Boat Festival Honorary Couples Award, 2004; Parents of Excellence Award (Parents Day Celebration) University of Denver Community Service Award

My Asian American Pacific Island identity is very important to me and I can identify some common shared values, which include (a) importance of family (b) respect for elders (c) being the 1st born male and the responsibilities it carries (hard work to make a life for your family) (d) education – very important to take up an occupation and do your very best (e) do not bring 'shame' to your family. Learn more about the "other" Asian ethnic groups (i.e., their culture and traditions and involve with the diverse community and learn more about their culture and activities.

I would leave the experts in education to draw up the curriculum for the lower grades, high school and college.

We need more teachers of Asian heritage teaching all grades. The APA students need to have teachers of Asian heritage so that they can identify with Asian teachers in various ethnic groups. They must be well versed in their cultural background to support the student's identity and encourage them to learn. For the non-Asian teachers, they should attend the various cultural activities of our Asian communities and then receive a certificate of attendance or some criteria to certify them. Likewise, our Asian language school should also teach the students about their heritage/culture and have the Colorado educational system involved in coordination with the curriculum.

The diverse Asian population, with its demographic location, generational stages of each, acculturation as well as the inter-marriages of our hapa (Caucasian/Asian) likely is very confusing on how they view their parents and grandparents' culture. This area sociologically and culturally requires further research and evaluation.

"My major in sociology and courses in cultural anthropology as an undergraduate, as well as my Master's degree in social work with specialization in adult/child therapist, has been invaluable and rewarding. The most rewarding part my job as therapist for 35 years is the response from my patients and clients. They tell me that I have made a difference in their lives.

# Donna B. LaVigne

Donna LaVigne, as immediate past chair of Region V, successfully furthered the goals of the region by bringing other Filipino organizations in Colorado to affiliate with NaFFAA. This section also recognizes Donna as leader of the Filipino American Community of Colorado (FACC); her volunteer activities as Vice-President of Fund-Raising for Uplift Internationale and her joining the medical missions in the Philippines for the last 10 years; her active work as member of the Broomfield City and County's Cultural Affairs and the Health and Human Services Advisory Councils; as current Treasurer of the Dragon Boat Festival; past co-chair of the Aurora Asian/Pacific Community Partnership; and Past member of the Governor's Asian Pacific American Advisory Council (GAPAAC).During her two terms as Chair, Donna successfully started and organized the annual "Filipiniana," annual events that recognize the achievements of Filipino Americans in Region V, showcases Filipinos and local talents and a venue for fund raising for worthy causes supported by NaFFAA. The NaFFAA Region V Regional Conference and Filipiniana 2007 featured the Philippine American Medical Symposium.

Donna, born in Aklan, Philippines, credits her late father for her passion and dedication to help others. She learned from his example that volunteerism is a natural part of life, not an option. To her, "it is more of a duty and obligation to get involved in community and humanitarian services." Bringing that concept with her to America, she continues to immerse herself in community projects, serving as President of the FACC. To her, FACC is her second home. "It provides us a security of having the members as our immediate family, where our children can learn the basics, as well as the most important heritage and culture of Filipinos, of hospitality, respect of elders and authority, and the practice of the *bayanihan* spirit."

Donna is recognized and honored with many prestigious awards. Some of them are as: honorary chair, of the 2005 Colorado Dragon Boat Festival; Humanitarian Award, Uplift Internationale; Outstanding Leadership, FACC; Leadership and Service, AT&T Broadband/GAPACC; Special Recognition, Aurora Asian Pacific

Community Partnership; and Most Distinguished Alumna, Northwestern Visayan Colleges, Philippines.

To strengthen cultural ties and cooperation among the different APA communities, Donna suggests that "we need to foster collaboration and understanding by supporting APA communities and business organizations, focusing on team building by preparing our youth for leadership development and supporting them in the arts, athletic, and political arenas and promoting APA pride by celebrating culture and recognizing contributions and achievements."

As an Asian American, she wants to preserve most the *bayanihan* spirit "the Filipino culture that embraces a powerful sense of extended family and community, where every one derives a satisfaction of working together."

## Silvino "Van" Simsiman

Van, as he is called in the FACC community, was born in 1935 in Cabugao, Ilocos Sur, Philippines. He is married to Fe and they have three children, Frances, Daniel and Theresa, and two grandchildren, Taryn and Griffin. He came to the U.S. as a student and first enrolled in Hartnell College in Salinas, California where he earned a associate's degree in Arts in 1958. In 1961, he earned his B.S. in industrial engineering from California Polytechnic State University, Obispo, CA. He officially obtained his Industrial Engineer California license in 1969. Moving to Denver, he graduated from the University of Denver, with a Master's degree in Business Administration in 1970.

"Van" describes his experiences with the Filipino Club of the Rockies (FCR), which became the nucleus of the Filipino American Community of Colorado (FACC). In his own words is a narration of his involvement and commitment to the Filipino community, which later expanded to the Asian Pacific American communities.

"My wife, Fe, and I joined the FCR on July 4, 1962 during an Independence Day celebration at the Frank Mendoza residence, where we met most of the members then. That was the first time we became involved with a group of Filipinos (or Filipino Americans) after almost a year trying to locate or contact them. We enjoyed the celebration – the

Filipino food complete with *lechon* (roasted whole pig) that was prepared at the site. We were very much welcomed among new friends and acquaintances. Forty-nine days later, on August 22, our first-born daughter, Frances, arrived. (Frances later became President of the FACC). From there, we became very active, involving ourselves in all aspects of FCR, including assuming leadership positions and being elected as officers in the organization.

"Serving as Secretary in 1963, I spearheaded the updating and improvement of the FCR constitution and by-laws and organization. Under the new organizational set up, I was treasurer in 1964-65 at which time, we implemented improved record/keeping and more timely collection of dues. Gaining more acceptance and influence, I was elected vice-president for 1966-67 at which time we begun considering formal incorporation of FCR. For lack of further interest, primarily due to membership apathy and FCR's own struggle for relevancy, the idea of incorporation became remote. I became president in 1968 and held the post for two terms (1968-69 and 1970-71. In my mind, I formulated what were needed to be done and so as Secretary in 1973, I gained FCR's approval to mandate a special committee to draft a new constitution and by-laws and re-organization plan. Then President Eusebio Sevilla appointed me to chair the committee and by summer 1973, we reported to the membership and won approval on November 28, 1973, by an enthusiastic 80% majority, for the reconstitution and re-organization of the Filipino Club of the Rockies into the Filipino-American Community of Colorado as incorporated in the State of Colorado. I was elected as its first president."

Armed with engineering degrees and a license, Van easily found a job at Samsonite Corporation as an industrial project engineer. Little known is his expertise in settling work standard grievances at the company. He was later promoted to the position of industrial engineering supervisor, charged with directing a staff of 23 engineers and technicians involving design of facilities for their new assembly plant. Another promotion as manager led Van to manage 38 engineers, which also involved union relations and work standards. He rose to higher levels to the point where he supervised a staff of eight professionals and played major roles in planning and control of a $40 million modernization program at Samsonite Corporation. After 21 years at Samsonite, he retired and opened his own business: Simsiman and Associates, where he managed an apartment rental and a dry-cleaning family business, which was dissolved in 2002. Van then worked for 10 ½ years in the Colorado Department of Health and Environment as an engineer, dealing with environmental programs in the Hazardous Materials and Waste Management Division.

Van has received numerous awards including the following: Life Member, FACC, 1986; Life Member Service Recognition Award, FACC, 2001; Certificates of Appreciation, FACC, various years; Outstanding Achievement Awards, FACC, various years; Parents of Excellence Award, Colorado Parents Day Council, 2005; Excellence and Achievement Award, given by National Federation of Filipino American Associations (NaFFAA Region V), 2005 Community Service Award, CAHEP, 2006-2007.

Never knowing when to retire and relax completely, Van became a volunteer/advocate and representative for the Filipino American community at the Colorado Asian Health Education and Promotion (CAHEP). In his capacity as chair of the Health committee, he became involved with studies of tuberculosis and tobacco use control among the Filipino community.

"I am willing to take any advocacy or leadership position to help enhance or advance any FACC interest," he says. "I extend these commitments to serve the APA community and I encourage and support any member of my family to do the same."

He continues, "Perhaps the greatest challenge, especially in the early younger days, was getting accepted in person, ideas or language, among older, stranger members in the FCR. Selling the vision of an expanded, more relevant Filipino organization such as what actually became the FACC, was a great challenge. The mobilization and maintenance of total consistent community support and enthusiasm in the fund raising and acquisition/maintenance of the *Bahay Kubo* were challenges as well."

Van would like to preserve for his children, the traditional family that is morally strong and with open and adequate family member support system. More rationally based aspects of Filipino culture should be preferred but the ethics of *bayanihan* (helping others); *tiyaga* (patience); or *pakikisama* (getting along) are always useful. Avoid *bahala na* (come what may) or the *gaya-gaya* mentality (keeping up with the Joneses or copycat).

To strengthen the cultural ties and cooperation among the APA communities, Van suggests networking and maintaining contact with various APA community organizations and leaders. In addition, collaborating and participating in pan-Asian affairs such as the Colorado Dragon Boat Festival, Asian Film Festival, or in the awareness campaigns on issues of both health and education disparities in the APA communities would be other ways to strengthen ties.

"The present generation of Filipino Americans at FACC has widespread appreciation of their parents or grandparents' culture. They have experienced and lived the culture at the *Bahay Kubo*. This has been one of the greatest achievements of FACC. We should not, however, expect or demand their complete conversion to the culture. That will be counterproductive. Let us let the young people make their choices of culture to live their lives. Remember, we parents are multi-cultural (mixture of oriental and occidental influences) ourselves in order to live comfortably in this great country!"

## Ratnamanirao Chunilal (Manu) Raval

Manu was born on November 1, 1922 in Dehgam, in the Gujarat region of the Old Bombay province of the British Raj. The family belonged to middle class and had inherited the intellectual aristrocracy of the Nagars – the highest stratum among the Brahmans. Manu attended elementary schools in Dehgam and in the small town of Vadharota, about 40 miles away from Ahmedabad. He is the eighth in a family of 4 brothers and 5 sisters. His father was among the elders of the Nagar group and was well versed in Sanskrit and scripture literature. His father was a courageous, upright, honest person with great regard for truth. His mother was a pious, compassionate, God-fearing woman, full of affection for the family and community.

Manu graduated with a Bachelor's degree in English literature in 1945 from the prestigious Elphinstone College of Bombay. He studied Economics and Sociology for his Master's and Bachelor's in Law, between 1945 and 1947. He speaks several Indian regional languages. He also knows Sanskrit and is a student of Vedas and Vedant, and secular Sanskrit literature. He married his college sweetheart, Chanda, who, too, at a young age was a freedom fighter, and later became a well-known poetess, playwright and a social worker. She received her Bachelor's in Sanskrit and Master's in Philosophy. They have one son who came to the

U.S, for graduate education. In 1963, he married a Caucasian girl from Ohio. Manu and his wife came for the wedding and migrated to the U.S., leaving behind a comfortable and predictable life.

In 1915, Mahatma Gandhi returned from South Africa. Manu was growing up at that time that Gandhi's nonviolent disobedience ideology was spreading. At the age of 12, Manu joined the Indian National Congress, which in 1947 brought independence to India.

Today, besides his work in international trade and business management, Manu continues his volunteerism in various social and spiritual organizations. He has held executive positions such as chair of the Hindu society of Colorado and Asian Roundtable of Colorado. He also chairs the Gandhi group of Colorado, which celebrates Gandhi's birthday and spreads the message of non-violance and harmony to all Coloradoans. He is also involved in writing a book on Patanjali's Yoga Sutram, a political prince who followed Gandhi and courted numerous jail terms and penury.

Manu believes that, "some of the most profound philosophy contained in the Vedic literature is a great human heritage, which the future generations of Indian Americans may neglect at their own peril. It may enrich the world-culture in nonviolence, truth and love for a greater peace and harmony of the human race the world over."

## Chris Wanifuchi

Chris is a Colorado native and the third daughter of Japanese American parents who migrated to Colorado during World War II. She and her husband, Howard, have two daughters, Leslie and Jennifer and two grandchildren, Lauren and Kyle. While working and raising a family, Chris attended school at night and received a Bachelor of Science, Business Administration degree (Magna Cum Laude) at Regis University. Some years later, she was accepted to the Regis University Master's of Nonprofit Management Program as a Colorado Trust Fellows in 2002. She later received a Master's degree in nonprofit management and graduated with honors.

Chris' professional background includes both working in the profit and non-profit arenas. She was the chief operating officer for

YouthBiz, a non-profit youth development organization. She was recently selected to be the Executive Director of Asian Pacific Development Center, where she plans to enhance their existing programs and services while looking into the future for new ways to serve the APA communities.

Her community involvement includes participation in many organizations such as the Denver's Commission on Aging, Denver Mayor's Asian Advisory Council, Asian Roundtable of Colorado and the Aurora Asian/Pacific Community Partnership.

Chris believes it is most important to preserve as much of her cultural heritage as possible, such as traditions, standards, language, arts, food, family, honor, respect, community and your religion. "Where you come from and knowledge of your ancestral heritage can truly define you as a person."

To help strengthen cultural ties and cooperation among the APA communities, she believes that "if you carry on your shoulders and in your heart a philosophy of inclusiveness and an unconditional belief that we are all human beings, one can bring together people and communities. I am an advocate for all APA communities to the rest of the world and to help bring down barriers that many face. I will be a single voice of many voices that say we of the APA communities are strong and alive. There also must be a sense of sharing and communication."

## Thomas J. Migaki

Tom Migaki was third in command under Mayor Wellington Webb. He served as manager of general services for the City and County of Denver, in charge of five agencies: Purchasing, Theaters and Arenas, Public Offices/Facilities, Utilities and Central Services. Currently, Tom is grants manager, Budget and Management Department of the City and County of Denver under Mayor John Hickenlooper. He is a Certified Public Accountant and affiliated with the American Institute of CPAs, N.Y. and with the Colorado's Society of CPAs in Denver Colorado. He graduated from the Harvard University, John F. Kennedy School of Government for Senior Executives in State and Local Governments (2003). He was a recipient of several awards, including the Wells Fargo Bank award, Asian Pacific Islander Employee Resource Group Award (2002) and the Martin Luther King Business Social Responsibility Award (2001). His community affiliations include the Asian Chamber of Commerce and the JACL Mile-Hi Chapter.

A Denver native, he attended South High School, graduated from the University of Northern Colorado with a degree in accounting and earned an MBA from Regis University.

His father, who lived in Portland before WWII, was interned at Minidoka. His mother lived in Nebraska and was not interned. "The irony is that some of my relatives in Nebraska had German POWs working for them during the war," Migaki says.

Migaki grew up in a culture that was both Japanese and American, partly because his Japanese-speaking grandparents lived in Denver. "I guess I was raised with Japanese values because they worked as a baseline you live by, how you work hard and do your best.

I would like to preserve the beliefs and history from Japan, history on immigrating to the U.S. The ceremony, dress, food, values and celebrations are all important parts of my culture that need to be passed along to my child, family and future generations. It is also important to remain connected with your country of origin through family, friends, business government and education. I think it is important for each Asian and Pacific Islander culture to keep their culture intact.

"APA culture is an important piece of American history. Personally, it gives me a sense of identity. Each Asian culture brought to the U.S. brings a unique perspective and contribution and becomes a part off what makes the United States of America the best country in the world.

I can help strengthen the cultural ties and cooperation by trying to bring in younger people, immigrants and new people into the organizations to participate in the various activities to help the Asian community. The immigrants and all other participants need to understand and be educated on the history and the issues Asians have had to deal with over the years in the U.S. such as the internment of Japanese Americans and that here in the U.S., APA's are a minority. We can enhance our visibility by becoming politically involved and also participate in community groups and non-profit organizations outside of the Asian organizations."

## Gloria Williams

Gloria was born in Minglanilla, Cebu, grew up in a loving family among six siblings and close relatives. She graduated from the University of San Carlos, with a B.S. in Accounting. She met Calvin Williams while he was on assignment for an oil company. They have two children, Jacob and Amanda. Gloria has worked as an accountant in different companies and currently works for SKLD Information Services.

Gloria Williams, FACC president (1998-1999) found a rewarding challenge of leading a community towards the end of the 20th century into the new millennium. Under her energetic leadership and together with a hardworking Board of Directors, the FACC thrived, receiving the most grants during her term and building a strong financial base for which the community can plan future projects. Gloria continued to build a strong rapport with other Asian organizations, particularly the Asian Roundtable of Colorado, where she was Secretary and later President, and the Aurora Asian/Pacific Community Partnership where she was a member of the Steering Committee and later co-chair. She has also encouraged the membership of FACC into the National Federation of Filipino American Associations (NaFFAA) Region V. making FACC more visible in the national arena. Internally, she passionately encouraged the Board of Directors to approve the improvement and repairs of the FACC building, also known as the *Bahay Kubo,* but most of all, she took pride in the achievements and accomplishments of the FACC members, such as the successful cultural productions: Republika, Balagtasan, and Maria Makiling. She encouraged the commitment of FACC to co-sponsor Uplift Internationale in its humanitarian projects in the Philippines. She is particularly proud of the youth members --- the future of our community, for already they are showing the same passion and commitment to FACC as their parents.

Gloria has been an inspiration, not only to the FACC members, but also to the greater Asian Pacific American communities. Her leadership style, coupled by her spontaneous sense of humor, has endeared her to all she comes in contact with. Gloria is a recipient of the Minoru Yasui Community Volunteer Award (2004). She is no longer the unsung hero.

Perhaps, her greatest strength lies in her ability to motivate members to make full utilization of their talent and abilities. She feels that we should give generous praise and adequate acknowledgement for their contributions. Gloria started during her term to invite groups outside of the Asian population to participate in the FACC Festival. "It is exhilarating to see FACC grow, become more international, knowing that you were a part of making it happen". She was the first FACC president to invite the Aztec dance group, Danza Azteca, and the Irish Dancers. "By knowing more about them and their customs and traditions, we learn to accept and appreciate each other." She encourages FACC members to see themselves as American and be actively involved in government and business.

## Kit Williams

"I was adopted from Hong Kong when I was 3 years old by two wonderful people and grew up in mostly white middle-class neighborhoods with limited exposure to the Chinese community. When I moved to Denver my tenuous ties to any APA community was severed for a number of years until Martha Lee insisted I attend the Asian Pacific Women's Network of Colorado with her. It was one of those classic moments in accidental volunteerism where I went to the restroom and came back to find that I was President Elect. Since then I have been active in a number of organizations serving Colorado's Asian communities. For me association with these organizations has provided a personal bond to a heritage and rich cultural background I had not known growing up. Being actively involved has also given me an opportunity to become friends with incredible leaders from various Asian communities."

She has been on the Asian Chamber of Commerce Board from 1997-2002 and again on the Board from 2005 to the present, totaling approximately nine years. "I learned about the Asian Chamber and became good friends with John Wright when I was running the Women's Chamber of Commerce (1992-1996) when it was co-located in Pena Plaza with the Asian, Hispanic and American Indian Chambers."

She first started with the Colorado Dragon Boat Festival in 2005, photographing the event and had quite a wonderful time to consider volunteering again in 2006 and 2007. "I joined the Board of Directors and look forward to becoming very involved with the festival as it welcomes its first international teams. She has also been involved with the Asian Public Media project to produce TV programs that highlighted the culture, contributions and diversity of Colorado's Asian communities. In 2006, she was selected as the featured artist for the Aurora Asian Film Festival. She photograph the opening and closing events for the festival and was the event's photographer again in 2007.

She participated in the A/PW network that brought together Asian women from the Metro Denver area and was elected its President in 1992. She was in the planning committee for the A/PW Achievement Luncheon in 1993 and 1994. Martha Lee asked her to facilitate a series of meetings in 1993 and 1994 that culminated in the creation of the APWLI, a national organization that trains APA women leaders through its intensive Fellowship Program and weekend Leadership Summits held throughout the U.S. She is a founding member of APAWI and was on its Board of directors from 1995-1997. "I also went through its excellent leadership training program."

To improve or increase visibility in Colorado, Kit says, "Until fairly recently we were a very small part of the Colorado population. With increased numbers comes increased visibility especially when individuals and organizations are now willing to do activities, such as: run for public office, be assigned to highly visible appointments, or seek appointments to public and private boards and commissions. The Denver Metropolitan area has a well-established support network (social, cultural, business, heath, and media) of Asian organizations. There are also groups like the Asian Roundtable and the Mayor's Asian Advisory Committee that strives to bring together organizations to work on projects of mutual interest; continue to bring the different APA communities together, and Continue to build and support organizations such as the Asian Public Media, Asian Avenue Magazine and the Colorado Dragon Boat Festival that give voice to the Asian population."

# Piangjai "Eed" Cefkin

Piangjai, better known as "Eed," is a proponent of multiculturalism. This has been evident based on her experience as a teacher, mentor and supervisor in a refugee camp in Thailand for Southeast Asians seeking asylum in the United States. She loves working with people of different cultures such as the Vietnamese, Hmong, Lao and Cambodians. The refugee program was funded by the U.S. Department of State. Her job was to give orientation to those refugees approved for resettlement to the U.S. Such service is essential in order to prevent "culture shock" when they enter the U.S.

Eed was born in a small town in the eastern part of Thailand toward the Thailand-Cambodian border. She grew up in a military base in Thailand and lived there until her father's retirement as sergeant major. Her mother had a family restaurant. Since Eed was the oldest in the family, she was given full responsibility to work in the busy restaurant and take care of her younger siblings.

"I learned to multitask," she said. "I appreciate the opportunity now; not then, when I was young." In many Asian families, the oldest child carries the obligation to look after the welfare of the younger siblings. The younger ones, in return, reciprocate by giving the oldest sibling high respect and love.

A milestone Eed said she had in life was when she had the opportunity to go to the U.S. as an exchange student. She stayed with an American family for one year (1976-1977). Her experience living in the U.S. was critical in understanding Western culture and such knowledge has been helpful in later years in her job as a teacher, mentor and supervisor in the refugee camp. She finished her senior year in high school in upstate New York in 1977. After that, she went back to Thailand and finished her B.A. in English and psychology at Thammasat University in Bangkok, in 1981. She taught English as a second language and cultural orientation, and later became a trainer/supervisor to teachers. Aside from Thai and English, she speaks fluent Lao and conversational Cambodian.

Refugees fleeing from the communists had inundated Thailand, because of its proximity to the other Southeast Asian countries. It was logical to establish a refugee camp where Eed worked in the language and cultural orientation program for refugees.

The refugee program offered English as a second language as well as cultural- and work-orientation courses, which include parenting, housing, transportation and how to live effectively to Hmong, Lao, Cambodian and Vietnamese refugees.

Eed met her husband, Jonathan Cefkin, at work in the refugee camp. He came as a supervisor, and then became the program manager overseeing the refugee program. He is well versed in intercultural relationship and was a Peace Corp volunteers in Africa. Jonathan is from Fort Collins.

Eed traveled on a job assignment to Manila and Bataan, Philippines twice for conferences in the refugee camps. After 10 years in the job, the family decided to move back to the U.S.

In 1992, the family moved to Fort Collins with their two children. Their daughter, Tarika, was 5 1/2 years old and son, Benjamin, was 2 1/2.

Eed's earlier experience as an exchange student in the U.S., working with diverse cultures in the refugee camps, as well as her marriage to an American citizen helped her adjust to the American way of life.

Her first job was at Colorado State University, in its catering service office. Later, she found a job as a Thai language instructor to soldiers in the National Guard in Denver. She still remembers how difficult it was to look for a house to rent. Was it because she had two small children or was it because of her Asian face? She told her husband to go look for a rental house alone, but Jonathan convinced her to come along with him, saying, "If they are prejudiced, we don't want that kind of landlord."

Eed is proud to say that she has been working non-stop ever since she came to the U.S. "My work," she says, "has been both challenging and enjoyable dealing with adults from multicultural backgrounds. From being an English teacher to immigrants and as an administrator of various organizations, I am comfortable and skillful in communicating with people who know little or no English."

Eed has worked as an instructor and later as a coordinator in adult English as a second language (ESL) in Aurora Public Schools. She was an ESL instructor at Community College of Aurora and a coordinator of Interpreter's Bank at the Asian Pacific Development Center (APDC). Currently, she is the case manager coordinator for Colorado Asian Health Education and Promotion (CAHEP).

Eed has been involved as officer or member of the Board with the Aurora Asian Pacific Community Partnership, Denver Thai Lions Club, Thai Cultural Connection, Founder/President, Wat Buddhawaran of Denver, Thai Buddhist Temple and with the CoTeSol, Colorado Teachers of English to Speakers of other Languages. The Aurora Chamber of Commerce honored her in 2002 with the award called: "Women Making a Difference: Unsung Heroes," Aurora Chamber of Commerce,

Differences in faith or religion have not become a problem to Eed and Jonathan because they are open-minded. Eed is a Buddhist from Thailand and is married to an American Jew. They were married in Buddhist rites. Both of them celebrate Jewish and Buddhist traditions and both honor and respect Buddhist and Jewish heritage and customs. The family is involved in the Thai community. Their children take Thai language, dance and classical music lessons. Both Thai and Jewish people have strong family traditions, which are very important to them.

When asked how they raise their children so they can keep their identity, Eed answered, "We want to make them proud of being unique as being Buddhist Thai and Jewish American."

Their daughter, Tarika, is now in college at St. Lawrence University in New York, majoring in speech and theater. As part of the study-abroad program, she was sent to Shanghai. Their son, Benjamin, plans to study ethnomusicology when he goes to college. At present, he is with a band "Thai Harmony," which plays Thai classical music, and the principal bassoonist with Denver Young Artist Orchestra.

Being model parents, they teach their children to respect elders, set good examples, good citizenship, diversity and some sense of volunteerism and community. They are proud to say their children have grown with some sense of purpose.

Eed wants to continue to connect with other Asian communities. "We have to know that we are all Asians," she says. "We have to appreciate all cultures. There should be an ongoing support for community events." She wants to see more Asian leaders working together and supporting educational efforts to enhance APA visibility. She also endorses Asian TV channels. Furthermore, she wants to dispel the common public perception that all Asians are Chinese. Many people have no idea that Asian Pacific Americans are diverse.

# Prapimpan "Patty" Coutts

Patty is secretary of the National Association of Minority Contractors, Colorado Chapter (NAMC/CO), the mission of which includes the promotion of education and training of minority contractors, the economic and legal interests of minority contracting firms, the advocacy of laws and governmental actions that concern minority contractors and the maintenance of the highest professional standards.

"Global transformation for humanity and world peace," are big words coming from a small woman from Thailand who in 1960 immigrated to the United States. "I stand up for humanity, for everybody, for all races," she continues. "I am a community activist. I fight for the rights of everybody." Furthermore, she says, "her life's passion is to serve both underserved and minority communities to make a difference."

Patty is half Chinese and half Arabian, and grew up in Bangkok, Thailand. She is the daughter of the late Dr. Chitti Chittvej, who was a general and a doctor of the Thai Army.

After two marriages and subsequent divorces and supporting her children, Patty managed to go to college and earned a Bachelor's degree in Communications and a Master's degree in Public Administration from the University of Colorado at Denver. She also worked at the Yum Yum Tree Restaurant and at Cherry Creek Inn. She tried her luck with the restaurant business in Denver's LoDo section, but those ventures failed. Was she discouraged? No. She was still smiling and bubbly because she had a mission to fulfill.

In her 48 years in America, Patty has been involved in many Asian groups. She served as vice-president of the Asian Pacific Development Center, where she started the annual festival of Asian Arts and Culture. She later served as Vocational Counselor of the Refugee Program of the Center. She helped launch the Asian Chamber of Commerce, serving as Secretary. She was chair of the Asian Education Advisory Council of the Denver Public Schools for two consecutive terms and later as Executive committee member. She also served as Co-Chair of the Aurora Asian/Pacific Community Partnership; Executive Director of the Thai Association of Colorado, Asian representative to the Kindred Spirits at the Denver Center for the Performing Arts, Board member of the Original Aurora Renewal and the Crossover Project; member of Denver Mayor's Asian Advisory Council and member of the Steering Committee of the Asian Roundtable of Colorado. She was involved in the Asian Trade and Cultural Center (ATCC), a bold venture to build a huge business center for Asian small businesses and cultural groups. Will she succeed? We will see for "Life is a journey through summer, fall, winter, spring and each one of us will have to do our part," Patty concludes with a smile.

# Chapter 7

# ASIAN PACIFIC AMERICANS IN THE FIELD OF EDUCATION

As pointed out in other parts of this book, Asian and Pacific Americans highly value education. The importance of education is seen in its emphasis by APA families and communities and by APA educational attainments. A discussion of the latter can be found in the chapter on APA issues and concerns.

The subject of education also encompasses APA educational activities. Over the years, many APA community organizations have offered programs, classes, or other activities on APA cultural heritage, Asian languages, and English language for immigrants. Several organizations have recognized the achievements of APA high school graduates, including the Asian Roundtable of Colorado, the Asian Education Advisory Council of the Denver Public Schools, the Aurora Asian/Pacific Community Partnership, and the Japanese American Community Graduation Program.

Given the emphasis on education by Asian and Pacific Americans, it is interesting to note that APAs are often underrepresented as professionals in the field of education, especially at the K-12 level.

Within higher education, Asian American studies courses were first developed in Colorado at the University of Colorado-Boulder in the early 1970s. Other institutions that currently offer such classes include Colorado State University, the University of Colorado-Denver, and the University of Colorado-Colorado Springs. Student service programs have also been developed to meet the needs of APA college students

This chapter begins with the stories of three outstanding Colorado APA educators, Ved Nanda, John Yee and Chiyo Horiuchi. Some APAs, such as Erin Yoshimura, are involved in personal training and coaching which is an individualized form of educational activity. This chapter concludes with responses of Peggy Lore and Le Reagan to a questionnaire as they relate their experiences as Student Directors at respectively University of Colorado - Denver and Colorado State University.

# Ved P. Nanda

Born and raised in New Delhi, India, Ved Nanda came to the U.S. in 1960 where he earned a doctor of law degree from Yale University. Besides being an internationally renowned scholar of international law and a humanitarian, he has worked tirelessly for world peace, mutual respect and the progress of Asian and Pacific Americans.

Professor Nanda is the vice provost at the University of Denver and John Evans University Professor and Thompson G. Marsh Professor of Law. He also serves as director of the International Legal Studies Program. In 2006, he was honored with a $1 million gift and a matching amount from the university to found the Ved Nanda Center for International Law. He is chosen to be the 2008 Honorary Chair for the Colorado Dragon Boat Festival.

Professor Nanda is past president of the World Jurist Association, former honorary vice president of the American Society of International Law and its counselor and a member of the advisory council of the United States Institute of Human Rights. He was formerly the U.S. delegate to the World Federation of the United Nations Association and on the board of directors of the United Nations Association. He also serves as an elected member of the American Law Institute, on the board of Human Rights Center of the American Bar Association and as a council member for the American Bar Association Section of International Law. Professor Nanda has received numerous national and international awards. One of his students, Secretary of State Condoleeza Rice wrote in a tribute to him, "I have the highest admiration for you, not only as a fine scholar of international law, but also as a genuine and wonderful person. You are a rare example of a great teacher successfully merged with a great scholar."

On human rights issues, Professor Nanda says it is unfortunate what is happening in Afghanistan, Pakistan and Burma, where human rights have been violated for long periods of time. But there has been progress on the positive side. In the United Nations, treaties have been signed by member nations, which they are obligated to follow. Treaties have been signed on issues such as women's rights, children's rights, and the elimination of discrimination but more needs to be done to implement these agreements. Professor Nanda feels that, although it is sad that there are so many countries and world leaders critical of the U.S. policies, no country can challenge the U.S. on military and economic fronts. The U.S. would like to see its own values of democracy, human rights and economy be accepted, yet this will take time and will be reflected only by its actions.

Over the last few years, with the trend of self-discovery in India, Prof. Nanda thinks it is not a bad idea to go back to ancient traditions and look at the philosophy of being part of a greater society -- if one suffers, everyone suffers; if one is happy, everyone is happy; if one is prosperous, everyone is prosperous. These represent core principles of Hinduism and Sikhism and perhaps all religions of the world. Sometimes it is necessary for nations, societies and communities to introspect and understand good practices based on sound moral values that will become a beacon of inspiration for our next generation.

In response to a question on Asian Pacific American identity, Professor Nanda says that APAs need to have their own identity; that it is very important to retain values on the importance of family, reverence for elders and parents, love of learning and hard work. On the question of discrimination, Prof. Nanda says it is important for APAs to have their own imprint in political settings. "There are many political decisions that affect their lives. APAs need to be more active, and he advises that young leaders start participating in school activities, school boards, service organizations, cultural groups and go from there. APAs need to have that kind of impact in order to be visible."

## John H. Yee

John Yee has been a teacher and community leader in the metro Denver area for more than five decades. His scholarly writings and his sense of history are profound, which make him one of the much-sought speakers in Colorado, not only about the past but also about contemporary issues and events.

John's life and voluntary civic and community services to the Asian Pacific American community in Colorado and to the mainstream society are in a nutshell "driven by his firm conviction that the world would be a better place if we could combine the science of the West with the wisdom of the East; that in these very troubled times, it is imperative that we search for meaning to create a better world, with less violence, with peace and less selfishness and more caring for our fellow man."

John is married to Nai-li Yee, an APA leader in her own right. He has a son and a daughter, from a previous marriage, five grandchildren and four great grandchildren.

John was born in Kunming, China in the province of Yunnan, which means "South of the Clouds." It is located north of Vietnam, and East of Burma (now Myanmar), in Southwest China. Kunming is the capital of Yunnan Province, and, like Denver, is a plateau 6,000 feet above sea level, located in a mountainous region. The city is the political, economic and cultural center of transport, science and technology. Consequently, Kunming has become the most popular center for tourism in Southwest China due to alluring highland scenery and numerous places of historical interests. During World War II, Kunming was the airbase for the Flying Tigers, formally known as the American Volunteer Group (AVG) in which John served with distinction. In addition, Kunming became the most important city in wartime-free China as the only port accessible to military aid from America. Consequently, Kunming became the home of many Chinese refugees from all parts of China fleeing from the invading Japanese. Kunming became Denver's Sister City in China, which was officially formed in 1987 during the Pena Administration.

The events leading up to John's entry to the United States centered on the Sino-Japanese war, which dragged on during the Second World War. The United States entry into the war against Japan made China an ally against their common enemy. The mutual cooperation between the U.S. and China resulted in military cooperation. When the AVG was formed in 1941, there was a need for an English language interpreter and John joined the college students from Southwest Union University, then located in Kunming, to train as an interpreter for the newly formed American Volunteer Group (later known as The Flying Tigers).

John provides us a brief background of the Sino-Japanese war, which led to the Second World War in Asia. Japan has long possessed the desire for territorial expansion. In 1894, the Japanese started the Sino-Japanese War. When China lost the war, China had to sign the Treaty of Shimonoseki in which Japan took Taiwan, and in 1910, the Japanese took Korea. In 1931, Japan created the Mukden Incident in which she invaded NE China and took Manchuria. China protested to the League of Nations, but to no avail. Then on July 7, 1937, Japan created the Marco Polo Bridge Incident near Beijing and invaded China and with its superior military force occupied a major portion of China by 1939.

After the fall of Nanking, (and the infamous Rape of Nanking by Japanese troops in which over 300,000 innocent Chinese men, women and children were massacred in the course of three weeks). The Chinese Nationalist Government moved its government headquarters to Chunking, in far away deep Yangtze River gorges of Southwest China in Szechuan Province, digging in for a prolonged war of self survival. No sooner than Hitler succeeded to take Paris in Europe, did the Japanese take French Indochina (which includes Vietnam). Using Hanoi as a base, the Japanese sent bombers to bomb major Chinese cities such as Kunming and Chungking. The Chinese had little to defend themselves. And the Japanese bombed China with impunity.

In 1940, with the help of veteran American pilot Claire Lee Chennault, China successfully negotiated for an acquisition of 100 fighter planes from the U.S. At that point, there was a need for volunteers to fly the airplanes, and since America was not at war with Japan at that time, volunteers were sought, offering $700 a month plus $500 bonus for each plane shot down. There was also a need for English translators for U.S. servicemen. As previously described, interpreters were mainly recruited from the Foreign Language Department of the newly formed Southwest Union University, the union of three top universities from North China (Beijing, Chinghua and Nankai).

Upon graduating from training, the students were made commissioned officers of the Chinese Air Force, and assigned to various departments of the Air Force to work with the American personnel. John was attached to the American Volunteer Group (AVG) under General Claire Lee Chennault and worked for the most part at Fighter Control Headquarters.

John worked for one year (1941-1942), with the AVG Flying Tigers, and when the AVG was demobilized, the AVG was replaced by the China Task Force and soon later replaced by the U.S. 14$^{th}$ Air Force, commanded by Claire L. Chennault, who was then promoted to Brig. General. This was after Pearl Harbor, and America had entered the war against Japan. In 1943, the Chinese wished to upgrade its Air Force. The Land-Lease Program under President Franklin Roosevelt gave aid to China to train pilots and navigators and other Chinese Air Force personnel in America. In 1944, John was sent to the U.S. for help in the training of Chinese Air Force cadets.

In 1944, he came to the U.S. and travelled through a long route by ship from India, Australia and finally, California. In 1947, he got sick and was confined at Fitzsimons Military Hospital and was scheduled to go to California to be shipped back to Shanghai. By a stroke of luck, at the last minute, a phone call from Washington came saying Chungking gave him permission to stay in America. According to John, "In life, people's lives are controlled by time and chance. He quotes: "And I returned under the sun to find that the race is not to the swift, nor battle to the strong, nor bread to the wise nor fortune to the man of understanding. But time and chance happeneth to them all." (Ecclesiastes 9:11)

One incident that John experienced and will always remember was the extent of prejudice and discrimination in America. In 1944, he related, he and two other Chinese cadets went to New Orleans for a weekend visit. On their return by bus to the Air Base in Biloxi, Mississippi, they had to take a bus back to Biloxi. They were the first ones in line, but the bus driver pushed them aside and did not allow them to get in the bus. Finally, one white man, also in line at the back, noticed them and asked the bus driver why he did not let them in, as they were first in line. The bus driver then allowed them to enter the bus but they had to go to the last three seats in the back of the bus. John, until now, deeply regrets why he did not take the name of that white man so he could thank him for going out of his way to fight injustice. Apparently, the noble truth of equality is still not self-evident to many people in this world.

After the war, he received a scholarship to the University of Denver, graduating with a B.A. in Social Science. In 1960, he graduated with an M.A. from the University of Colorado, Boulder, major in history and minor in education. He then began teaching in the Aurora Public Schools. Later he taught at University of Denver and Metropolitan State College. John says, no matter what you do, if through your work, you have made a difference in someone or some people's lives in a positive way, then this sojourn has not been for naught.

John has volunteered countless hours in many Asian Pacific organizations for the last fifty years. He has been active in the Denver Sister Cities International since 1985 and was responsible for the choosing and founding of the Denver Kunming Sister Cities Committee, which was established in 1987. He also served as chairman of the Board of Denver-Kunming Sister Cities Committee from 1994-2004.

He is a past member of the Asian Chamber of Commerce, the Aurora Asian/Pacific Community Partnership, a lifetime Mason and Rotary Club member. In addition, he has led tour groups (including educational travel groups to visit China and Southeast Asia. Guests often used his home for many of the gatherings of Asian groups, offering his Chinese cuisine to promote good will. Recently, John, together with other Denver officials, accepted a gift from Kunming to the City of Denver - a bronze peacock sculpture, measuring 12 ft. long and 17 ft wide, which is now installed in a place of honor in the Denver Botanic Garden.

Recognized for his numerous contributions and voluntary work, John has received many awards, among them are the following: 1966 – Distinguished Service Award, from Americans by Choice Citizens Committee Citizens Day; 1998 – Martin Luther King, Jr., Humanitarian Award; 2001 -- We The People – Vision of America Award from the International Channel; 2002-2003 – award for his participation in the China, Burma (now Myanmar), India Theatre of War, where in WWII he was named Commander of the Colorado Chapter of the American Veterans of China, Burma, India Theatre of War; 2004 -- Honorary Chair, Dragon Boat Festival; 2005 – Minoru Yasui Volunteer Award.

**Memorable excerpt from a speech delivered during the We the People Award Ceremony, 2001**

"I think one of the problems we face in the world today, is that during the past fifty years, science and technology has advanced so fast, it has surpassed anything man has achieved over the past 5,000 years of history. So that today, we are living in a Global Village and yet, in human relations, we have not advanced at all. In fact, we have gone backward. Witness an increase in broken homes, youth problems, drugs and violence. There is no correlation between a standard of living and the quality of life."

# Chiyo Horiuchi

Chiyo Horiuchi, at 88, has lived a fulfilled life and is still going strong, doing fun things like ceramics, reading, golf or working out at the gym. She gave up skiing at age 86. She actually won a gold medal in the senior competition at Peak 9 in Breckenridge, Colorado. A very well educated woman, Chiyo has an Ed. D. degree from the University of Northern Colorado, an M.A. in elementary and secondary education and special education from the University of Denver, B.A. in Oriental studies from the University of Washington and has taken some post-doctoral courses at various universities. She has publications on special education and memberships in many professional organizations. Long after her retirement in 1988, she was still busy participating actively in several groups, including the Denver Mayor's Commission on Cultural Affairs and the Asian Education Advisory Council.

Chiyo was married to the late Robert Horiuchi with whom she traveled the world. They have two children in the San Francisco Bay area and three grandsons whom they visit often. Their daughter, Lynne, has a Ph.D. in architectural history from the University of California-Santa Barbara, an M.A. in art history and an M.A. in Italian language from Middlebury College, and B.A. in fine arts from the University of Colorado. Her son is an established guitar musician who has been recognized by Quincy Jones.

Chiyo remembers fondly her childhood, her school days and her first travel to Japan at age eight. That was when she first dreamed of traveling to other countries. Chiyo was born in Seattle, Washington and was raised in a bilingual, bicultural family. In her own words, she was "American during the day at school and was Japanese after 4 o'clock when she went to a Japanese language school." At home, her mother spoke Japanese to them. Her father, a successful businessman who owned five corporations, believed that all his daughters should go to college. Chiyo was in her senior year in the University of Washington when the war broke out in December 1941. In September of that year, a professor already warned her that Japanese Americans should move inland and prepare to become self-sufficient because a U.S.-Japan war was imminent. She thought that was crazy, believing she was an American through and through. Little did she realize that she would be one of those sent to an internment camp because she was of Japanese descent. Her experience in camp during the war years had a big impact on her life and work later on.

Her greatest contribution to Colorado is her work with special education students. For 15 years, she served as a consultant to the Colorado State Department of Education. Since the late 1960s until she retired in 1988, she worked extensively with handicapped students. She initiated the first high school programs for all handicapped in the Littleton School District, establishing work-experience and study programs. As a teacher for eight years, she worked directly with special education students, focusing on their preparation for life in society, school, family and work. She contacted and worked with city businessmen, industries, and parents to provide handicapped students opportunities to learn and work on jobs. But it was not always work and no play. For example, she integrated high school athletes with her students for after school volleyball. On one occasion, the students invited then-Governor John Love and his wife to a dinner, which they cooked. While the Governor could not attend, Mrs. Love came and ate dinner with them, listening to loud music the students' preferred. Chiyo was happy the Governor's wife enjoyed the evening so much.

During the years she was teaching, there was little tolerance for special education kids. Many years later, new laws forced the community to treat them equally. Now they are integrated into regular high school programs, except for the most severe cases. She felt her own sense of helplessness at camp during World War II was similar to what the special kids were experiencing. Her teaching experiences and consulting helped her "view the whole state and the varying status of education in Colorado." She visited all special education programs as well as provided the training and leadership for teachers at the state level. She was invited as a speaker and presenter in many in-state and out-of-state conferences to talk about handicapped children and their education and training and gainful employment. Among her useful research and publications, Chiyo, together with Dr. Dennis E. Mithaug (now at Columbia University), followed-up on Colorado handicapped students to find out how they fared after graduation from high school. Results of this study were published in 1983 and showed that students found mostly part-time jobs after high school and there was a great need for social adjustment.

Chiyo's travel wishes were fulfilled when she joined her husband on assignment to Afghanistan. They lived there for two years and she taught at the American International School at Kabul. Later, she had the opportunity to travel to three African countries (Kenya, Uganda, and Tanzania) by car, traveling a total of 5,000 miles when Bob was working for those countries.

On May 1, 2005, Denver Mayor John Hickenlooper issued a proclamation designating the day as "Chiyo Horiuchi Day in Denver, Colorado." This was in recognition of her lifelong work in special education as teacher, professor, consultant in the State of Colorado and her contributions to the Asian Education Advisory Council and numerous community cultural and social organizations was recognized. On June 25, 2006, she was selected by the Stellar Women Organization, a 6-year-old organization that was founded with the sole purpose of honoring women of accomplishment to thank them for being role models and mentors.

Presently, she is on the board of Auraria Library, the Japanese School of Colorado and member of the Welcome Colorado Club, Japanese American Citizens League, and Lowry Little League. Her wish is to see all three grandsons graduate from college. One grandson graduated in 2007 from the University of California-Los Angeles. Another is attending the Berklee College of Music in Boston. Her third grandson is thinking of returning to college. He just retired from bike racing in Europe. They are all individuals!

## Erin Yoshimura

Erin Yoshimura, Chief Empowerment Officer and founder of Empowerful Changes, is a certified trainer and life coach who focuses on empowerment – whether it's in one's career or personal life – through emotional intelligence training, coaching and personal branding. She has created training programs for clients including NBC affiliate KUSA, Raytheon and Making Connections-Denver.

She's conducted workshops, lectures and keynote speeches for Colorado State University, Denver Public Schools, St. Mary's Academy, Overland High School, the Cherry Creek Arts Festival, Japanese American Citizens League, and the Federal Correctional Institution in Englewood, Colorado.

She is a certified personal brand strategist through Reach Branding Club, certified emotional intelligence trainer through San Diego-based Six Seconds Emotional Intelligence Network, received coaching and leadership training through Coaches Training Institute (CTI) of San Rafael, California and is also a certified professional co-active coach (CPCC) through CTI. She has undertaken more than 700 contact hours of leadership and coaches training, cultural diversity and emotional intelligence seminars. Erin has also trained with Lee Mun Wah ("Color of Fear") of Stir Fry Seminars in Berkeley, Calif., a nationally-recognized Master in diversity and communications training and is currently enrolled in their certification program.

She writes a blog called "Wasabi Woman" for *DenverPost.com*, and also writes a coaching column in *East West* magazine. She has appeared often on TV and radio as a coach and spokesperson.

Erin's career before becoming a trainer and coach was in high tech, where she was an East Asian product manager, IT project manager and IT change management analyst. What she loved most about her jobs was leading multicultural teams - whether they were made up of people from various ethnicities, in different countries, spread across different sites throughout the U.S. or even in different departments within the same building. Now she combines her intercultural corporate experience and passion for emotional intelligence with professional coaching, workshops and training to teach empowerful communication and cultural intelligence skills. Erin's mission is to introduce people to more possibilities through training and coaching so they can live life by choice, not by circumstance!

Erin says “Two of my favorite Japanese traditions are bon odori and New Year’s oshogatsu. Bon odori is where Japanese Americans and many other ethnicities, regardless of their religious beliefs, dress in their yukata (summer kimono) or hapi coats, don colorful Japanese fans and dance in memory and tribute to their ancestors. It’s a way to celebrate our culture while paying respect to our ancestors and family members who are deceased.

Every New Year’s Day (January 1st), families prepare several savory Japanese dishes (osechi-ryori) ranging from tempura, nishime, a variety of sashimi and seafood, pickled vegetables and rice dishes to bring in the New Year. Many of these dishes are only enjoyed at this time of year and signify good luck, good health and prosperity. For instance, kuromame (sweetened black beans) are to be eaten by every family member whether they like them or not. And, an odd number of beans need to be eaten. We start out New Year’s Day by eating o-zoni, which is a light, fish-based soup filled with Japanese vegetables and freshly pounded mochi paddies. This signifies good luck for the rest of the year. New Year’s Eve is also a busy day filled not only with food preparation but also cleaning out the “old dirt” to ensure good luck for the New Year.

The most common cultural values that I hear are: self-effacement; don’t bring attention to yourself; avoid conflict for the sake of harmony; hold back and refuse politely when offered things; respect and honor your elders and people of higher authority; shikata ga nai -- it can’t be helped.

As a community, we need to continue to dialogue with each other and learn the differences and similarities in our culture. We also need to be open-minded on how cultural values can sometimes clash and learn to work together and hold both with equal importance.

We’re not only the most ethnically diverse group; we also have a lot of issues to address in terms of different generations (immigrant/first generation, second generation, etc), socio-economics, and multi-racial as well as historical/political issues. On top of this, we have issues in regards to what it means to be Asian Pacific American and how we merge our ethnic culture with American culture.When I attended public school, the only close representation of Asian culture taught was when we studied Japan. Contributions made by Asian Pacific Americans need to be integrated into the American history curriculum. Many people don't know that there was a Japanese American concentration camp at Granada, Colorado and that there was a bustling Chinatown in Denver until it was burned down. It's no wonder that we're still considered foreigners in our own country. Since the month of May has been declared Asian Pacific American Heritage month, it would be great to tap into this by providing short educational presentations from different ethnicities. This would require planning and organization but I'd think that teachers, especially in primary grades, would be willing to have guest presenters.

Many do not know nor even care why it is important for us to know and remember that period in American history when Japanese Americans were incarcerated in camps during World War II. The yearly remembrances and commemorations held in Colorado and elsewhere may not be enough to keep the memories alive.

The main injustice is how this important part of American history is still not given more than two paragraphs in high school American history books. Although my great-grandparents, grandparents and parents were all interned, I don't feel like I can completely convey their experience. I believe the Japanese American community, whether they have internment in their family history or not, have all been impacted differently and all stories make up the Japanese American experience. There are some Nisei (second generation Japanese Americans) still alive today who can answer this best.

## Peggy Lore

Peggy Lore is Director, Asian American Student Services at University of Colorado in Denver. She is an American-born Chinese from North Carolina. She grew up in New York, where she graduated with a B.A. in English from Syracuse University. She then enrolled at the University of Colorado Denver and graduated with a Master's degree in English. "It is difficult to talk about myself," Peggy says. "I have met so many wonderful students, staff, faculty, and community members in my work. Twenty years have flown by since I began working at UCD."

In teaching American literature, some students were surprised why, as a Chinese American, she could teach the subject. She is also bothered with the negative publicity on Chinese exports, which has been going on recently.

Since Peggy has direct contact with university students, she is one of the best persons to interview regarding APA students and their perspectives. "The construction of Asian American identity is a fragile state," says Peggy. "I think the idea of trying to form an Asian American identity is like nailing Jell-o to a wall in some instances because it is affected by many things. When people think of APAs, they think of them as being foreign, even if they were born and raised in America." In answering some questions, she was passionate about the following.

**Perceptions about APAs as Viewed by the General Society**

We have few problems and/or we have language problems. We are fairly invisible in the public eye except around Chinese New Year, food, and cultural events and when something happens in Asia (i.e. Chinese food import/scare) that impacts the U.S. population directly. Recent flooding in the Philippines and China and storms in Japan get very little press although the human losses are great.

**Racial Stereotyping in Schools and in the Workplace**

APA students are seen as high achievers or as having language difficulties that impede their progress. Teachers have very little multi-cultural training and that has not changed over time. Schools and society in general still view race issues in black and white. Because we are in the West/Southwest, they also view issues in black, white and brown. The training a teacher gets focuses on these particular ethnic groups. The low numbers of Asian Pacific Americans in teaching and administrative positions exacerbates this lack of direct contact or knowledge.

**Lack of Understanding and Knowledge of the Diverse APA Communities and Cultures**

This has been a continuing problem and this lack of understanding and knowledge exists internally and externally in our communities. Some changes have occurred when you see younger generations of students from various APA communities come together, for example through the Asian Student Alliance and CAAPA. The students interested in intra-ethnic group work seem small in number but this could be said of Asian students joining Asian American clubs – at least on this campus. The current Asian Student Alliance Club consists of Hmong, Vietnamese American and Thai students.

I think we have faculty who don't see leadership potential in APA students because they appear quieter. It think there are faculty who assume APA students may be international students (rather than permanent residents because they speak with accents). We have faculty who assume APA students cheat because they work in groups or speak in a language other than English. Ironically, APA students, particularly international students, have commented often that they have a lot of anxiety in courses that require group work where the faculty lets students form their own groups. Many times, APA students, (particularly those who speak with distinct accents) are not selected by non-Asians for group work.

## How APA Cultures Influence APA Students' Patterns of Behavior and the Way They Look at Things

I think APA students consider the ramifications of their choices more often than not in asking, "What will my parents think/want or what will this do in my family?" The response to this question has to consider whether or not a student was born and acculturated here and how long they have been here if they are immigrants.

## Working with APA Students

I work a lot one-on-one with students by presenting myself as a resource. There are many students I have worked with for years as they complete their education and it is always a joy to see the transitions over time. Many students have questions about balancing family expectations with personal goals. When I first started here, almost every student I worked with wanted to be an engineer. They, and more significantly, their parents, heard that engineering would lead to good, high paying jobs. Fortunately, many of these students had the academic skills needed for engineering so they were able to achieve their personal goals as well as their parents' goals for education. But, there were also many students who had other skills. Some students who were going into engineering really had a passion for other areas, like music or the arts. For these students, I tried not to take sides – being among the first American-born APA generation myself, I am very familiar with the tug of cultural wars that goes on for students. Many times, in talking to these students, it was to help them find ways to fulfill their goals – perhaps through clubs or performance classes while they were also struggling through their major courses, or, it was taking the time to listen as a student would think through his or her choices. I believe that this listening, giving the students the support and space to come to their own decision has been the most productive way to assist them.

More resources and information on APA communities would be helpful for all Americans to understand the diversity and richness of their cultures.

She feels strongly that "Whatever challenges there are, they are outweighed by the opportunity to assist APA students and their families. It brings great joy to be able to work with them and to give back to the community." Two current challenges are: a) unclear messages from the university about their interest in and commitment to diversity. For example, Ward Connelly has come to Colorado to try to get his anti-affirmative action bill (which he calls a "civil rights bill") on a referendum. The university, through advice from its legal counsel is asking that the Education Opportunity Programs (American Indian, Asian, Black, and Hispanic) re-organize and remove ethnic specific references in names as they relate to the delivery of services. So, it is proposed that "Asian American Student Services" would not be a program name. We could still deliver services under a broader umbrella of, for example, Multi-cultural Affairs or First Generation Student Services. I'm not opposed to serving a broad first generation student population. However, I do have a concern about not being able to use ethnic specific references. I think the ethnic names: 1) support the institutions stated commitment to diversity; 2) are symbolic and concrete representations of diversity for the campus and the greater community; 3) help students who want to meet with someone from their racial background for whatever reason identify a resource; and 4) because there is no legislation or law that has passed that specifically states that you cannot provide services under ethnic specific names. I am working to develop a proposal that will address the needs of APA students. I maintain open communications with administration. I seek student, community and academic support.

b) Competition for resources and the stereotype that Asians do not need services or do not need them as immediately as other ethnic groups. There have been discussions by UCD to try to become designated a Hispanic-serving institution. This would allow UCD to apply for certain earmarked federal dollars. There is great emphasis on creating programs, applying for grants that state that they serve all students, but the staff that are hired and the recruitment efforts favor Hispanics.

There is no discussion about getting more APA students except when a few people like me ask questions. I don't object to recruiting all students, but I think stereotypes and realities about APAs seeking education, not making waves, etc. make it difficult to raise issues. But the difficulty doesn't stop one from asking questions. I would really like to see more APA community members participating in efforts like the Blue Ribbon Commission on Diversity and other groups. I also apply for whatever funds are available.

APA's shared cultural values that should be preserved by our people. I hope that young people will continue to value history and recognize the struggles of past generations that have led them to this point in their lives. I hope that they will pass on: a) pride in who they are and what they and others have contributed; b) a passion and love of family; c) a respect for experience; and d) a desire to maintain the language of their ethnic group.

Her recommendations to enhance the visibility of APAs are: run for political office, participate on boards, run for school board, and create more scholarship opportunities, collaborate on projects with other ethnic groups in addition to working with the dominant culture, and speak-out on issues such as immigration, English-only, etc.

She notes that – “My most treasured awards have been certificates from the APA student organizations I’ve worked with, recognition from DPS’s Asian Education Advisory Council board, a university staff award, a UCD staff award, and the Richard Castro Social Work award.”

## Le Reagan

Le has been Assistant Director of Asian Student Services, at Colorado State University. He notes that perceptions of APAs are dependent on geographical locations, immigration status, socioeconomic status, educational level, etc. “I was born and raised in Oregon and the APA community there is much different than Fort Collins. I know Denver has a pretty large APA population/community, but I have not been exposed to it enough to is much different than Fort Collins. I know Denver has a pretty large APA population and di**verse** community, but I have not been exposed to it enough to understand the dynamics of it.”

APAs living in a predominately white community with a minimal number of APAs tend to be of a higher socioeconomic and educational status. With that status, they often are seen as a model minority. In terms of their APA identity development, they may see themselves as white and thus act that way to assimilate into the general society. Besides the color of their skin, they are basically considered white by nonAPAs until the issue of race is brought up.

In certain areas on the West/East Coast, there are higher numbers of recent immigrants from Asia and they tend to be of a lower socioeconomic and educational status. They tend to live in more closely knitted communities, but that is usually perceived by outsiders as isolation/segregation from the "mainstream" community. Gangs are also more prevalent, thus instead of seen as a "model minority," they are labeled as low class troublemakers who don't belong in the U.S.

In general, with the manipulation/misinterpretation of statistical information, APAs are seen as a "model minority" in terms of their perceived high educational attainment and socioeconomic status. Despite this, they are still seen as passive, perpetual foreigners, and do not possess the "qualities" of a leader. The following are his thoughts.

## Racial Stereotyping

As a result of the "model minority myth," APA students are typically encouraged by schools (teachers and advisors) to pursue areas such as math and science. This discourages them from pursuing other areas like social work, student affairs, teaching, etc. Areas of math and science tend to be "robotic" in nature and typically do not involve much "leadership." Thus APA students are encouraged to take that route because of their perceived lack of leadership qualities.

In the workplace, APAs are seen as "great" workers, but not exceptional workers who will quickly get promoted to leadership roles. They are seen as passive and good at their specific work but "not possessing" the aggressiveness and leadership qualities to elevate themselves to a higher position. Thus a glass ceiling exists for APAs in the workplace.

## Portrayal of APAs in the Media

In general there isn't that much representation of APAs in the media. APA men are portrayed as the most emasculated males of any racial group. They are portrayed as nerds, asexual, "gay," as "great male companions," etc. Even when they play roles that are typically seen as "masculine" such as martial artists and heroes, they are still somehow desexualized in terms of them being able to become sexual/sensual with a female character.

APA women, on the other hand, are excessively sexualized, eroticized, and perceived as submissive. This perception creates fetishes among predominately white men due to the power dynamics of them not only by having power over a woman, but also because the APA woman is seen as being powerless and submissive to their sexual fantasies. So basically as a result of the media, no one wants to hook up with APA men, but it's okay to "do it' with APA women.

## Lack of Understanding and Knowledge of Diverse APA Communities and Cultures

APAs are diverse racially and geographically, but most people just clump them together as Chinese, Japanese, Hawaiian and others.

I believe Southeast Asians are the fastest growing APA population in the U.S., but there is little knowledge and recognition of them. The Hmong and Mien are relatively ignored and unknown.

Generational status is typically ignored too. First generation SE Asians have totally different needs and experiences than third generation Chinese/Japanese, but that is rarely recognized by the mainstream population.

## Working with APA Students

Coming from Oregon State University where there was a much bigger APA population and sense of community, it was a little difficult adjusting to an environment at CSU that lacks a sense "APA community."

Most of the students here come from predominately white communities and don't necessarily recognize their APA identity. Many are still in the developmental stage of denying their APA identity and wanting to be "white" so that they won't be perceived as "outsiders." This makes it more difficult to connect them with our office, because they don't want to be different and step outside of the mainstream.

Due to the model minority myth, students are under enormous pressure to succeed academically; otherwise they would be looked down upon. This not only comes from their classmates and professors but also from their families. APA students who do poorly in math are basically asked, "What's wrong with you?" as though they are genetically engineered to excel in math.

I went to a Hmong cultural show at CU Boulder last year and learned a few things about the Hmong population in Colorado. I didn't realize that Colorado has the fifth largest population of Hmong in the U.S. The reason why that was a huge surprise for me was because I am only aware of fewer than five Hmong students at CSU! That doesn't seem that representative. Furthermore, one of our Hmong students just transferred back to Denver after her first year here. I went to Oregon State University, and Oregon isn't even ranked in the top ten in terms of the number of Hmong, but when I left OSU, we had about 40 Hmong students. That's up from five when I started school there in 1999. The reason for that was active recruiting of Hmong and Southeast Asian students. These populations are highly underrepresented in higher education. We went to community centers, high schools that they attended, community events, and met with families to educate them about college. The goal wasn't to simply recruit them to OSU but to educate them about the benefit and experience of college. Most of the work was done by current Hmong students, and they spreading the word to their community.

My overall point is that the APA population is extremely diverse so we need to start working on providing the support to specific APA populations and not just provide general support. I would love to start connecting with the Hmong and other Southeast Asian communities but our resources are limited and the university wants our office to focus more on retention than recruitment, which to me is unfortunate for these populations.

One of the biggest cultural values of APAs is collectivism. This value of collectivism in comparison to Western individualism can at times create a lot of burden/pressure for students. Many APA students (especially recent immigrants) go to school not only to make a better life for themselves but also for their family/parents. They are expected to financially support their parents/family. So when they do badly in school, they are not only failing themselves but also their family and this adds a lot of unnecessary pressure, which results in depression, suicides, and erratic behaviors.

## Programs for APA Students

The biggest focus for our office is the retention of first year and new transfer students, so we do a lot of programs around that. Some programs that I directly work with:

We have peer mentors that reach out to all APA first year and new transfer students to help them with the transition to CSU. For those that live in the residence halls, the peer mentors occasionally visit them to check on them and let them know about our programs and events. They implement social programs such as movie nights, ice cream socials, and Wii nights to get the APA students connected with one another. They also implement academic programs to help with their academic success and career goals. The peer mentors take a course about basic counseling skills, Asian American identity development theory, issues facing APA students, and different resources available on campus for students.

The PALS Program is a big brother/big sister type of program where we pair mostly CSU APA students with APA K-4 graders in the community. They get together every other Sunday at CSU for two hours and do various activities such as cultural crafts and games. Most of the little kids are adopted, so it's a good way for them to connect with someone that looks like them.

TEA Time (The Experience of All) is a bi-monthly series where we have craft and cultural food demonstrations; workshops on things such as how to deal with homesickness (a big issue for Hawaiian students) and career development skills; and we frequently bring in special guests (mostly CSU APA staff/faculty members) to talk about their experiences as an APA and issues affecting APAs.

ATAPA Project (Ask the Asian/Pacific American) is a program to actively educate CSU and the community about issues concerning APAs. For the first project we interviewed various people on campus and created a DVD talking about the representation of Asian Pacific Americans in the American media. It was a great project and created a lot of buzz through our presentation of it. It challenged the current representation of APAs in the media and offered some strategies on how to be critical viewers of the media and proactively create change.

A program that the office does that I'm not directly involved with is the Jump Leadership Program. It's a program geared toward first year APA students and it focuses on the development of their leadership in terms of their APA identity. As mentioned before, society don't see APAs as leaders and this workshop helps them to better understand their APA identity and that they, too, are leaders and can develop to be great leaders.

## Resources and Information on APA Communities

I think there are a lot of resources out there to help non-Asian Americans understand the diversity and richness of APA cultures. The issue is accessibility and whether they truly want to understand our cultures. Americans are one of the most ethnocentric people in the world and typically see non-whites as foreigners and thus don't care much to better understand them. I believe the information and resources are out there and it depends on whether we use them and how we use them.

**Biggest Challenge**

My biggest challenge is reaching out to APA students and helping them connect with their APA identity. It is not something I can force on students rather, they will need to discover themselves and hopefully become a support-resource. I continue to reach out to students by attending their club events and reciprocally inviting them to ours. I have seen many students who were initially hesitant to connect with our office, but once connection is initiated, they gain better understanding of themselves. This allows them to give back to the community by serving as a support-resource to other APA students. "Connecting" involves not only sending e-mails and flyers but also the process of relationship-development.

**APA's Shared Cultural Values**

I think APA's shared cultural values are an important component of their identity, so they all should be preserved. They should not, however, be "showcased" all the time, but they should be aware and not be ashamed. They need to adapt their shared cultural values so that it will work best for them in the real world.

**Enhancing the Visiblity of APA in Colorado**

I think Colorado does a pretty good job of creating visibility of APAs, since there are big events like the Dragon Boat Festival and are represented in the news media, but that's only one type of visibility. APAs may be physically visible but the issues they face are not as visible. There is a need not only for "Asian" cultural shows but also for a more "APA" focused educational events and programs. With the perception of being seen as perpetual foreigners, the dominant society has yet to distinguish "Asians" from "APAs." When society understands this better, they can begin to understand the ethnic breakdown of the APA population. I think the best way to truly enhance APA's visibility in Colorado is through politics, by being actively involved with social issues in the community and making sure our voices are heard.

## Conclusion

I've only been here for a little over a year, so I'm still somewhat trying to adjust to the culture here and figure out why things are the way they are. Most of the programs/events I do here were already established before I came, and I've just been trying to improve or make changes to them. My students have recognized me for my mentorship and by my colleagues for my continued active support of them and their programs/events.

# Chapter 8

# PERSPECTIVES OF THE YOUNGER GENERATION OF ASIAN PACIFIC AMERICANS

This chapter focuses specifically on the younger generation of Colorado's Asian Pacific Americans. It features the stories and personal views of several individuals who talk about their experiences growing up as APAs in Colorado. These stories cover such important themes as the challenges they faced and their accomplishments, families and values, and sense of ethnicity. All of these individuals were able to surmount difficulties and excel in their studies.

The second and later generations of APAs are much more acculturated to American society than Asian immigrants, but they still retain core APA values and identities. They believe in the importance of education as a way to succeed. Many are very pragmatic and outspoken. They tend to be fairly independent, making decisions about what is good for them but at the same time taking responsibility for their actions.

APAs in Colorado are proud of the younger generation and have high future expectations for them in their economic and civic endeavors and also as leaders of APA communities. Besides the individuals in this chapter, additional members of the younger generation of Colorado's APAs appear in other parts of this book, for example along with their parents, including John Sie, Lily Shen, Ding Wen Hsu, Vinod Tewary and Mercedes Huang.

## Joseph Jefferson

Joseph Jefferson is currently an elected official and law student. He is a member of the Englewood City Council and was elected when he was 27 years old. He is probably the youngest legislator elected to serve on the Englewood City Council and he diligently represents District 1. Son of Shiou Yun Wan Jefferson, owner of the Twin Dragon Restaurant, his campaign was based on a commitment to serve the community, fiscal responsibility, and economic improvement. Joseph knows that his family has realized the "American dream" in Englewood and he wants to ensure the continued opportunity for success and quality of life that was available to his family.

Joseph was born and raised in Englewood. He attended J.K. Mullen High School and went on to Cornell University in Ithaca, N.Y. and graduated with a B.S. in hospitality management. For him, Cornell had the best business program because it provided a solid background to support his mother's business. After graduating, he worked as a stockbroker at Morgan Stanley. He later enrolled at the University of Denver Sturm College Of Law. He will graduate in May 2008 and plans to take the Colorado bar examination soon after.

Although he regrets that he is not fluent in Mandarin Chinese, he has learned many good Chinese values from his mother, values like love of family, respect for elders and hard work. He remembers being carried by his mother, sometimes being carried piggyback as a child while she worked in the restaurant. His mother's example has grounded him and provided him with a unique prospective.

What does the future hold for him? Joseph plans to begin a career in law and continue to pursue his political duties. He hopes to have his own firm and company some day. He is an entrepreneur at heart, like his mother. Although he is just beginning his work in politics, who knows what the future may hold? He may even become the first governor of Colorado of Chinese descent. Only time will tell. With his mother's full support and his education, realistic ambitions and hard work, there is every reason he will surely succeed in whatever endeavor he may set his mind to pursue.

## Payal Kohli

Payal Kohli emigrated to the U.S. from India with her parents at age nine. After graduating as valedictorian from Eaglecrest High School in Aurora, she entered the Massachusetts Institute of Technology in Boston. There she graduated in 2002 with a perfect 5.0 GPA in a double major in biology and brain and cognitive science, with a concentration in economics. She was also the president of the South Asian Association at M.I.T and was a very active member of their cultural programs. During her first year at

M.I.T. she was faced with her parents' divorce but that did not deter her from her ultimate goal. Upon completion of her undergraduate education at M.I.T., she was accepted into Harvard Medical School's prestigious HST Medical Program as one of 30 out of 4300 applicants. She pursued her medical career along with some very valuable research, which was published in the *Journal of Immunology* and presented at an international conference. During her medical school career, she was awarded the Ghiso Fellowship. She was also a teaching assistant for several first and second year medical school courses. At her Harvard Medical School graduation in June 2007, she was one of the two students to be honored with magna cum laude in a special field. She is presently pursuing her internship and residency at Brigham and Women's Hospital at Harvard. She plans to specialize in critical care medicine and is the recipient of the prestigious Beecher Scholarship, which will allow her to be on the Harvard faculty after completing of her residency training. Her hobbies include photography, reading, classical Indian dance and music.

In the section below, Payal discusses some of the social/cultural challenges growing up and going to school in the U.S.

"Even though America is considered the world's greatest melting pot with equal opportunities for all minorities, it is often not the personal philosophy of many individual Americans. During high school, there were many instances when the color of my skin, not the knowledge I held, determined how well I performed. For example, despite being the senior-most member of the newspaper's editorial staff, I was required to take an English test before being granted the title of 'Editor-in-Chief' because 'I grew up in a country where English was not the primary language' . Similarly, my English literature teacher insisted, despite my impeccable performance on the written and oral exams, that a foreigner could not master English literature more than a 'true American.' Roadblocks were put up at every step of the way by those very individuals in my high school who existed to support the students. I will always remember how one of the guidance counselors in my high school violated my trust in the most profound way by photocopying my application and personal essays for another 'American' student who was applying to the same colleges."

"On a personal level, having lived half my life in India, I found assimilation to be difficult and awkward. Having an Indian name and accent made social encounters more cumbersome. I remember my aunt suggesting that I change my Indian name from 'Payal' to 'Polly' in order to make my transition to this culture easier. I must admit that the suggestion tempted me... I desperately wished to fit in and obliterate all possible differences that might make me stand out against my American peers. However, the cost of altering my identity, in the most basic way, was too heavy a price to pay. It was only after I realized that my uniqueness, including my name, empowered me culturally did I truly begin to assimilate and discover that I was a product of East and West. I'm still 'Payal' and I often find myself proudly explaining the definition and origin of the word to my peers and colleagues."

"Many social and cultural practices were much different from what I had grown up with. Indian values emphasized family, obedience and education. American values, in contrast, focused more on independence and the individual. I found myself often wavering between the two, eventually striking the perfect balance for myself. High school and college, difficult times for any teenager were compounded with the conflicting messages from home and school. While all my peers were drinking, dating and partying, my parents repeatedly instilled the principles of discipline, dedication and self-restraint. Being a product of two starkly different cultures left me searching for a way to find my own path -- a way to integrate my cultural and moral foundations with the expectations of the society around me. I found a way to express and practice my Indian values amongst the South Asian community by becoming president of the South Asian Students Association at MIT. I found my place among my Caucasian peers as well. "

"I think the most important advice I can give to the other APA students is to forge your own path. In this modern society, it is very easy to succumb to pressure from society (or from one's parents) and we sometimes feel we have to do things to 'fit in.' It's important to realize you are different from your Caucasian counterparts and your Asian counterparts in India. You are unique in a special way and that should be cherished and emphasized rather than minimized. You should take the best from both cultures and remember to be true to your values and to yourself. Don't try to be someone you are not. And remember to respect your parents, above all, since they have made tremendous sacrifices for your success."

# Annie Guo

Annie Guo, 22, graduated as valedictorian from John F. Kennedy High in Denver. She was the recipient of the Asian Education Advisory Council (AEAC) award in 2004; the President's Student Service award; Outstanding Student of America award, and many more. She has a Bachelor of journalism degree in advertising from the University of Missouri at Columbia. Annie is the current marketing director of *Asian Avenue Magazine*. She contributed the article, "Growing up in America" where she expresses her personal feelings quite well.

"Growing up in the Denver Public Schools is a unique experience. From elementary through high school, I was in a surprisingly diverse environment with a large percentage of Hispanic and Caucasian students, and a few African American and Asian American students as well.

Even so, with a lack of Chinese American friends, it was hard for me to accept my "Chinese-ness." There was so much I didn't understand when I was younger. In elementary school, I wanted to fit in with my classmates, my predominantly Caucasian friends. As an Asian American, I often denied aspects of my culture. I was embarrassed to speak Chinese in front of my friends. I hated telling them to take off their shoes in my house. And I denied that I ate the seaweed sitting out on the kitchen counter. "Oh, I don't even know what that is. My parents eat that, it's weird."

I recall experiencing subtle racism at my elementary school. Kids would yell "ching, chong" to me on the blacktop and ask me why I looked different. A very vivid memory I have is of a Caucasian boy not letting me get in line for milk. He would repeatedly step in front of me to block me from the line, pulling his eyes, as an imitation of "Chinese" eyes, and singing, "aliens aren't allowed to have milk." I cried in the school bathroom that day, but never told the teacher. I was so embarrassed and didn't want to bring additional attention to the incident. I never told my parents either. I felt my parents already had enough pressures of their own, dealing with discrimination in the workplace, let alone having to worry about what was going on in Denver's elementary schools.

At that age, you convince yourself that the cool thing to do is to be like everyone else. I didn't appreciate my parents enough then. And I often took for granted the cultural values and traditions they instilled in me. When my mom would pack me fried rice for lunch, I'd often not eat it and just tell my friends I wasn't hungry. I'd go home and beg for "normal" sandwiches and "Lunchables" like the other kids were having. I also remember being upset that my parents couldn't hang out with my friends' parents, like the other kids did. I didn't understand the language and cultural barriers, and the difficulties other nonAsian parents didn't have to deal with when building their parental friendships.

But now that I'm older, I appreciate growing up in a Chinese American home, having the best of both worlds: hamburgers and dumplings, Christmas and Chinese New Year, and Chinese dramas and the Opera Colorado. And I have so much respect for my parents, especially as first generation immigrants coming to the States for their kids to have a better life. I can't begin to imagine completely starting over in a new country, learning a new language, eating new foods, and meeting new people. Leaving the state for college was even hard for me!"

At the University of Missouri, I lived with a Caucasian roommate who told me, "Wow, I've never actually seen an Asian person before," on the first day we met. She was from a small town in Missouri with a graduating high school class of 20. Let's just say it was a rough first semester dealing with comments like, "Chinese sounds so funny... Do all Asians have small feet?... Look there's your sister on TV, what is she saying?" Yes, Amber thought it was funny to refer to every Asian person she saw as being a relative of mine. Her intentions were good, but she definitely grew up in a home lacking any sense of worldly or cultural understanding.

Living with her roommate took a lot of patience but ultimately fueled my passion for getting involved in the Asian American community, which was about 4% of the student population at Missouri. "I felt it to be a personal mission to help our own community and at the same time educate others who are different from us, as to what it means to be an "Asian American". This term seems so new to people. Asian American? We were often immediately grouped with the Asian international students on our campus. That continues to be a challenge Asian Americans deal with today, having to prove that we are American. Although we grew up in the States, speak perfect English, and are immersed in American culture, our appearance gives us an instant 'question mark' as to our American-ness."

"I still dealt with racial pressures in college, ten years after the ching chongs; I was now dealing with racial hate mail and harassment, after organizing an Asian American Awareness Week at the university. The Asian American student group organized an educational campaign entitled: Race is not black and white. The campaign had a double meaning: 1) race is not a black and white issue and often falls into a grey area, and 2) typically race conversations revolve around issues between the Caucasian and African American communities. Often, Asians and Hispanics are overlooked in the discussion. It was a very successful event because although the Asian American population was small in number, we were powerful in conviction and voice. It was empowering to see a group of Asian Americans stand up together to spread cultural awareness, as we passed out flyers and fortune cookies with Asian American facts. For the most part the event was received well by the university, but there were some inappropriate remarks made by students, one of which was "why don't you guys go back to your own country"?

Alas, racism still exists today. What's hard about the race subject is knowing when race is involved. People hate it when minorities "pull the race card," but sometimes race is indeed a factor. You never really know. I have been with a group of Asian friends and not let into nightclubs, while the doorman repeatedly lets other people around us (who are not Asian) into the club. I have been in the car when an Asian friend is pulled over and treated poorly by a Caucasian police officer. I have seen an Asian man get bullied by a Hispanic man while waiting in line for the bus. Are these racially charged incidents? Can't really say, sometimes there's just no way to tell.

Now that I'm older, I see my experiences in a new light. I couldn't be more proud to be an Asian American. Post-college I joined the *Asian Avenue Magazine* team to continue this mission of bridging differences and spreading cultural awareness and appreciation. I hope to become a mentor to Asian American elementary students so that their "Asian self-appreciation" takes place much earlier than mine. It wasn't until college for me. But for the next generation of children, I'd like to help them realize how lucky we are to be Asian Americans - and how proud we should be."

# Jocelyn Chao

Jocelyn Chao, daughter of Frank and Wendy Chao, has successfully blended her Chinese culture with American ideals and she knows it. She is aware that she is appreciated wherever and whenever she performs her Chinese folk dances. She is a perfect example of one who is living in the best of two worlds. She has been performing traditional Chinese folk dance for over 20 years throughout the country and the world. She also has volunteered at two Chinese language schools to teach Chinese folk dancing.

Jocelyn graduated with honors with a Bachelor of science degree in business management in 2006 from Babson College, Babson Park, Massachusetts. She was a Presidential Scholar, admitted into the honors program, Multicultural Scholar, Women's Leadership Scholar, executive vice president of the student government association, and was selected as the only student body representative to work with a committee of faculty and deans to develop recommendations for curriculum revision. She completed an honors thesis on the representations of businesswomen in the media.

She took coursework on business analysis and valuation and strategy, conflict and cooperation at Harvard University (2005). She also took coursework on bargaining and negotiation at the London School of

Economics (2004). Jocelyn was selected as one of 12 national student advisory board members for the American Association of University Women. (2004-2005). She was awarded a scholarship for "outstanding contributions and services to the community" at the Lt. Governor's Conference on Youth Education (2005) and was recognized as one of the 10 outstanding seniors (Fall, 2005).

Jocelyn currently works as a senior consultant for Navigant Consulting Inc., manager and member of the *Colorado Chinese News* and the *Asian Pacific Business Journal*. In 2004, she served as a consulting intern to the senior manager at BearingPoint Inc., London, England.

Joycelyn says "During my childhood, I thought I was no different from any other kid on the playground, even growing up in an environment where 95% of my classmates were white. While I went to Chinese school on Sundays, practiced Chinese dance and ate fish balls and pickled bamboo, I didn't think that I was any different from the blonde-haired, blue-eyed girl down the street. However, I do remember the first time that I felt like an outsider. I was in second grade and walking back from recess with another girl. Before we walked in the classroom, she stopped walking, looked at me and asked, 'Why is your face so flat?' She didn't mean any harm by her question and, at the time, I had no idea what she was even talking about. But when I went home I looked at myself in the mirror and realized that I wasn't like all the other girls I went to school with. My eyes were dark and almond-shaped, my face round and my hair dark and thick. While this event may not seem momentous, it was the first time I realized that my ethnicity would always define a piece of who I am. While I am proud to be an American and feel blessed to have many privileges and freedoms, it has always been important to me to embrace my Chinese culture—such as celebrating Chinese holidays, speaking Mandarin and practicing Chinese folk dance. On a deeper level, traditional values are very important to me and being an Asian female, I was taught to always work hard, be modest and have a quiet demeanor. Thus, my biggest challenge had been to embrace both traditional Chinese values with more western ideals such as individualism."

Jocelyn tells how she developed poise, confidence, grace and pride in her Chinese culture. "I have been practicing Chinese folk dance for over 20 years now. My first performance was for my grandmother's 80th birthday celebration in Taipei. It was actually my grandmother's wish to have my mother perform a Chinese folk dance. However my mother politely declined and handed down the responsibility to her four-year old daughter. So for a month straight, I went to dance lessons to master the Chinese ribbon dance. My mother tells me it was from that first performance that my love for the stage blossomed. I have since performed all over the world in Singapore, Taiwan, New York, Boston, Los Angeles and many other places. While I do enjoy the spotlight, what I cherish the most about Chinese folk dance is that I am able to share the beauty of the Chinese culture with so many others."

As an Asian American, I believe that we have strong cultural values. When I was growing up I was told to work hard, listen to my parents and do well in school. I value the discipline and work ethic that was instilled in me through my upbringing and credit this to the success that I have achieved so far."

Jocelyn thinks APAs are stereotyped in the media. "While there has been a significant increase in the number of positive Asian American role models in the media, there is still room for improvement. On that note, I believe that the most important role models are not those that we see on television or films. I believe that it's our everyday role models in the community: parents, teachers and mentors."

## Piya Sorcar

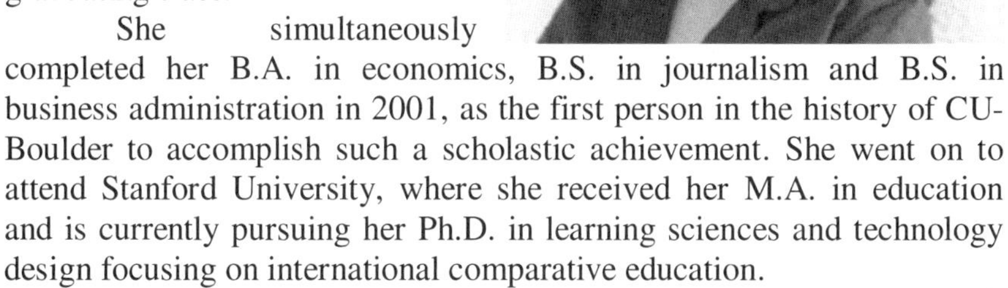

Piya was raised in Arvada and graduated summa cum laude from the University of Colorado at Boulder, where she was a President's Leadership Scholar and the winner of the Chancellor's award for most outstanding academic achievement in her graduating class.

She simultaneously completed her B.A. in economics, B.S. in journalism and B.S. in business administration in 2001, as the first person in the history of CU-Boulder to accomplish such a scholastic achievement. She went on to attend Stanford University, where she received her M.A. in education and is currently pursuing her Ph.D. in learning sciences and technology design focusing on international comparative education.

Professionally, Piya is the founder of TeachAIDS, a non-profit organization she started at Stanford, dedicated to creating and distributing research-based HIV/AIDS education around the world. As the basis of her Ph.D. research at Stanford, Piya developed the primary set of curricula distributed by TeachAIDS. She was previously an economic research analyst with Analysis Group in Denver and also held positions with IBM, TiE, and NBC 9 News in Colorado.

Throughout her life, Piya has also been heavily involved in the performing arts. She was nominated for a regional Emmy award for acting in the lead role in "Deepa and Rupa: A Fairy Tale from India." The film was the winner of numerous international awards including the Gold Plaque at the Chicago International Film and Television Festival.

Piya says "The support of my family has meant everything to me. My parents served as my role models and mentors and were always an inspiration to me. My father is an engineer; artist, author, producer, and entrepreneur, throughout his life, and my mother became an entrepreneur, starting an Indian cooking school program, which has now taken off in a big way. They both always encouraged me to pursue my dreams." It is obvious her family has shaped her life, nurtured her spirit, and guided her destiny with their love. This accomplished young lady's presence, achievements and example, make her a role model for other younger students to follow. Piya is married to Shuman Ghosemajumder, a member of the product management team at Google.

## Jessica Lauren Pasion

Jessica, daughter of Wilbert and Editha Pasion, graduated in 2005 with honors from Grandview High School. She was part of the varsity swimming team for all four years and became the team captain during her senior year. She qualified for the State championships during her sophomore, junior, and senior years. Jessica was also a member of the Spanish Honor Society

Jessica is currently attending Regis University pursuing a Bachelor's of science degree in nursing. She is scheduled to graduate in May of 2009. After receiving her Bachelor's degree, she plans on continuing her education to receive her Master's degree and then to become either a nurse practitioner or a nurse anesthetist.

Jessica has always put her religion and her family at the very top of the list of what is important to her. Her Catholic beliefs and the influence that her family members have had on her have helped shape her into what she is today. She feels that the morals and beliefs that have been instilled in her during the early years of her life helped her make correct decisions and to continue to grow from the different daily experiences. Education is one of the keys to the successes in her life. Furthermore, Jessica also puts a great value on her friends who gave her their full support through the years. She has learned a lot of lessons in life from them.

Jessica wrote the following in an essay about growing up in two different cultures. "Being a second generation immigrant, I feel that it is important for my generation to continue to teach the knowledge, values, and traditions of our cultures to the generations after us. Our cultures are so beautiful and interesting and they set us apart from everyone else. Although I grew up greatly disliking the fact that I was different from the people I went to school with, I now cherish the qualities that make me unique. I eventually learned how wonderful it was to be not just a Filipino or just an American, but a Filipino American."

"I realize that, because of my mixed culture, I am not ignorant of the fact that everyone comes from a different place with something different to offer to this country. If we continue to lose these qualities that identify us as being part of Asia, an area that is so great and diverse, we will no longer be Asian Americans, but just Americans."

Jessica is an active member of the Philippine American Society of Colorado (PASCO) where she has been a dancer for the Dance Repertoire since 1994. She was a youth director from 2003 to 2005 and a dance instructor for the Dance Repertoire from 2007 to the present. She is also a member of the Couples for Christ (CFC) Youth (1997 to the present) and the Philippine Nurses Association of Colorado (2007 to the present).

## Rahul Neil Sarwal

He was born on October 24, 1992 in Columbus Ohio. Most people call him by his middle name, Neil, which he appreciates as it is easier on the tongue and as such preferred by his American (Caucasian) friends and teachers. This middle name was given because his parents wanted to provide a name with dual meaning and recognized both in the U.S. and India. Indian names are typically selected with profound meanings. The earliest meaning of Rahul, found in the Upanishads, is "conqueror of all miseries".

He was raised by his family based on a selected set of Indian customs and with a strong influence from his paternal grandparents. Currently, he lives in Parker, Colorado, and his lifestyle indicates a reduced influence of his Indian culture. “Perhaps that is the inevitable influence of my American friends and all the time spent with popular media – TV and video games”. He states, “Perhaps I envy my American friends, as I think they have a pleasant lifestyle – easy-going and unburdened with cultural constraints and taboos. My parents prefer that I use all my spare time in order to do well in academics and leadership groups. I have friends who are Indian, as well, and some are in a similar situation, sharing the burden of dual cultures. However, I also respect the friends who live in more orthodox homes and are more in tune with their religious roots of Hinduism.”

Indian culture heavily emphasizes respect for grandparents. He observes, “Learning Indian customs is a fascinating exercise, for example children in India are asked to touch the feet of the seniors/elders as a sign of respect. But with the blend of an American lifestyle, I am not required to follow that practice and just give my elders a hug. When looking at American teenagers today, some are just outright rude to their elders but that is not the style of many Asian-American children like me. I do have respect for my grandparents but perhaps a bit reduced from the degree my parents’ respect them, and that could also be due to our physical separation, as they live in India.”

He has a younger brother, Ashwin, and feels that it must be quite challenging for his parents to handle two boys, with unique interests and personalities, as in his candid opinion, he notes, “we can both be quite stubborn.”

“Many of my American friends aren’t exactly ambitious which is why they have a more care-free lifestyle with most of their time spent at playing, and relatively less time spent on chores and homework.” He is working hard in the Douglas County International Baccalaureate (IB) program and attends school with students who are also extremely ambitious and so he has his circle of friends at school who get along quite well. “My parents also prefer I spend my spare time with such ambitious students.”

He notes, “When I visit India I observe a land of extremes. There are the very rich people and the people ridden with abject poverty. India isn’t as uniformly advanced as the U.S. but there is a sense of emerging greatness. Even though air-conditioned malls and super-markets are now being built at a fast pace, there are still many indicators of the third world status that Indian people were used to till a few years ago. The IT (Information technology) centers have created islands of grandeur immersed in an ocean of a lower economic class of people pulling rickshaws (tricycle taxis driven by humans) or hawkers of fresh vegetables, going street to street and shouting for customers. My parents, who grew up in India, mention that there may well be a new social revolution driven by a fast expanding middle class – I will take their word for it, as I cannot verify such a comparison."

For the youth, the U.S. life can be convenient, but Neil feels an under-lying pressure of acculturation, especially due to being a child of immigrants who want to succeed in their new homeland. "At times, my parents don't exactly approve of my being careless or lazy as they were raised in a society that was more competitive and high-strung. I have noticed that the parents of my American friends are much more lenient with fewer conditions unlike my Indian friends who have strict parents."

Currently, Neil has very good grades. He is in the National Honor Society program. He is a second-degree black belt candidate and plans to earn this degree quite soon. He is also a very good piano player and participates in numerous local and state competitions.

"I am very proud of my parents – what they have achieved as immigrants and what ambitions they have for me. I hope to fulfill my dreams and ambitions by working hard and achieving the American dream for myself. Hopefully I will make my parents proud."

## Lauren Alyssa Gonzales

Lauren, 15, daughter of Sam and Mary Gonzales and granddaughter of Nestor and Elnora Mercado, dreams of becoming an orthopedic surgeon or an anesthesiologist someday. She attended Nativity of Our Lord Catholic School, was a member of the Junior National Honor Society, went to Holy Family High School during her freshman year and is now a sophomore at Broomfield High School, taking advanced classes and maintains a 3.5 GPA. Her favorite subjects are in the math and science fields including her current classes in honors algebra and biology.

As part of the Filipino values, customs and traditions, she would like to preserve are respect for elders, strong family ties, and faith in the Catholic religion. She is involved with her grandparent's activities with the Filipino community and goes to annual Filipino festivals and community events.

She is a member of the United States Figure Skating Association (USFSA) and the Rocky Mountain Figure Skating Club. She started skating at age eight when her brother was playing for a hockey league. Her schedule includes three hours of training five to six days a week including 6:00 AM sessions, off-ice training and conditioning. Her competitive free skate levels include pre-juvenile, juvenile, and intermediate. She has won several gold and silver medals in competitions locally, statewide, and regionally. She is a recipient of a bronze medal at the Southwestern Regional Championship held in Dallas, Texas, October 2004. The Southwestern region spans 12 states. She was an eighth place pre-qualifier at the Southwestern Regional Championships held in Arvada, Colorado, October 2005, a finalist at the 2007 Colorado Championships as an intermediate lady. She has achieved the pre-silver level in freestyle dance and the freeskate junior level in moves in the field in November 2007. Currently she competes at the novice level. Her goals are to achieve the senior level freeskate and moves in the field before high school graduation in 2010. As a member of the Rocky Mountain Figure Skating Club, Lauren showcases her talents as a soloist in ice show fundraisers. She has volunteered as a figure skating instructor assistant in the Learn-To-Skate Program and volunteers at a variety of figure skating competitions as a runner, ice monitor, hospitality sponsor, and registration assistant.

## Joseph Hemschoot

Joseph "Joe" Hemschoot, 14, only son of Paul and Teresita Hemschoot of Lakewood, Colorado, is a sophomore at Lakewood High School. He loves sports and currently is team captain of both the football and baseball teams at his school. His academic grade point average is 3.8 and his favorite subject is mathematics. His goal in life, after high school and college is to go into financial management. He is proud to be Filipino American. He has played the piano for seven years and is a member of the Jefferson All County Orchestra.

At 6'1" and already well-built at 14, Joe started playing football when he was seven years old. He was a member of the Little Lake Football League and his team won the championship three years in a row. Later, he became a member of the Midget Major Football League. He was voted MVP of the Freshman Football League at Lakewood High School.

Joe wants to be a role model for young people. High on his list of Filipino values are respect for elders, desire to excel in school and close family ties. He enjoys eating Filipino food like adobo, pansit, lumpia, sinigang, and nilaga. A popular student in school, Joe is well adjusted and does not mind if he is perceived by some as a Mexican. He is also involved in cultural presentations at the Filipino American Community of Colorado. He is scheduled this year to go to the Philippines as a humanitarian volunteer to build houses for the poor under a program called Gawad Kalinga, which means "give care."

He hopes to get a sports scholarship to a university and dreams of playing in the National Football League someday.

## Payal Sorcar

"Growing up in the United States has been amazing. Ever since I was a child, my mother and father have always given me opportunities to explore my East Indian heritage, whether it was through participating in my dad's Indian animations for children, learning traditional Indian dancing, or learning Bengali, our mother tongue. They also shared with me many American traditions that I fell in love with. These experiences have made me very proud to be an Indian American. I feel very fortunate to have such intimate insight into two beautiful cultures and hope to instill this pride into my future family."

Payal Sorcar Sutton, the youngest daughter of Manick and Shikha Sorcar, graduated from the University of Colorado at Boulder in 2002, with a B.A. degree in psychology and a minor in dance. Early on, Payal began her research career studying juvenile delinquents and their social and family interactions. Payal carried on her love for research, and now works as a clinical research associate at a prestigious Massachusetts-based bio/pharmaceutical corporation with operations in

51 countries. Here, she is part of the process of bringing new medical devices and medications for such indications as Alzheimer's disease and HIV/AIDS to the global marketplace. She travels around the country monitoring research data and ensuring that all Food and Drug Administration requirements are met at medical sites. Prior to this, she worked at a comprehensive clinical research and development company as a clinical research coordinator where she got the experience to collect data directly from patients with central nervous system disorders.

Since she was a child, Payal has assisted her father in composing music for many productions, coordinating dozens of dancers for massive theatrical performances, and choreographing fusion dances for multi-cultural productions held throughout the U.S. and India, including her father's production entitled "Enlightenment of Buddha" which was the winner of the Artistic Award (the Oscar of laser industry) at the International Laser Display Association annual contest at Rimini, Italy. When she is not doing these things, Payal works with her family's production troupe and choreographs many of the world touring performances. For years now, she has been teaching children from various backgrounds to express themselves through different dance forms and to enjoy life though the arts.

Payal says that one of the most challenging problems for Asian Pacific American youth is their search for identity. "Balancing the two cultures can be tricky at times. My advice to you is to never forget your roots. The Asian American culture and community is much a like a tightly-knit family, full of wisdom and ready to support you in any challenge you may face. I'm fortunate to have not only had my father's art and cultural productions to educate me about my heritage, but also my mother's tireless devotion and care in raising us."

Payal is married to Benjamin Sutton, a research scientist specializing in molecular biology.

## Alisa Rushford

Alisa Rushford, 18, daughter of Giselle and John Rushford, grew up participating in many activities of the Filipino American Community of Colorado (FACC). Her mother, Giselle Rushford, served as FACC president for two terms and has raised her children in an atmosphere of both Filipino and American cultures. John, of Irish descent, served as FACC director for several terms.

Alisa says "I am very fortunate to have grown up in a biracial family because it gave me a unique perspective on both cultures. How I blended these together was by staying active in my Filipino community, and living the day-to-day experiences as an American youth."

Alisa graduated from Northglenn High School and is enrolled at Metropolitan State College in Denver.

She says "I am very proud of my Filipino roots and eagerly express my background to others. I view my parents' cultures as exact opposites. But since their cultures have become so integrated with each other, for me it seems normal within my house. On the contrary, my mother's side views me as the "white cousin", and on my father's side I'm the granddaughter that has long beautiful black hair and tan skin complexion."

"My mother has also instilled in us a family closeness which I think is relevant to most Filipino families. At dinnertime we were always required to eat with everyone around a dinner table, which is very rare to find in many other American homes. On my father's side I would like to preserve his ideals on education and reaping its benefits."

"I can help strengthen the cultural ties and cooperation among the Asian Pacific American communities in Colorado by being actively involved in my Filipino community. I can do this by dancing the dances of our ancient history, hosting festivals to educate the interested and staying loyal to my roots. Because most of the people who come to our festivals are of the older generations, I want my generation to be more aware of the diverse cultures in our country. The only time they gain interest is when they are older and they are introduced to a small fraction of a culture they probably only heard about in their high school history class."

"APA culture is very important to me since it's the culture that I have been brought up in and it's the culture that I want my children to imbibe."

"I don't think that the Colorado school system has included enough APA culture in their curriculum. It's understandable that public schools have to cover a lot of material in a short amount of time, but it would be in the best interest for the students to be exposed to cultures other than their own. In my own experience, it felt like many of my fellow students were very ignorant towards other cultures and unconsciously became insensitive to their minority peers. In reality it's not their fault that they are this way -- it is the system that they were brought up in and also due to their lack of exposure to other cultures."

# Chona Palmon

Chona Palmon, daughter of Jeff and Emy Hackenberg of Littleton, Colorado, is among the youngest elected directors of the Filipino American Community of Colorado (FACC). Because of her 15 years experience as a FACC dancer and as beginning choreographer of the FACC dance troupe, she has a great opportunity to use her talents as cultural director for the next two years. She will be leading a team of outstanding young Filipino American women who will be performing and entertaining audiences in the future.

Chona was born in Davao City in the southern Philippines and immigrated to Colorado with her mother and sister, Lulu, when she was nine. Now 25, she is married to Vireak Touch and they are proud parents of a little girl, Skye Palmon, age three. She graduated from George Washington High School in 2001 under the IB program and computer magnet. She will be attending classes at University of Colorado Denver in the fall of 2008. She relates her most satisfying experience as lead role in the "Alice in Wonderland" musical when she was a pre-teen. She had always considered herself as a shy person, but her confidence was boosted when she began dancing. Chona has started choreographing some Filipino dances, making some changes in moves and steps to make them different without deviating from the Filipino style. She also enjoys performing contemporary American dances. She was also able to work with other organizations and perform with other Filipino organizations.

Growing up in America, as an immigrant, has not always been easy for Chona. She used to be embarrassed of her heritage and had fears of being an outcast in school because she looked different. "I am thankful that my mother was involved in an organization as the FACC. Because of strong bonds among the members and the continued education about our heritage, a strong sense of pride of being Filipino was instilled in me." The Bahay Kubo has been a second home for Chona. "Here, I have a Lola (grandma) a Lolo (grandpa), a Tita (aunt) or a Tito (uncle). It was at FACC that I learned to dance and appreciate the dances, the different Filipino foods and being a Filipino. I feel proud of having my own identity that I am unique and I stand out in a crowd." Chona knows she belongs to a small minority, but she has learned to accept that she is not alone. She enjoys learning about other cultures. Her husband is Cambodian and she has found common traditions such as close family ties. At the same time, she has also learned to respect different practices, her husband being a Buddhist and she a Catholic.

## Somxai Vue

Somxai Vue entered the U.S. in the late 1980's as a refugee along with his mother, three sisters and two younger brothers. He was only 14 years old. In Colorado, he enrolled and graduated from Northglenn High School. Later, he enrolled at the Metropolitan State College of Denver and graduated with a B.S. in computer information. Finally, in 2003, he graduated from the University of Colorado Denver with a Master's degree in computer information service. Presently, he is working at Lattner, Ruben, Fishman, Brown, Saul, P.C. as Information Technology Manager.

Somxai represents the younger Hmong generation, smart and proud of his cultural heritage. His biggest challenge here in America is the language barrier, which he thinks is generally true of those born overseas. His mother, up to this time, has a hard time adjusting to American life because of her difficulty in understanding and speaking English and adjusting to a different culture. In time, he and his sibling have overcome the language barrier and are succeeding in school. In the meantime, their family has maintained their own rich Hmong culture.

According to Somxai, the secret to living in a new cultural environment is by learning and adapting as best one can. He believes that the Asian Pacific American culture is very important to him. There are ways one can help strengthen the cultural ties and cooperation among APAs. One way is to volunteer and give back to the community, not just to the Hmong community but also to all other communities.

"Mainstream society does not have enough information for them to understand the Hmong cultural heritage in Colorado," says Somxai.

Somxai recommends networking, to be inclusive and to reach out more. "I think the present APA generation is losing its grip on their parents' and grandparents' culture. I think the culture will be lost. Lastly, the APA communities should come together and form coalitions. They should encourage volunteers to help the community."

# Chapter 9

# ASIAN PACIFIC AMERICAN ISSUES AND CONCERNS

## Introduction

Since the mid-1960s, Asian and Pacific Americans have been stereotyped as a "model minority," especially in the print media. This characterization was first applied to Japanese and Chinese Americans and then later to other APA groups and it has been heavily criticized by APA scholars and community activists. It generally portrays APAs as all having achieved high levels of education and income and of not experiencing any problems. This stereotype ignores important socio-economic differences both within and between APA groups. It also ignores other factors. For instance, some APA groups, on average, have relatively good levels of household income, but these households often have two, three, or more persons contributing to this income. Also, many APA households are fairly large, so the amount of income per person may not be high. The model minority stereotype tends to mask significant APA economic, educational, and social problems. For example, in the 2000 census, the Hmong, Cambodians, and Laotians were recorded as having poverty rates of 38%, 29%, and 19% respectively, well above the national average. In addition, these groups along with Chinese and Thais were recorded as having 20% or more of their adult population that had less than a high school education.

Large proportions of the adults in several APA groups have limited English-language proficiency. APAs, especially those from lower-income backgrounds, experience difficulties in obtaining affordable housing, adequate health care, and access to other social services. In fact, because of the model minority stereotype, many people argue that APAs no longer need public services such as bilingual education, government documents in multiple languages, and welfare. Finally, the model minority stereotype ignores continuing incidents of prejudice and discrimination. While it is the case that many APAs have taken advantage of educational and economic opportunities to achieve a comfortable lifestyle, and that some have attained much more, APAs need to become more visible so the true nature of their socioeconomic diversity is no longer hidden. When only stereotypes and limited information prevail, APAs will be the recipients of flawed policy decisions that affect their social well-being.

In this chapter we will discuss seven overarching issues that affect APAs today. While this may not be an exhaustive set, these issues have been selected based on the experiences and interviews with Colorado APAs from all backgrounds: a) education, b) other youth issues, c) immigration, d) health and social wellness, e) political participation, f) career development, and g) race relations.

## Education

A good education is strongly valued by Asian Pacific Americans. APAs are not that different from many other Americans regarding the importance of education. However, the APA emphasis on education, the high percentages of APA students who attend college and the significant APA enrollments at institutions such as Harvard and Stanford have contributed to a variation of the model minority stereotype - that all APA students excel academically and attend so-called "elite" universities. APA educators across the U.S., including Russell Endo at the University of Colorado Denver, have been critical of this stereotype. Numerous studies show that there are differences in educational achievement within the K-12 APA student population due to many factors, including social and economic background and English-language proficiency. And while APA students attending suburban K-12 schools often do well, those attending inner-city schools are more at-risk for academic difficulties. Endo argues that more research is needed on APAs in higher education. He points out that about 40% of the APA students in the U.S. attend community colleges and most of the rest are not at "elite" institutions. His research on APA students at four-year public colleges and universities in Colorado shows that overall APA student achievement - as measured by grades, dropout rates, and graduation rates - usually is lower than that of white students; this also is true at many other public institutions across the U.S. Although many APAs go on to earn graduate and professional degrees, the educational characteristics of Asian Pacific Americans at all levels need to be much more visible.

## Other Youth Issues

There are APA youth who may feel alienated from their parents, families, schools, and communities. Such youth feel misunderstood and under-appreciated. There is considerable pressure for them to accept the values of people from their parents' generation. They feel they have to compromise their individuality and live a life that is quite different from their non-Asian peers. They may also feel that they are victims of prejudice and discrimination by others at school. The dichotomy of the multicultural life they lead may not be fully understood by them or their parents, teachers, and non-Asian friends. The social isolation of these APA youth makes them susceptible to joining gangs. A small proportion does turn to gangs for social support and to obtain a sense of belonging and acceptance as well as material benefits. APA gangs exist in Colorado and their activities have raised concerns. APA communities are concerned about this problem and the racial profiling of all APA youth as gang members by law enforcement authorities.

## Immigration

As mentioned earlier in this book, the 1965 Immigration Act has lead to a dramatic increase in Asian immigration to the U.S. Because of the provisions of this and subsequent immigration laws, there have been large numbers of Asian migrants with professional backgrounds such as medical doctors, engineers, nurses, and teachers. Specific recent immigration policies have encouraged the migration of software developers on temporary H1B visas. The number of Asian immigrants to the U.S. is limited, and there are long waiting periods for potential migrants. This is especially problematic for individuals who are trying to reunite with other family members already in the U.S. Once in the U.S., Asian immigrants encounter many social and economic challenges. They may also face anti-immigrant sentiment and attitudes that immigrants are taking away jobs from other Americans and are an unnecessary burden on social, health, and other public services. However, the fact remains that APA immigrants contribute more to the US economy and society than they receive in the form of support and social programs.

## Health and Social Wellness

Cultural barriers and inequalities in income and education underlie many health disparities in the U.S. In general, populations with high disparity that suffer the worst health status are also those that have the highest poverty rates and the least education. Disparities in income and education levels are associated with differences in rates of mortality and morbidity and cancers, heart disease, diabetes, obesity, hypertension, low birth weight etc. Data for the Asian Pacific American population is quite limited, and available data may be reduced in value since it often is on APAs overall and not specific APA groups. It is essential to have disaggregated data in order to make accurate policy decisions. Without such data, it is impossible to understand the health status and contributing factors specific to each APA group. Even though health indicators suggest that the APA population overall is one of the healthiest in the U.S., there is great diversity within this population and marked health disparities exist for specific APA groups and even economic and regional subgroups. The health and social wellness of APAs is discussed further in the chapter on health and medical services.

## Empowerment and Adequate Representation

In general, Asian Pacific Americans don't participate in electoral politics to the degree that they could. There are historical and cultural reasons behind this. Differences within APA groups and, in some instances, the absence of strong relationships between groups also hampers political activity. This is unfortunate because, though APAs are one of the fastest growing populations, they still only comprise a small percentage of most political jurisdictions outside of Hawaii's and a handful of other areas such as San Francisco. The importance of greater political participation is something interviewees throughout this book emphasize, and besides allowing APAs to have more of a voice in policymaking, this would increase their overall visibility.

However, APAs have not been totally absent from American politics, especially in Hawaii and on the West Coast. The first APA from the U.S. mainland to become a member of the U.S. House of Representatives from California was Dalip Singh Saund. More recently, prominent Asian American politicians include U.S. Senator Daniel Inouye (Hawai'i), former governors Gary Locke (Washington) and Benjamin Cayetano (Hawai'i), Governor Bobby Jindal (Louisiana), U.S. Representatives Mike Honda (California) and David Wu (Oregon), and a number of APA state legislators, mayors, and city officials including Minnesota State Senator Mee Moua and California Assembly members Van Tran, Alberto Torrico, and Leland Yee. Beyond elected officials, scores of APAs across the country have been appointed to government cabinet positions, commissions, and boards. Currently the U.S. Secretary of Labor is Elaine Chao and Norman Mineta was the U.S. Secretary of Transportation.

In Colorado, APA participation in electoral politics lags behind that of APAs in places like Hawai'i and California but again has not been totally absent. From 1962 to 1964, Seiji Horiuchi served in the Colorado House of Representatives and was the first person of Japanese descent outside of Hawai'i to be elected to a state legislature. More recently Stanley Matsunaka served in the Colorado Senate from 1995 to 2003 and was Senate President for two years; Matsunaka also ran unsuccessfully for the U.S. House of Representatives in 2002 and 2004. In addition, a handful of Colorado cities have had APA mayors, including Fort Collins (Richard Suinn) and Pueblo (Melvin Takaki).

## Career Development

The careers of APAs, including those in Colorado, are often hampered by the "glass-ceiling" effect. APAs in this situation, especially professionals, find that their careers get off to a good start but eventually plateau or hit a "ceiling." In large organizational and institutional settings, this usually happens because APAs stop being promoted to higher supervisory or executive positions. Sometimes this is due to discrimination; a company, for instance, doesn't want "too many" APAs (or other peoples of color) in highly visible positions. Lack of access to mentors and informal support networks may also hinder APA career advancement. However, negative stereotypes are a major contributing factor. APA professionals allegedly lack the communication skills or leadership abilities required for promotion to higher positions. APAs are stereotyped as being good at doing things but not as having the skills or personalities for directing the work of others. The abilities and achievements of the APAs interviewed for this book clearly point out the fallacy of such stereotypes.

In her keynote speech at the Colorado Governors Asian Pacific American Advisory Council Summit Conference former University of Colorado administrator Jean Kim accurately described the glass ceiling phenomenon for APAs. She said, "....the high floor-low ceiling experience is influenced by a set of stereotypes about APA professionals: that we are good at our jobs, hard reliable workers but not leadership material; that we are not good at interpersonal and communication skills, that we are good followers but not good leaders...More APAs need to sit at the decision-making table to make and influence policy."

## Race Relations

Race relations have always been a problem of deep concern to all Americans. Racism is the practice of racial discrimination that claims to find racial differences in character, intelligence, etc.--- that a particular race is superior or inferior to another. A vital key to improving race relations is the need to understand and appreciate every group and how they have enriched the cultural and social fabric of American society. Among other things, this requires extensive educational programs in schools and communities.

Race relations are an ongoing issue that a responsible American society must address. By describing a few examples of racism against APAs, we hope to make this aspect of the experience of Colorado APAs more visible, but also to encourage actions by everyone working together to deal with this continuing concern.

On February 18, 2008, the online *Campus Press* of the University of Colorado, Boulder published an opinion essay by Max Karson, entitled, "If It's War the Asians Want... It's War They'll Get." In that article, Karson wrote, "they hate us all."..."I say it's time we start hating them back." ... "That's right, no more tolerance. No more cultural sensitivity. No more 'Mr. Pretend-I'm-Not-A-Racist. ... It's time for war. But we won't attack their bodies or minds. We will attack their souls." Karson went on further to call for "volunteers" to join him in catching the Asians with huge butterfly nets, hog-tying them, forcing them to eat bad sushi, then waking them up after four hours of sleep with megaphone shouts.

The moment this essay came online, the Internet was filled with messages, letters, and articles by angry Asian Pacific Americans condemning this article as racist, offensive, irresponsible, outrageous, shocking, insensitive, discriminatory, hateful, unacceptable, negative, cruel and more. These messages called for actions by the university administration, resignations of *Campus Press* advisers and editors, and even the expulsion of the writer. Three examples are reprinted below:

In a letter to the university president, regents, and deans, APA community leader and spokesperson, Mary Lee Chin wrote:

> "...The School of Journalism in our "flagship university ideally should teach disciplined, responsible and principled journalism. It is reprehensible that the school allowed the publication of this derogatory article under the guise of free speech. ...There is the burden and fine challenge of responsibility that comes with the privilege of free speech. If the author wants to publicize it on his personal blog, so be it, but NOT in a publication supported by the School of Journalism as a teaching lab. Why would the role models, faculty advisor, educators and editors in the school think this insulting and one-sided diatribe was an effective way to dialogue about race?"

In another message, Erin Yoshimura stated:

> "While this was 'meant' to be satirical, not everybody gets satire...I had a strong negative reaction after reading this and have to say that I felt fearful; fearful that it would cause harm for APA students at CU. I have heard how deeply racism and stereotyping has impacted students and faculty of color. I don't think CU-Boulder has advanced enough in diversity and inclusiveness practices to allow this type of column to be posted

> regardless if it's satire and meant to be funny. It's putting a lot of faith that all readers will get the humor and not act out any of Karson's suggestions."

The editors of *Asian Avenue*, an APA magazine, wrote:

> "Unity can only occur when we recognize each other's differences and celebrate them. We need to come together as a people. This article took a step back, bringing us further away from unity. People are different. We're not all the same height, weight, or color. Pointing out these differences is obvious and at this point in human history, quite juvenile. As we progress into the future our goal is to evolve towards unification as one collective group of people."

The university chancellor, the dean of the School of Journalism and Mass Communications, and the editors and adviser of the *Campus Press* quickly issued apologies and pledges of action to repair the damage this controversy caused. Chancellor G.P. "Bud" Peterson issued a statement about "this poor attempt at social satire, laden with offensive references, stereotypes and hateful language." He reaffirmed his commitment to building a campus that embraces diversity in all its forms. Cassie Hewlings, editor of the *Campus Press*, also issued an apology on behalf of her staff, stating that Karson's satire was not published to intentionally incite controversy and offered the hope that they "will learn from this experience and better their publication."

Amy Herdy, adviser for the *Campus Press*, responding to a note from Theresa Simsiman (of Sacramento, CA) admitted sadly that she did not realize the magnitude of racial divide on the university campus. "Students of color feel wounded and excluded, and many do not feel safe." Journalism dean Paul S. Voakes met with the five editors of the *Campus Press* and decided on immediate "next steps," which included enhanced coverage of the campus controversy; establishing a student diversity board to provide editors with regular feedback from students with a diversity of backgrounds; inviting student organizations to discuss specific concerns with editors; adopting an opinions policy to determine standards and acceptability of opinion columns; scheduling diversity awareness workshops for the entire staff and workshops for opinion writing and editing to be presented by experienced professional editors.

About a week after Karson's column first appeared, nearly 200 university students rallied outside the University Memorial Center and met with Chancellor Peterson. They demanded the resignations of the *Campus Press* faculty adviser Amy Herdy and editor Cassie Hewlings.

On the same day, Bill Johnson of *Rocky Mountain News* devoted the entire page of his column "Rocky Talk" to this furor. He titled it " 'Just Move On' Won't Work for Offended CU Students." The news media subsequently reported that Karson's duties with the *Campus Press* had been suspended pending restructuring of the opinion section.

The column written by Max Karson and published in the *Campus Press* is a form of racism against all APAs. It is sad to know that racism still exists in America, especially among intelligent students at great universities. This column also raises concerns about other forms of anti-Asian activity---such as racial slurs, vandalism, and even physical violence---and their prevalence not only on university campuses but elsewhere as well.

Below, we describe another incident at Colorado College in Colorado Springs.

Asian and APA women are often stereotyped as "China dolls" or "Asian babes," as being exotic, subservient, or compliant. In March 2002, the Colorado College campus newspaper *The Catalyst* carried a racially offensive fake news brief that made demeaning references to Asian women and an article targeting blacks. The news brief stated: "A freshman from Colorado College expressed his disappointment at the lack of hot Asian girls, 'Man, where are all the hot Asian chicks?' There has to be one in Colorado Springs who wants to be my some 's---y-f---y". This statement was so offensive that the *Asian Pacific American Times* editor and managing editor drove to Colorado Springs the next day to attend a student rally expressing anger at the editors regarding this offensive matter. They also interviewed the college president, who had already issued an apology. Reprinted here is the *APA Times* report:

March 29, 2002. *The Catalyst* – Colorado College's student newspaper – published as an April Fool's joke two articles, one targeting blacks and the other about a fictional freshman who was disappointed he could not find any "hot Asian babes" on campus. The publication caused immediate outrage among students, faculty and administrative staff.

April 5, 2002. *The Catalyst* published an apology from President Kathryn Mohrman and editor, Audrey Thompson. Comments and reactions from students were also published in this issue. The outrage continued..

April 9, 2002 - At a press conference, Vachon Brakett, co-president of the Black Student Union, enumerated seven initiatives which they had presented to President Kathryn Mohrman and demanded their implementation within the week. Kathryn Mohrman stated that even though these articles were published as an April Fool's joke, they were tasteless and unfortunate. She cited the need to create more of an understanding of minorities and wants her apology to be published in P/AAT. Since we did not have a chance to ask questions during the press conference, we relayed to President Mohrman that as Asians, we were much offended by the publication and would like to voice our concerns and warnings that this should not happen again.

Another common stereotype of APAs is that they are "foreigners." Nestor and Nora Mercado relate their experiences with this stereotype: "Since we immigrated to America in 1970, we have experienced many instances when people, mostly whites, are surprised to know that we speak English and even more surprised when they learn that we publish our newspaper in English. They think that because of our brown skin, we would naturally have difficulty in understanding and speaking English. We are first generation Filipino immigrants and we still have the Filipino accents and pronunciation. We know we are understood at work, in church and in the community at large, yet we have learned through the years living in Colorado that most people assume that those who have brown or yellow skin and slanted eyes are foreigners and therefore do not speak English well. This perception is especially annoying to APAs who have been born and raised in America."

Racism in Denver when bussing and desegregation were in full swing is related below in an interview with Frances Campbell. She relates the brutal realities happening in schools and society at that time. In her own words, she describes her experiences from grade school through high school and college and later at work.

## Frances Simsiman Campbell

Fran was born in Denver, Colorado, in the 1960s and grew up during the years when APAs were not as common in neighborhoods or in schools or shopping centers.

Amazingly, Fran grew up strong and more determined to know more about her roots and her culture. As a second generation Filipino American, born and raised in Colorado, she struggled and succeeded through the years. A third generation of Filipino Americans serving the community with the same fervor and dedication continue as daughter Taryn

Campbell and son, Griffin Campbell now serve in various capacities in the Filipino American Community of Colorado (FACC). Fran talks about her biggest challenge while growing up in a pluralistic society in the U.S.

"The biggest challenge I had during my school years was "ignorance" about my cultural identity. Not just ignorance from my classmates but also my own ignorance. In the Denver Public Schools in the late sixties, there were just a few ethnic minorities living in the suburbs. I knew as soon as kindergarten that I looked different than everyone else. None of the kids were outright cruel to me but I was peppered everyday with questions – "Are you Chinese?" "Are you Japanese?" "Do you speak English?" "Where are you from?" "Do you eat rice?" When I was very young I was embarrassed by these questions because I didn't really know the answers…and after continued questions my embarrassment turned to shame. I remember one boy nicely explaining to me that I was an "oreo toe". I didn't know what that was for the longest time...my toes looked fine to me…so I didn't know how to respond to him. Of course he meant "oriental".

There was another APA boy in first grade named Donald. For some reason the other kids really picked on him. They teased him about the way he talked, laughed at the shape of his eyes and scorned him because he smelled like "fish". I was terrified, really terrified, that some of that teasing would be turned to me because I looked like Donald. So I tried my best to be as "un-Asian" as possible. I became a tough little tomboy, I physically distanced myself from my family when in public…I even told some of the kids who had asked if I was Chinese that "no, actually I'm Jewish". I was really just as ignorant as those kids.

Junior high was instantly less innocent. Not only had we moved to a new neighborhood that summer where I would have to re-establish all that I had built up to protect myself – but Denver was instituting school de-segregation that fall – court-ordered "bussing". Everyone was mad at everyone. There were white adults picketing in front of my junior high school in southeast Denver. They were shouting at the kids on the busses, telling them to go home. Did they mean me too? I wasn't even sure. And on TV, I saw black adults picketing in Montbello and north Denver, shouting for equal rights. Did they mean equal rights for me too? I wasn't even sure. There were bomb threats and duck and cover drills and times when the students and teachers had to stay in the padded wrestling gym for hours until the police said it was safe to leave. There were police cars driving around everyday that fall. All the kids "ganged up". I didn't see rich kids versus the poor kids or the nerds versus the slackers. What I saw were blacks with blacks, whites with whites, Mexicans with Mexicans. There were only two APA kids in the whole school – me and one other. I didn't have anyone to gang up with. Luckily the first friend I made was a really nice Mexican girl, so I ganged up with the Mexicans. The other APA girl ganged up with the whites.

Fairly soon after I started at Hamilton Junior High, the beatings started too. The first time I was beaten up was by a black girl named Tammy. I had thought she was my friend. Tammy cornered me against the brick wall during lunchtime. She called me an "ugly gook". I didn't know what that was. She slapped my face over and over until my nose and lips were bleeding. I had never felt pain like that before – I was stunned by how much it hurt. Her friends were laughing. Then the bell rang and she left. I walked home right then and when my mother saw me, she walked me right back to the school and told the principal to let me back into class.

The second time I was beaten was by a white boy with glasses named Arnie. He called me a "chink". I didn't know what that was. He banged his lunch tray against my hands until my fingers felt broken. His friends were laughing at me. I picked up my lunch tray, with all my lunch food, and banged him over the head with it. I was sent home but Arnie wasn't – and when my mother saw me, she walked me right back to the school and told the principal to let me back into class.

The third time I was beaten by a Mexican girl named Darla. She told me to stop trying to be Mexican. I had no idea what that meant. We beat each other up actually - pulled hair, pinched, bit, and rolled around on the floor. I didn't go home this time so my mother didn't know about this one. I was beaten up several times after that - but I didn't bring it home anymore.

Later that year, Tammy, the black girl that first beat me up apologized to me. She said that her friends were pushing her around because she wasn't "black enough" – she wasn't bussed but actually lived in the neighborhood. We became friends again, although after Hamilton Junior High I never saw her again. She even told me I was pretty. And even though I didn't know what a "gook" was, I know she didn't mean it. It was all ignorance.

Thomas Jefferson High School came with its own set of problems and my cultural identity wasn't always the priority on my "angst" list. But, by the time I finished high school and then college, my cultural ignorance was vastly improved – which meant that in turn, I was better able to deal with other's ignorance.

I can only speak for myself on the subject of court-ordered bussing – but as hard as it was for a kid, as an adult I am glad that I was able to go to school with such a diversity of students. Court-ordered bussing gave me the opportunity to learn and struggle alongside all different kinds of kids. I'm a better adult for it because I have no reservations learning and struggling alongside anybody. And as a parent living in the suburbs, I regret that my own children are not exposed to the same opportunity.

My biggest personal challenge in society at large in regards to my cultural identity is determining the difference between ignorance and deliberate prejudice – and then, once determined, choosing to respond with compassion or my enraged gut reaction. The dilemma is that the difference between ignorance and bigotry can be quite subtle, nowadays, so that it can be imperceptible.

For instance, a gentleman that I work closely with (a non-APA) made an off hand remark about Filipinos. He may have meant it jokingly but I was insulted...at first. I realized his was an awkward attempt to ingratiate himself to me and, although misguided, there was no malice intended. We discussed it as friends and were better co-workers for it.

Last summer at work, I was repeatedly berated as an "ignorant nigger" by a female patient. She may have been ignorant but her intent was to hurt and therefore she was deliberately racist. I was instantly deeply hurt – it was like I was back at Hamilton Junior High again. Because this incident happened at work there were many legal and administrative procedures, which followed the assault and it basically was handled by management, so the incident was "out of my hands" and no longer my problem alone. In the end, I forgave my seriously ill antagonist and let it go without a response – her challenges were far more difficult than mine.

Denver society has changed so much since the'70s and early '80s – and it's changed for the better. I am no longer the only person of color at the mall, or the only person of color at work, or even the only person of color at the rodeo. Ethnically diverse populations have increased quadruple-fold and mutual understanding has multiplied proportionately. But I think the challenge to society, as a whole is to guard against complacent apathy. I hope no one would be naïve enough to think that bigotry and intolerance have disappeared from Denver's landscape. I know personally that it hasn't.

All of us who have a strong connection to our minority ethnic heritage have to "adjust," to some degree, each time we walk through the door of our home. The reality is that we live in two worlds and there is a threshold dividing our minority identity with the rest of the majority world. But personally, I don't care to concede to that threshold too much just because I'm a member of the minority. There is so much more to me than just my ethnic heritage. I'd rather share myself than change myself.

The FACC is my work, my school, my family, and my respite. Since I have been fortunate enough to be in the FACC literally since birth, it has been only natural to emulate the leaders that I have watched all my life. I've witnessed the best aspects of leadership, as well as the worst. My teachers were the FACC leaders, especially my father – and they allowed me to learn under their wings. As my own skills in non-profit administration developed, my teachers eventually became my peers when I was elected President of the FACC.

My role in the APA community is a natural extension of what I have learned at the FACC. It is a natural progression for me – from serving my family to serving my hometown.

FACC is so much a part of our lives. Our family is there and our friends are there. The very best of everything Filipino is at the FACC – not just the traditions but also the attitude, the heart, and the fun of being Filipino is at the FACC. My children don't only keep up with their cultural heritage, they revel in it.

I'm fortunate that my husband Greg was not only amenable to learning my Filipino heritage but also very enthusiastic. It would have been very easy for Greg to separate himself from all of that – his own family was not very keen on their own cultural identity. But he didn't. When he and I were in the Philippines over a decade ago, there was nothing that he didn't want to learn, no one he didn't want to meet, or nowhere he didn't want to go. There was also nothing that he didn't want to eat! (Even I balked at some of the foods!) As my children learn about their heritage, their Dad is right there alongside learning too. I'm very fortunate."

To strengthen cultural ties and cooperation among APA communities, Fran has these suggestions: "Consider that, when I was a kid, only a handful of APA organizations existed in Colorado. Now there are numerous APA organizations addressing many different social issues. I'm a Denver native and I know for a fact that APA communities have never been stronger in the Denver metro Area. I believe that the balance between individual ethnic organizations (such as the FACC) and the umbrella organizations (such as the Asian Roundtable of Colorado) is just right. It gives everyone the opportunity to participate and contribute.

However, there are so many organizations right now and many new organizations being created - we are at risk of actually diluting our strength. I think we should continue with what exists right now and improve upon those. I think that we should continue to improve on the fantastic APA programs that currently exist...with one exception – we need to increase the number of APA representatives in public government office. Visibility will naturally increase from there."

Spreading her influence, Fran accepted the challenge to serve as executive director of the Asian Public Media of Colorado / "Colorado Asian Today;" co-chair of the Mayor's Denver Asian Pacific American Commission; facilitator-coordinator of Filipino Heritage Camp; APA liaison for the Colorado Department of Public Health and Environment Emergency Preparedness and Response; and member of the Jefferson Center for Mental Health – Cultural Competency Task Force.

Being involved in the Filipino Heritage Camp in Colorado, Fran shares her cultural heritage and would like best to preserve some beautiful customs. She says, specific to the Filipino Heritage Camp, "What I would most like to preserve and share is everything that can't be found in books or on the Internet. The parents and children at FHC can easily learn about the customs, traditions, history etc on their own – anybody can "google" Filipino. What we can teach at camp is something that is uniquely Filipino - our hospitality, our love of family, our respect for elders, our humor and our idiosyncrasies. Teaching the 'heart' of being Filipino is not easy and can really only be done through example and representation. So that is what the FACC volunteers try to do every year at camp. Interspersed between dance class and history classes, the FACC volunteers present all of those qualities I listed – just by being together. "

It is not unusual that APAs hear embarrassing comments such as: "You speak such good English." or "Where are you from?" Below is reprinted an article by journalist, Gil Asakawa, who felt that he is not taken seriously as an American but as a foreigner.

In his article "We Speak Such Good English", Gil mentions that most Japanese Americans have probably heard this backhanded compliment, and then suffered through a variation of the following conversation.

"Really, your English is so good, what nationality are you?"

"American."

"No, really where are you from?"

"California."

"Oh, you know what I mean. Where's your family from?"

"California."

Then the other person walks away thinking you're a jerk who's being difficult. But what's difficult is the inescapable feeling that you were not being taken seriously as an American, not just as an American citizen but also as a person who is American.

Non-Asian Americans often think of us as foreigners, even if we happen to be third, fourth, fifth or even sixth generation Japanese Americans. Not even hapas, or mixed-race JAs, are exempt. I've heard of hapas who get this version of the conversation: "Oh, you're half Japanese? Which parent is American?"

The fact is, almost all Americans, APA or otherwise, came from someplace else. Japanese have been living in the United States since the 1880s, but many people still assume we're newcomers - Fresh off the Boat, or FOB - when they first see us. It's irritating, because in most ways, Japanese Americans today are much more American than Japanese. Sure, we may have black hair, "slanty" eyes and "yellow" skin (who decided we're yellow, anyway? I've never thought my skin looked yellow). But in our speech, mannerisms, our values, and perhaps most important, our spirit, we're Americans.

Japanese Americans aren't Japanese. Some of us may be more connected to our roots than others, and a few of us might be able to actually make the transition and live and work in Japan someday - be Japanese. But most of us wouldn't be considered Japanese by someone from Japan. Which is interesting, when you consider that so many Americans have a problem, considering us Americans?

I should mention that when I speak of Japanese Americans, I'm making a generalization, and one that I don't even fit completely. I consider Japanese Americans as a group to have been in the US for several generations. I know that many Japanese come to live in America every year, and many become naturalized citizens. My family moved to the States in the mid-'60s when I was a kid, so we're somewhat recent immigrants.

But the immigrants that set the standards of JA culture began arriving in 1885, and most of us can trace our families to grandparents or great-grandparents who came to America in the early 20th century.

And that's what makes us different from the Japanese. It's not that we've had a hundred years to become more American. It's that Japan has changed so much since the era when our ancestors arrived in Hawaii and California.

In historical terms, those immigrants way back then were raised in a poverty-stricken rural country that was just starting to find its place among the world's modern industrial nations. That first wave of Japanese came like earlier Chinese immigrants had: to make more money then they could at home, and to return to Japan as wealthy men (they were almost exclusively men).

The values they brought with them to the United States were ones that had been in existence for centuries, based on duty and obligation, extolling hard work and perseverance. It's not that those values are gone today, but I don't think they're as pervasive and powerful as back then.

The popular culture has of course also changed, since not even radio was around when those ancestors climbed aboard ships in Japan for the long trip across the Pacific. For them, an evening might be spent gambling over Jan Ken Po (rock-paper-scissors) - a game that didn't require any pieces or skill. And, language has changed a lot too. Even Japanese who moved to the States in the '60s like my parents find it hard to follow all the English words that are now used in Japan.

Japan was going through the Meiji era when the first immigrants left the country. The Emperor Meiji was the one who came to power after Commodore Matthew Perry opened Japan up to Western ways. During the last part of the 19th century and early 20th century, Japan was busy playing catch-up with the West, soaking up all things European and American and introducing industry to its society. The death of the Meiji Emperor in 1912 was followed by the brief rule of his son during the Taisho era, and then when he died in 1926, his son Hirohito, who was familiar to Americans as the one who ruled over Japan during World War II and the postwar decades, ushered in the Showa era (each emperor's reign is designated by a name, and that name comes to signify the emperor as well as his era). The government first approved the limited emigration of Japanese laborers to America during the Meiji era after the US banned Chinese immigration in 1884, which caused a need for low-paid laborers.

Because so many of the Issei--the first-generation of immigrants--came to the US during the late 1800s and early 1900s, they brought with them values and ideas firmly embedded in the Meiji and Taisho eras. It's Meiji and Taisho values - language and food and traditions - that define Japanese American culture. Our identity is dictated by Japanese culture of a century ago, kept alive through oral traditions, annual festivals, family picnics and even funeral traditions.

As the first immigrants, who thought of themselves as sojourners, began to settle and stay in the U.S. and raise families, the next generation - the Nisei - became the first true Japanese Americans, because they were American citizens by birth. That didn't necessarily mean much - they faced prejudice not just in their communities but also in the media (thanks to the Hearst newspaper chain's harangues about the "Yellow Peril"). And of course, when WWII broke out, citizenship didn't prevent JAs from being rounded up and herded into concentration camps away from the west coast.

Over the decades in the US, laws were passed to restrict the influx of Japanese immigrants and to prevent the Issei from owning land or property, but they JA community thrived in spite of the obstacles. However, the Nisei became the only hope for JAs to establish themselves as Americans when the Immigration Act of 1924 completely banned further immigration from Japan.

Suddenly, those Nisei bore the responsibility of being good Americans and at the same time, preserving the culture their parents brought with them. That culture became the time capsule version of Japanese culture that JAs live by today. And that sense of responsibility led to the great lengths JAs have gone to, to assimilate into the American mainstream.

No wonder why we speak such good English - it was part of our self-defense mechanism!

We now feature Giselle Rushford, a Filipino American who has been working in the business world as a facilitator, consultant and community leader.

## Giselle Rushford

Larush Consulting principal Giselle Rushford emigrated from the Philippines to the U.S. over 37 years ago. She completed her undergraduate studies in finance at the Golden Gate University in San Francisco and completing her graduate studies in management and computer information systems at Regis University in Denver. She is an Asian Pacific Women's Leadership Institute Fellow, True Colors Certified Facilitator, and Loden Institute Certified Diversity Facilitator.

She retired from AT&T after a career of almost 30 years of managing multimillion-dollar projects for Fortune 500 companies. She was instrumental in the recovery of the communications services of several clients after the 9/11 attack. She is a results-oriented professional with in-depth experience in business, telecommunication, computers, management and people development.

Giselle supports several nonprofit organizations in their strategic and long-term planning as well as team building processes. She founded a senior immigrant program that helps the elderly in their acculturation process into the community. She also co-founded an employee resource group at AT&T to help Asian Pacific Americans integrate and develop as productive contributing members and volunteers of the community. She served an advisor to the national organization and still serves in the same capacity to the Mountain Region Chapter after completing two terms as president. She co-founded the National Federation of Filipino American Associations (NaFFAA) Central Region and is a charter member of this service organization. She served as the president of the Filipino American Community of Colorado, a 54 year old nonprofit organization for two terms—2000-2001 and 2006-2007.

When asked what her accomplishments were, she answered by saying that she made a difference.

Giselle contributes the following article about her experience as Asian Pacific American consultant and as diversity workshop facilitator in the business world.

# A Diversity Experience

A little known internal newsletter for a Fortune 500 company caused such a ruckus that it precipitated its demise as well as the advent of company-wide diversity training for this said corporation. What happened? In early 1990s, a monthly newsletter was trumpeting the globalization efforts of this multinational corporation by depicting a cartoon of worldwide communication links with people in Europe and Asia, engaged in talking with each other. However, instead of a person in Africa, the cartoonist depicted a monkey on top of a tree linked with other countries. Also upon close inspection, a roach is depicted in Mexico as linked with the world.

This cartoon would have gone unnoticed had the employees who read the newsletter ignored it. But instead of being silent, someone leaked the cartoon to the media. The next few days, the corporate switchboard was bombarded with calls from outraged shareholders, customers and the public questioning the appropriateness of such depictions of its global customers in Africa and Mexico. As a consequence of the public outcry, the entire editorial staff was fired (there was no person of color in the staff) and the newsletter was cancelled and eventually replaced with a differently named publication.

The company is AT&T, which hired a consultant to improve its corporate image and revamp its diversity program; it came to light that it had none. The consultant hired had successfully sued AT&T for gender bias in the 70's and coined the phrase "glass ceiling." She told the corporate leadership that it needed to include on its leadership team people who reflected its customers and employees if it was to successfully compete in the global market. At the time there was no one in the pipeline to fulfill those leadership roles. As callous as it may sound, improving the bottom line is the end-all in a corporation, particularly this one. Based on a study of the company she conducted, the consultant also recommended that the company go through a diversity awareness and sensitivity training conducted by employees who have the passion and credibility to deliver the company's message of inclusion and plurality. It was in this environment that the company recruited managers of color, gays, lesbians and people with disabilities to go on special assignments to facilitate diversity workshops across the business unit of thousands of employees. I was one of them who had been asked to facilitate canned diversity awareness workshops for three years, zigzagging various time zones.

In this assignment of which I was the only Asian Pacific American (there were 60 of us) I actually found my voice as a woman and a person of color in a world of work where results and accomplishments were keys to success. It was an experience in itself to be the only APA face in many places where they have never seen one in a leadership position. The only Asian they said they knew was the laundress or the Chinese restaurant owner in the strip mall. I heard various stories not normally heard in a corporation of pain, inequity, guilt, denial and insensitivity. Each workshop was memorable and I conducted about a hundred or so in a span of three years. Most of the workshops (two days) started with suppositions that discrimination was in the past and it no longer existed in this particular organization in this day and age (mid 1990s). As we went through the workshop, revelations surfaced on how much prejudice did exist (especially when the group was mixed) and towards the end, awareness began. Most of my successful workshops had been with diverse groups. It was quite a challenge when the group was homogenous.

In one of my workshops, I was disheartened to hear an elderly employee who went through the workshop and her final words were "birds of a feather should flock together and so do people." During the entire workshop, she had alluded to the validity of segregation while hearing her coworkers described the negative impact of prejudice on their lives and careers. However, my most amazing experience had been an "aha" from one of my participants who is now confined to a wheelchair as a result of a car accident. He was able to articulate the feelings of helplessness and the hopefulness that the workshop had brought to him. I never realized how powerful giving someone a voice can be until I heard that man summarized the goal of the workshop in his own words.

I conducted my last workshops in California where an APA face was normal but considered an anomaly to be in a facilitator role. It was pretty remarkable to see Asian Pacific Americans in positions of leadership but heart-breaking to hear that many have not budged from their positions for years. In retrospect, they had hit the "bamboo ceiling." (For more information about this phrase, read *Breaking the Bamboo Ceiling: Career Strategies for Asians*) Many of the Asian Pacific Americans at AT&T went into technical careers and most were pigeonholed in the stereotypical engineering positions. Although most had joined the corporation with college several degrees, many APAs struggled with their careers while their white counterparts with fewer degrees thrived. Furthermore, creating an employee network within the corporation did not materialize in a more successful APA community. Finally, they were just as concerned if not more impacted with the cost cutting measures of layoffs, outsourcing or demotions.

AT&T poured millions of dollars into diversity initiatives as have other corporations, but few have implemented initiatives with benchmarks including executive compensation based on their diversity metrics. Has there been a systemic change within the organization because of two-day diversity awareness workshops? Difficult to tell since they had undergone so many changes, such as divesting, mergers, acquisitions, etc., that the tracking system and mechanism in place have been lost in the process. Does the corporate boardroom embody color, gender or other diverse makeup that reflect our society? Not quite, but they are trying. Do we have laws in place that protect us from discrimination in the workplace? Yes, we do, but implementation is spotty and discrimination is so subtle now: it is like fresh air; you know it is there but you can't touch or put your finger on it. Have we made headway in our country's political leadership? Yes we have—just look at this year' potential presidential candidates—a woman, a black man and a white man with a disability. The future holds promise for a Latino or APA presidential candidate.

There are many similar incidents to continually remind us that prejudice is still out there, and we need to be vigilant so we can challenge inequity when we are confronted by it. Anything less can make the struggle even harder and our voices weaker.

Finally, this chapter concludes with an opinion column on affirmative action written earlier by one of the book's authors, Nestor Mercado.

## On Affirmative Action Programs

The need for equal opportunity for all Americans was born out of historical experiences, which culminated in the passage of the 1964 Civil Rights Act. The United States government, through affirmative action has provided the machinery through which minorities can have equal access to employment, housing, education and public and social services. While there is logic in the move to scrap present affirmative action programs, there are two compelling reasons to be apprehensive of such actions.

First, in a laissez-faire policy, which is characterized by free enterprise and competition, there are regulations the government has to set up. Thus, our economy is said to be more of a "mixed economy." In an analogous comparison, all citizens should be given the opportunity to compete in a free society and our government has that obligation to see that equal opportunities do exist. Second, the historical experiences of minorities who were discriminated against because of race are well documented and cannot be ignored. It is safe to say that this psychological pattern of discrimination and prejudice still exists, maybe to a lesser degree now. It takes time and effort for us to appreciate the diversity of American society from which we draw strength.

Providing opportunities for minorities may not be enough. It takes a real reorientation by the business world and the public to accept that cultural diversity is part of the changing American society. It will take massive educational programs to realize that each culture has something to offer and the more we learn from other cultures, the more we become appreciative and tolerant. Until this happens, we cannot just have the concept of equal opportunity to be decided by free market mechanisms through pure competition. There is still a need for some kind of affirmative action, without quotas, geared towards a sensible policy of assuring equal rights and opportunities to all Americans.

# Chapter 10

# ASIAN PACIFIC AMERICAN COMMUNITY AND RELIGIOUS ORGANIZATIONS

Community organizations are the life blood of Asian and Pacific American groups. They perform many functions, such as preservation of cultural heritage, providing specific services, advocacy and securing APA rights, enhancing economic and educational pursuits, conducting religious services, and providing an array of social activities. Community organizations are a vital element in the infrastructures of APA communities and are essential to their sociocultural and economic well-being. They offer vital social, cultural, economic, political, and religious support systems and communication links.

Many community organizations were originally initiated by the first waves of immigrants to Colorado from a particular APA group. Upon their arrival in Colorado, these immigrants created an informal structure with people from their homeland to help address various social, economic, and other essential needs. Eventually, they established formal structures utilizing community organizations or in some instance utilizing the Colorado branch of a national APA community organization, working to address these important community matters. Successive generations of individuals and groups modified the organizations in their community or created entirely new ones. With the advent of increased APA political activism, beginning in the late 1960s, Asian Pacific Americans from specific groups began working together in pan-Asian organizations to advocate for their rights and needs and to better organize APA people. Chapter 10 focuses on community organizations that are specific to various APA communities; chapter 11 focuses on pan-Asian community organizations.

The selected community organizations described in both chapters are the ones that have lasted and flourished through the years. They are meant to be only a representative set and not inclusive of all APA community organizations in Colorado. The discussion in this chapter begins with national organizations that have local chapters and local affiliations, including the National Federation of Filipino American Associations (NaFFAA), the Japanese American Citizens League (JACL) and Organization of Chinese Americans (OCA). Some selected

APA religious organizations and churches are covered in the last part of this chapter.

**The following APA organizations are listed in alphabetical order by Asian ethnic groups.**

## CHINESE AMERICAN COMMUNITY ORGANIZATIONS

**Chinese American Council of Colorado** has three goals: to promote traditional Chinese family values, foster the political influence of Chinese Americans, and to work with legislators and others to promote equal rights for all Asian Americans. Its mission statements are: To preserve culture and heritage by sponsoring cultural activities and exhibitions; to enhance human rights and welfare of all ethnic groups; to encourage cooperation and communication among all ethnic groups in Colorado and to establish a community activity center for Colorado Chinese population.

**Colorado Chinese Club (CCC)** aims to promote the Chinese American heritage through social events, festival celebrations, seminars and public exhibitions. CCC hosts the annual New Year celebrations, summer picnics, volleyball contests, and annual meetings and elections of officers and board members.

**Denver-Kunming Sister Cities International**

Mission statement: World peace through people contacts and understanding. It is a people-to-people, grassroots contact between international cities and arranges for exchanges among professionals in various fields, including students, doctors and government officials. The founder and driving force is John Yee.

### Organization of Chinese Americans (National)

Mission statement: "To embrace the hopes and aspirations of Chinese and Asian Americans in the United States." Founded in 1973, OCA is a national, non-profit, non-partisan advocacy organization of concerned Chinese Americans. OCA is dedicated to securing the rights of Chinese American and Asian American citizens and permanent residents through legislative and policy initiatives at all levels of the government. OCA aims to better the lives of the 10 million Asian Americans across the country.

**OCA Denver chapter** is one of 44 chapters across the nation engaged in developing leadership and community involvement among its members. OCA's primary objectives include: promoting active participation of Asian Americans in both civic and national matters; securing social injustice, equal opportunity and equal treatment of Asian Americans; eliminating prejudices, stereotypes and ignorance of Asian Americans and promoting cultural heritage of Chinese and other Asian Americans.

**Summit Choir, Colorado.** The mission statements of Summit Choir are to establish a non-political organization with the primary purpose of cultivating and interest and love of music; to promote cordiality and friendship among various social groups; to advance cultural exchanges between people East and West; to perform at appropriate social and cultural events. Summit Choir performs at various celebrations and concerts in Metro Denver area.

# FILIPINO AMERICAN ORGANIZATIONS

## National Federation of Filipino American Associations (NaFFAA)

The National Federation of Filipino American Associations (NaFFAA), a non-partisan, non-profit national affiliation of more than five hundred Filipino-American institutions and umbrella organization is the voice of Filipinos and Filipino Americans throughout the United States.

NaFFAA was organized in 1997 by then Philippine News publisher Alex A. Esclamado, TLC Beatrice CEO & President Loida Nicolas Lewis. Armando 'Doy' Heredia is NaFFAA's Executive Director. NaFFAA has been fighting for the rights of Filipino veterans and other issues and concerns affecting Filipino Americans around the country.

## NaFFAA Region V

In 1998, Colorado was the first state that became part of Region V. The first Chair of Region V was Nestor J. Mercado (Chair Emeritus), followed by Dr. Jaime A. Yrastorza, Donna B. LaVigne and Florliza J. Obana, current chair. Region V member organizations, under the leadership of Donna LaVigne, worked together to raise funds to build Colorado USA Village in support of the Gawad Kalinga movement to provide low-cost housing for the poor in the Philippines. Colorado member organizations include: AnCop Foundation (USA) (CO), Asian

Gold, Bayanihan Society of the Queen of Peace Church, FACC, PASCO, Philippine Heritage Foundation, Philippine Rondalla of Denver, U.P. Alumni Association of America, Colorado Chapter and Uplift Internationale. "Saklolo" was the fund raising event that led to the birth of the Colorado USA Village in the Philippines.

**Filipino American Community of Colorado (FACC),** the oldest Filipino American organization in Colorado has for its mission statement - to maintain, preserve and cultivate the Filipino culture and heritage, and help all its members reach those goals.

The early Filipino settlers tried to form a fraternal organization, Masonic in character called Caballeros de Dimasalang. This was organized as a branch in Denver in 1935.

Benito Bautista created the existing social group into a club. Frank Mendoza encouraged Filipino Americans living in the Metro Denver area to affiliate. Liborio Meneses drafted the constitution and by-laws and on January 1954, the Filipino Club of the Rockies (FCR) was born, with Benito Bautista elected as its first President. Mostly social in nature and in activities, the FCR lasted for 20 years.

President Eusebio Sevilla mandated a special committee in 1973 to meet during the summer for the sole purpose of drafting a constitution and bylaws. The organization was incorporated as the Filipino American Community of Colorado, a non-profit organization. In November 1973, Silvino Simsiman was elected as its first president for the year 1974-1975. In January 1977, the community was granted tax-exempt status.

In the book, *Fulfillment of a dream*, author Nestor J. Mercado, traced the idea of FACC having its own *Bahay Kubo* or a community center. Jess Villar conceived this dream during his term in 1976-1977. He organized the Cultural Center Committee, which was continued by succeeding presidents Nestor Mercado and Cesar Palencia. Funds were raised for the Bahay Kubo. It was President Ralph Acosta, however, who vigorously pursued this dream. A solid plan and concerted efforts were made under his leadership. Vice-President Emil Pischel introduced the "bingo" as a vehicle for financing the purchase of the "Bahay Kubo." Pepito Castellanes secured the State Raffle/Bingo license and Lu Eurich is credited for faithfully organizing and working at the bingo project. Finally, on March 30, 1988, the dream of two generations of Filipino Americans in Colorado was fulfilled – The Filipino American Cultural Center at 1900 Harlan St., Edgewater was purchased. This building is now being used for meetings, cultural performances and special events not only by FACC members, but also by other Asian Pacific American organizations.

## Filipino American Community of Southern Colorado (FACSC)

Based in Colorado Springs, FACSC was founded on January 1, 1993 by Mr. Ron Nono. FACSC is a non-profit organization and does not charge any membership fee.

A brief history: In 1978, a group of 20 people elected Lolita Mangindin as the president of the "Filipino-American Association." Later that year, the "Philippine International Association of Colorado Springs" was formed and elected Lolita Mangindin as its first president. In 1993 and FACSC was born.

FACSC goals include: to unite Filipino-American families in Colorado; to build stronger interpersonal relationships among Filipino-American families; to teach and promote the diversified cultures and customs of the Philippines; to assist all newly arriving families in Colorado; to support the military community, especially Filipino American military and their families stationed at Fort Carson, Peterson Air Force Base and Air Force Academy, and to create a better living environment for all Filipino-American families in Colorado.

Current FACSC President is **Grace Morris.** Born and raised in Manila, she attended Malate Catholic High School and the University of Santo Tomas. She served as an officer of the Society of St. Vincent de Paul in Malate, Manila. Through this experience, she developed the desire and the enthusiasm to help people in need. She came to the United States with her husband, George C. Morris in 1992. They have a daughter, Giane and a son, Geordan.

Grace has introduced several new programs to the FACSC, particularly those to help members in the community and also in the Philippines. Currently, she is working with Marlene Perez of AnCop (Answering the Cry of the Poor) to support the Gawad Kalinga project. They are raising funds to build houses for the poorest of the poor in the Philippines.

As a community leader in Colorado Springs, she has the Filipino American Community alive and vibrant in that part of the State.

**Maria Teresa del Gallegos Gieseke**, Tita Mateng or Tita Terry, as she is fondly known to her friends and relatives, has been an active member of the Filipino American Community of Southern Colorado (FACSC) since 1999. Since her husband is a U.S. Air Force retiree, Mateng joined the Air Force Academy Parish of St. Michael's Church, where she was assigned Chair of the Social Committee. Every year, she and members of her committee hold a big social event to share the Filipino culture, including food, dances and entertainment amidst a Philippine setting. Due to her successful leadership, she is considered the Matriarch of Colorado Springs.

Born and raised in Manila, Mateng attended Maryknoll College from grade school to high school. She graduated from the University of the East with a B.A in Commerce.

Mateng also serves as the link between the Colorado Springs and Denver Filipino community. With friends in both cities, she has "bridged" cultural and philanthropic activities and projects to help people in need. She is now involved in the Gawad Kalinga project of building a village for the poor people in the Philippines.

**Philippine American Society of Colorado (PASCO)**

PASCO was founded in 1984. A 501(C) (3), the nonprofit organization is governed by elected officers and members of the board. PASCO is dedicated to cultivating, preserving, promoting and sharing the Philippine culture and heritage through educational and cultural opportunities that would enrich and enhance the lives of its members and the people of Colorado.

The founding members of PASCO are: Abraham Barbero (Founding Father), Amelia Ashmann, M.D. (1st President) with Serge Abad, Mario Rivera, Tina Estudillo, Fred Carino, Zaida Koh and Linda Pilapil serving as the first set of officers and board members. The following served as PASCO presidents: Ben Pernea, Romy Magalong, Minda Gloria, Linda Pilapil, Pepito Castellanes, Edith Pasion and Elbert Eloriaga (current president)

The PASCO Folk Arts Dance Repertoire performances in the community and helps spread and promote the Filipino culture. PASCO's regular classes help educate the youth regarding their heritage.

PASCO sponsors community functions during major holiday such as Easter, Fourth of July, Halloween and New Years Eve celebrations. Other projects include scholarship grants to deserving high school graduates and youth who volunteer and support PASCO activities; fund raising activities to generate funds to assist the Philippine victims after a natural disaster.

## University of the Philippines Alumni Association in America (UPAAA) Colorado Chapter

by Dr. Erlinda Rojas-Santos
Pharmacist, Educator, Researcher (retired)

The UPAAA-CO was founded by Dr. Erlinda Rojas-Santos in 1997 after she attended as lone delegate from Colorado, the UPAAA General Convention held in Atlantic City, New Jersey. Starting with ten members, the organization grew to 61 in 2005 including members within the whole State. The first set of officers was inducted by Philippine Consul General Teresita Marzan from San Francisco at an auspicious occasion marking the Centennial of Philippine Independence. The association is registered officially at the Philippine Consulate in San Francisco, pursuant to regulations.

The University of the Philippines is unquestionably the premier university in the Philippines, the acclaimed national university, and the apex of Philippine education. It has evolved into a "multiversity" with seven autonomous universities within the University of the Philippines System (UP Diliman, UP Los Banos, UP Manila, UP Visayas, UP Mindanao, UP Baguio, UP Open University). Its graduates are renowned as the top leaders in the nation, counting several Philippine Presidents, Supreme Court Justices, Department Secretaries, heads of top business corporations, governors and mayors and other high positions, community leaders in all continents across the globe, executives and professionals in all fields of endeavor. Dr. Santos worked for the official accreditation of the chapter with the UPAA based in the UP Diliman campus giving the chapter lifetime accreditation. At a later date, the UPAAA-CO received full affiliation to the National Federation of Filipino-American Associations in America (NaFFAA).

The purposes, goals and objectives of the UPAAA Colorado Chapter are: (1) to bind and serve UP alumni in the Colorado and Rocky Mountain Region and promote their economic, social, cultural and

political well-being; (2) to establish and maintain open lines of communication between the University and its alumni in this region, particularly helping the upgrade of its faculty by sponsoring professorial chairs, raising funds for medical research and student scholarships, and expansion and improvement of its libraries, equipment and facilities; (3) to promote and disseminate the Philippine culture and preserve and maintain our Philippine Heritage; (4) to serve as a link or bridge between the Philippine consulates, federal, state and local government agencies, professional and community organizations and the Filipino-Americans in the community on events, news, and programs; (5) to participate in continuing education, seminars, in-service training, conferences, conventions and reunions.

# ASIAN INDIAN COMMUNITY ORGANIZATIONS

## India Association of Colorado (IAOC)

Mission statement**:** to promote the cultural and social activities and interests of the Indian community of Colorado; to promote friendship among all persons interested in the culture of India; to foster international understanding and goodwill.

IAOC preserves, and celebrates Indian culture and special festivals events. The Association provides a forum for exchange of social and cultural views, open to persons of Indian origin.

**Colorado Kannada Koota** is an association of Colorado residents hailing from Karnataka, India.

Mission statement: to promote, preserve and maintain the cultural and linguistic heritage of Karnataka, to foster the interests of Kannadigas, and to enrich the diverse cultural mosaic of Colorado with the best of Indian traditions. The Colorado Kannada Koota started in the early 1970s. In addition to music, dance and other cultural programs, several members of the Kannada family organize to promote humanitarian causes and such events as annual Mother's Day picnics. It is a Colorado Kannada Koota tradition to provide an opportunity for men and children to show off their skills in cooking to honor their loved one and mother, respectively. The day is filled with fun and games, where children gang up to beat their parents in both physical and mental games.

## JAPANESE AMERICAN ORGANIZATIONS

### Japanese Americans Citizens League (JACL)

The national Japanese American Citizens League (JACL) was founded in 1929. The JACL mission statement is to secure and maintain the civil rights of Japanese Americans and all others who are victimized by injustice and prejudice. The leaders and members of JACL also work to promote cultural values and preserve the heritage and legacy of the Japanese American community. JACL is today the oldest and largest Civil Rights organization focused on Japanese and Asian Americans. Over the years, JACL has been instrumental in a series of legal actions eliminating discriminatory laws. This list includes: naturalization rights for Issei Japanese Americans, elimination of more than 500 local, state and federal laws discriminating against Issei aliens, elimination of immigration laws discriminating against Asians, repeal of laws authorizing detention, in time of emergency, without regard to due process guarantees, repeal of anti-miscegenation laws prohibiting marriage between persons of different races and formal repeal of Executive Order 9066.

After a 10-year effort, the Civil Liberties Act of 1988 was passed, under which the United States government formally apologized for the imprisonment of Japanese Americans in World War II and monetary redress for those directly involved.

## Mile-Hi JACL

The Denver-based chapter of the Japanese American Citizens League (JACL) was born 70 years ago. The Mile-Hi JACL has been an active civil rights and educational organization since 1938. The local JACL organization's first president, Dr. Shimpei Sakaguchi, set the path and leadership that has endured and prospered through to 2003. Many people are not aware that there was a significant number of first generation Japanese Americans living and working in Colorado, Wyoming, Nebraska, Utah and New Mexico in the late 30s. For Colorado residents, that number would swell by the end of World War II. This is due in a great part to the leadership, of then Governor Ralph L. Carr (1939 – 1943), who with the highest of principles and understanding of our Constitution, strongly spoke out against the Japanese Internment Camps. Governor Carr opened Colorado to Japanese Americans in the middle of the war. Camp Amache held as many as 8500 Japanese. Along with members from the Denver JACL, Kasumi Miyamoto, then president of the Ft. Lupton JACL, met with Governor Carr in 1940 to reaffirm our support and loyalty as citizens of this country.

## JACL Tri State Region

In 1946 and 1947, the Denver JACL played a significant role to connect the JACL organizations from Colorado, Nebraska and New Mexico together. This became the Tri State Region. Denver JACL hosted the 9th Biennial National Convention in 1946. Minoru Yasui was a regional representative at this time.

## Japanese Association of Colorado

It was founded in 1903. Its mission statement is: To provide support for Japanese American community events in Denver. Among their accomplishments, JAC provided educational scholarships to graduating students of Japanese American ancestry in the Denver metropolitan area, hosted a community picnic for individuals of Japanese and Japanese American ancestry in Denver, participated in the annual Dragon Boat Festivals; hosted a traveling group of musicians from Japan.

## KOREAN AMERICAN ORGANIZATIONS

**Korean American Coalition (KAC)** was incorporated as a non-profit organization in 1983, to serve as the vehicle to overcome the many barriers in the pursuit of full and meaningful participation in American society. Their priorities include advocacy, empowerment, outreach, organization, and multi-generational collaboration. KAC emerged as the voice of the Korean American community during the 1992 Los Angeles Riots. They provided relief assistance to affected businesses with a $500,000 grant from New York Life Insurance. KAC served the underserved Koreans first in Los Angeles and rapidly grew to become the voice of all Korean Americans. Through the years, KAC registered voters, processed citizenship applications, coordinated forums, seminars, internships and leadership conferences. KAC developed relations with media, government agencies, elected officials and leaders of other ethnic communities.

### Rocky Mountain Korean Lions Club (RMKLC)

Mission: to serve. L=Liberty, I=Intelligent, O=Our, N=Nation S=Safety

RMKLC offers free health screening to Korean Americans through the 9-Health Care; provides college scholarships to senior high school students; conducts Peace Poster contests for children ages 11-13; and serve meals to the homeless through volunteers.

## LAO-HMONG ORGANIZATIONS

### Lao-Hmong American Coalition (LHAC)

President-Emeritus/Founder: Yang Chee

The Lao-Hmong American Coalition (LHAC) was founded on September 16, 1995 exclusively by the former allies of the United States – the Lao-Hmong Special Guerilla Units (SGU) veterans and their American counterparts who side-by-side fought the U.S. "Secret War" in Laos.

LHAC, the national organization, is a non-profit organization. The Coalition has no outside funding. It relies solely on its limited financial resources from membership dues and generous contributions from private donations. There are no paid staff/officers. Its headquarters is in Colorado with chapters in several states.

Some of its primary missions include: to educate the citizens of the United States about the profound connection that binds the two distinctive people together as eternal brothers and sisters in the fight for a common goal: Freedom - to promote greater public awareness and better understanding for the Lao-Hmong people's historical contribution to, especially the U.S. during the Vietnam War, to inform, advise and educate the Lao-Hmong about the inevitable social and cultural changes/shock that may affect them as life progresses through acculturalizations in a new society, to promote the cultural, social economic, educational and humanitarian developments of the Lao-Hmong people within the U.S. through transitional changes, adaptations and integrations; but not total assimilations, to identify and develop worldwide awareness of the issues concerning the well-being of the Lao-Hmong people domestically, as well as internationally, through constructive and peaceful means, to promote unity, foster harmony and encourage mutual respects among diverse communities and to be productive and contributing citizens of our adopted country – The United States of America.

## Hmong-American Association of Colorado (HMAAC)

The mission of this association is to protect, preserve, promote, develop and advocate for the rights and interests of the Hmong community in Colorado and to be successful within the larger community.

Some of the goals are: to promote social, economic, cultural and educational success for the Hmong community; to promote, protect and support the rights and interests of the Hmong community; to preserve and develop Hmong tradition and culture; to network with local, State, Federal government, agencies, and with other organizations and communities; to establish programs and provide services to help Hmong become self-sufficient and better citizens

The Hmong-American Association of Colorado (HMAAC) was established in October 13, 1992 by the members of the Hmong community to address the challenges faced by the community who are much in need and underrepresented.

Their services include: Elderly Service Program, Youth Leadership Program, (In 2006, HMAAC successfully helped Shaw Heights Middle School, Westminster High School and Ranum High School to establish Hmong student clubs to encourage academic success, leadership development and cultural awareness among the Hmong youth): Outreach Program (A special needs project for several families who have children with disabilities to provide them with the necessary resources and workshops to understand and assist the needs of their child's disability); Adult Program (The program currently offers two

English classes for adult students to become more proficient in reading, writing and speaking the English language) Hmong Language Class (The class teaches students of all ages how to read, write and speak Hmong appropriately in the Hmong language, Cultural and Health Festivals)

**TAIWAN**

## Taiwanese Association of Colorado

**Mission statement:** to help the Taiwanese Americans in Colorado to improve their quality of life.

# TIBET

## Colorado Friends of Tibet

Colorado Friends of Tibet (CFT) registered as a Colorado nonprofit organization in March 1994. With hundreds of members throughout the State of Colorado, their mission is to help Tibet and preserve this unique cultural heritage. Their support goes to help improve the health, education and welfare of the Tibetan refugees in India and Nepal and improve the living conditions of Tibetan children who continue to escape from Tibet in search of freedom. In addition, CFT helps to preserve Tibet's culture by making it available to the people of Colorado by organizing events such as the 1997 visit of His Holiness the Dalai Lama and the Colorado tour of the Tibetan Institute of Performing Arts.

Tibet was once one of the world's most remote, self-contained and religious civilizations. Hundreds of Tibetans have settled in Colorado, and CFT works closely with the Tibetan Association of Colorado, especially with regard to China's increasing crackdown on Tibet and Tibetan demonstrators since March 10, 2008.

# VIETNAMESE AMERICAN ORGANIZATIONS

## Unified Nationalist Vietnamese Committee of Colorado (UNVCC) 1st President: Mr. Sum C. Nguyen

The UNVCC is an organization of American and Vietnamese soldiers who fought during the Vietnam War. As a non-profit organization, the Committee has promoted the interests and the culture of the Vietnamese Americans in Colorado. It has also vigorously promoted close relationship with other Asian organizations and state and local officials. They have established a Community Center named after

Nguyen Khoa Nam, a renowned general of the Republic of Vietnam Armed Forces who committed suicide when South Vietnam fell to the communists. They have held the following activities: teaching Vietnamese courses for their youth; offering English classes for adults conducted by Mr. Michael Kemp; citizenship classes as well as orientation classes for new American citizens, particularly on the political process. The Committee began efforts in establishing a Vietnamese cemetery in the Denver Metropolitan area.

## Vietnamese Community of Colorado (VCC)

Past President: Dr. Duong Nguyen

Its mission is to serve as umbrella group of Vietnamese community organizations in Colorado. Established in 1993, VCC promotes Vietnamese Americans in the Colorado community, preserve Vietnamese culture and heritage, encourage communication and cooperation among ethnic groups in Colorado and provide support to local communities including city and state government.

Charter members include: Vietnamese Elderly Association, Vietnamese Mutual Assistance Association, Quang Tri Association, Tay Son Binh Association, Vietnamese Women Volunteer Association, Vietnamese Community of Colorado Springs, Vietnamese Air Force Association, Vietnamese Navy Association, Nhu Lai Temple, Vietnamese Catholic Church and the Vietnamese Student Association (Denver).

The following article is reprinted to describe the organization and activities of this Vietnamese organization for seniors in the words of its founder.

## The Vietnamese Elderly Association of Colorado

In the words of Thong D. Nguyen, "I have described the loneliness of most elderly Vietnamese in America in a previous asiaXpress.com article as reprinted in Chapter 1. This is a true situation for many Vietnamese now living in Colorado. Fortunately, we have a Vietnamese Elderly Association of Colorado (VEAC) in Denver. Many elderly Vietnamese have joined this association, although its membership is still modest - about 200 people. This is a non-profit organization having the guiding principles to reach goals pertaining to social security, religion, culture, and wholesome, healthy entertainment. The purpose of the association is to unify all Vietnamese and American Vietnamese refugees, 50 years old and up, with no discrimination of religion or sex.

The purpose also provides spiritual and physical help to all members, especially to members having problems (e.g., an accident or a sickness) according to the capacity of the association. The association organizes English and Vietnamese classes, the American citizenship class and also special- interest classes for elderly people. The VEAC sets up travel opportunities, picnic outings in public parks, in mountainsides etc. Besides these activities, the VEAC organizes many lectures on health care, social problems, and American or Vietnamese cultural literature."

The VEAC also has a Senior Center with magazines, newspapers, TV and VCR for use by elderly people. The Center also offers coffee, tea and cookies for refreshment. The VEAC warmly invites all Vietnamese elderly people to join the association to build up solidarity and friendship between the old Vietnamese refugees while far away from home, and also to dismiss the loneliness, which disturbs us everyday.

## RELIGIOUS ORGANIZATIONS IN COLORADO

Many Asian and Pacific American religious organizations and churches in Colorado have been organized over the years. They often blend religious and cultural practices. Many have experienced substantial growth in attendance and in the scope of activities, which include community gatherings and other social events. The rest of this chapter discusses a very small sample representative of the many APA religious organizations and churches in Colorado.

### The Bayanihan Society of Queen of Peace (Aurora)

It is a prayer group that was formed more than 24 years ago by a group of inspired Filipino parishioners of Queen of Peace Catholic Church. The First President was Virgie Rogge followed by Rudy Bautista, Serge Abad, Manny Avante, Mrs. Josie Delumpa, Lito Santos and Gloria Castillo. The current president is Ed Anolin. Over the years, the Bayanihan has served the Filipino community in various ways, including prayers, prayer vigils, songs, Eucharistic ministry and lectors. It spearheaded the acquisition and the subsequent enshrinement of Our Lady of Antipolo when the new church at Queen of Peace was built. The Society is also a member of the NaFFAA Region V. Although the Filipino community started it, the society accepts into its fold anyone who is interested and believes in its ideals and purposes regardless of age, gender or national origin.

In order to share Filipino culture throughout the year, selected traditional Filipino religious fiestas are celebrated in the church with the Queen of Peace parish community: Santo Nino Fiesta, Santa Cruz de Mayo, Antipolo Anniversary and Virgen delos Remedios.

**Gloria Castillo,** immediate past president, has been serving the Queen of Peace Church under several capacities: as member of the Ministry Council, as president of the Bayanihan Society, as coordinator of the Eucharistic ministers and Cantor of the Santinig Choir. In addition, Gloria has been visiting the sick, doing volunteer work for the elderly in the community, driving them to medical appointments and health functions. She is often called to lead prayers for the sick and for the dead all over the metro Denver. She has also served as interpreter for Tagalog and Cebuano for court and medical cases. Gloria has served as member of the Board of Directors of the Philippine American Society of Colorado (PASCO) for more than 20 years. She also sings and dances with the FACC Mano Po Singers and Dancers. For her services and contributions to the Queen of Peace Church and the Filipino community, Gloria has received numerous awards. A graduate of Far Eastern University, Manila, with a degree B.S. in Pharmacy, Gloria came to the United States in 1973 in search for better economic opportunities. She has five successful children, four boys and one girl and four grandchildren. Gloria has found peace by becoming active in the Queen of Peace Church and serving as volunteer in the Filipino community.

**Couples for Christ (CFC) – Queen of Peace Catholic Church.** CFC is a movement intended for the renewal and strengthening of Christian family life. CFC believes in marriage as an indissoluble institution as taught by our Lord Jesus Christ; that God created marriage primarily for love between man and woman, and for the procreation and proper rearing of children; that God created man and wife with equal personal worth and dignity; that God ordained order in the family by giving the man the role as head of the family and the woman as helpmate and support; that it is the responsibility of parents to educate their children to become responsible and mature members of society. It is led by Bart and Marlene Perez, Emil zand Imee Guardiano of Youth for Christ and Joyce Dennison. Many Filipino families and youth who are members of the Queen of Peace Catholic Church belong to CFC.

## Tri-State/Buddhist Temple (Japanese)

A short history of the Japanese Buddhist Temple is included here as it relates to the early Japanese settlers in Colorado. Japanese immigrants settled in and around Denver in the early 1900s. Many were Jodo Shinshu Buddhists. In 1916, the Tri-State Buddhist Temples' headquarters was formed and called Denver Buddhist Church. The first headquarters was at 1942 Market Street. During World War II, Japanese-American citizens were forced into relocation camps. Simultaneously, many Japanese-Americans from California were evacuated to Colorado where they lived as "regular" citizens as opposed to "prisoners" of the relocation camps. To serve them, the Denver Buddhist Church structure was enlarged. In 1947, the new temple was dedicated and the name Denver Buddhist Church was changed to Tri-State Buddhist Church. In 1965, it became a separate Church and in 1981, the name was designated "Temple" instead of "Church". In 2002 (37 years after the initial separation), Denver Buddhist Temple merged with Tri-State Buddhist Temple resulting in a single Board of Directors and treasury under the new title of Tri-State/Denver Buddhist Temple (TSDBT).

Jodo Shinshu Buddhism emphasizes everyday Buddhism for ordinary people, rather than monastic Buddhism for spiritually strong (singularly-minded) people. Jodo Shinshu brings moments of joy and *shinjin* a rich tradition and expresses a living experience of Buddhism.

Japanese Americans who became Christians go to Simpson United Methodist Church.

## The Hindu Temple and Cultural Center of the Rockies (HTCC)

Its mission is to provide a forum for religious worship and celebrations, and for cultural, religious, and spiritual development activities based on Hindu / Vedic / Sanatan-Dharma tradition. The HTCC celebrated its 11th anniversary in 2007. The Temple, which is open five days and seven evenings a week, offers Bal Mandir program for children and Yoga classes for adults. HTCC purchased a new land at 7200 South Potomac St., Centennial, Colorado for the construction of a new Temple, scheduled for completion in 2010. Its priest Acharya Kailash Chandra Upadhyay was born in a Brahmin priest family in the foothills region of the Himalayas, now known as Uttaranchal Pradesh in India. In 1981, he earned his *Shastri* degree from S. Sanskrit University of Varanasi, U.P., India and in 1983 from L.B. Shastri Sanskrit Vidyapeeth, Delhi.

**The Hmong Community** consists of refugees from the mountains of Laos and Vietnam. Many Hmong immigrated to the United States as refugees from the Vietnam conflict. Pastoral care, worship and religious education are available through **All Saints Parish in Denver.**

**Iglesia ni Cristo (INC)** (Tagalog, "Church of Christ") claims to be the true Church established by Christ in 1914 by Felix Manalo, its founder. The majority of its members are Filipino ex-Catholics.

**Saint Lawrence Korean Catholic Church**

The Korean Catholic community finds parish life and worship available at St. Lawrence Parish in Aurora. Pastoral care and religious education programs are provided in Korean. Well over 200 Korean families are served by this church. There are many other Korean churches not listed here.

**Queen of Vietnamese Martyrs' Catholic Church (Wheat Ridge)** Over 1, 200 Vietnamese families participate in the life of the Queen of Vietnamese Martyrs' parish in Wheat Ridge. Mass and programs are available in Vietnamese. Community gatherings occur after the Sunday Mass; lunch is included.

**The Sikhs in Colorado**

The Sikhs are a community in Northwest India founded by Guru Nanak in the 15th century. He saw how much misery war between Hindus and Muslims brought to the Punjab and how caste intolerance dehumanized the lower castes. He preached a gospel of universal brotherhood and love that would then lead to a love of God. He was against the fanaticism and intolerance of the ruling Muslim class and meaningless ritual and discrimination against lower castes and women, which was a part of Hindu life. His religion was an austere monotheism that disapproved of idol worship and the caste system. It was based on the work ethic *Kirit Karo* (work hard), *Wand Chako* (share what you earn with those less fortunate), *Nam Japo* (take the Name of the Lord). He emphasized the role of the Guru, or teacher, as a guide of the community (Sangat) of him singing (Keertan) and breaking bread together (Langar).

The community had its own language, traditions, literature, beliefs and philosophy. The Sikhs had 10 Gurus, including Guru Nanak, and had to take up arms and become a fighting force to counter fierce bigotry by the Mogul emperors who tried to forcibly convert them. The last Guru, Guru Gobind Singh, developed the "Five K's" to mark the soldier saint (Khalsa). They were: Kes (uncut hair), Kara (steel bracelet), Kirpan (sword), Kanga (comb), Kacha (underwear). The rag-tag army of peasants was able to counter and defeat the Mogul army in the 17th century.

There is no fatalism but a will to conquer hardship that explains the entrepreneurial spirit of the Sikhs. They also believe in giving women an equal role with the men. They do believe in Karma and the transmigration of souls like the Hindus.

### Simpson United Methodist Church

In 1908, Rev. Hichiro Shirato and Mr. Hamanosuke Shigeta and around 80 Japanese and Caucasians voted to become part of the Japanese Methodist Episcopal Mission. They moved to several places in Denver until 1935 when they purchased facilities at 2501 California St. in Denver. World War II had a profound effect on Americans of Japanese ancestry. Japanese Americans who were forced to leave the west coast found support and community in the California St. congregation. In 1943, the California St. Church held its first English language service. By the early 1960's, the congregation moved to 3401 High St. in Denver in a merger with the "Caucasian" Simpson Methodist Church. In 1967, the current facility, now called Simpson United Methodist Church, in Arvada was completed.

The church holds a yearly free Doll and Cultural festival called Hina Matsuri, a Doll Festival, featuring martial arts, Kimekomi dolls, Yo Yo, music, calligraphy, origami, tea ceremony, brush painting, bonsai, ikebana, Japanese dance (Nihon Buyo) Taiko and archery. They also offer classes on Japanese culture and language.

### Wat Buddhawararam of Denver
### The Thai Buddhist Temple in Denver, Colorado

**(วัดพุทธวราราม นครเดนเวอร์)**

The first Theravada Buddhist temple in Colorado known as Wat Buddhawararam of Denver was established in 1976 (or in the Buddhist Era year of 2519 B.E). The word "Wat" means 'temple' in Thai. The name 'Buddhawararam' means 'The dwelling place of the Buddha". A group of local Thai people living in the Denver-metro area at that time purchased a building which was up for sale from the Salvation Army. The building was a former Greek Orthodox Church that had passed into the hands of the Salvation Army and was being used as a storage depot for donated goods. The building was registered to be a Buddhist temple under the provisions of the laws of the State of Colorado, and received the permit to operate as a religious institution on the 25th of March 1976 (2519 B.E). The purposes of the operation of the temple are to provide a place of residence for Buddhist monks, novices and nuns, to provide a facility where local Thai and temple members can gather for social functions and making merit, to provide space for meditation classes, to provide a facility for a Southeast Asian cultural center, to accommodate classes for Thai language and culture as a part of Buddhist Sunday school

Since 1979, the temple has had Sunday schools teaching Thai language and Thai culture, as well as basic principle of Buddhism to children of Thai people and to people in the general public.

Now, the temple has a large number of members from the Denver metro area and throughout the state of Colorado, as well as from surrounding states. The temple operates its formal functions through a board of directors and a committee.

# Chapter 11

# PAN-ASIAN AMERICAN ORGANIZATIONS

This chapter describes selected pan Asian community organizations. Pan-Asian organizations present an opportunity for individuals from many APA groups to work together on common goals. Such organizations also provide an opportunity to examine and discuss common interests and for greater communication, understanding, and unity between APA groups. Pan-Asian organizations have many of the same general goals and functions of organizations that are specific to particular APA communities.

The Pan-Asian organizations in this chapter have been grouped into four categories: cultural, business, professional and advisory. Cultural organizations include the Colorado Dragon Boat Festival (CDBF), the Asian Roundtable of Colorado (ARC) the Aurora Asian/Pacific Community Partnership, and the Boulder Asian Pacific Alliance (BAPA). The business category contains the Asian Chamber of Commerce (ACC), which has successfully supported the APA businesses in Colorado. The professional organizations include the Asian Pacific American Bar Association (APABA) Colorado and the National Association of Asian Pacific Americans (NAAPA). The advisory councils category includes the Denver Asian Pacific Advisory Commission, the Asian Education Advisory Council (AEAC) and the Governor's Asian Pacific American Advisory Council (GAPAAC). A few other pan-Asian organizations are covered in other chapters, for example chapter 12 on APA health and medical services. As mentioned previously, these organizations are meant to be representative, not inclusive, of all such organizations in Colorado.

## A. Cultural Organizations

# Colorado Dragon Boat Festival: A Community-Driven Event

The Colorado Dragon Boat Festival (CDBF) has become, in a few short years, the most recognized and celebrated Asian American-Pacific Islander cultural event in the Rocky Mountain region. From an audience of 15,000 in its first year, 2001, the Festival has grown to over 100,000 spectators. It has received many accolades and awards. For example, Westword anointed the Festival as "Best New Festival" of 2001. The Rocky Mountain News called it the "Best City Festival" in 2003. And, in 2007, 5280 Magazine described the event as "One of Colorado's greatest festivals..."

**Crowds along the shore at 2003 Festival**

A number of Asian Pacific American festivals and other celebrations have been held in the Denver metro area. These events were important individually, but they also collectively set the stage for the success of the

**Eye dotting ceremony**

Dragon Boat Festival. For many years, the Aurora Asian/Pacific Community Partnership with partners Denver Film Society and the City of Aurora hosted the *Aurora Asian Film Festival*, a showcase for recent featured documentary films with Asian themes. The film festival is currently on hiatus. The Asian Pacific Development Center mounted *Passport to Asia*, which included Asian American entertainment and vendors.

At its peak, *Passport to Asia* drew 10,000. The *Cherry Blossom Festival* at Sakura Square has been a Denver tradition for over 35 years. Sponsored by Tri-State/Denver Buddhist Temple, the thriving *Cherry Blossom Festival* draws 25,000 spectators to celebrate Japanese-American culture, food, music, dance, and arts and crafts. And, the Boulder Asian Festival, produced by the Boulder Asian Pacific Alliance, typically occurs during the third weekend in August.

Formal planning for a dragon boat festival began in 2000. Ding Wen Hsu, then president of the Chinese American Council of Colorado, had heard that John Chin, then president of the Denver Chapter of the Organization of Chinese Americans, was working with Howie Solow, founder and chief instructor of the Shaolin Hung Mei Kung Fu Association, on developing a dragon boat festival in Denver. She contacted John Chin to discuss collaboration as she was interested in doing such a festival.

Chin and Solow had worked together producing a number of successful cultural events, and Solow had participated in dragon boat racing festivals in the New York City. Solow felt that such a festival would be very successful in Denver. Chin and Solow began preliminary investigations into the possibility of such an event as early as 1995. The collaboration of Chin, Hsu and Solow and their respective organizations established the critical mass needed to make the Festival a reality.

**Howie Solow, John Chin and Ding Wen Hsu with Denver Mayor John Hickenlooper**

When the three festival founders met, they found that they shared a common vision. All three believed that the festival should be a Pan-Asian event celebrating all of Colorado's Asian American and Pacific Islander communities. Moreover, they felt that the festival needed to be "community-owned" with local AAPI communities guiding its goals and direction. They also envisioned three key elements as fundamental to the success of the festival: dragon boat racing using traditional dragon boats; an entertainment stage featuring local Asian Pacific American performers; and a marketplace with the foods, crafts and other merchandise of local AAPI businesses. The CDBF's emphasis of these three elements, the inclusion of all of Colorado's Asian American and Pacific Islanders, and the fundamental premise of community "ownership" made this event different from other dragon boat festivals of the time.

While Chin, Hsu and Solow each had some experience in planning and executing special events, they recognized that they needed a skilled and enthusiastic team to execute a festival of the scale and scope that they envisioned. They recruited a team called the Steering Committee to share responsibilities overseeing the myriad of festival details. Each member of the original Steering Committee was a long-standing community volunteer in the Asian Pacific American communities. The Steering Committee members shared a common festival vision and were committed to putting on an event that conveyed the diverse richness of the local APA communities and promote a strong sense of cultural pride. The Steering Committee has been critical to the initial and ongoing success of the event. Over the years, the festival's planning and execution has become increasingly complex. The time commitment of the Steering Committee is enormous, becoming literally full-time as the dates of the festival approach. At another level, the Steering Committee is seen as a role model for effective collaborative working relationships. The first Steering Committee was made up of, as pictured, Karen Nakandare, community relations; Hong Wilkins, entertainment; Patty Quinn, treasurer; Mary Lee Chin, marketplace, Ding Wen Hsu, chair; Joanne Tabellija, corporate relations; True Nguyen, venue; John Chin, marketing, and Howie Solow, race logistics. (Stella Yu, not pictured, was also on the Steering Committee. Erin Yoshimura and Gil Asakawa, pictured, joined shortly after it was founded.)

One of the first tasks that was undertaken was to reach out to the local APA communities to garner their support for the festival. Meetings with community leaders stressed that the organizers were stewards of the festival envisioned to be an enduring community-based cultural institution. The festival concept was generally well received albeit not without skeptics and received numerous expressions of endorsement and support. Also, CDBF was also incorporated as a non-profit organization in 2001.

From its inaugural year, the Festival has been a success. In 2001, festival organizers privately hoped for an attendance of 3,000. Crowd estimate by the Denver Department of Public Safety was 15,000. Attendance reached 30,000 in the second year. And, spectator numbers have continued to grow as the event became better known. The excellent reputation of the event has also increased general awareness and appreciation of Colorado's Asian Pacific American communities. The Festival has been a success in other ways. The event is a great source of pride for the APA communities. It is often cited as a successful model for Asian Pacific American community cooperation and collaboration. The Honorary Chair and Honorary Patron are coveted positions honoring APA community leaders who are outstanding role models.

The Festival continues to improve existing elements to increase spectator enjoyment. Additionally, it strives to add new elements intended to entice previous spectators to return while attracting new spectators to attend. 2007's *Cultural Unity* – a hip-hop venue – and *Explore Asia* – an in-depth exploration of Filipino, Mongolian and Hmong cultures – were instantly popular. In 2008, the Festival will enter the international ranks of dragon boat racing as CDBF will host the American Dragon Boat Association international competition.

Over the years, CDBF continued to rely on an all-volunteer Steering Committee – now called the Operating Committee –to plan and execute the Festival. By late 2003, there was a growing feeling that the CDBF organization needed to evolve so that CDBF remained agile and responsive and to ensure the sustainability of the Festival. The event's increasing sophistication and complexity necessitated year-round planning. As a result, the Operating Committee could only focus on the Festival details. Long-range planning, sustainability and other fundamental concerns received only minimal attention. Moreover, festival organizers envisioned other opportunities to promote cultural awareness and education. At an all-day retreat, it was recognized that there were, in fact, two critical parts of the Festival. There was the Festival as an annual event, and there was a Festival organization. It was decided that the CDBF organization would be made up of two parts. A Board of Directors would provide strategic direction and governance for the organization called the "Colorado Dragon Boat Festival." The Board would also be involved in CDBF fundraising. The Operating Committee would focus on executing the event. This structure allowed for the organization to produce the Festival, but begin working on other strategic initiatives that would foster CDBF's continued success and stability. Another key organizational change was the use of part-time contractors – specialists in festival operations, e.g. logistics, volunteers, marketing, and corporate sponsorship – to supplement the work of the volunteers on the Operating Committee.

CDBF has been driven by vision, mission and values statements that have been consistent since its inception. The passion of festival organizers for the event is articulated by the vision, mission and values. These statements provide a context for all strategic and operational decisions made for the festival organization and annual event. The statements are as follows:

**Vision.** The Colorado Dragon Boat Festival (CDBF) will be recognized as the premier organization celebrating and promoting the culture, contributions and accomplishments of Colorado's Asian Pacific American communities.

**Mission.** The mission of the Colorado Dragon Boat Festival is to build bridges of awareness, knowledge and understanding between the diverse Asian Pacific American (APA) communities and the general public through cultural education, leadership development, and athletic competition.

**Values**

* Community Pride and Ownership - The CDBF is community-driven, taking direction and guidance from all of the APA communities.
* Collaboration - The CDBF seeks to foster understanding and cooperation among the APA communities and the general public.
* Business and Community Development - The CDBF helps promote and strengthen APA businesses and community organizations.
* Leadership and Team Building - The CDBF provides opportunities for athletic competition and leadership development.
* Creative and Innovative Programming - The CDBF strives to present fresh, fun family-oriented events and programs with special emphasis on the arts, cuisine and crafts, and youth expression supporting healthy and vital APA communities.

**Alisa Zimmerman with daughter Mimi at 2007 Festival.**

In 2007, CDBF hired a full-time Executive Director, Alisa Zimmerman, to oversee the Festival organization and day-to-day operations. Previously, Zimmerman was the Cultural Affairs Manager for the City and County of Broomfield. She was also well versed in business operations, economic development, marketing and performing arts management.

With Zimmerman's hiring, the Festival is now poised to work on key strategic initiatives. Over the next three years, CDBF will continue to evolve and grow in keeping with its vision, mission and values. A critical initiative is expanding the Festival's infrastructure and financial base. Promising opportunities include national corporate sponsorships, foundation support, other revenue streams, and philanthropic efforts. Another endeavor for CDBF is educational outreach, an integral element of the CDBF vision and mission. Festival organizers have also long-considered other events, such as an Asian New Year Celebration, that can draw general and APA populations.

As CDBF enters its eighth year, the Festival, as an event and as an organization, is undergoing fundamental change. Key individuals who have been with the Festival for most, if not all, of its growth and evolution are leaving or planning on leaving. A sister organization, The Colorado Dragon Boat Race Association, intended to be an autonomous organization, was started by CDBF to support and promote the sport of dragon boat racing. As the Festival continues to grow in size and scope, the financial pressures increase dramatically. Growth also means that the CDBF organization struggles with staying true to its vision, mission and values. At the same time, the foundations of the Festival are solid and CDBF will continue to be an important APA presence.

For more information on the Colorado Dragon Boat Festival, contact Alisa Zimmerman (720) 524-7221

## Colorado Dragon Boat Festival Trivia

Selection of Sloan's Lake. CDBF holds the event at Sloan's Lake because of a fortuitous conversation with Giselle Rushford of the Filipino American Community of Colorado. As the organizers were considering sites, Rushford suggested Sloan's Lake offering to house the festival at their nearby community center if rain occurred. There is some question as to where the first year's audience of 15,000 would have fit if there was a rain out.

2001 Champions. The Mongolian team emerged as the first year champions. They were aided in this win by Z's Dragons, the Denver Public Safety Team. In their semi-final heat, the Mongolians were tied with Z's Dragons. Captain Brian Gallagher, head of the Z's Dragon team, suggested a coin toss rather than a potentially exhausting run-off. The first toss revealed that the Mongolian team captain needed to be taught how a coin toss worked. The Mongolians won on the second try.

Food Sell-out. In 2001, food vendors were unsure about the size of the crowds and badly underestimated the demand for food. Many vendors had to replenish their food stocks within an hour of the marketplace opening.

Marketplace Vendors. Two vendors show the range of the festival marketplace. Tuong An, an Asian Gifts store located at the Far East Center, has been a popular marketplace vendor since 2001. Another marketplace favorite for many years has been Rosa Linda Mexican Restaurant, a well-known Denver establishment.

Honoring World War II Vets. In 2003, CDBF honored Asian Pacific Americans who served in World War II. Honorees include Medal of Honor awardee, George Sakato.

First International Performer. In 2006, the Festival had its first international performer, Dalgunn, a young woman from Mongolia. She may have also been the festival's youngest solo performer.

**List of Honorary Chairs**

Stan Matsunaka, John Yee, Bill Hosakawa, Dr. Jamie Yrastorza, Donna LaVigne, George and Helen Yoshida, Dr. Susanna Choi, Prof. Ved P. Nanda

**List of Honorary Patrons**

John and Anna Sie, Jimmy and Linda Yip, Leo K. and Linda L. Goto

**List of Board Members** (Past & Present)

Paul Chan, Violet Chan, John Chin, chair 2003 to 2007, Fay Chu Fong, Jim Fore, Bei Lee Gold, Ding Wen Hsu, chair, 2008, Donna LaVigne, Sami Nakazono, R. Tony Smith, Howie Solow, Ken Tapp, Yume Tran, Kit Williams, John Wright and George Yoshida

## About the Authors:

**John Chin** retired as the Chief Academic Officer at Front Range Community College in 2004. He is still active in higher education as a consultant. John recently completed three years as the founding chair of the Colorado Dragon Boat Festival Board of Directors. A lifelong community volunteer, he currently volunteers as vice chair of the board of directors at the Asian Pacific Development Center; board member of the Shaolin Hung Mei Kung Fu Association; chair-elect, Community Relations Council at the Denver Center for Performing Arts; member, President's Community Advisory Council at the Denver Museum of Nature and Science and interim chair, Business Advisory Council, Denver March Pow Wow.

**Ding-Wen Hsu** is co-owner and Chair of Board of Directors of Pacific Western Technologies Ltd. (PWT) in Denver, Colorado. PWT specializes in information management, and environmental management. Currently, PWT employs over 100 employees in Colorado, Texas, New Mexico, Montana, Tennessee, and California. Hsu, a native of Taiwan, has been very active in the Asian and Chinese American communities in Denver since she moved to Colorado in 1978. Currently, she is the chair of Board of Directors of Colorado Dragon Boat Festival, the largest Asian American annual event in Colorado.

**Howie Solow** is the President and Board Chair of the Academy of Chinese Martial and Cultural Arts and Chief Instructor for the Shaolin Hung Mei Kung Fu Association. SHMKF has been a fixture in the Denver metro APA community for over 13 years performing at the area's major cultural events including Asian New Year celebration at the Far East Center; Colorado Dragon Boat Festival; and Denver Parade of Lights. Solow is Vice President of Engineering and Operations at Peak Pilates in Boulder, Colorado, where he designs and manufactures Pilates exercise equipment.

Notes on photographs: All photos property of the Colorado Dragon Boat Festival. Festival photographers included Mike Bush, Kit Williams and Kyle Andrews.

# Asian Roundtable of Colorado

(APA Umbrella Organization)

The Asian Roundtable of Colorado is the umbrella organization of Asian Pacific American organizations in the State, which was formed to empower Colorado Asian and Pacific Islander communities by providing a forum to discuss and act upon issues of mutual concerns.

**Brief history,** by Stella Yu

In January 1993, The Asian Cultural Center organized the first outreach summit attended by more than 60 people to explore the concept of forming a pan-Asian organization. Subsequently, a task force was formed under the guidance of Lelanda Lee, and supported by the resources of the Asian Cultural Center, Asian Pacific Development Center and the Asian Chamber of Commerce. Bylaws and corporate structures followed, and the Asian Roundtable of Colorado was formed, with Ramani Kandan and I serving as the first co-chairs. Later, I became the first president of this organization and helped achieve its nonprofit tax-exempt status. Our first task was to outreach to all Asians through a grassroots effort. A very successful family event was held at the Alameda Center represented by different Asian groups of metro Denver, where various Asian cultures, cuisines and service organizations were introduced to the public. This provided the basis for continued communication among the many Asian groups of metro-Denver and a conduit for government and the community at-large to reach Asian Pacific Islanders of Colorado.

George Kuwamura, Manu Raval, Gloria Williams and Lily Shen (current president) have provided continuing strong leadership of the Asian Roundtable of Colorado. The Asian Roundtable currently includes over thirty Asian Pacific organizations from many different Asian communities. ARC's signature project is the Asian Heritage Month Community Celebration, which is held annually during the month of May. This free event showcases the culture and cuisine of Asia through cultural performances and an Asian luncheon buffet.

# Stella Yu

## 1st Co-Chair and 1st President of Asian Roundtable of Colorado

Stella Yu has been one of the movers and shakers of the APA communities in Colorado. Here is her story, which can serve as an inspiration for the younger generation.

"My first experience with APA organizations was serving as member, officer and later as President of the International Students Association at the University of Hawaii when I was undergraduate student of Fine Arts. While operating my bi-lingual graphic design and printing businesses in Denver in the 1980s, I became involved in the forming of the Asian Cultural Center and served as vice-president under Stanley Pouw for a while. I later participated on the board of the Asian Education Advisory Council of the Denver Public Schools, and was among the early leaders of the Colorado Dragon Boat Festival.

The Asian Community has given me a sense of "family" in Colorado. In the early days when the APA community groups were still in isolated pockets, I received huge support from many when a personal disaster struck in the early 90s. Not only do I have an obligation to pass on the kindness that I have received, I enjoy much ease and comfort among people who share my cultural roots. It is gratifying to see the APA community grow and the different groups reach out to jointly make Colorado a better home for all."

As Program Manager of the Denver Arts Program, Stella tells how she generated much enthusiasm in creating a mural from over 100 groups. The Denver Environmental Mural Project is part of the Art Miles Mural project, an international effort to support UNESCO's Decade of Peace and Non-Violence Among Children of the World, 2001 - 2010. Art Miles' goal is to engage people throughout the globe in the peaceful activity of making art to promote peace. Art Miles aim at completing twelve miles of big paintings grouped under twelve themes; among them are Peace, Health, Environment, Heroes, Music, Sport, and others. These 5 feet by 12 feet canvases are meant to be joined and displayed around the Great Pyramid of Giza at the end of the decade. The founders of the project requested participation from the City & County of Denver, and she became the program manager to help them reach the goal of completing the first mile, with the theme of "environment" being the focus. Denver's citizens tend to be environmentally and internationally conscious, and many community groups participated.

With the help of two part-time staff, support from a few Denver City Agencies, especially Environmental Health and Public Works Department, and many enthusiastic volunteers and sponsors, the project gained momentum in the early spring of 2004. Through outreach, workshops and educational support, more than 120 community groups participated and completed over 150 murals within three months. The goal was to display the Denver murals during an Earth Day celebration in April, alongside another 500 that had been painted worldwide.

As the Denver mural project progressed, it became apparent that a mile of paintings of one theme might set a world record. Guinness World Records began to take an interest in this mural activity in Denver. In the end, a world record attempt was made and 10,912 feet of paintings on various environmental topics were completed. They were displayed, measured and celebrated at a public ceremony held on the rolling hills of Barnum Park at 6$^{th}$ Avenue and Federal Blvd in Denver. The murals are currently kept in San Diego and are exhibited at various occasions throughout the world.

Stella is also involved with Asian Public Media of Colorado, which is featured in the chapter on Media.

## Aurora Asian/Pacific American Community Partnership

Contributed by Frankie Anderson

The Aurora Asian/Pacific Community Partnership (the Partnership) is a nonprofit organization working together with the community toward creating and maintaining a high quality of life for all Asian Pacific American residents of Aurora. Established in 1991 and currently operating as a program of Spirit of Aurora (a 501(c)(3) organization), the Partnership has initiated a variety of projects and events that have been consistent with its mission--providing business assistance, cultural awareness programs and educational services, with a goal to improve communication with all Aurora's citizens while promoting the City's diverse cultural interests.

The Partnership, founded in 1991 by Aurora's then Mayor Paul Tauer, has traditionally been staffed by the Aurora Business Development Center, with an APA community leader serving as Co-Chair, elected annually. The Partnership's initial function, with guidance from the Honorable Mayor Tauer and the City of Aurora's Small Business Coordinator, was to identify and get to know the Asian businesses along East Colfax Avenue in Aurora. Many Asian businesses had located along this unique retail strip, and friendships were fostered through the Partnership. What began as a business development endeavor grew into a larger cultural focus. Subsequently, the Aurora Business Development Center has continued to serve Asian businesses throughout the city of Aurora as part of its overall focus, and the connection to Asian business remains strong.

For ten years, through 2007, the Partnership's signature event was the Aurora Asian Film Festival, which offered a cinematic journey to Asia and the Pacific Islands, allowing for the filmmakers' perspectives on the rich and varied cultures of Asian/Pacific Islander and Asian Pacific American peoples. The festival received professional support from the Denver Film Society and was held in conjunction with the City of Aurora. Award-winning feature films and documentaries were screened at prestigious international film festivals prior to being selected for the Aurora event. The festival often featured North American premieres. This unique four-day weekend of entertainment was held at the historic Aurora Fox Arts Center and nearby Fletcher Plaza, complete with outdoor gala receptions, including Asian cuisine and entertainment. The event expanded to feature Asian visual artists during receptions at nearby local art galleries.

The Partnership Steering Committee members thoroughly enjoyed the annual selection of well-deserving recipients of the Aurora Asian Education Awards. Over seven years, highly intelligent, talented and service-minded Asian youth (and a few adults), received awards for their outstanding achievements, from Elementary grades through High School Seniors. Middle School and High School nominees were asked to write an essay on the given year's theme, and the responses reflected great promise for future APA leadership in Colorado, the U.S. and abroad. The next stage of the awards program will involve more APA students in an expanded program to include other cities throughout the Colorado Front Range and, eventually, the Western Slope. As APA educational issues come to the forefront, the Partnership plans to spearhead effective change through new educational initiatives.

Over the years, the Partnership sponsored many important forums (e.g., on immigration, working with the police, etc.), community activities (e.g., entering Asian-themed floats in the annual parade and holding an annual holiday gathering, etc.) and performing arts programs. The Steering Committee will continue building friendships in Aurora as members seek to exchange cultural ideas by sponsoring various new programs—featuring both traditional and contemporary APA cultures—throughout the city. The Partnership is also faithful to support other pan-Asian events in the metropolitan area, adding a level of cohesiveness to its mission. For more information, visit www.auroraasian.org.

APAs appreciate people who support their efforts, activities and their causes. In this section, we have included fellow Americans, Frankie Anderson, John Wright, and Jeffrey Seifried who have been steadfast and loyal supporters of APAs over the years.

## Frankie Anderson

### Secretary of the Aurora Asian/Pacific Community Partnership

**Frankie Anderson** has been a loyal and steadfast supporter of APA activities since she became secretary to the Aurora Asian/Pacific Community Partnership in 1992. In addition to Partnership activities, Frankie worked hard for the success of the Aurora Asian Film Festival and the Awards Program, she was also actively involved with the Colorado Asian Health Education and Promotion (CAHEP). While doing all these, she learned to love and play Balinese music as member of the Gamelan Tunas Mekar ensemble.

Frankie Anderson gives administrative support to the City of Aurora Business Development Center. She has held that position since 1992 while simultaneously serving as Secretary to the nonprofit Aurora Asian/Pacific Community Partnership. She coordinates the meetings of the Partnership and the many logistics of Partnership activities, including the decade-long Aurora Asian Film Festival. After seven years of implementing the Partnership's Aurora Asian Education Awards Program, she and several APA leaders are spearheading the development of an Asian education initiative that is broader in scope and purpose for the benefit of all Colorado APA students. Frankie volunteers on various committees for APA programs, most recently the Colorado Asian Health

Education and Promotion's annual Health Disparities Symposium. One of her strengths is being a resource coordinator, connecting people with people and building friendships along the way. Frankie is a founding member of the Denver-based Balinese music ensemble, Gamelan Tunas Mekar, established as a community orchestra in 1988. Having traveled to Bali to study the traditional and new music of the island, the gamelan combines her love of music with a fascination for Asian/Pacific cultures. She has served as the group's President in the past and currently as a Board of Director. For many years, she was President of the Colorado New Music Association, producing an annual music series that included world music concerts. Her interests in the arts and culture keep her active in the community, and her talents in music are also utilized in her local church.

## A note from Jeffrey Seifried regarding the Partnership officers and members

I will never forget my first meeting, as co-chair with the Aurora Asian Pacific Community Partnership members. I had just been hired by the City of Aurora and one of my assignments was to staff the Partnership. There I found myself with 12 or 15 people representing eight or 10 different local Asian-American communities – Thai, Filipino, Chinese, Indonesian, Korean, Vietnamese and others. I was so impressed – the group was enthusiastic and committed and very interested in more involvement and communication with the City of Aurora.

That was the beginning of a meaningful and rewarding relationship with dozens of Asian-Americans that took so much pride in their cultures, their children and their communities. We had the pleasure of educating, problem solving, supporting, and entertaining the Aurora community together for more than seven years. I learned a lot about Asian cultures and how they differ, but most of all I learned how much we have in common. The Asian American community rallied around the idea of establishing an Asian Film Festival in 1997 and we all saw over the next ten years the passion, insight, creativity and sensitivity that Asian filmmakers bring to their art. It was a treat to work with my friends in the Partnership to bring these extraordinary and revealing works of art to Colorado audiences.

# Boulder Asian Pacific Alliance (BAPA)

Mariagnes Aya Medrud, together with Narayan, Ramani Kandan and Shirley Fong (now in San Francisco) co-founded the BAPA in 1994.

It is a grassroots coalition of representatives from the diverse Asian Pacific populations, organized to become a more active part of the Boulder community and to impact social change.

BAPA represents Hmong, Laotian, Cambodian, Vietnamese, Korean, Chinese, Japanese, Filipino, Malaysian, Indian, Thai, Nepalese and other groups of Asian Pacific background. Recent arrivals come from Mongolia and Tibet. BAPA holds annual Asian Cultural and Asian Film Festivals.

"The differences among the Asian Pacific communities separate and isolate us from each other as well as from the larger Boulder community. We are not seen as viable members of the community and are largely invisible. We are often not included in the policy-making decisions that affect our communities. The Alliance is actively working to integrate the Asian Pacific population into the larger Boulder community." -- Mariagnes Aya Medrud.

# B. Business

## Asian Chamber of Commerce (ACC)

The Asian Chamber of Commerce (ACC) was incorporated in the state of Colorado in September of 1986 as a nonprofit organization. The mission of the ACC is to promote awareness of the Asian business community, and to assist in its economic development. The ACC provides workshops, business networking, business consulting, financial planning and international trade leads.

The ACC has a volunteer board of directors comprising 18 members that represent all Asian ethnicities and countries, as well as those who are interested in Asian business and cultures. The ACC's membership has grown to over 470 individual, small business, and corporate and nonprofit members. ACC has five working committees that provide the drive and backbone of this organization. They hold monthly business-after-hours meetings, hosted by different ACC members, which enable members to showcase their business or facility and make meetings interesting. ACC offers an excellent overall networking and referral service.

**John Wright**, President of the Asian Chamber of Commerce, has been supporting the APA businesses and communities for many years. .

John Bernard Wright was born in Montclair, N.J., the son of a Chase Manhattan banker. He graduated with a B.A. in Foreign Affairs, "summa cum laude" from the University of Cincinnati, M.A. in East Asian Studies at Cornell University, and received a Certificate on Construction and Business Management Institute from the University of Denver.

As President of the ACC, his responsibilities include keeping the 18 Board of Directors aware of the issues and concerns of the Asian business community and maintaining focus and direction of this non-profit organization.

Some of his experiences include the following: Program Administrator, Visiting Scholars Coordinator, Harvard Yenching Institute, Harvard University, Cambridge Massachusetts. Special Affiliations: CSU Minority Scholarship Council; Denver Museum of Nature and Science (Member); Co-Chair, Denver Sister Cities International Convention, 2000: Leadership Denver Class of 2004; Colorado Dragon Boat Festival, Board of Directors, 2005-present.

John enjoys traveling especially to Asian countries.

# C. Professional

## Asian Pacific American Bar Association (APABA) of Colorado

Organized in 1990, APABA of Colorado provides mutual support for Asian American attorneys, judges, law students and the general Asian community in Colorado. Their goals include: to advance the professional growth and interests of Asian American attorneys, judges and law students; to improve the access of the Asian American community to legal services and to promote the interests of the Asian American and broader APA communities.

APABA is affiliated with the National APABA (NAPABA) and they participate and vote at the Colorado Bar Association Board of Governor's meetings. Their committees include: Activities, Community Services and Membership and Communication Committees.

### National Association of Asian Pacific Professionals (NAAAP) Colorado

NAAAP-Colorado is part of the National Association of Asian American Professionals (NAAAP), which was founded in 1982, as a 501(c)(3), non-profit, volunteer organization consisting of professionals and business leaders in the greater Denver area. NAAAP is dedicated to the improvement of the Asian American community by promoting leadership, career development, educational exchange, professional networking, social networking, and civic responsibilities. Currently NAAAP has a national network consisting of more than 4,500 members with chapters across the country. The membership is open to anyone regardless of ethnicity, socioeconomic status or creed. Current members include individuals from a range of backgrounds that include managers, entrepreneurs, and professionals in the community.

NAAAP-Colorado began its operation in October of 2006 with representatives from various major corporations in the greater Denver metro area. With support from corporations such as Sun Microsystems, Kaiser Permanente, Coors, Wells Fargo, and local organizations such as Asian Chamber of Commerce, NAAAP-Colorado has already hosted number of successful events in the area.

## D. APA Advisory Councils

### Asian Education Advisory Council (AEAC)

It was established in 1985 by the Denver Public Schools Board of Education; AEAC works to improve educational opportunities and to improve quality education for all students in general and Asian students, in particular. The Council consists of diverse Asian ethnic representatives, 14 community professionals and parents plus 7 DPS certified educators, including the coordinator of the council.

AEAC's educational commitments include: to function as a communication link between the Asian community and the Denver Public Schools; to advise and make recommendations to the Board of Education and the Superintendent; to communicate the needs of students, parents, and the community to the Denver Public Schools; to identify and assess research that has application to Asian students and the community; to act on behalf of the educational interests of Asian students, parents employees and community; to assist the school district in developing programs to increase parent education and involvement; to identify needed programs on the basis of school district statistics, policies and community concerns; to relate the policies, programs, and activities of the Denver Public Schools to the community; to evaluate the effectiveness and annual achievement of the council and to report to the Denver Public Schools' Board of Education.

Ba Vovan, Vietnamese American and Community Specialist with the Denver Public Schools, was the first coordinator who successfully organized and managed this council.

**Denver Asian Pacific Advisory Commission (DAPAC)** was formerly called the Denver Mayor's Asian Advisory Council. \ The Commission serves as a support liaison and facilitator between the APA community in Denver, the Agency for Human Rights and Community Relations and the office of the Mayor of Denver. Further, it is the Commission's objectives to act as catalyst, educator, collective voice and to respond to issues and/or advocate based on community assessment of need and to create awareness and visibility of APA communities to the community at large. The purpose is to promote the work of the Commission as a resource to community outlets and government entities within the City/County of Denver; to facilitate linkage of community services to the APA community; to actively recruit and increase Commission membership to include representation of the multiple APA communities and their diverse issues and to function proactively with work on Commission's identified top issues.

## Karen Nakandakare

In the past, Karen served as co-chair for one year and have been a member for over five years of the Denver Asian Pacific American Council.

Karen currently sits on the DNC Volunteer Committee and is co-chairing an evening event with Tom Migaki for APA delegates and others when they come to town. They are deciding on the date, venue and program.

To mobilize APAs and be more visible in the community, Karen suggests that APAs should register and vote and get others (family and friends) to do likewise. "Sounds simple but it is amazing how many people don't want to get involved and then complain. I am not saying this about our APA community. This happens universally. Sometimes, people mistake being vocal with being visible in society. Being selective which group you support and how you support is a key factor." More change can take place from inside vs telling people what they are doing ineffectively. Karen Nakandakare is one of the first Asian recipients of the Minoru Yasui Volunteer Award.

## Governor's Asian Pacific American Advisory Council (GAPAAC)

GAPAAC was organized by Daniel Oh during the two-terms of Gov. Bill Owens. Council Members from the various APA groups brought issues and concerns to the attention of the Governor through panel discussions, symposia and meetings.

**GAPAAC members pose at the Governor's Mansion.**
***Seated L-R: Toy Nieme, Lily Shen, Purnima Voria, Chiyo Horuichi, Suegie Park and Donna Lavigne. Standing L-R: Carolyn Takashita, Eric Sung (behind her) Nestor Mercado, John Chin, Sum Nguyen, Peter Lee, Daniel Oh, George Kuwamura, Tong Heng, John Yee, Alok Sarwal & Richard Lin.***

Among GAPAAC's activities and accomplishments were:

On June 18, 2000, GAPAAC supported, "Celebrate India" working with event chairperson Purnima Voria. The event was held at the Donald R. Seawell Grand Ballroom at the Denver Center for the Performing Arts to promote the rich cultural heritage of Asian Americans through understanding and awareness and to bring unity in diversity.

On May 13, 2001, GAPAAC presented "Celebrate Asia" to showcase the contributions of APAs to the state of Colorado at the Denver Center of Performing Arts.

On May 19. 2001, GAPAAC held the Colorado Asian Pacific American Summit. "Making our Voices Heard," at the Front Range Community College. This very successful workshop provided a forum for members of APA communities to discuss relevant issues important to APAS. Based on this Summit, GAPAAC prepared a report on the proceedings and recommendations to be implemented by the Governor.

On August 4, 2002, an offshoot of the Summit, GAPAAC presented a Media Workshop, the results of which are also covered later.

## Daniel Oh

Daniel Oh is one of the most visible Korean community leaders in Colorado and is nationally well-known. In 2003, he was the recipient of the Martin Luther King, Jr., for humanitarian services in Colorado. He has also received the Outstanding Service Award as Chair of GAPAAC. He was the founder and moving spirit of GAPAAC. Some of the issues of the APAs were brought to the attention of the Governor through seminars, panel discussions and meetings.

Daniel has a Ph.D. in philosophy from Strassford University in England. He has a professional Real Estate and Multi-Lines of Insurance Broker Licenses. He is also the Vice-President of Re/Max Commercial Alliance and a Senior Broker with Dunton Commercial Real Estate Co. He was the Event Co-Chair, American Cancer Society, Relay for Life, APA Colorado (2005-present); Denver Mayor Asian Advisory Council (1997-present); Executive Vice-Chair, Asian Roundtable of Colorado (1996-1997); Steering Committee Member, City of Aurora Rehabilitation Authority (1996-1997)

Awards include: Certificate of Outstanding Service as co-chair and member of the Aurora Asian Pacific Community Partnership (1994-1998); Outstanding Service Award, Korean Chamber of Commerce, Colorado (1998-1999). Daniel got involved in civic and humanitarian services. "I have always been motivated to help people and the community, especially the poor people. One way I could attain this goal was to be a Catholic priest, so I entered and graduated with a B.A. in

Theology and a Master of Theology in Korea. In Colorado, I finished a Master of Divinity at St. Thomas College in October, 1979, just short of being ordained a Catholic priest. I left and became a layman."

To further strengthen cultural ties among APA communities, Daniel encourages APAs to get involved particularly in the field of education, such as having more Asian ethnic teachers in public schools. An important focus is the next generation, preserving family values and respecting elders. However, the children have now become independent and highly influenced by Western culture. There needs to be a balance between tradition and innovation.

Daniel is married to Irene and they have four daughters, all born in the U.S. Susie graduated from Northwestern University with a degree in journalism and now works in Chicago; Eunice, graduated from University of Northern Colorado in the field of teacher education and now works in Washington, D.C.; Janice is now working in the Justice Department in New York, and is Director of the Asian Outreach Teaching America Program; Anita, the youngest, is working in a Chicago hospital. Hopefully, she will continue on in the medical field.

Daniel is very much involved with the reunification of South and North Korea. He is the president of the National Unification Advisory Council (NUAC) Denver Chapter.

"Basically, the reunification of the two Koreas is more focused on economic and cultural cooperation, more so than a political agenda. Despite sharing the same culture and language, North and South Korea remain separate. The (NUAC), Denver Chapter, hosted a luncheon recently at American Legion to educate people about the diplomatic progress being made to bring together North Korea and South Korea. With economic cooperation and understanding, North Korea would provide labor while South Korea would provide capital and technological know-how. North Korea has the raw materials in the ground, while South Korea has none. Established in 1981, NUAC has 31 members in Denver, Colorado Springs and Pueblo."

Daniel concludes that the future for Korean reunification is not simple and will involve long-term plans and action.

# Chapter 12

# ASIAN PACIFIC AMERICANS IN INTERNATIONAL HUMANITARIAN SERVICES

Many Asian and Pacific Americans have been driven to work with people in America and around the world who are less fortunate than themselves. Such individuals are, in part, motivated by the longstanding American tradition of giving money, resources, and time to benefit other people, groups, or causes. But for many, Asian cultural values that have been brought to America also play a role. For instance, in China, the tradition of sharing wealth and time is deeply rooted in Confucianism and Buddhism. Buddhism stresses the value of compassion and service to others, and Confucianism emphasizes the value of benevolence and obligations or responsibilities. When Asian immigrants first arrive in the U.S., many struggle to survive but share financial, informational, skills-based and other resources with one another. As immigrants, their children, or succeeding APA generations become more financially and economically secure, they are better able to help those who have greater needs and to even make substantial investments in large-scale and visionary projects. This chapter provides a glimpse of some of the humanitarian activities by APAs in Colorado.

The chapter is organized into four sections. The first features four remarkable APAs who are involved in international humanitarian services, devoting their lives to helping others in Asia and elsewhere. These individuals are Dr. Jimmy Yrastorza of Uplift Internationale, Jimmy and Linda Yip of the Nathan Yip Foundation, Dr. Theodore Ning, founder of Friendship Bridge, and Mila Glodava. founder of Metro Infanta Foundation. All have made a difference in the world.

The second section is about the Colorado Heritage Camps where Colorado APAs have connected with individuals who have adopted children from orphanages in less-developed countries. Every year, APAs share their cultures and experiences with adopted children and their parents during annual camp activities in Snowmass, Colorado.

The third part of this chapter is devoted to a project in the Philippines called *Gawad Kalinga* (meaning Give Care). This movement, which involves the humanitarian efforts of Filipino Americans, has spread to Colorado. Other humanitarian fundraising projects developed within the last ten years are also mentioned.

In the last section of this chapter, four Peace Corps volunteers, truly the ambassadors of goodwill, tell stories of their worthwhile experiences while serving in the Philippines. Because of their experiences, they have become attached to and connected with the Filipino American community in Colorado.

The materials in this chapter were taken from interviews, contributions by various writers, information from editorials and articles previously published in the *Asian Pacific American Times*.

## Dr. Jaime Yrastorza

Dr. Jaime Yrastorza is the founder and president of Uplift Internationale (UI) Inc., a humanitarian organization based in Colorado. UI adopted the name of the project: *Operation Taghoy* (a Visayan word for whistle) and focused only in the Philippines. Its care is limited to children with facial deformities – primarily clefts of the lip and palate. The deformity prevents the ability to whistle, as well as other functions of the mouth and face, which normal people take for granted. The venue of UI activities are the rural regions where there are known children with the deformity and local expertise is unavailable. Foreign medical and surgical missions, as caregivers target the needs of the indigent population. The staff includes also non-medical personnel. The guiding parameters of *Operation Taghoy* are unique: willingness to

a) repeat visits to a host venue while targeting the rural regions;
b) provide surgical and adjunctive care, which is either not readily available at the venue or beyond the means of the patients;
c) invite participation of local peers who may thereafter establish an on-going *Operation Taghoy* cleft clinic with subsidy by UI.

The concept of sharing ownership as envisioned by the medical mission is to engage its present local supporters, namely, the Rotarians, members of the health associations and government officers to assist in identifying potential individuals, corporate and/or foundation benefactors from within the community, the province or the nation.

Dr. Yrastorza was born in Ormoc, Leyte in the Visayan Region in the Philippines. He graduated from high school in 1948 at the Ateneo de Cagayan, Misamis Oriental. In 1949, at the age of 18, he decided to come to America on his own. He enrolled at the University of Minnesota, Duluth and graduated with a B.A. in psychology in 1953. Then he enrolled at Washington University, St. Louis, MO and graduated with a DMD (Doctor of Dental Medicine) in 1957. Later at Georgetown University in Washington, D.C., he graduated with an M.S. in Oral Surgery in 1961. He established his 4-year residency, specializing in maxillo-facial surgery. There, he met his wife, Patricia Leverly, who was a nursing student. They have five children.

From 1963-1965, he had his private practice. At the same time, in 1991-1995, he was a consultant oral surgeon in Wheat Ridge, Colorado. During his private practice, he served as the Department Head of Oral Maxillofacial Surgery at the Lutheran Medical Center and a Clinical Associate Professor at the Veterans Hospital in Denver. He is a member of the UN Development Program in the Philippine, where he helped develop a training program in his specialty at the St. Porres Charity Hospital in Manila.

Dr. Yrastorza was a recipient of the 2003 National Federation of Filipino American Associations (NaFFAA) Lifetime Achievement Award. He was also chosen as the Honorary Chair of the Colorado Dragon Boat Festival in 2004. In 2002, he was honored by the Metropolitan Denver Dental Society (composed of the American Dental Association members) for his outstanding service to his profession and to the world community.

Lately, Uplift International received the very prestigious ABS-CBN Global and Gawad Geny Lopez Bayanihan Pilipino Award for 2007.

# Linda and Jimmy Yip

Jimmy and Linda Yip must have discovered the secret of living and doing things right, for everyone who sees them can see a glow of peace and joy on their faces. Their secret is fulfilling the dying wish of their only child, Nathan, who was killed in a car accident at age 19. Instead of living in grief and anger, the couple decided to devote their lives helping educate children in impoverished countries -- Nathan's dream to be his life's work after college.

Nathan, who was born and raised in the United States, felt very fortunate to live in this country where education is available to all who are willing to study. Early on, Nathan had already developed love and compassion toward the needy -- admirable qualities he surely imbibed from his parents. He also learned this at Kent Denver High School, where he was vice-president of Future Givers, a group, which encourages students to help others through philanthropic efforts. Through their travels to rural areas, especially in China and Mexico, they witnessed first-hand the poverty and the lack of educational opportunities for the children. The Yip family, with Nathan's wish, planned to establish a foundation for the purpose of helping these children when Nathan finished college.

**The Nathan Yip Foundation**

Upon Nathan's sudden tragic passing in late 2001, their plan materialized earlier than expected. In 2002, the Nathan Yip Foundation was born. The mission is to keep the spirit and passion of Nathan Yip alive by providing schools and educational needs of the children and ongoing support. Through donations by individuals, corporations and through fundraising projects, the Foundation is supporting the following projects:

## Completed Projects

### Nathan Yip School of Hope, Hunan Province, China – November 2006

The Foundation provided funds to build a 5,000 square foot school to accommodate 400 students and a basketball court for 100 students and three teachers.

### Nathan Yip School of Hope, Jiangxi Province, China – April 2006

The Foundation built a two-story, 6,000 square foot school and basketball court to accommodate 400 students and nine teachers.

### Orphanage, Kiglai, Rwanda, Africa – April 2005

The Foundation contributed $30,000 to help rebuild the orphanage.

### Don Bosco Vocational School, Guangdong Province, China

The Foundation provided full-year $600 scholarships for 15 children at the school for 3 years.

## Ongoing Projects

### Shitan Salesian Children's Center, Guangdong Province, China

The Foundation gives ongoing monetary support to the school whose mission is to provide room, board and education to children from severe home environments until they are ready to attend university.

### Yangtze River Elementary School, Guangdong Province, China

The Foundation built a new 17,000 square foot school fully equipped with a library and athletic facilities.

### Loreto School, Loreto, Baja California Sur, Mexico

The Foundation provides ongoing financial support to the school, to educate students in isolated coastal areas of Baja California, Mexico preparing them for sustainable employment.

## New Projects in 2007-2008

### Arbol De Vida Children's Home, Juarez, Mexico

The Foundation subsidizes teacher salaries at the school outside of Juarez that provides food, shelter, clothing and education for 65 orphans.

### Bai Sha Elementary School, Guangdong Province, China

The Foundation has built a new building with eight classrooms to enable the school to enroll 600 students.

### Marian Children's Home, Fujian Province, China

The Foundation is assisting with the construction of a five-story children's home for mentally and physically challenged children and abandoned girls so they may have a permanent and loving home.

One hundred percent of donations go directly to the projects and are channeled through the Salesian Fathers, who have been faithfully helping the projects for the last six years. Unpaid dedicated volunteers continue to help the Yips and their partner, Fred Miale, keep the Foundation going.

Jimmy studied in a technical school in Hong Kong. He came to the United States as a student in 1970 and enrolled at the City College in New York. He started a restaurant business, first in New York, then in Pueblo Colorado and finally in Denver. Succeeding in this venture, he went on to open two more restaurants called Cusine Unique. Jimmy later started with partner Fred Miale, Omnivest International, Inc., a real estate and land development business. Later, they developed an insurance company called Peliton. These two companies established the Yip family comfortably in Colorado, allowing them time and means to travel and to fulfill their dreams to help others.

Linda came to Denver from Taiwan in 1979. She has a degree in political science from Taiwan. After meeting and marrying Jimmy in 1981, Linda continued working. Since Nathan's death, she continues to devote her life to philanthropic projects. People had urged them to sue the family of the teenager responsible for Nathan's death, but she said, "What for? If we can fulfill Nathan's wish to help others, we will be happy." A fascinating note about their projects: Linda and Jimmy always attended the opening ceremonies to inaugurate the newly finished buildings, but it always rained heavily before and after each ceremony. It took them years before they realized the significance of the rains. Nathan's name in Chinese is *Haw Ling* – means 'heavy rain.' Now, Linda and Jimmy say, "Nathan has always been with us." As they travel two or three times a year to visit the schools and orphanages, they are gratified and happy to see the children grow and develop into productive citizens in their countries. Nineteen of the children from the dormitory they built in Mexico have gone on to college. By providing the educational opportunities to these children, they hope they can help end the cycle of poverty that exists in these countries. They always say, "The more you give, the more you have, and the more blessings you receive." For their humanitarian efforts, Linda and Jimmy Yip were recognized as Colorado Dragon Boat Festival Honorary Patrons for 2007.

# Dr. Theodore (Ted) Ning

Dr. Theodore (Ted) Ning is the founder and executive director of the Friendship Bridge, a not-for-profit organization that uses micro-credit and health educational programs to improve the lives of Vietnamese and Guatemalans.

He and his wife, Constance Ning, also founded Friends of Children of Vietnam, an organization that facilitated the adoption of hundreds of Vietnamese orphans across the United States.

For nearly 20 years, Friendship Bridge provided Vietnam with medical supplies, as well as volunteer teachers, nurses, doctors, public health officials, physical and occupational therapists and two dentists to teach local care providers modern advances in healthcare and hygiene. Since 1994, TFB has provided micro-loans to women to establish small home-based businesses while providing them with monthly health care classes. This program has been so successful that it is now being replicated in Guatemala.

Friendship Bridge invited more than 30 Vietnamese doctors, nurses and physical therapists to visit the United States with sponsorship by the University of Colorado, Health Sciences Center. "Training the Vietnamese people to help themselves is the most important kind of philanthropy Americans can do". Dr. Ning believes. "Primary care, though effective for one person, doesn't improve the system. I want teaching to be our priority, and where you go is to the places where local people are taught."

Dr. Ning began medical school at the age of 19, at Northwestern University, graduating in 1968 at the age of 25, Dr. Ning worked in the U.S. Army, as captain and physician. However, his medical training was never used as he was assigned as an engineer with the 101st Airborne Division. In essence, his job was to look at the many problems caused by poverty in Vietnam and finding solutions within cultural context. The best way to help the Vietnamese was, sending them medical books, training them about sanitation and other healthy day-to-day activities.

# Mila Garcia Glodava

When Mila Garcia Glodava received news of the calamity that befell her hometown in November 2004, she did not waste any time responding to calls for help. Her growing network of fellow expatriates from Infanta, Quezon, Philippines, raised nearly $50,000 for emergency and rehabilitation relief for their town submerged in water, mudslides and mountain debris.

I was glad to have Metro Infanta Foundation to turn to," said Glodava, who created the foundation in 1996 to complete her Asian Pacific American Women's Leadership (APAWLI) fellowship. The APAWLI Fellows were required to spearhead an Impact Project that would eventually benefit about 25 people. "You do not have to save the entire world to make a difference," said Glodava, whose endeavors usually start small, often simply as a dream. "We must turn ideas and dreams into action."

Glodava is a doer. She is a woman of style, grace and smarts to balance family, work, church and community. A veritable power when it comes to contacts and committees, Glodava has been involved in many major events in the Asian community as well as the Archdiocese of Denver. She has received numerous awards for her works for justice, inclusion and dignity of the human person, and her commitment to the principles of Catholic social teaching.

She was named a Minoru Yasui Volunteer by the City and County of Denver, a Woman of the Year by the Arvada/Northwest and the Colorado Business and Professional Women, a Peacemaker by the Archdiocese of Denver, and a Woman of Distinction by the Mile Hi Girl Scouts. She also received the Manuel L. Quezon Medal of Honor, the highest award a citizen of her province can receive for distinguished service.

Her advocacy work for marginalized women resulted in a book she co-authored –"Mail-Order Brides: Women for Sale" (Alaken, Inc., 1994) – used by social workers, researchers and the media. She has appeared on "60 Minutes," "Geraldo Rivera" and "Montel Williams." She has been quoted or featured in local, national and international publications, including the Reader's Digest. Glodava was awarded a fellowship to the Salzburg Seminar where she participated in a global round table on the role of nonprofit organizations in the public sector. As a publicist and fundraiser at St. Thomas More Catholic Church in Centennial, Colorado, Glodava can boast of millions of dollars raised, teaching others worldwide about giving to support their mission.

It was Glodava's fundraising experience that led her to reach out to the Philippines. Although she has lived in the United States since 1972 (after marrying Mark Glodava, a New Jersey native and former Peace Corps volunteer), Glodava often thought of the poverty and numerous people in need in her native land as well as the influential positions of fellow expatriates. Glodava recognized a match: people in need of help and people who have the resources and willingness to help. "My goal was to emulate the work of grassroots organizations and community foundations," said Glodava, "offering opportunities to serve and to make a difference – to touch hearts and to change lives."

Thus, Glodava put her fundraising prowess to work. To date, Metro Infanta Foundation has raised nearly $500,000 for projects benefiting Infanta and beyond. Additionally, through Glodava's connections and influence, she has facilitated sending nearly $250,000 directly from funding agencies to worthy causes in the Philippines.

Grants took form in the awarding of scholarships which Glodava's husband and children, Kirsten and Kevin (and Kevin's wife Trish), support financially. The foundation also supports religious and civic causes – building water tanks and churches or distributing pencils and computers. The foundation also has published a book, "*Labong ng Kawayan* (Bamboo Shoots): *Walking through the Pathways and Streets of Infanta*" (Socio Pastoral Institute [SPI], 2002) which was distributed to schools and colleges in Infanta and neighboring towns. Further, the foundation is spearheading the reconstruction of an old elementary school building ravaged by a typhoon many years ago.

"These are concrete ways we have manifested our support," Glodava said. "And we have only just begun!" She is not content, however, in distributing charitable grants, "in giving fish." Rather, she believes in teaching people "how to fish." Besides, it has become increasingly difficult to seek funds for international causes, even for the Catholic Church.

So, what's the alternative? Stewardship as a way of life! "Stewardship is a life of thanksgiving for God's blessings," said Glodava, "and in return we give back to God a portion of our blessings to benefit others. Giving is an expression of a personal and loving relationship with God and is based on a need to give, rather than giving to a need. It is a Christian way of life."

Glodava, who has a Bachelor's degree in education from St. Paul College (now University) of Manila, created the Office of

Communications and Stewardship at St. Thomas More in 1989. She has seen the fruits of the stewardship lifestyle. The parish, which is home to nearly 6,200 families or about 21,000 individuals, is blessed with more than 8,000 volunteers serving in 300 outstanding ministries and programs. It has fostered vocations to the priesthood and religious life for about 25 young men and several young women. Additionally, St. Thomas More's offertory collection has grown from $1.2 million to $4.5 million.

Thus, Glodava has learned many tried and true ways to provide resources – both human and financial – to carry out the parish mission to "go and make disciples." Why not teach this successful approach for sustainability? In 2002 Glodava introduced stewardship to the Prelature of Infanta at the invitation of Carmelite Bishop Julio X. Labayen. Since then Glodava and her pastor, the Rev. Andrew Kemberling, have been teaching the Spirituality of Stewardship nationally and internationally. The International Catholic Stewardship Council has recognized their efforts with numerous awards, including the *"Archbishop Thomas J. Murphy Memorial Award."* In addition, Our Sunday Visitor, a national Catholic publishing company, is considering publication of a book on stewardship at St. Thomas More.

Meanwhile, Bishop Labayen saw what stewardship could mean to the Philippine Church in its desire to become a self-sustaining "Church of the Poor." As a result, the bishop requested Cardinal Ricardo Vidal, Archbishop of Cebu, to convene a group of dioceses and, eventually, the entire Catholic Bishops' Conference of the Philippines to share the message of stewardship. Cardinal Vidal agreed.

Today, the Philippine Church is slowly embracing the stewardship lifestyle. In fact, many believe it is a key to its "renewed integral evangelization." "They (Glodava and Father Andrew) have transformed our way of looking at the Church of the Poor," said Cardinal Vidal. "We have come to realize that to be the Church of the Poor we must be instruments of God's gift. Stewardship is discovering God's gift to us; it is sharing our giftedness to the Church."

"It is humbling to be a part of the Church renewal in the Philippines," said Glodava, who feels a need to give back to her old country. "I have a strong sense of mission, which is shaped by my Philippine heritage and the values of faith, family, education and service." She knows, however, that she could not possibly do it alone. "I am grateful to the many people, especially my family, who have supported me along the way. And I thank God for this grace."

Indeed, it is God's grace that gives Glodava the drive to make a difference. She may not be saving the entire world, but she's making a real difference - touching hearts and changing lives.

**Colleen Smith**, a Denver-based writer, contributed to this article.

## COLORADO HERITAGE CAMPS

As Asian Americans, most of us have always looked at the American people as the embodiment of compassion, the symbol of freedom and the shining example of generosity and their desire to help people around the world. This was expressed by Carlos Bulosan, one of the first Filipino-American writers of consequence to write in English in the U.S. He wrote, "America is not bound by geographical latitudes. America is not merely a land or an institution. America is in the hearts of men that died for freedom; it is also in the eyes of men that are building a new world."

If America is in the hearts of men, then, surely it is found in the Colorado Heritage Camps (CHC), a post-adoption resources organization based in Denver. CHC is a highly respected organization, which has been running heritage camps for 15 years. Without fanfare and publicity, the CHC has projected clearly a universal image of care and concern unmatched by other people in the world. There are ten such cultural camps held annually in Colorado that provide post-adoption acculturalization programs for American parents and their adopted Asian children. These adopted children come from countries such as China (two camps), Korea, Philippines, India, Vietnam, Cambodian, African/Caribbean, Latin America, and Russian/East European/Central Asia. With the increasing pace of adoption by Americans of Asian children in recent years, there is a growing need to bridge the cultural gaps between parents and their adopted Asian children. Every year, APA communities have been the logical sources of cultural information in these camps.

Adoption of Asian children transcends race and culture. Families from all over Colorado attend these annual camps and gain a fuller appreciation of the varied and beautiful culture from each country. At the same time they help build a community of people with similar experiences. Friendships are formed, strengthened and renewed each year – friendships that transcend cultural differences and barriers across the oceans.

American adoptive parents are quite serious in understanding and appreciating the culture of their adopted children. They also utilize the services of indigenous ethnic groups who have direct experiences of their own culture and history.

Indeed, America is in the hearts of men and women in our everyday lives, both ordinary and extraordinary Americans and unsung heroes such as those found in the Colorado Heritage Camps. These are the real people who make America the greatest country in the world. These are the hearts of America, as viewed and envied by the rest of the globe, offering inspiration as well and raising their hopes for a better future for their countries and their children's children. The Colorado Heritage Camps surely represent all these.

Listed alphabetically are the heritage camps who have adopted Asian children, with brief descriptions of their activities.

**Cambodian Heritage Camp** is a family camp where campers from age 3 to 18 plus their parents, participate in classes, workshops and family-oriented special events presented by Cambodian Americans, adult adoptees, professionals in the field of adoption. The campers, themselves enthusiastically share their perspectives and expertise with adoptive families. More than 40 Cambodian American young adults serve as counselors, acting as warm and caring role models and mentors to the children as they participate with them in cultural classes. Adult family members attend cultural and adoption-related workshops ranging from Cambodian cooking to the blessings and challenges inherent in the adoptive families. Founded and run by adoptive parent volunteers.

**Chinese Heritage Camp** was one of the first camps in the country exclusively created for families with children adopted from China, offering programs for infants through middle school.

**Filipino Heritage Camp**

One of the ten cultural heritage camps is the Filipino Heritage Camp (FHC). The Filipino American Community of Colorado (FACC) has had the privilege of assisting the camp with volunteers composed of counselors, teachers and facilitators. They had the opportunity to meet and interact personally with adoptive parents and their adopted Filipino children.

Sharon Cuartero, a counselor, who was adopted at the age of two by an American Jewish family said, "I was deeply moved by the parents and the obvious love they hold for their children. They helped me gain a better understanding of the pain, the struggles and the countless joys that adoptive parents go through and what my own parents have endured."

Fran Campbell, FACC president, noticed "What really struck me the strongest was the absolute dedication of the adoptive parents to remain side by side with their children during their exploration of their cultural identity."

**Indian/Nepalese Heritage Camp** is a family camp with programming for each member of the family. Campers from age 3 to 18, plus their parents, grandparents, family friends, etc. participate in classes and workshops taught by adoption professionals, parents, and cultural community members.

**Korean Heritage Camp** is the flagship heritage camp, entering its 17th year! They are proud to be one of many camps held around the country for Korean adoptees, but they are slightly different than most. The majority of Korean Camps are for "kids only." The Korean Heritage camp is for the entire family, from infants through teens, and for parents.

**Vietnamese Heritage Camp** was the first camp in the country, exclusively created for families with adopted children from Vietnam. At the YMCA Snow Mountain Camp, an American couple attending the Vietnamese Heritage Camp in the same place, had this to say, "We have too much here in the United States and we want to share such good fortune with others."

## Gawad Kalinga

Gawad Kalinga (GK) is a non-governmental organization that means Give Care. It is building houses for the poorest of the poor in Philippines and is providing infrastructure for good jobs. It supports developing health programs, education, livelihood and community centers. The holistic approach to solving poverty through the leadership of Executive Director, Antonio Meloto, has gained the respect that it now enjoys. GK encompasses both private and governmental institutions, including the Catholic Church, numerous religious organizations, domestic and multi-international businesses and donors from all over the world. GK started in Bagong Silang, Cavite City in 1995 when Mr. Meloto tried to work with gang members in the slum and crime-infested area. He knew something had to be done to break the cycle. The first house was built in 1999. From then on, GK has inspired Filipinos of all faiths and foreigners. GK's 777 project of building 700,000 houses in 7,000 communities in seven years (by 2010) is succeeding.

Dylan Wilk, a British philantrophist, traveled around the world to search for a charitable organization worth supporting. He found GK and now he loves the Philippines and the Filipinos. He sold one BMW and with the money built one entire village called BMW Village. Dylan Wilk, dubbed as GK's effective poster boy and head of the International Partners of GK, has been traveling around the US to talk about GK. He said, "More than newly-built houses, I saw transformed lives. We were entering rather dangerous slums, breeding grounds for thieves and kidnappers, yet in the middle of that was an oasis, the colorful GK village. I saw people smiling, men working, children laughing. I've seen other projects across the world, but I have never seen anything like GK. This really worked."

Filipino Americans in Colorado are now part of this movement. A Colorado Village in Isabela, Luzon, now almost completed, has been constructed through the efforts of the Colorado Couples for Christ (through ANCOP USA - Answering the Cry of the Poor) and other member organizations under the NaFFAA Region V. More and more

Filipino Americans around the US are joining the movement and are also building GK villages all over in the Philippines.

Antonio Meloto was awarded the 2006 Ramon Magsaysay Award for community leadership. He is being recognized for "inspiring Filipinos to believe with pride that theirs can be a nation without slums." Gawad Kalinga Community Development Foundation is given the 2006 Ramon Magsaysay Award for community leadership. The organization is being honored for "harnessing the faith and generosity of Filipinos the world over to confront poverty in the Philippines and provide every family the dignity of a decent home and neighborhood." The Ramon Magsaysay Award is Asia's highest honor and is widely regarded as the region's equivalent to the Nobel Prize.

The GK program will succeed, such as: (1) Fighting poverty could be the rallying point for people of different faiths, especially in Mindanao. For decades, Christians shudder at the thought of belligerent Muslims and avoided entering their towns. Now, through GK, they suddenly find the courage to cross their safety and comfort zones to show solidarity and friendship with their Muslim brothers. (2) Behavioral changes have to occur first with the prospective recipients before any program can start, Building relationship and trust among people who have been abused throughout their lives is key to the success of the program. Volunteers are the backbone of GK. (There are more than 150,000 volunteers who are serving two to five years). (3) The holistic approach is an important component "where houses are not only built, but include a livelihood program, a value enhancement, and a sense of pride and camaraderie.

GK is spreading outside the Philippines. In July 5, 2005, the GK program was launched outside the Philippines at Papua, New Guinea. Through GK, there is hope for the Philippines and perhaps for the world.

In Colorado, NaFFAA Region V, under the leadership of Donna LaVigne, gathered the member groups to work together to raise funds to build Colorado Village, U.S.A., now housing 30 families in Catbagan, Isabela, Philippines. Two outstanding leaders of the community are featured here for their unwavering volunteer work for Gawad Kalinga: Natee "Babes" Anolin and Joyce Dennison.

Natee "Babes" Anolin was Gawad Kalinga Partnership Services Director in Colorado. For many years, Natee and her husband Ed Anolin, have been actively involved in the Fil/Am community in Colorado, and have participated in various fundraising projects. "But this Gawad Kalinga project," she says, "is not only a fundraiser but a Partnership in rebuilding the land of my ancestry- the Philippines. As we build a GK Colorado USA Village in the Philippines, we are partnered with respective recipients of each home. Imagine, we will be a part of the beneficiaries' growth and their new livelihood. I never thought that a simple, working person like me could be a part of this Great Commission of the Lord. "

Joyce Dennison has been very active in supporting Gawad Kalinga in Colorado. "The Philippine government chose Gawad Kalinga (GK) to spearhead the rehabilitation efforts for the typhoon victims because of its efficient track record in building low-cost houses that involves many sectors of society including businesses, private citizens, leaders, the government and even partners from foreign countries. The effort doesn't stop in just building villages consisting of 50 homes each; rather; it is a holistic effort providing education for the children, health care, livelihood training, and community empowerment.

## ANCOP International Colorado

(**AN**swering the **C**ry **O**f the **P**oor) Couples for Christ – Colorado

The Colorado GK Village was initiated by the Couples for Christ in Colorado under the leadership of Bart and Marlene Perez, CFC **u**nit leaders and ANCOP branch coordinators.

With the help of NAFFAA (National Federation of Filipino American Association) Region V, in early 2005, GK gained wide support. The group pledged a GK Village to help the victims of the Philippine typhoons that hit the Luzon area. A majority of the GK partners for the Colorado Village were Filipino-American groups as well as the members of CFC. United for a worthy cause, answering a call to hearts and a plea for help, CFC along with the organizations put on benefit dinners, dances, GK presentations, Almusalan (Pinoy Breakfast), GK Cowboy Night, and a local coin bank drive.

## More Humanitarian Movements

When tragedy, calamities and natural disasters, such as typhoons, floods or earthquakes occur in an Asian country, APA organizations and dedicated groups of men and women come together and show a willingness to aid both local and home countries during their time of need. These are inspiring stories about their efforts to help the victims. The following are just a few examples of such APA groups.

**2003: The India Association of Colorado,** working with event-lead Alok Sarwal, in collaboration with the University of Denver and several other Asian Pacific American organizations, held its fund raising concert on January 30, 2003. The event raised $16,500, which benefited India, Indonesia and Sri Lanka. The Asian communities in Colorado came together in an unprecedented show of support to raise funds for the victims of the Tsunami. This special event was supported by multi-ethnic communities, in collaboration with the University of Denver and several Colorado Asian Pacific American organizations. This tsunami Relief fund-raising concert showcased the culture and arts from the countries most affected, specifically India, Indonesia, Sri Lanka and Thailand

**In 2005, The Chinese American communities** in Colorado raised $26,000 for the tsunami victims. It is also right to acknowledge the general public, including children in and out of schools who contributed in their own way to help the tsunami victims.

### Philippine Humanitarian Projects

Some of the humanitarian fundraising projects initiated by the Filipino-Americans are: – Earthquake Relief Project (Bayanihan) May 11, 1991; Mt. Pinatubo Project (Bayanihan, FACC, PASCO) May 9, 1992; World Youth Day project, Sept. 1994; and The Trial of Alice in Wonderland (Philippine Heritage, FACC) Nov. 4-5, 1995.

## The Peace Corps

**Continuing Quest for World Peace**

"Ask not what your country can do for you; but rather,
ask what you can do for your country." President John F. Kennedy

This 19-word nugget from President Kennedy's inaugural address in January 1961 found fruition two months later. By an executive order on March 1, the 35th American president conceived the Peace Corps as an instrument of promoting international goodwill and understanding. "Our Peace Corps is not designed as an instrument of diplomacy or propaganda or ideological conflict. It is designed to permit our people to exercise more fully their responsibilities in the great common cause of world development." On Sept. 27, 1961, Congress approved legislation authorizing Peace Corps with the mandate to "promote world peace and friendship," through three goals: to help the people of interested countries in meeting their needs for trained workers; to help promote a better understanding of Americans on the part of the peoples served; to help promote a better understanding of other peoples on the part of Americans.

International terrorism, the instability in the Middle East, the threat of another attack on the U.S. and the threats of the use of nuclear weapons are anathema to the second and third goals of the Peace Corps mandate, which is to promote international understanding. World peace and prosperity are ideals that emerged after World War II; and certainly the Peace Corps has generously contributed to the attainment to those ideals with its thousands of staff and volunteers helping the recipient countries help themselves.

The Peace Corps has operated in many Asian countries such as the Philippines, India, Indonesia, Pakistan, and others. The impact of Peace Corps volunteers has been profound. For example, in Denver, Peace Corps returns have developed long-term relationships with the recipient families in the Philippines. Here in Denver, they are the most active members of the Filipino American communities, often contributing their time, money and talent to the organizations. On the average, they seem to be more "Filipino" in terms of culture than many among our Filipino immigrants. Other Peace Corps volunteers assigned in other countries have the same pleasant experiences that they proudly remember and pass along to the potential PCVs. It is important for the Peace Corps to continue its noble mission and its quest for world peace and understanding. For as long as the ideal of human brotherhood lives, the Peace Corps will also continue its role for Americans.

## Stories by Peace Corps Volunteers

The following are stories of the experiences of four Peace Corps volunteers who were assigned in the Philippines: Jay LaVigne, Georgette Chiappa Johnson, David and Arlene Lipman.

## Jay Lavigne

Assigned to Balete, Aklan

Jay LaVigne, current President of the Filipino American Community of Colorado (FACC) graduated from Purdue University, West Lafayette, Indiana, with a degree of B.S. Industrial Management and has a law degree from University of Denver. He was assigned to Balete, Aklan, where he worked in a rural bank, doing various projects including marketing and depositor analysis. He learned that housewives in the Philippines had 10 times more money in their accounts than men. Jay also taught college. Jay is married to Donna Bandiola whom he met in Aklan. They have a daughter, Mahal, a senior in Colorado State University.

I had no real deep impressions of the country before I got there – a third world country that had some connections to the US and the scene of many WWII battles. However, I have an unusual perspective in that I was an American who lived and worked in the rural Philippines. Most Filipino Americans were Filipino when they lived there and have never really lived and worked there after moving here. One memory I have is during Donna's and my first trip back to the Philippines, Donna commented on how dusty it was, and asked why everyone was always honking their horns: in general she was a little taken aback at how it was in Kalibo– I didn't think it had changed at all – it was the same place I loved when I was there. My approach is that the US is neither better nor worse than the Philippines -- they are simply different. Filipinos are not more or less polite than Americans, we are simply polite in different ways and often we do rub each other the wrong way because what is okay in one culture is not in another.

Regarding the Philippines itself, I loved the country and the people. It was really cool that they like Americans. I admired that they could take so much comfort from being around family and that they were there to help each other.

It was interesting to me that this extended family did create a great social safety net but also made it more difficult for those who wanted to work hard to succeed. As one family member got ahead, the less fortunate would often increase their demands for assistance.

Every day was an adventure and full of memorable moments. Perhaps my trips to Boracay, which occurred before electricity and vehicles, were truly special. At the time, there was one two-story building on the island. Long stretches of white beach were undeveloped, only a few boats were ever pulled up on the beach.

One day I endeavored to walk around the north end of the island. At the time there was nothing. The island features the main beach on the west but around the north side, many coral hills rose up out of the water to create small white beaches no more than 40 feet wide, were you could see no sign of human life except the small path that came down one side of the beach and then went up the other.

On the very north of the island is a larger beach with, at that time of year, bigger waves than on white beach. As I came through the coconut trees on to the beach, out in the surf a few feet was an ati (what we in Kalibo call the aboriginal people) – he had nothing but a bahag (loin cloth) on and was looking intently in the water for a fish to shoot with his small bow and arrow.

It was stunning to think that this man was living in essentially the same fashion as his ancestors, hunting with a bow, wearing animal skin clothes and knowing little or nothing about the world outside his own village and his hunting grounds. What a contrast.

I do wonder, a bit sadly, about whatever happened to him and his family as the island developed explosively during the late 1980s. I hope he could find a new home that would let him continue his traditional existence.

It was amazing how quickly and easily the Filipinos assimilated us Peace Corps volunteers into their towns and their families. There were never any signs of impatience or being inconvenienced by us being around. Perhaps it is the fact that in the rural Philippines there aren't any strangers, just friends you haven't met yet. So being so far from home did not mean being away from those who thought of you as family.

It is clearly a mindset that we at the FACC need to continue working on recreating in our own events and at the center.

## Georgette Chiappa Johnson

Assigned to Mamburao, Occidental Mindoro

Georgette went to Kean University, New Jersey, and graduated with a B.S. degree in Social work. She served as a Peace Corps Volunteer (PCV) from Oct. 1975 – Oct. 1978, where she was assigned to Mamburao, Occidental Mindoro.

Georgette has many good memories of

her experiences in the Philippines. First was her attendance of the "Ali-Frasier Thrilla in Manila" fight on Oct. 1, 1975, her birthday. She felt so sad and lonely, being so far away from her family in a new country. But everything changed as soon as she began her volunteer duties.

Georgette was an outreach nutrition social worker in the barrios working in the Municipal Bureau of Agricultural Extension. Operation Timbang was her assignment where she weighed children and checked them for degrees of malnutrition.

She remembers one case in particular: Little Willie from the barrio of Kasoy. He was severely malnourished, was abused by his stepmother. He almost died. The family was extremely poor. They lived in a broken down nipa hut, barely having enough rice for all. Willie would pick up the rice droppings from the other's plates and that's all he ate!! Through my intervention, we saved Willie. I found a nurse who would adopt him. Happy ending: After a long drawn out court proceeding, Nading adopted Willie. He is now a healthy adult, married, and proudly boasts about his little girl.

Georgette taught many educational classes as a PCV, among them: Nutritional classes for Mothers, Backyard gardening, and raising rabbits.

I had no knowledge of the country. Before leaving the U.S., our group met in California where we quickly learned a little about the country, culture and programs. This was a great opportunity for me to travel, work and learn all pretty much at the same time. After Peace Corp, I learned a lot! Being an American, I felt privileged being able to live in another country! The people were great. Once I learned Tagalog, I was able to become more acculturated and fit in better because I was not a tourist. I was living there! People were very friendly, sometimes too friendly! I met the First Lady Imelda Marcos, pychic surgeon Sister Josephine, just to mention a few. I made many friends and became ninang (godmother) a few times. I learned how to live in the barrio -- without running water or electricity, made daily trips to the market and attended social events a lot.

Some of her memorable moments in the Philippines included: dealing with the US marines when they came to Mamburao for war games; being in a horrible typhoon where the roads were flooded so much, the water was up to my neck!; taking a banka (boat) trip to "Apo" reef where a lighthouse stood; went snorkeling and saw beautiful things in the South China Sea; learned how to weave cloth in Baguio; hard the killing of a pig for the first time.

Being over there totally changed my life. I met many great people and still keep in contact with some. My kumadre (mother of my godchild) keeps me informed with the Mamburao news. I have loved the Philippines and its people so much that as soon as I returned to the U.S., I searched for Filipinos so I could talk to them. When I moved from New Jersey to Colorado, I immediately came in contact with the FACC. This was mainly because I wanted to continue my cultural experience and keep it alive within myself. I find the Filipino families very similar to my New Jersey family. Being involved with the FACC keeps me grounded as I grow along with my children. I have a special connection with the FACC since I have learned so much and have become part of the FACC family -- friends who will be my friends (like family) till I die!

## David and Arlene Lipman

Assigned to Toril, Davao City and Tagbilaran City, Bohol

I really didn't think about joining the Peace Corps until I met and married David Lipman. He wanted to apply, so after much discussion, we applied. We finally heard that we had been accepted in February 1970. I was on top of a mountain studying snow flakes when I learned we would be going to the Philippines. Where is the Philippines? I discovered that this Asian country is made up of over 7000 islands. We packed up our apartment, visited our families and left for training in Saxons River, Vermont! After spending over 300 hours learning Cebuano, the language of the central islands, we were declared ready to leave the chilly East coast and go to the warm tropical Far East.

We were assigned to Toril, Davao City. David worked with science teachers in Dalao district and I with math teachers in Piedad district. Toril is like a suburb to the main city of Davao, but still part of the city. Toril had a daily market with fresh meat, fish and chicken as well as fruits, vegetables and rice. Twenty-thousand people were considered residents of the district of Toril. The various barrios (now they are called barangays) ranged from sea front villages to villages up near the top of Mt. Apo, which is the tallest mountain in the country and a dormant volcano. Our school districts went from the central schools to small primary schools on the mountain.

We soon became close to our "family" of Juanito, a banker his wife Christita (we called her Nang-Tita, a Cebuano title for an honored woman) a school teacher and their seven sons and daughters. Nang-Tita called us her "American son and daughter"! Juanito's extended family included a total of 15 siblings and their families. We were included in social activities by them and many other new friends from our schools. We soon added a helper to our household, a high school girl who did laundry, marketing and house cleaning. Patring ended up living with us the whole time we were in the country. A couple of dogs and cats completed our house.

After our first two years, we extended our Peace Corps tour by accepting a new assignment in the province of Bohol. We moved to Tagbilaran City with Patring, as well as our dog and one of our cats. There we worked with the math-science supervisor for the school division that made up the entire island. We ended up doing a training project that gave every one of the elementary school teachers (5000 of them) a week long seminar in methods of teaching modern math and another one in process approach science.

Each week we would each travel to four or five of the towns in the province where the seminars were being led by our "core teachers" that we had trained. That year in Bohol, there were some U.S. Army rangers conducting training exercises. We organized a volleyball game between some of the soldiers and PCV's. We called it "War and Peace"!

The 3 1/2 years we lived in the Philippines have truly shaped my life. Toril and Tagbilaran are as much my "home towns" as Laramie, Bountiful and Hickman Mills, where I lived when I was younger. I have Filipino memorabilia decorating my house.

When we first arrived in Denver, I met Ralph Acosta who introduced us to the Filipino American Community of Colorado. FACC has become our Filipino family here in Denver. I love going to club meetings where I can still talk Cebuano and eat some of my favorite foods like lumpia and pancit. The ladies gave me my baby shower before my daughter Rachael was born and both my girls have grown up in the community. Rach thought that she was a Filipina when she was little and Becca is proud of her connections to the group. Some of our friends joke that we are reverse coconuts, white on the outside and brown on the inside. I sing in the FACC- Mano Po choir and have learned to play the banduria to be part of the Rondalla. I am proud that David and I are now Life Members of the FACC.

Sometimes it seems like Peace Corps was another whole life. It was mostly a wonderful time. There were some difficulties, to which I can look back and laugh. In 2002 we joined the Uplift Internationale medical mission and returned to the Philippines after 28 years. We went "home" to Bohol on that trip and found some of our friends there. The next year we went on the mission a second time and this time visited our Toril home. It was a great time to see Nang-Tita and Patring. Recently I met someone who had had attended a seminar in Toril as a young teacher. I asked her if it had been useful. She said it had been good. It was nice getting validation, 30 years later!

# Chapter 13

# HEALTH AND MEDICAL SERVICES FOR ASIAN PACIFIC AMERICANS

## Introduction

Asian and Pacific Americans represent both extremes of socioeconomic and health indices with more than a million APAs living at or below the federal poverty level, but APA women having the highest life expectancy of any other group. Factors contributing to poor health outcomes for APAs include language and cultural barriers, the stigma associated with certain conditions, and lack of health insurance. In 2002, the ten leading causes of death in the U.S. for this population were cancer, heart disease, stroke, accidents, diabetes, infections (influenza, pneumonia), chronic lower respiratory disease, suicide, kidney ailments, and sepsis.

Many immigrants from Asia come from less-developed countries. Such countries are characterized by widespread poverty, malnutrition, and insufficient medical services. Due to these factors, immigrants are exposed not only to tropical diseases but also ailments such as tuberculosis and other respiratory and cardiac problems. Also, there is a high rate of liver cancer and lung cancer-related deaths among this population.

The rate of cervical cancer among Vietnamese women is five times that of white women. APAs have among the highest rates of tuberculosis and hepatitis B in the U.S. Asian Indians have an unusually high rate of coronary artery disease, and parasitic infections are particularly widespread among Southeast Asian refugees. Nationally, the APA population shows a trend of having one of the lowest rates of cancer deaths, ranging from 119.5 and 134.2 per 100,000. In Colorado, APAs consistently have lower rates of cancer deaths than most other groups. Recently, the average rate has been over 105.8 per 100,000,

This chapter describes two main community organizations that provide health and mental health services for APAs and then profiles a few APA professionals in these fields. While all of us are very grateful for services of numerous other medical experts, we have tried to focus on a few individuals who have a track record of community service for the under/uninsured and vulnerable APA people.

## Asian Pacific Development Center (APDC)

The Asian Pacific Development Center is a community-based, nonprofit, 501(c)(3) organization founded in 1980 to serve the needs of a growing population of Asian Pacific Americans throughout Colorado. APDC operates a licensed Community Mental Health Clinic designated by the Colorado Department of Public Health and Environment, youth programs, various health promotion programs and a multicultural Interpreters Bank. The mission of APDC is to empower Asian Pacific Americans through promoting the understanding and appreciation of cultural diversity. APDC provides clinical services to APA communities as a specialty mental health clinic through Federal, State and local grants. A trained professional bilingual staff provides culturally-competent services that include: assessment and evaluation; individual and group counseling; case management services; victim assistance services; mentorship, after school, and youth leadership programs; health promotion; interpretation/translation services; as well as cultural competency training and consultation. Services provided are linguistically and culturally appropriate.

APDC has served APA families in the Denver metro area for over 20 years. It offers family strengthening programs, therapy, translation services, substance abuse counseling, and many programs for APA youth. One such youth program is the Asian Youth Center. It provides a safe, healthy place to have fun and is open to all APA youth, with mentoring support. This program matches APA adult mentors of college age and up with APA kids age 10-14 to serve as role models.

The philosophy of APDC is that APA communities need to stand up often and voice relevant concerns as a community. The most critical role for APA communities is to stand together united and set aside any differences that divide when called upon among the general community at large. With the many inter-generational families living now in Colorado, it is paramount that we continue to build bridges and bring everyone together.

The current CEO, Chris Wanifuchi, plans to enhance existing programs and services while looking into the future for new ways to serve APA communities. This will be a continuation of behavioral health services, youth programs, interpreting/translation services through the Interpreter's Bank, health education and awareness, ESL programs, and internships. She says "as our community changes, so should APDC reflect those changes and become one of the premier agencies for the APA communities.

## Colorado Asian Health Education Promotion (CAHEP)

This organization has roots in the Colorado Asian TB Elimination Project (CATEP), started in 2001, involving a coalition of APA leaders focused on eliminating Tuberculosis (TB) among their community members in Colorado. Recognizing that health disparities existed in Colorado's APA population, beyond just TB, the organization was reorganized in 2005, with a new focus, to include all relevant infectious and chronic diseases and became an independent nonprofit 501(c)(3) organization. Previously it was using fiscal agency services of organizations such as the Filipino American Council of Colorado. From the start, CAHEP has made significant positive impact on disease prevention and behavior changes in APA community by tailoring interventions that precisely meet the needs of each ethnic group.

Currently CAHEP works in a coalition of over fourteen Colorado Asian Pacific American ethnic populations. For over seven years, it has developed effective partnerships with immigrants from China, India, Thailand, Vietnam, Korea, Philippines, Laos (including people of Hmong ethnicity), Cambodia, Myanmar (Burma), Japan and others. CAHEP's organizational model has developed and evolved to be agile and effective and supports directly helping the vulnerable APA populations throughout Colorado. It provides screening and early detection of diabetes, asthma and other pulmonary diseases, allergies, all cardiovascular diseases, tuberculosis, osteoporosis, and when requested by the community, cancer screenings. It provides an analysis of test results and preventative health care education at the point of care. It also provides chronic health training for people determined to be at-risk and self-management of all chronic diseases. In other words, CAHEP covers the continuum of care from the point a person is diagnosed to be at risk of a health abnormality. CAHEP's strong partnership with major medical organizations and medical centers in Colorado makes for a viable care-model that benefits the APAs.

The vision of CAHEP is based in large part on providing health and human services at the grass-roots levels. Many APAs face an enormous burden due to lack of medical insurance, language challenges and cultural barriers. They also lack understanding of the existing medical systems in Colorado. APA immigrants often are burdened by an approach to preventative health care based on knowledge they brought with them when they immigrated. There is a lack of trust of anyone other than their leaders, close friends, and family. Such individuals can typically become part of the statistics of health disparity. Organizations such as CAHEP are necessary for providing early detection of diseases, preventive health education, and support for clinical visits or follow-up care for those who have been assessed to be at-risk. The cooperation of APA communities, working with CAHEP, allows them to take matters into their own hands and determine the best paths to healthier living. Multi-lingual case-managers and community leaders working with medical providers, stakeholders and public health experts can provide a best-case approach to problems. True multi-ethnic partnerships are the key to a program based on a pragmatic and realistic model.

So an organization such as CAHEP plays a significant role in serving vulnerable individuals. Due to the increasing urgency of this work and the associated human costs of delaying such services, CAHEP provides navigation and referral support with all major clinics, medical providers, and other health programs that accept uninsured individuals, sliding-scale charges, and Medicare and Medicaid insurance. For over two years, CAHEP has been providing case-management for all of the APA populations it screens, and it supports comprehensive follow-up care for all infectious and chronic diseases so that no one is left unserved. It has also developed an effective program for Chronic Disease Self-Management utilizing multi-lingual and multi-cultural trainers, so individuals are now taking charge of their medical problems with vital support from CAHEP and qualified trainers from Stanford's nationally recognized system of action and self-empowerment.

CAHEP provides a comprehensive program of health and wellness outreach and education, health-related risk screenings, and follow-up care. It covers the continuum of care.

It's community health promotion events, offer health education, and risk-assessment screenings in a reassuring and culturally appropriate setting.

Health-promotion events and outreach takes place at community-organized sites such as churches, temples, cultural centers, some 9HealthFair sites, and conducted in partnership with community leaders and community providers. Up to six months after each event, at-risk individuals are contacted to assess their adherence to the self-management program and to see if they require additional support. To date, more than 120 Health Promotion events have been held and in the past three years more than

7,000 AAPI individuals have been educated and/or screened for chronic and infectious diseases. CAHEP also organizes an annual symposium to bring together stakeholders and national experts for addressing health disparity and family health care issues in a cultural relevant APA context.

Executive Director and co-founder Alok Sarwal mentions that – "These community, needs-driven, health care programs incur substantial cost in time and money and cannot succeed without the passion, energy and vision of the community leaders, community medical providers, sponsors and the people who are now empowered in working with this organization." CAHEP is making a significant impact and has also been recognized by state foundations and federal Health and Human Services organizations for its outstanding contribution.

**A Korean community-based health screening is shown below**

## D.J. Ida

Misperceptions persist about the mental health and well being of APAs in the United States. APAs continue to be the fastest growing ethnic population in the country, yet they still lack adequate resources to address their diverse needs. Many in the mainstream health care fields view them as a homogenous population with few if any problems. There are numerous challenges to the field including the lack of accurate data, research and evaluation. In addition, there is a serious shortage of trained, bilingual personnel who can support culturally competent services. There is also a need to identify, design and implement successful intervention strategies, particularly in geographical areas with limited AAPI resources. The issue of stigma and shame in the community must also be addressed with greater involvement from consumers and families.

As a champion of these issues, Dr. D.J. Ida, Executive Director, National Asian American Pacific Islander Mental Health Association (NAAPIMHA) is at the forefront. "D.J." graduated from the University of Colorado, Boulder with a B.A. in Asian studies & sociology (1971), M.A. in guidance/counseling (1977), M.A. (1987) and a Ph.D. in clinical psychology (1989). She served as a counselor, therapist, consultant, intern, staff psychologist, in various clinics and health centers in local, state and national agencies, notably, as Director, Child and Adolescent Services for the Asian Pacific Development Center in Denver (1990-2000).

In the area of organizational development, D.J. was responsible for the establishment and growth of many programs, centers, and clinics for children and adolescents connected with mental health services, such as for the National Association of Multi-cultural Behavioral Health Associations. Working tirelessly, D.J. started serving as a member of various Boards, Committees or Councils, such as on the Hmong National Development, Inc., Advisory Council, Washington, D.C.; on the Research and Training Center for Children's Mental Health in Florida; on the National Advisory Council – U.S. Dept. of Health and Human Services, Center for Mental Health Services; as Technical Partner for the National Center for Mental Health Promotion and Youth Violence Prevention, Educational Center; Founding Board Member of the National Alliance of Multiethnic Behavior Health Associations, Washington, D.C.; on the Executive Committee of the National Mental Health Association; on the Steering Committee of the Annapolis Coalition on Behavioral Health Workforce Education; on the National Council of Asian Pacific Americans (NCAPA), Washington, D.C.; Georgetown University Child Development Center, Washington, D.C. She has also participated on the panel of professional experts in mental health for two CAHEP Health Disparity Symposiums.

D.J. Ida has established a strong pattern of contributing to the APA communities, and brings excellence to all her endeavors. Her recognition as a leading expert in her field with a far-reaching impact beyond Colorado is significant. Certainly she deserves the gratitude of the country for her total dedication and contributions to mental health services for Asian Pacific Americans.

Her association's mandate, then, is to advocate on behalf of APA mental health issues, to serve as a forum for effective collaboration and to network among stakeholders of community based organizations, consumers, family members, service providers, program developers, researchers, evaluators and policy makers. Moreover, NAAPIMHA will endeavor to work with direct service providers, such as nonprofit community-based organizations, to augment this effort. Such a collaborative effort will only increase the likelihood of developing comprehensive, culturally competent services to meet the needs of APA communities.

## Amelia C. Ashmann

"My main interest is community service by preserving the health of my patients and providing ways of healing illnesses through scientific and evidenced-based medical practice. One of my greatest dreams is promoting and preserving the Filipino culture and values through the performing arts," says Dr. Amelia Ashmann, a respected physician, a dedicated community leader and volunteer and an inspiring role model for all Asian Americans.

That was her statement in 1996, when first interviewed. After 35 years of medical practice, five years in Michigan and 30 years in Colorado, she retired in April 2007. Amy, as she is fondly called, has multiple interests - spirituality is one of them. She developed this by reading literature on spirituality and medicine, a growing trend, and her entering the Denver Catholic Bible School, a four-year course, leading to completion in 2003. Amy discovered the truth and the beauty of her faith. Enlightened by the simplicity and skill of how the Catholic Biblical School imparts knowledge, Amy and Dolly Banzon, a fourth year biblical school student shared their knowledge of the Scripture to the community by forming a Bible study group and bringing Thomas Smith, Executive Director of the Denver Catholic Bible School and the Denver Catechetical School, to the Philippines in June 2007.

These lofty goals in life have been and are now being fulfilled by Amy after a successful private practice as an internist with hematology and oncology subspecialty.

Born in Claveria, Cagayan, Philippines, Amy developed early in life the desire to help others from her parents and brother who were models of sharing and caring people. Her late brother was an engineer who built artesian wells, clinics and medical missions for the poor in their community. Her older sisters were dedicated school teachers and her youngest sister, a cardiovascular anesthesiologist, is also involved in medical missions.

Dr. Ashmann finished her medical degree in Manila Central University. She finished a rotating internship practice in Jose P. Reyes Medical Center in Manila and at Malden Hospital in Massachusetts. She completed an internal medicine residency in Detroit Macomb Hospital and W. Beaumont Hospital in Royal Oak, Michigan. This was followed by a fellowship in Hematology at the Harper Hospital and Detroit Receiving Hospital. She was a consultant of internal medicine, hematology and oncology at Ypsilanti State Hospital and later at Metropolitan Hospital in Detroit.

She moved to Colorado in 1976, and after the delivery of her first child, started her medical practice. She volunteered at the American Medical Center and Cancer Research and later became the director of the Outpatient Department where she participated in cancer research and outpatient cancer chemotherapy treatments. She participated in many cancer screening programs including Channel 9 health fairs.

In Arvada, she practiced for 30 years. Included in this practice were Preceptorship of medical students from the University of Colorado Health Sciences Center, Preceptorship for registered nurses needing more clinical work, medical assistants, mentoring a foreign medical graduate prior to placement and high school students trying to go to the health care field.

Dr. Ashmann is now an active emeritus of the Clear Creek Valley Medical Society and the Colorado Medical Society and an active member of the American Medical Association. She is in the Honorary staff category at the Centura St. Anthony Hospital Systems for Central and North in Denver and Westminster, respectively. She is an Emeritus staff category at the Exempla Lutheran Medical Center in Wheat Ridge, Colorado. She is a member of the Catholic Medical Association currently in formation.

Throughout her medical career, Dr. Ashmann had treated her patients with fairness and respect, love and compassion, always giving her best to anyone that came to her. She maintained her expertise and keeping up with the advances in medicine by attending weekly continuing medical education conferences and attending national conferences pertinent to her specialty, like the Mayo Clinic, UCLA, UCHSC, Cleveland Clinic and other subspecialty meetings to name a few.

Her non-medical memorable experiences include her participation in the 1990 Adams County Festival of the Arts and Culture (Celebrate Asia), which she coordinated with the Asian Pacific Development Center. She was a board member of Uplift Internationale, a Charter member of the Asian Roundtable of Colorado, vice chair of the National Federation of Filipino American Associations (NaFFAA) Region V, Founding President of the Philippine American Society of Colorado and the Philippine Heritage Foundation (for the performing arts), Board Member of the Philippine Rondalla of Denver. She coordinated the Philippine Centennial Celebration in 1998. Now retired, she continues to be active in medicine by being a committee member of the Continuing Medical Education Committee at the Exempla Lutheran Medical Center as a volunteer for the Emergency Preparedness for the Colorado Medical Society in conjunction with the Clear Creek Valley Medical Society and supporting the development of the Catholic Medical Association.

What people do not know is her quiet way of giving free medical help to patients whenever asked, especially those without medical insurance, travelers needing emergency care and indigent patients.

Amy attributes her blessings in life as gifts from God and is thankful for the support of her husband, Marshall. They are now grandparents to two boys, sons of Lorraine Eloriaga, their daughter, who has a Bachelor's degree in Interior Design. Arthur, her son, has a Bachelor's degree in Information Technology and is completing his Master's degree.

She has lived up to her Hippocratic Oath. Amy is fulfilling her dreams and is truly serving as a role model for younger Asian Americans.

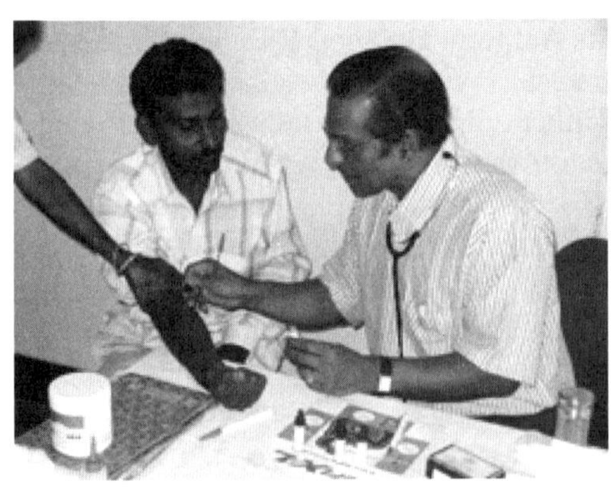

## P.K. Vedanthan,

Dr. Vedanthan is a board-certified allergist, who has been practicing in Ft. Collins, Colorado, since 1976. He was born and raised in the city of Mysore, India and received his medical degree from the University of Mysore. He had training in medicine and pediatrics at Brown University in Rhode Island and he completed his fellowship in allergy and immunology at the National Jewish Center, Denver.

Due to increasing needs for asthma education in various parts of the world, Dr. Vedanthan established the non-profit organization, International Asthma Services (IAS) in 1986. Along with different teams of volunteer physicians and other volunteer medical personnel, IAS has been conducting asthma camps, educational seminars, and public symposiums in different countries. He resides in the U.S. with his family. He is also the co-chair of the Diversified Physicians Section of the Colorado Medical Society and serves as the senior medical consultant to CAHEP.

He notes, “If you are a Native American, your likelihood of dying from heart disease, liver disease, SIDS (Sudden Infant Death Syndrome) is at least twice what it is for whites. If you are an Asian American, the chances of being uninsured are at least 25% higher than the general population. If you are Vietnamese, your chances of dying due to cervical cancer or liver cancer are in each case significantly greater. If you are a Pacific Islander (including Indians) chances of having tuberculosis or hepatitis B infection are higher than any other ethnic group in the nation. Why are these differences so glaring and obviously bothersome? Is this an ethnic problem, a genetic problem, a social issue, a language barrier, or lack of doctor-patient communication?” He remains extremely concerned on such issues. “In the same town with all the modern facilities available, the chances of you suffering or dying are greater if you happen to be a ‘minority’ in this country. This is hard to swallow especially in this nation, supposedly the richest and most powerful in the world”. He feels that we can do much better in Colorado and the entire country.

His organization has conducted several free asthma camps with the help of Rotary International and local Rotary Clubs in different parts of the world. Nearly 31,000 patients have been evaluated at such camps. Educational materials, as well as some equipment and free medications have been distributed. The organization has assisted the local physicians in educating patients about asthma, conducts continuing medical education for the physicians, has started a no-smoking clinic and holds educational seminars for various communities. Our doctors also appear on the radio and television for mass education. He has helped develop respiratory care centers in Karnataka, Mombasa and Nairobi, Manila, and Port Louis with fully functional Pulmonary Lung Function Lab facilities for both in and outpatient evaluations and treatment. When in the U.S., he works with CAHEP to develop and conduct interventions in the Asthma and Allergy area for APA people. He truly believes in the tremendous benefit provided by organizations such as CAHEP. He has devoted his life to helping the underserved and needy here in Colorado and in many other countries and is truly a role model for others in his profession.

## Suegie Park

Suegie Park is an immigrant from South Korea. Her determination to accomplish her goals in the United States is inspirational. I volunteer to give back to the country I adopted and love and to the community, especially to those with health issues. This country has given me so much. This is the only way I can return what I have received."

Suegie had two wishes when she was in Korea. One was to study and learn more about the U.S., the country she considered the greatest in the world. When the U.S. opened immigration, especially to those in the medical field, she immediately applied for an immigrant visa. Her other wish was to give better educational opportunities to her children. She was already married to Nobok Park and had two daughters when she finally arrived in Arlington, VA in 1975. She earned a degree in pharmacy in Korea when she came, but she did not have money to further her study in an American university. Although she learned English in Korean schools, she needed to know how to speak and write English better. Where will she get the money to enroll in college? With luck on her side, she found magazines next to a dumpster near her apartment. She took them home and saw a flyer inviting the reader: Want to go to college? Join the U.S. Army! So, she did. She took the test, passed and became a payroll clerk, worked for four years and finally got her tuition paid for studying by the G.I. Bill from U.S. government.

Suegie had attained a degree in pharmacy in South Korea. She studied at the University of Colorado, Boulder and obtained her B.S. Pharmacy Degree in 1983 and her Doctor of Pharmacy Degree (Pharm. D.) from the University of Colorado Health Science Center at Denver in 2005. She said it was hard studying and working as an intern, and mother of two children, later as a clinical pharmacist at St. Lukes/Presbyterian Medical Center for 13 years.

Besides her medical credentials, she has been involved with the Korean Heritage Camp (KHC) for over 16 years, as a community coordinator. Every year, she organizes camping activities of American parents from all over the world, who have adopted Korean children and want to learn the Korean culture. She started fundraising from the Korean-American community to support these activities by soliciting donations from church groups, businesses, groceries, restaurants, private sectors and Korean organizations, such as the Korean Association of Colorado, the Rocky Mountain Korean Lions Club, Korea Daily Advisory Council Member and Korea National Unification Council Member.

She has been coordinating with the 9Health Care program since 1995, sponsored by 9News, a valuable program for Korean Americans. As a pharmacist, she has served as a professional consultant, translating informational material from English to Korean. She has been chair of the scholarship committee of the Rocky Mountain Korean Lions Club for over 10 years. Together with her husband, she established Rocky Mountain Korean Lions Club in 1987, and this committee encourages the Korean younger generation to pursue higher education. A volunteer organization, the International Lions Club is the largest nonprofit organization in the world, with four districts in Colorado.

As though this was not enough, for the past 12 years, she has conducted and participated in research on prostate cancer prevention trials (SELECT) funded by the National Cancer Institute.

She was a vice president of AEAC (1998-1999) and has encouraged Korean parents to be more active in the Denver Public Schools to improve the system. Currently, she is working for CAHEP as a case manager and human services specialist, for CAHEP supported services to the Korean community such as: health screenings, follow-up care, disease self-management trainings and culturally appropriate interventions.

She says, "I always thought America was the best country in the world. I found a lack of respect for parents, and I still do not approve of young couples kissing openly in public. But most Americans I know are so kind and generous, especially when donating to worthy causes and to victims of natural disasters, not only in the U.S. but all over the world."

Suegie now wants to preserve Korean values and traditions for her family and future generations, such as respect for parents and elders. "I want my children to be caring and respectful. As parents we have to listen to them and love them".

# Edith Pasion

Edith was born in Pamplona, Camarines Sur, hometown of her father Valeriano Ayo. Her mother, Luisa Dungca hailed from Minalin, Pampanga.

She graduated from high school at the Saint Paul College and obtained her Bachelor of Nursing from the University of Santo Tomas in Manila. After graduation from nursing school, she worked at Bacacay Rural Health Clinic as part of the government program of assigning new graduates to serve in the remote areas of the Philippines. It was one of the most exciting experiences she had as a new nurse, serving the underprivileged citizens of our country. It was also her first experience of being independent from her family, which prepared her for life in the United States.

She worked briefly as a clinical instructor at the Family Clinic School of Nursing and as an Industrial Nurse for Edward Keller Company while waiting for her H-1 working visa, after which she was recruited to work at the Kansas City Hospital for Osteopathic Medicine. In Kansas City, Missouri, Edith was surrounded by a supportive group of former classmates and new-found friends and together they were able to adapt to the culture and lifestyle in the US.

Through mutual friends, she met her husband Wilbert Pasion who just got out of the U.S. Air Force after serving for four years. They made Colorado their home – a wonderful place to raise their family. They have a son Eric, a graduate of University of Colorado with a degree in Computer Science. He now works at the Computer Department of University of Utah. Their daughter Jessica is a junior in college at Regis University. She is pursuing her Bachelor Degree in Nursing and hopes to become a nurse anesthetist. She has been employed at St Joseph Hospital in the Intensive Care Area for 25 years, as a relief charge nurse, preceptors to new and experienced nurses who are new in the critical care area.

In addition, she is an active as Steering Committee Member for the Aurora Asian/Pacific Community Partnership, 2000- present; President-Philippine American Society of CO, 2003-2006; Vice President- PASCO, 2001-2003; Board Member-PASCO 1999-2000;

Chair for Survivor- Asian Pacific Community Relay for Life- 2006; Planning Committee Member- Sallow and as Volunteer to San Jose, Antique Mission for Uplift Internationale, 2006.

Edith has been doing volunteer activities since her elementary grades in places such as: classroom, school libraries, sports and extra curricular activities. She is the Founding President of Philippine Nurses Association of Co (PNACO), Incoming President of PNACO is Helen Franz. She was Co Chair- Aurora Asian/Pacific Community Partnership in 2007; Member- Susan Komen Multicultural Advisory Board and a Filipino Case Worker for CAHEP.

## John Van Wu

Dr. John Van Wu is a medical doctor, community leader, inventor and business pioneer. Dr. Wu began to show an interest in computer programming at the age of 14. He created and wrote many computer software programs that could be converted into multi-languages. He wanted to spend his time creating software, but his Asian parents insisted that he should get a stable career as medical doctor. His love for technology and finding ways to help Asian people kept him pursuing many businesses that promote Asian cultures.

During his early years, his family moved to several Asian countries including Vietnam, Malaysia, Hong Kong and eventually they immigrated to the United States in the late 70s. He graduated from Pomona High School in Westminster, and attended the University of Colorado, Boulder, graduating with honors and two majors in the same year, Biochemistry and Environmental Biology. He went on to finish his medical training at Johns Hopkins Medical School in 1996 with specialization in internal medicine, liver cancer and pain management. He is the youngest medical professor emeritus in his alma mater. He is also a visiting professor and an annual guest speaker at Beijing, Tokyo, and Hanoi University Medical School. This amazing young man speaks English, Chinese, Vietnamese, Malaysian, French and Spanish.No wonder Asian patients flock to his clinic in Denver, Colorado.

During his extensive travels abroad, volunteering his medical skills in Asia, Dr. Wu realized that there was not one multulingual Asian website that would serve the rapidly growing Asian communities worldwide. He saw an opportunity to create a website to help billions of people worldwide. Dr. Wu feels it is now time for him to expand his community services not only for his patients in Colorado but also for Asians all over the world. How can he help more people? Using a state of the art multi-languages website and graphics design, ABIDOOO was started in January 2006, with the original goal to help Asians compete on the internet, "E-shopping." Now the website is a comprehensive database and can be searched in numerous languages: English, Chinese, Vietnamese, Korean, Japanese and many more. In addition to business information and directory, ABIDOOO now offers access to entertainment and educational programs for children. Particularly for new businesses, ABIDOOO includes free assistance to start-up businesses, free online classified, competitive website hosting and development, to name a few. The category on E-Tips contains useful advice and tips on various topics including car troubleshooting, dating, investment, health care and cooking. ABIDOOO's ultimate goal is to reach the biggest markets in the world: China and India then eventually Southeast Asia and Europe. ABIDOOO started with just a few hundred hits a week during the first month, now growing to over 1 million hits daily worldwide. Dr. Wu decided not to limit its potential by marketing it to Asians only. ABIDOOO aims to maintain a non-political and purely journalistic approach of neutrality, which is something hard to find these days in most businesses.

Regardless of his success, Dr. Wu remains humble, saying, "I have the best staff working for me and they deserve all the credit." Once the ideas were conceived, the research and recruitment of talented international programmers and web developers worldwide were the hardest first steps for the company. Dr. Wu spends many nights without sleep to enable to hold a live worldwide conference with his staff because of time differences between America and Asia. In May 1, 2007, the website Abidooo.com officially launched on the World Wide Web. Since then, with the goal of being "the next most user-friendly and multi-lingual search engine," it has developed into a success story.

One of the main objectives of the website is to be more than just a traditional search engine, such as Google and Yahoo, by providing a full range of services to its customers. Therefore, it aims to be exclusive by being a one-stop information, entertainment, and business media. At this website you can search for information in many languages with special keyboard character support, play free educational as well as recreational games, watch free videos and over one hundred fifty domestic and international television channels, buy and sell both Asian and International merchandise on E-shopping. The website's other function is to promote all businesses to worldwide Asian community markets.

A man with full dedication to his family and community with deep passion in technology, John describes himself as "The Solution Visionary." His primary goal has always been to make life easier for people by giving them what they want -- the exact philosophy behind his website.

For a man who has worked tirelessly for years and achieving many awards, Dr. Wu has began another chapter in his life to focus on family and community. In 1997, he married Audrey and they have two children. They also established the John and Audrey Wu Children Health and Education Foundation in 2000, which focuses on Asian rural community education issues and promotes children health care. Dr. Wu has also established philanthropic foundations for the causes of medical research, Asian arts, community service, and literature preservation.

# Chapter 14

# ASIAN PACIFIC AMERICANS IN CREATIVE ARTS

The creative arts encompass a number of areas including painting, writing, poetry, filmmaking, photography, pottery, sculpture, dance, theater, singing, and musical performance. The contributions of Asian and Pacific Americans to the creative arts in America have been vast and diverse and have been occurring for more than a century. The creative arts have also been critically important for APAs themselves. They have greatly enriched the quality of the lives of APAs. They have provided venues and opportunities for APAs to express and speak for themselves, to reflect their heritage, and to shape their cultures and identities in America. APAs take great pride in their artistic accomplishments and continue to develop their talents and expand their artistic horizons in America.

Adequately describing APAs in the creative arts is a complex task that, for several reasons, is beyond the scope of this chapter introduction. First, the creative arts encompass a number of different areas. Second, each of these areas has many specific forms and styles, and each of these, in turn, will vary in different cultures in Asia. For instance, the many forms and styles of dance found throughout the Philippines are different from the many forms of dance found throughout Korea. What complicates the picture is that when Asians migrate to and settle in America, their creative activities may mirror those left behind in their Asian homelands, but, over time, they often change and evolve in response to cultural influences in America and to transnational influences from the changing cultures of their homelands. Thus, Japanese American instrumental music may be very traditional in nature, or it may reflect the influences of American jazz, or it may be influenced by the changing contemporary music scene in Japan. A final complication is that APA groups differ in the degree to which their creative activities change and evolve in America. Again, this chapter introduction cannot provide a comprehensive discussion of APAs in the creative arts. What it will do is give some examples of music and dance in Asia and then a few illustrations of changes due to American influences. Readers who are interested in additional information should consult the appropriate materials in the reference section at the end of this book. This chapter will then feature several outstanding APA creative artists in Colorado.

Korean music and dance were originally a means of religious worship and this tradition continued through the Three Kingdoms Period. More than 30 musical instruments were used during the Three Kingdoms Period. Particularly noteworthy was the *hyeonhakgeum* (black crane zither), which was created by altering the seven-string zither of China. Also notable was the *gayageum* (zither of Gaya); the 12-string *gayageum* is still played in modern Korea.

In the Philippines, there are three basic indigenous styles of music styles: southern, northern and other. The southern style of music usually involves five different instruments including the kulintang, the *agung*, the *gangdinagan*, the *dabakan* and the *babedil*; the northern styles reflect Asian gong music. In addition to the instruments used by southern and northern music styles, other instruments used in the Philippines include log drums, flutes, bamboo zithers and the *Kudyapi.* Hispanic cultures from Spain and Mexico have greatly influenced the development of Filipino music. The *Harana, Kundiman* and the *Rondalla* style of music developed as a result of the fusion between indigenous music styles and traditional Spanish and Mexican music. Today the influence of Spain and Mexico is still present in modern Filipino music. Modern popular music in the Philippines still has a Hispanic flavor.

In Vietnam, *Nhã nhạc* was the most popular form of imperial court music, specifically referring to the court music played from the *Trần Dynasty* to the very last *Nguyễn Dynasty* of Vietnam. It is based on earlier Vietnamese imperial court music which, in turn, was influenced by the music of the Chinese *Ming Dynasty*'s imperial court. The lion dance was imported from China into Vietnamese culture where it developed its own distinct style. It is still performed today, primarily at traditional festivals such as Tết (Lunar New Year) and Tết trung thu (Mid-Autumn Festival) but also during other occasions such as the opening of a new business.

Indian Classical dance is an expression of life for many people in India involving the body and emotions. Indian Dance is based on texts from Sanskrit, an old Indian language of Hinduism. The dance drama performance is made up of four aspects; the devadasi with its emotions, *mudras* (hand gestures), *rasa* (the audience experience) and the *rasika* (an audience member). The major Indian classical dances are: *Bharata Natyam, Kathakali, Kathak* and *Manipuri, Kuchipudi, Odissi* and *Mohini Attam.* In addition, there are innumerable folk and tribal dances spread all over the country. In Colorado we have many Asian Indian dance teachers and performers, and one will be featured in this chapter.

The work of two APA musicians nicely illustrates some of the

American and Western influences on APA creative artists. Californian John Jang is a nationally renowned composer and pianist. Born in Los Angeles, Jang has produced more than ten major recordings, and he and his ensembles have performed in venues all around the world. His work is influenced by Chinese folk music, African American spirituals and jazz and classical European styles. One of his recent works, *Two Flowers on a Stem*, has characteristics similar to Chinese folk songs but placed in a jazz ballad context; it is played using Western musical instruments and the traditional Chinese erhu. Another recent composition, *Island: the Immigrant Suite No. 2,* is designed for a Western-style string quartet and a Chinese opera singer.

Minnesota-based Tou Ger Xiong is a young Hmong American hip-hop and rap artist. Born in Laos, he and his family came to America as refugees and settled in St. Paul. Xiong incorporates traditional Hmong stories and rap music in his performances. Much of his work is motivated by the hardship and difficulties Hmong face living in America and by his search for cultural identity. Two of his recent compositions are titled *Go Hmong Boy Go Hmong Boy Go: A Rap* and *We Are Hmong: A Rap*. Xiong and Jang are examples of musicians whose work is a fusion of Asian and American/Western influences. The work of many other APA creative artists, such as writers and painters, often shows such influences.

Because of time and space constraints, not all of the outstanding Colorado APAs in the creative arts were interviewed for this chapter. One who was not deserves special mention. Gus Lee is a nationally-known ethicist and leadership expert who perhaps is best known as an award-winning author. He has written six national best-selling books including the novels *China Boy*, *Honor and Duty*, and *No Physical Evidence*. His latest book is a nonfiction exploration of leadership titled *Courage: The Backbone of Leadership*. Lee grew up in California but now lives and works in Colorado Springs.

We now showcase some examples of APA creative artists in Colorado. These individuals are exceptionally talented but have also worked very hard to keep their arts alive by sharing and teaching them. Their efforts represent their earnest desire to maintain and shape APA cultures, and such efforts greatly enrich the cultural diversity and vitality of Colorado and the entire nation.

# Art in Multi-Media

## Manick Sorcar

In 1997, "The Denver Post" addressed him as *"The Animation Man."* In 1998, Colorado's "Jefferson the Magazine" selected him as one of the *"Top 100 People"*, in 2000 he was given the *"Excellence in Arts"* award from the National Federation of Indian American Associations, and in 2005, The *Voice of America* lauded him by telecasting a special feature on him. Welcome to the world of Manick Sorcar, who has been blessed and profusely showered with many talents in art and science, which have given him international recognition and made him the renaissance man of our time. His creative work ranges from being an accomplished electrical engineer, a lighting designer, an author of university texts to award-winning artist in a variety of media including fine arts, animation, cartoons, music direction, and stage shows mixing live performance with laser graphics. He has earned a series of international film festival accolades and the *"ILDA Artistic Award"* - the Oscar of laser industry. He is the first Asian American to receive this coveted award from the International Laser Display Association, twice.

What's the secret of his success? "There is no secret", says the self-made man who is originally from India and set a bright example of the success story of an Asian American in the U.S. "I believe in what my father taught me and which, I pass on to my children and others: you can do anything - if you love it and put your mind to it".

Manick is a full time electrical engineer by day abiding all the rules and regulations of codes; but it is at night when he retires to his basement studio and immerses into the world of art where no rules apply but his own. This is where we see the real man. The nighttime production is an outpour of his incredible love for India and her culture, which blooms like flowers in a variety of ways expressing his emotions and allowing the world to share the beauty of it. It is the sight of his love for art in everything, including his lighting design in electrical engineering, which made him what he is today.

Manick came to the USA in 1970. After receiving his Master's degree in electrical engineering from the University of Washington, Seattle, in 1972, Manick (formal name Prafulla C. Sorcar), took up a job as a junior engineer at Howard W. Butterweck and Co., a reputable electrical consulting engineering firm of Denver, Colorado. In two years, he was promoted to become its Vice-President when the company re-incorporated changing its name to Butterweck–Sorcar Engineering, Inc. In the next three decades, under his supervision, the corporation did the engineering services for numerous multi-million dollar land-mark project, which lit a good portion of Denver's skyline, e.g., lighting design for Denver International Airport concourses, Colorado Convention Center, Convention Center high-rise Hyatt Hotel, Rapid Transit Stations around the city, Denver Justice Center, to name a few. His artistic lighting designs reached other parts of the world including palaces for Saudi Arabian princes and Sport Centers in Japan. After the death of Mr. Butterweck in 2000, Manick bought the company and changed the name to Sorcar Engineering, Inc., of which he became the CEO/President. Under his formal name, he is the author of several books: *Rapid Lighting Design and Cost Estimating* (McGraw-Hill, 1979) was a feature selection by the Architects' Book Club; Energy Saving Lighting Systems (Van Nostrand-Reinhold, 1983), and *Architectural Lighting for Commercial Interiors* (John Wiley and Sons, 1987). The last two books were used as a text for Illuminating Engineering and Architectural Engineering at several universities in the U.S. and in India.

It is the art side of Manick, which stormed the world, and interestingly, it was his deeply rooted family values of Indian culture that gave him the opportunity to explore and get international recognition. In 1974 Manick married Shikha in Calcutta and returned to Colorado to make Denver their home. Being a father who loves his home country very much, Manick had the strongest desire to instill upon his two US-born daughters, Piya and Payal, the Indian culture, the good things about his country, the beautiful customs, traditions, and language. These influenced him to compose Indian children's songs, create animation and other productions. When the girls were 4 and 7, he wrote children's songs in his native language Bengali and produced two cassettes: "Santa Claus come with me to India" and "Clap-Clap-Clap" which were sung by his daughters. These became popular both in the US and in India and were recorded by CBS in 1984 at that time in 45-rpm discs. This caught the attention of the American Cablevision of Wheat Ridge, Colorado which provided him the opportunity to apply his talent in painting and animation with the songs, resulting in two 30-minute programs "East Meets West", and "East Meets West, II". The programs were instantly popular with American children, and became a great source of inspiration for the whole family to produce more. The gap he was trying to bridge at home soon became the cultural bridge between East and West. He then made his first animation movie mixed with live action, entitled "Deepa and Rupa: A Fairy Tale from India," which took the world by storm. Produced in English, and his daughter Piya as the leading actress, the 30-minute show was shown on several PBS stations around the U.S. and nationally telecast in India. It went on receiving a host of top awards including the Gold Plaque at the Chicago International Film Festival and nominations for three Heartland Emmy Awards. Manick's desire to teach his children Indian values went beyond his wildest dreams. Schools began inviting Manick and Shikha to make presentations of their animation and talk to students about their culture. Inspired, he went on to make more movies: "The Sage and the Mouse" (1993), winner of the Gold Medal at the International Film Festival of New York, "Sniff" (1993), winner of the CINE Golden Eagle, "The Woodcutter's daughter" (1997), Finalist at the New York Festivals, and "Rule of Twenty-One" (2003), which won the Bronze Plaque at the Columbus International Film Festival. Produced in English, all were based on fables of India introducing culture of another land to American children.

It was in early 2000 Manick started experimenting and succeeded in making animation with the cutting edge technology of laser by using the strong beam of light as a painting brush and space as a canvas. He invented "SorcarScope", a technique through which life-size laser animation could be safely mixed with live action on stage, which brought revolutionary results. On March 2006, his "Enlightenment of Buddha" which integrated live action with laser animation on stage won the First Place in international contest and received the *ILDA Artistic Award* from the International Laser Display Association in Italy. In April, 2008, at the time of writing this article, Manick's "Reflection", a laser-art scene from his forthcoming stage production won the First Place in Laser Photography in international contest and received his second *"ILDA Artistic Award"*.

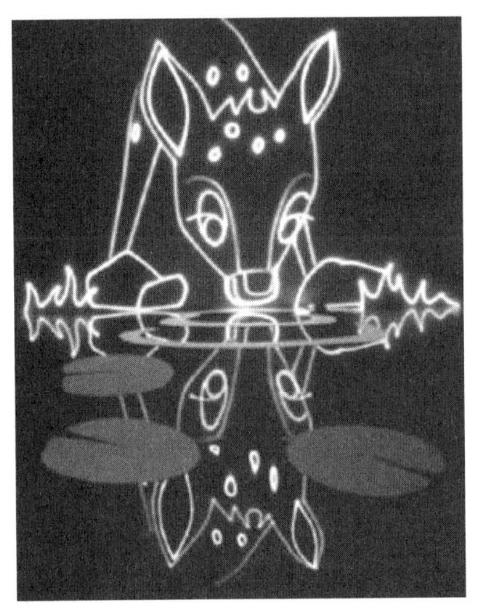

Manick's love of art is seen in everything he touches. His current 8,000 sq. ft residence in Arvada, which is designed by him and decorated with his own arts, was featured in the Rocky Mountain News, and visited by the Asian Art Association of the Denver Art Museum. His gallery in the 3000 sq. ft. basement displays original, amazing creations in various conventional and unusual media. As far as we know, he is the only artist who has created portraits of famous personalities, using actual newspaper articles about them to reveal the portrait of the subject, such as Mother Teresa, Princes Diana, Gandhi, President Clinton, Mayor Wellington Webb of Denver, etc. Meticulous and a perfectionist, Manick is the artist we know who has painted the portrait of U.S. president Jimmy Carter on one side of half a peanut. Still more amazing is a painting of Abraham Lincoln on a grain of rice, distinctly visible only under a magnifying glass. How about portraits of various poses of Mahatma Gandhi made out of black onion seeds, which appear from afar like charcoal paintings! Another part of the gallery has the giant size portrait of a meditating Buddha collaged with pieces of floor tiles. Then, there is a three-dimensional life-size sculpture of the street musicians of India, carved out of layers of Styrofoam. What looks like a white marble carving is anchored to the wall of his family room.

Manick is also an accomplished cartoonist and has published cartoons in several newspapers and magazines. He is the author of The Melting Pot: Indians in America and Spices in the Melting Pot – two popular books of cartoons dealing with the life of Asian Indians trying to assimilate with the mainstream in the U.S.

Pieces of his original works, including scenes of his animations, have been displayed in Colorado, including the Foothills Art Center, Golden, Colorado; Denver Center for Performing Arts (DCPA); and at the annual Arvada Art Studio Tours.

Manick's artistic productions have kept the family close together. His daughters, Piya and Payal co-directed and choreographed the dances for all the shows, while his wife is the production coordinator and costume designer. Their shows are an extravaganza of state-of-the-art laser light technology with intelligent lighting interacting with live performers, which they take around the world when there is a break from engineering work.

Manick has a big heart and is a great humanitarian. His contributions include the special stage shows they did for the Tsunami victims, Kids 4 Kids: Raising awareness about child abuse, raising funds for 9/11 victims, and performing at the Silver celebration ($25^{th}$) anniversary of the Asian Pacific Development Center (APDC). Manick, his wife Shikha, and daughters Piya and Payal have taken an active part for several years in the East Indian Heritage Camps for adopted children from India.

# Calligraphy

## Harrison Tu

Harrison Tu, Chinese American calligrapher, is the founder and president of the Rocky Mountain Chinese Calligrapher Association and owner/publisher of the Chinese American Post. He also teaches at Colorado College and at NAROPA Institute in Boulder.

Harrison is an expert in the art of brushwork and calligraphy, the oldest art form. He says, "The more you understand calligraphy, the more you can understand the world. It's high beauty, yes, but it's also a meditation, an activity that involves the arms, center and spirit." Harrison is also active with the APA community, sometimes demonstrating his special art and talent at special events. He was a member of the Governor's Asian Pacific American Advisory Council (GAPAAC) and many other Chinese organizations.

# Paintings

## Steve Lumanlan

**Panaghoy Nang Puso"(Harana)**
**Acrylic 18x24 2003**

If a picture paints a thousand words then the viewer of this whimsical painting can clearly see the depiction of a cultural courtship in the Philippine barrio. Here the young girl receives her admirer in the house, under the strict supervision of her "lola" (grandmother). The beau pours his heart out in a song as he serenades the girl who has captured his heart. From her expression, the girl is obviously thrilled at the harana and that the boy has already won her heart. But could he win Lola's approval? Not if his singing continues to cause "bantay" the dog to howl. (By Maria Concepcion Panlilio)

Steve Lumanlan of Aurora has painted many portraits of prominent people in the Philippines throughout his illustrious art career spanning over forty prolific years

The Archbishop of Caceres was so impressed with the stunning life-like character of his canvas cloth version that he immediately commissioned Lumanlan to paint the portraits of the past 30 bishops of Naga. Inevitably, his reputation as a great portrait artist spread like wild fire in the art community. What followed was a succession of art commissions for prominent figures of families throughout the country, which included: Maj. Gen. Thomas Moorman of the U.S. Thirteenth Air Force, Congresswoman Juanita L. Nepomuceno, and the portrait of Pope John XXIII, which was hand-carried by Bishop Emilio Chinese to the Vatican and presented to the Pope.

Another gift in 1961,that of U.S. President John F. Kennedy, was sent to Washington. In a letter to Lumanlan, Evelyn Lincoln, personal secretary to President John F. Kennedy, states in part: "The very fine portrait that you did of the President has been received and he asked me to send you this note of thanks."

In 1963, the JAYCEES of Angeles City nominated Lumanlan for the Ten Outstanding Young Men (TOYM) of the Philippines for his contributions in the field of Art.

.

## Lito Santos

Over the years Lito Santos has actively represented the Philippines, albeit unofficially, through his art, poetry, dances and songs at several cultural and artistic activities, including "ARTIST ASIA", an annual art show sponsored by Wells Fargo Bank in downtown, Denver. This versatile artist has not limited his creative prowess to painting landscapes and portraits in all mediums. He is also a sculptor, creating figures from wood, clay and plaster. In one collaborative effort, he has designed the stained glass window backing the statue of Our Lady of Antipolo at the Queen of Peace Church. Blessed with the gift of words, Santos also writes poetry. Lito established his own company called EARTH CA after his children's names. He has been active in the community since moving to Colorado in 1975. He served as past president of The Bayanihan Society of Queen of Peace of Aurora. Santos' latest works feed his homesickness for the Motherland, his longing for the past. "They are a depiction of my remembrances," he laments, "my solace, a big part of my life emotionally."

**Lito Santos, artist, poet, sculptor, singer, composer and choreographer poses in front of a mural size painting in his art studio and gallery.**

# Jam Wong

**Jam F. Wong displays his landscape paintings.**

With a smile as big as his heart, blended with a touch of mischievousness, Jam is an artist whose creative spirit touches everything he does. Jam, an architect by profession, retired from Wong Strauch Architects and has resumed his hobby – painting.

# Maria Concepcion Panlilio

Maria Panlilio of Conifer, Colorado, has been drawing since she discovered the magic of pencil at age one. A prolific artist who draws energy from the beauty of nature, Panlilio has always taken on life with untiring passion. By the time she was eight years old, she was already writing and illustrating her own comic books. At 14, her first illustrated short story was published in a comic book in the Philippines; and at 18, one of her stories was adapted for a TV drama series. In the U.S., her first romance novel was published at 27. In 1997, tired of her corporate persona, she traded her briefcase with a backpack, and for nearly two years, she explored and hiked many of the Pacific Cascade volcanoes. Inspired by the splendor of the snow-shrouded peaks, she immortalized the volcanic mountains on clay and canvas. The ornate tones of her brushwork bring Monet richness to the canvas. Each scene is a cherished memory from her life and those of her growing customer base.

Represented by Violeta of California, which featured her handmade ceramic vases in its L.A. showroom, Panlilio designed many of the huge collector vases where she has carved and painted most of the Pacific Northwest volcanoes.

Between art and her international travels, Panlilio is immersed in her literary endeavors as a freelance writer and columnist. She hopes to publish a novel someday.

**Mother and Child**
**Oil on canvas, ca. 2004, 24x30**
**Collection: the artist**

# Ceramics

## Nelfa Querubin Tompkins

**Nelfa Querubin-Tompkins,** born in Iloilo, Philippines, now lives and works in Golden. After becoming one of the well-known printmakers in the Philippines, she pioneered studio pottery at a time when clay was not accepted as a fine art medium. More importantly, she formulated her own clay bodies and glazes, used found materials, fashioned her own tools and constructed her own wood-firing kilns sourced on site from the earth of her native Miag-ao, Iloilo, where she built her ceramic studio. For these and her excellent output, she was one of the recipients of the prestigious 1980 Cultural Center of the Philippines Thirteen Artists Award, in recognition for her contribution to the indigenous movement in Philippine contemporary art.

She said: "The mystery in the materials and processes of clay, its endless color, textures, forms and shapes, drive my creativity with boundless joy."

**Prize-winning ceramic art by Nelfa Querubin Tompkins exhibited at Foothills Art Center, Golden, Colorado**

Tompkins was a consistent winner of major awards in fine arts since 1969 in the Philippines and in Colorado. She had 17 solo exhibitions including 2 retrospectives, participated in national and international exhibitions, and was active in group shows and fine art festivals in Southwestern States. She was featured in international and national magazines and art books. She did workshops as visiting artist in art centers in Colorado and in the Philippines and was invited as guest lecturer in universities and art groups.

Querubin-Tompkins' works are in the permanent collection of Central Bank of the Philippines, cultural center of the Philippines, University of the Philippines in the Visayas, design center of the Philippines, private collectors in the Philippines, Asia, Europe, Middle East, USA, and Vance Kirkland Museum of Denver, Colorado.

# Performing Arts

## I Made Lasmawan

Master Balinese drummer and composer I Made Lasmawan is the Artist-in-Residence for the Denver-based Gamelan Tunas Mekar, a community orchestra that studies and performs the music of Bali, Indonesia. Since coming to Colorado, his influence as a Balinese musician and instructor has spread throughout the region. Pak Lasmawan teaches Balinese *gamelan* (Indonesian for 'orchestra') at Colorado College in Colorado Springs, the University of Wyoming in Laramie and the University of Colorado at Boulder. With an unusual 'storehouse' of creative energy, he is currently beginning a *gamelan* at the University of Colorado at Colorado Springs and is a graduate student at CU Boulder's School of Music as an ethnomusicologist. Additionally, he teaches Balinese music and cultural workshops throughout the United States and Canada, often composing and arranging traditional and new compositions for specific events. It should be noted that the Balinese *creasi baru* (new creations) are a vibrant part of everyday life in Bali that perfectly balance the music and dance of tradition.

Pak Lasmawan was born in the village of Bangah, in the Baturiti region of the regency of Tabanan, Bali in 1958. Strongly influenced by his family and involved in the arts since childhood, he entered KOKAR

(Conservatory for Traditional Performing Arts) in Denpasar, Bali, and graduated in 1977. He continued his studies in 1978 at STSI (Indonesian College of the Arts) in Surakarta (Solo), Central Java, and studied traditional Javanese music, receiving his Traditional Indonesian Music degree in 1983.

Pak Lasmawan has since traveled throughout the world, including Belgium, France, England, Singapore, Japan and Mexico. He is a prolific composer who taught Balinese music at STSI from 1983 until 1990, when he was invited to San Diego State University to teach Javanese and Balinese music. In 1992, he was invited by the Indonesian Embassy's Cultural Attaché, a choreographer, to perform with him in Aspen, Colorado, at which time an instant bond of friendship was made with members of Gamelan Tunas Mekar that continues to this day. In 1996, Pak Lasmawan led Tunas Mekar in performance at the international Bali Arts Festival in Denpasar, placing the Colorado orchestra 'on the map' as the second U.S. group to participate in this prestigious event.

In collaborations with the Indonesian Consulates of both Los Angeles and Chicago, and with the Indonesian Embassy in Washington, D.C., Pak Lasmawan brings Indonesian culture to life in the Rocky Mountain region and beyond. Most recently, he traveled with Gamelan Tunas Mekar to Chicago, Houston and Montana to perform several major concerts.

He lives in Colorado Springs with his wife, Ni Ketut Marni, a professional Balinese dancer, and his three talented sons. When in Bali, Pak Lasmawan continues to play a leading role in the development of his home village's *gamelan* ensembles.

## Dolly Banzon

Dolly Banzon, from Davao City, Philippines, has distinguished herself as an effective promoter of the Filipino culture through her production and choreography and participation in Filipino folk dances and concerts. She has been the lead choreographer in the Filipino community for many years. She brings to audiences dance presentations on behalf of the Filipino American Community of

Colorado, the Philippine American Society of Colorado and the Philippine Heritage Foundation. She heads no formal dance group but is a consultant choreographer to organizations interested in cultural presentations for their special events. Her choreographic style is distinctly Bayanihan.

Most noted among her presentations to name a few are: Fiesta Pilipinas, Pista sa Nayon, Kalayaan, Kasarinlan, Indak Pilipino, Gabi ng Kasoutang Pilipino (Philippine attire Fashion Show), Sayaw Pilipinas, etc. She has also participated in Asian festivals, sponsored by the Asian Pacific Development Center, as well as, for other community organizations.

Dolly is well regarded for her tireless efforts in instilling the correct interpretations of Filipino dance, music and song. She not only teaches the dance steps – she continually inspires her students by instilling pride in the Filipino culture and heritage. She carefully describes the historical and cultural influence of each dance and the significance of the different costumes.

For her efforts and dedication, Dolly has been honored with many awards, among them are: one of the six Most Outstanding Asian Women of Colorado in 1994 in the field of Arts and Culture; Lifetime Achievement Award from the Philippine Heritage Foundation; the Distinguished Artist Award for Lifetime Achievement from the Philippine American Society of Colorado (PASCO) and the NaFFAA Region V 2006 Lifetime Achievement Award.Dolly has a B.S. degree in English from the University of the Philippines and worked as head of the Personnel Department of her father's business in the Philippines. A deeply spiritual person, she has touched many lives through motivational talks to various groups and individuals. Her transformational journey during her four-year study in the Catholic Biblical School has inspired her to share her knowledge with her Filipino brothers and sisters in the Philippines. Together with Amelia Ashmann, M.D., and in conjunction with the Catholic Biblical School through its previous director, Thomas Smith, they introduced the Bible Timeline in the Philippines. Her goal, with the help of the Denver Catholic Biblical School, is to establish a sister institution in Davao City.

## Dancers of Wat Buddhawararam

There is a unique Thai music and dance program in Denver. To preserve Thai culture, the Thai community members in Denver and Wat Buddhawararam of Denver arranged to have volunteer instructors come each year from Thailand to teach Thai music, dance and language to local adults and children. Ms. Pornnapa Boontha came to Denver in 2000–2001 and volunteered to teach and perform classical Thai dances at Wat Buddhawararam. She came back to Denver to live in 2003, married a local Thai software engineer and together they ran a convenience store a dry cleaning family business. She holds a BA in Acting from a university in Thailand and enjoys state performances. She has been training her own children, who were born in Thailand, to appreciate both Thai and American cultures. She teaches her children to 'wai' (Thai greeting by putting palms together on your chest and bending your face down to your hands) when they meet older Thai people and to greet non-Thai people by saying hello. She continues to speak Thai language at home. She hopes her children will learn to assimilate US culture and arts, while being proud of their Thai heritage.

She wants to see Asians work together to improve social and economic conditions for the future Asian generations.

# Namita Nariani

Namita Nariani was indoctrinated into Indian dance at the age of three. She has learned various forms of Indian classical and folk dances, from esteemed gurus in India, but her specialty is in the classical dance form of "Kathak" which is derived from the word "Katha" meaning story telling. She is a guest teacher for the Department of Humanities and the Dance Department of the University of Colorado at Boulder at undergraduate and graduate level. Namita is a cultural resource to various public schools in Colorado. She has lectured for four years on the problems and positives of an immigrant's life. She has been invited to participate in discourses at Lutheran School of Theology and other religious organization relating to dance as a form of worship. Namita was a guest choreographer with "Up with People" and a master teacher at Cleo Parker Robinson's "8th annual Summer Institute".

An Architect by profession Namita moonlights as the Founder, Lead Choreographer and the driving force behind Mudra Dance Studio, a non-profit Indian dance studio. She started by teaching three students in a borrowed basement in 1993 and now has a studio with over seventy students and eight different classes. The Studio is one of a kind, non-profit studio, teaching Asian Indian classical dance form of Kathak along with various folk and contemporary dances. She has become a source of inspiration and a guiding light for scores of Colorado area first and

second generation immigrants. Mudra has won acclaim in national and international performances.

The success of Mudra Dance Studio has propelled her to achieve her vision of service to humanity, peace and harmony through annual dance ensemble productions dedicated to various humanitarian causes, and donating upwards of $25,000 to grassroots organization like CED Society- Supporting orphanages in Himalayas, Colorado Heritage Camps and Red Cross for natural disasters. Each ensemble production has focused on the subjects of strife and conflicts, internal and external, and harmonizing these conflicts through acceptance and integration by love and affection to bring about universal peace.

Namita's vision extends beyond dance as a form of entertainment. She has been instrumental in starting an annual Mudra awards program since 2002 for the Asian community in Colorado. Each awardee is nominated and selected by a panel based on merits and criteria as defined for the award.

As a testimony to cultural diversity and integration, Mudra has choreographed and performed dances with music from different cultural sounds; on Japanese drums with "Denver Taiko", on African drums with "Bantabe" and integrating Indian folk dances to their music. Mudra has choreographed and dances for inmates, kindergarteners, churches, Temples, with Cleo Parker Robinson for "Granny Dances to a Holiday Drum" and with "Up with People".

In response to how and why she started Mudra, Namita responds "As an architect, the artistic side of my life has always influenced my career. I handled my architectural practice with passion, utilizing the importance of heritage, culture and ethnic roots as a basis for the design the client prefers. I feel passionate about this form of communication that crosses all barriers - Dance. It helps me overcome all obstacles in life, and it is a great platform for me to be able to create bridges between cultures, generations and languages. I was lucky to have found committed students and supporters who made this very enjoyable and satisfying."

When asked which aspect of Indian culture helped her husband and her raise their children, Namita says, "Both of us were raised in families that loved and respected our individual cultures and we also appreciated, revered and learned from those around us. That taught us not just acceptance, but also, loving, learning and embracing nuances of different cultures, languages and religion That is the essence of our upbringing, and we are proud to bring up our children on that same foundation. We were always taught that all men and women should be treated as equals and we strongly enforce that in our psyche and with our daughters. They can accomplish anything in this world, as long as they feel passionate about it."

She notes that the diversity of the Asian Pacific cultures represented in Colorado is magnificent and as APA people we need to promote and expose all the positive energy that emerges from these cultures: through festivals, cultural exchanges, student exchanges and discussion platforms to help the younger generations understand and accept differences and actually feel the similarities that exist. This world is a beautiful place, because of all the different cultures, colors, languages and religions of people that inhabit it. That is what should be celebrated, appreciated and promoted. I am hoping our children and the next generation will be able to do so, and eradicate the hatred, intolerance and bloodshed that exist at this time. As an ambassador of Asian Indian culture in Colorado, she states, "Indian cultures are very diverse and beautiful. Their traditions of dance, music and traditional ceremonies at conventions, fairs and festivals, and through articles or stories about the culture emphasize all the positive aspects of the culture and the country. We should promote this starting from the elementary, middle and high schoolers. Indian culture should be revered as an old culture that is rooted in values derived from all the issues and challenges that are faced by people of all origins. We should learn to celebrate life the way all the diverse languages and cultures of India do, in a language that can be understood by all who live in this great American melting pot – the arts.

## Christina Yeh

The Christina Yeh Dance Studio was established by Christina Yeh, Dance-Master, Choreographer and Instructor.

Christina Yeh is a graduate of Chinese Culture University, Taiwan, with a dance and music major. She focused on the art of Chinese dance as a performer, instructor and choreographer. She is a professional dancer, practicing dance since age 10, and has received numerous citations and awards for excellent dance performances. She interprets Chinese culture and traditions through various dance forms in individual and group performances. Her dance students, including children and adults, perform for many schools, corporations, organizations and cultural events around metro-Denver. Christina has regular dance classes at Christina Yeh Dance Studios in downtown Denver and Centennial. Christina is also a beloved Chinese folk dance instructor of major Chinese language schools in metro-Denver.

# Musical Performances

## Josefina "Pepita" Tuason

Josefina Tuason ("Pepita" to many of her friends) had been playing violin with the Aurora Symphony for 10 years when she decided to extend her music skills to mandolin. Soon thereafter, she founded and directed the Philippine Rondalla of Denver and, later, the Note-ables International. Pepita has conducted the Philippine Rondalla, plays mandolin with the Note-ables and has arranged music pieces for both groups. They are her dreams come true.

Pepita graduated from the University of the Philippines with a Bachelor's degree in Speech and Drama, and from the State University of New York with a Master's in Communications. She also went to Syracuse University on a UNESCO Fellowship. Pepita's rich career in the Philippines includes a faculty appointment at the UP Institute of Mass Communications, Production Manager of Radio Veritas, producer-director of a nationally broadcast public affairs television series and columnist for the Manila Chronicle. In the U.S, Pepita has made a career of public television, having worked at TV stations WCNY in Syracuse, NY, KTSC in Pueblo, CO and KRMA in Denver. Outside of her public television career, music remains Pepita's avocation of a lifetime.

The rondalla is the Philippine counterpart of a string orchestra. The Philippine Rondalla of Denver, under the direction of Josefina (Pepita) Tuason, was formed in 1997, with the mission of preserving and promoting Philippine musical traditions and sharing them with Filipino and American communities in Colorado.

The musical instruments used in the Philippine Rondalla of Denver include bandurrias, lauds, mandolins, guitars, bass and percussion. Although coming from various professional and personal backgrounds, the Rondalla members share a common love of music and an appreciation for diverse cultures. In its short history, the Philippine Rondalla quickly built a reputation for being the leading ambassador of Filipino music in Colorado.

Within the Philippine Rondalla is a small ensemble that has performed with, and independently of, the larger group. The Note-ables International has been a part of the Philippine Rondalla from its inception, but has maintained additional repertoire that expands on typical Rondalla programs. In its performances, the Note-ables International conveys the same musical flair that characterizes rondalla music.

The Philippine Rondalla has not performed as a large group for some time, but the Note-ables International, which the Filipino community still refers to as a rondalla, continues to perform music in the rondalla tradition. Through the Note-ables, the Philippine Rondalla, and all that it stands for, lives on.

# Malou Mateo Stirman

## Filipino American Songwriter, Arranger, Conductor

"This is my home', one of her compositions, evoked an unmistakable way of tugging at the heart and mind, bringing tears to the eyes of singers and audience alike."

A singer, composer, arranger, acoustic guitarist and conductor, Malou Mateo Stirman hails from a family of musicians. Her older brother Ponciano, a flamenco guitarist and her older sister, Zeny, a mezzo-soprano, both have degrees in music education. Malou was born in Leyte, Philippines. She studied at Centro Escolar University in Manila with emphasis in Mass Communications.

Malou has been performing on and off stage since she was five years old. At age six, Malou won her first all-level amateur singing contest. Consistently, she performed on school plays and participated in programs all through high school. She wrote scripts and choreographed musical scores in high school. After a couple of years in college, she went on to perform as a musician professionally, starting as a bandleader in Subic Bay, Philippines. She fulfilled contracts outside the country as well, ending in Guam. Malou has continued to make music a part of her life in America.

Malou lent out her civic sensibility through a collaborative work for the FACC, by writing for and directing a chorus who sang during "Pagdiriwang," a show created to celebrate the pre-centennial of the Philippine independence from Spain. As artistic director for the Filipino American Community of Colorado, she subsequently created musical performances for various occasions of significance: Fiestas Filipinas, Maria Makiling, Balagtasan, as well as Republika. The latter is a musical, depicting intimate glimpses of the principal players in the Philippine Revolution against the Spaniards. The controversies underlying the accomplishments of the movement were very well played out in a musical dialogue that was both melodically and textually balanced, bringing out both the angst and elation that are present in a dynamic premise. "This Is My Home," an inspired composition, was sung by the Jubilee Chorus for FACC's 50$^{th}$ anniversary celebration in 2004. The song plays out the journey of the early Filipino Coloradoans, culminating in a vital community, which offers a home from which dreams and aspirations are lived out and shared. Perhaps, this is one of her best compositions, in her unmistakable way of tugging at the heart and mind, bringing tears to the eyes of singers and audience alike.

Malou earned a degree in Music from the University of Colorado, graduating *cum laude.* She is currently the Director of Music at Holy Ghost Church, a catholic church in downtown Denver. Through her grassroots vision, a Good Friday musical reading of the Lord's Passion and the ancient Tenebrae service have become significant additions to the already traditionally rich church.

# ORGANIZATIONS

## Kaci Kopec of Polynesian FiaFia Group

Kaci Kopec, granddaughter of APA leaders George and Helen Yoshida, is a performing dancer with the Polynesian Fiafia group. Hula is an essential aspect of the Hawaiian culture for the hula dances and chants pass on the stories of the culture. The hula dances and chants teaches about respect of one another and oneself, appreciation of natural phenomenon the cycle of life and death, how to live life with "HA:" or breath.

The performing dancers of the group are reminded about the importance of humility, and hula is a lesson in patience and humility. The performers of Polynesian Fiafia are mindful of the importance of humility and sharing "HA" and "MANA" with those for whom they dance and perform. When dancing the hula, the dancer must be one with the dance. King David Kalakaua stated " Hula is the heartbeat of the Hawaiian people." The tradition continues and the base message to all is "Hold On To Your Culture."

## Polynesia-Pacifica Foundation of Colorado

Polynesia-Pacifica Foundation of Colorado is a non-profit organization founded in 1996 with the mission to preserve, promote and share the diverse and rich culture of Polynesia with residents of Colorado. Polynesia-Pacifica provides opportunities for the general public and for educational institutions to experience the culture, traditions, histories, music, arts, languages, food, and dances of Polynesia in a beautiful, enjoyable and positive way. Polynesia-Pacifica Foundation's goals are cultural enrichment, youth development, and education of the Coloradan community at large about the Polynesian culture through performances, workshops, arts and craft demonstrations, exhibits, and other cultural forms. PPFC not only provides the general public with a source of education and point of contact with the Polynesian culture, but also spreads cultural diversity awareness.

Helen Simms is the founder and Executive Director of the Polynesia-Pacifica Foundation of Colorado.

### Jr. Wahines Polynesian Dance Troupe

This dynamic group of young performers takes their audience through an exploration of native Polynesian dances that includes Hawaii, Tahiti, Samoa, Tonga, Cook Island and New Zealand. They entrance the crowd with authentic costumes and fast-moving Tahitian dance, followed by a very athletic execution of an ancient hula as well as the soft, gentle arm and hand movements of modern hula. An amazing feat of twirling a poi ball enthralls spectators through skill and precision. This well-applauded and professionally performed program showcases a true taste of diversity presented in a "talk-story" format that incorporates narration to provide a rich cultural context in which their audience can understand each island cultural showcase. The Jr. Wahines holds the distinction of being the only dance group in Colorado to showcase dances from six island cultures of the South Pacific.

## Pacific Pride and Island Hearts

Pacific Pride and Island Hearts is a non-profit organization. The association consists of the parents who help organize and support the goals of the group. The officers of the group are: Sandy Bodnar,

President, Carmen Duenas, Vice President, Relva Sami, Secretary and Vae Lefano, Treasurer.

The Pacific Island Dancers of Colorado Springs, Colorado have been performing for 14 years. Their goal is to help perpetuate the Pacific Island culture through their dances. They perform for private shows such birthdays, anniversaries, graduations, retirements, and weddings. Their goal is to share the feeling of Ohana (family) through their dances.

Every year they host a luau, dinner and a spectacular show. The performance includes various dances from Hawaii, Tahiti, Samoa, New Zealand, Fiji, Tonga, Guam, Rapa Nui and the Cook Islands. The costumes are authentic and handmade. Each island showcased is sure to catch your attention and mesmerize. At their luau, they have a special dedication to men and women of the Armed Forces, which is sure to bring a tear to your eyes. Ever since September 11th they have vowed to perform this dance until all our men and women are safely back home.

# FILM FESTIVALS

## AURORA ASIAN FILM FESTIVALS

## Asian Films: A Reflection of our Diverse Culture

The Annual Asian Film Festivals hosted by the Aurora Asian Pacific Community Partnership for several years reflected the varied and rich Asian cultures in the medium of films. This was started in 1998. Included were films from China, Hong Kong, Indonesia, Thailand, Tibet, Vietnam, India, The Philippines Korea and Japan. The festivals provided the audience with a window of opportunity to appreciate the richness of Asian Pacific cultures through the medium of film. These films mirrored the unique cultures, traditions, mores and idiosyncrasies of the Asian countries. The Film Festivals provided the stimulus for learning and understanding the differences among the peoples in the Asian Pacific regions.

Although Asians share a common value system such as respect for elders, strong family ties, strong desire for education, each home country is unique in itself. Some films depict historical influences and others reflect contemporary life in various home countries.

The 8th Aurora Asian Film Festival, for example, offered a variety of themes, settings and emotions as shown in 11 films produced by independent filmmakers representing eight Asian countries. Sample titles enjoyed by the audience included "Electric Shadows" from China,

"19 Revolutions" directed and produced by Sridhar Reddy, a Thornton, Colorado born writer, The Overture, from Thailand and the "Crying Ladies" from the Philippines.

The 10th Aurora Film Festival in 2007 culminated a grand effort to bring forth a cinematic journey to Asia and the Pacific Islands, allowing for the filmmakers' perspectives on the rich and diverse cultures of Asian/Pacific Islander and Asian Pacific American peoples. It was an educational process of discovering art, addressing current issues, looking at a 'moment in time' and being moved by that moment. Although the City of Aurora was highly supportive of the Festival, unfortunately, the Festival lost two other major sponsors and its partner, the Denver Film Society, due, not to any bad feelings or disappointments, but rather to a change in goals and priorities. The Partnership Steering Committee and the Festival's planning committee felt that it would be possible to continue to promote Asian film one film at a time throughout the year by collaborating with different film screenings as opportunities arise. The Aurora Asian/Pacific Community Partnership will hold a place on their web site for announcements of new screenings in the future at www.auroraasian.org.

# BOULDER ASIAN FILM FESTIVALS (BAFF)

The BAFF holds their annual Asian Film Festival in conjunction with the Boulder Asian Cultural Festival, which attracts 20,000 visitors on the Pearl Street Mall. They show a variety of entries (shorts, documentaries, features animations and screenplays) by Asian producers, directors, writers, including Asian characters, subjects, locations or motifs.

The Boulder Asian Cultural Festivals offer food, art performances from the Shaolin Hung Mai Kung Fu lion dancers, Denver Taiko and many other cultural demonstrations for young and old.

# Chapter 15

# ASIAN PACIFIC AMERICANS IN MEDIA

Asian and Pacific Americans have always had a complex relationship with the media. When early Asian immigrants were coming to American during the late 1800s and early 1900's, newspaper stories about them were comparatively rare, and those that were published depicted the immigrants in a very negative and stereotypical manner in order to justify their economic exploitation or to argue for their exclusion. In order to counter this lack of coverage and to improve communications within their own communities, Asian immigrants began to establish their own newspapers. In Colorado, the first Asian immigrant newspaper was the Denver Shimpo, which began publication in the Japanese American community in 1908. A long tradition of APA community news media continues today with the publication of several newspapers, magazines, and online media that are described in this chapter, including the Asian Pacific American Times, Colorado Chinese News, Asian Avenue magazine, Nikkeiview, and Asiaxpress.com. Coverage of APAs outside of community news media, for instance by the Denver Post and Rocky Mountain News, has improved over the years but still tends to be sporadic and newspaper stories occasionally depict APAs in an inaccurate manner.

Historically, films mostly portrayed Asians in Asia, often in a very negative and stereotypical manner. More recently, there have been better-quality films about Asians and a small number of feature-length motion pictures about APAs. Much of the latter is due to advocacy efforts by APAs and the increasing number of prominent APA actors and actresses, directors, screenwriters, and independent film production companies. In addition, over the past several decades, APAs have produced many documentary films about their history and communities. Feature-length films and documentaries are occasionally shown in Colorado theaters and have appeared annually at Asian film festivals organized by APAs in Boulder and Aurora. Also, over the years, a small handful of APA filmmakers have worked in Colorado.

The historic pattern of television coverage of APAs has mirrored that of film, except that, even today, there is little TV programming that deals with APAs and few APAs appear regularly on television, especially on prime-time shows. The major exceptions are APA journalists who anchor TV news broadcasts or work as news field reporters. Three such individuals in Colorado are featured in this chapter, Adele Arakawa, Christine Chang, and Raj Chohan. Local APA communities have responded to the lack of TV programming by creating Asian Public Media, which is described in this chapter.

Colorado Asian and Pacific Americans are aware of the critical role media plays in their lives as well as the lives of nonAPAs. They have been actively working to increase their media visibility.

This chapter begins with special interviews with the three Asian American TV anchors and an article on Mary Lee Chin, a nationally known nutrition and media consultant who has been involved in training media people and is an active spokesperson for many issues affecting APAs in Colorado. This is followed by a brief history of the Asian Pacific American Times, the primary inspiration for this book, a discussion of the 2002 APA Media Workshop, a landmark event which brought together for the first time some of the well-known APA journalists in metro Denver from print, television, and online media. The highlight of this workshop was the keynote speech of invited guest speaker, Victor Panichkul, then president of the Asian American Journalists Association. Wendy Chao, Gil Asakawa, Joe Nguyen and Chritina Yu Tai Guo, owners/editors/publishers of print and online media are also featured in this chapter, which concludes with an article on Asian Public Media of Colorado.

## Adele Arakawa

**(Photo credit: 9NEWS/Andy Schaeffer )**

Perhaps the most visible Asian American in Colorado is Adele Arakawa, who has been 9NEWS (KUSA-TV) anchor since 1993. Adele has been in broadcasting since 1974, starting first in radio and moving on to television in Knoxville, WTVK-TV in 1981. Adele's work took her and her family to Chicago in 1989, where she worked for CBS, WBBM-TV as anchor for the weekday evening newscasts.

In 1993, she moved to Denver where she has anchored the weekday evening newscasts at 9NEWS (KUSA-TV), since then. In a telephone interview with her for this book, Adele says radio and television broadcasting is a tough and competitive profession, where you learn to do almost everything in the field. When she started, she filled different roles including video photographer, reporter, producer, and news anchor. It's not as glamorous as many people think, nor the compensation that high. One must continue to work long hours and one may be on call to cover breaking news. Her advice to young APAs who want to enter this profession: get a degree in their area: business, education, political science, including law and medicine as they are all needed. In addition, one must be up-to-date with computers and all their upgrades. Journalism is useful as one will be asked to edit their scripts. Although there are tele-prompters in the studio, there are no scripts out in the field. One must know how to speak well and ad lib on the spot – another qualification for a TV anchor. Adele says she will be live at the Democratic National Convention in 2008.

She considers the question, on how to enhance visibility of APAs in Colorado, a tough question. Compared to Los Angeles or Chicago, where there is a large Asian population base, there are much less APAs in the television broadcasting field in Denver. APAs need to portray a positive image. Aside from the Colorado Dragon Boat Festival, APAs must break into business. The success of one individual is the success of the community.

She grew up in Hawaii and moved to Tennessee when she was six years old. Yes, she experienced being called "Nip" or "Jap" and other names when she was going to school but her mother told her to just ignore them as they are ignorant. She did ignore them and they did stop.

Adele attended Tennessee Tech University and later graduated from University of Tennessee, Knoxville.

With so much experience behind her, Adele has received numerous awards including five regional emmys in the Heartland Region NATAS awards, including three for best anchor. In 1997, the emmy was awarded for coverage of the Oklahoma City Bombing. In 1999, the recognition came for coverage of the Columbine shootings. Another emmy for best anchor was awarded in 2004. Additional emmys include Outstanding Newscast, and in the category of "Interview and Discussion" in 2001. She has also received a national 1st place award in 1991 for reporting from the Asian American Journalists Association. The report was a three-part series on the 50th anniversary of the bombing of Pearl Harbor.

Adele served as president of the Chicago chapter of the Asian American Journalists Association in 1992. She is a member of the Japanese American Citizens League, and the Japanese American Service Committee.

Arakawa is Adele's mother's maiden name, which she took as an air name in her teens. Adele's mother is of Japanese descent from Maui, Hawaii, Her grandparents are from Okinawa, Japan. Adele and her husband are avid golfers and are into racing cars. Adele and her husband celebrated their 30th anniversary in 2007. Their son, who is now 23, majored in journalism, following the footsteps of his Mom.
(Information taken from phone interview and from 9NEWS website with permission.)

## Christine Chang

Christine Chang, born in Taipei, Taiwan, moved to the United States when she was 8 years old. She grew up in Houma, Louisiana, a small town, where she started learning about the exciting life of reporting for a TV station. She credits her parents for allowing her to decide on her own career to follow. An only child, she did not have much contact with her relatives in Taiwan, but she was raised by loving, caring parents.

Christine graduated from Northwestern State University in Natchitoches, LA., specializing in broadcasting and photography. She began her career as a weekend anchor/reporter at 31LAX in Alexandria, LA. She then moved to Eugene, Oregon where she worked as a weekend anchor/reporter for KEZI-TV, after which she moved to Las Vegas where she was morning anchor/reporter of KINV-TV. In February, 2004, Christine joined 7NEWS, where she started as a weekend morning anchor/reporter progressing to Monday-Friday morning newscasts and some noontime assignments. She also has a series of special reports throughout the year. Her next series is on cancer research.

Her advice to young APAs aspiring to work in television news media is to have a passion to live, a true desire to learn what's going on around you and enjoy sharing this information with enthusiasm. To be in this profession, one must be well informed and be like a sponge and soak up information and be able to express this in a clear, interesting manner. Christine says her career is an adventure and a challenge, a sacrifice and to be on call 24/7. Behind all the perception of glamour and prestige, are years of work and moving around. She can count on her fingers on one hand, the few times she was able to spend Christmas with her family.

Since she came to Denver, Christine has been volunteering in many Asian community events, often serving as emcee for celebrations or anniversaries. She says she wants to share the love her mom and dad showered on her with the rest of the community, not just Asian. Quoting from an earlier interview with asiaXpress.com, Christine was really surprised about Denver's huge Asian-American population. "There are so many groups out there with different events throughout the year. It's not just the Chinese New Year. Definitely, I will take advantage of getting involved while I'm here. The more that you can get involved with different organizations and events, the more you can appreciate the community. This is one way for APAs to become more visible."

Among her Asian role models, she thinks Connie Chung is huge. "She really opened the door for a lot of Asian-American journalists to come in, especially as a woman. I've always admired her during her career. I've followed her all along. Ann Curry on the Today show, is another one," Christine notes, "Thank you again for considering me to be a part of your book. It's truly an honor, to say the least."

(Information taken from a phone interview and from asiaXpress.com with permission)

# Raj Chohan

Raj Chohan is an award winning general assignment reporter and the driving force behind CBS4's critically acclaimed news franchise "Reality Check." He also hosts KBDI's flagship public affairs roundtable "Colorado Inside Out."

Raj has been with CBS4 since 1998, after doing stints in Rockford, Illinois and Grand Rapids, Michigan. After arriving in Denver, Chohan quickly picked up the station's coverage of the JonBenet Ramsey murder investigation in which he broke several significant stories. He has also covered the Columbine shootings, the western wildfires, and the Ward Churchill controversy. Other distinctive stories include the execution of serial killer John Wayne Gacy in Illinois, and the story of a Michigan school teacher who was persecuted for being gay. Chohan's investigative work exposed two rival teachers who illegally used school records to undermine the gay teacher's career.

Chohan's reporting has won two regional Edward R. Murrow awards (2003, 2007) along with First Place reporting awards from the Colorado Broadcasters Association (2006) and the Michigan Associated Press (1997,1998). He has also received numerous Emmy nominations.

In 2007, Westword newspaper named Chohan one of Denver's Best TV Fact Checkers.

Raj notes – “My father came to the U.S. in the early 1960s. He met my mother, an American, and they were married. I was born in 1966. My sister was born in 1972. I grew up in suburban Chicago. While my father is an engineer, I decided to pursue a career outside of the "normal expectations" for an Indian son. Most of us grow up knowing there are two options: become a doctor or become an engineer. I chose something different. I was first exposed to journalism while writing for my highschool newspaper. I enjoyed the flexibility of the work and the variety of assignments. However, in college I chose to study art and music during my undergradute years. I also wrote music and performed in a rock band. While in graduate school I became curious again about journalism and took a job at a small radio station at my college where I reported and anchored weekend newscasts. After deciding that I would like to continue in journalism, I applied for a television photography/reporting job in Rockford Illinois. This was my first TV job.

Ultimately I joined the media because it was exciting and different. Periodically, this career has given me a front row seat to history. I have covered just about every kind of story imagineable.

I think we Asians generally do a good job of leading by example. There are stereotypes which most new immigrant groups face in the first generation or two. For Indians, these include pop culture caricatures of the convenient store owner, the hindu mystic, the technical geek, etc. These sterotypes will fade over time as we continue to set an example of hard work, good citizenship, and economic success. The American disposition recognizes the best in human potential. There is no other country on earth in which a person can start with so little, and yet achieve so much. Americans are ultimately good people, and I believe they are color blind when it comes to talent and merit. We should be proud of our accomplishments here and the wonderful opportunities this great nation has given us.”

# Mary Lee Chin

She is a nationally known nutrition and media consultant, spokesperson for nutrition and food corporations and for the American Dietetic Association, is a sought-after speaker. She consults the media regularly on significant and controversial health and food issues and nutrition trends. Her challenge is to help people attain the pleasures of eating well while making wise food choices using science-based and realistic information. Mary Lee serves on numerous Advisory Boards, Committees, and Commissions in Colorado. She is a recipient of Denver's "2007 Women of Distinction" Award from Girl Scouts of America-Mile High Chapter, and selected by Denver's 5280 Magazine as one of "22 to Watch in 2002." She also serves as an expert witness on food and health related issues in federal and legislative hearings. At the University of Colorado Health Sciences Center, Mary Lee was the clinical nutritionist for the Pediatric and Adolescent Clinic Outpatient Departments; Chief Dietitian at the Barbara Davis Center for Childhood Diabetes; and Clinical Instructor in the Departments of Nursing, Dentistry and Child Health Associate Programs.

Mary Lee volunteers as trainer for the Center for African American Health of the Metro Denver Black Churches Initiative and serves as the Cultural Education Chair of the Colorado Dragon Boat Festival. Mary Lee's numerous publications focus on the subjects of potential of media, marketing for dietetic professionals and plant biotechnology.

Born outside of Boston, Massachusetts., Mary Lee grew up very close to her family and she has carried on this tradition to her own two sons.

In her own words, Mary Lee expresses her thoughts on her Chinese heritage and American influences.

"I love being an American and sharing many traditions of my Chinese culture with our Anglo community of friends including celebrating holidays and introducing customs and traditions, such as Chinese New Year. This serves both as a point of pride for me, and an increase of understanding of another culture to our friends."

Mary notes, “I love to cook, and it is a gift I give my family and friends to serve my mother's classic dishes. I just submitted 10 of her recipes for inclusion in a new cookbook, The Asian Grandmother's Cookbook, due out on 2009.”

“I believe it is important to pass our culture and traditions down to our children, providing the opportunity for them to experience and take pride of their ethnic heritage. Lastly, and what Asian families seem to share across the board-- education, education, education!”

“APA culture provides me a richness and depth to my soul, shaping who I am, and how I interact with the world. It also is a gift that distinguishes me from the greater culture in which I do so much work, as it provides me an additional dimension of attitude and pride. I like being an Asian American as I believe that gives me the best of two worlds.

I was one of the original organizers of the Colorado Dragon Boat Festival. Frankly, it has been a source of immense satisfaction to work cooperatively with so many diverse Asian communities, have them learn about and respect each other’s cultures, as well as positively present our heritage to the greater community. In the process, they, as well as I, have established many new friendships across the diverse Asian ethnic community. This already has shown to be of value as we work cooperatively on issues and projects important to our community. Most recently I was appointed to the Denver Asian Pacific American Commission. In that capacity, I aim to enhance the quality of life and promote the welfare of our APA community especially those who are most in need.”

Mary believes that APAs, should enhance their visibility by no longer being silent, nor accepting or ignoring bad things that happen. They need to contradict their traditional characteristic of being the model minority--never complaining and just insulating ourselves with family and taking care of our own. “Instead we band together to become a stronger voice to change things for the betterment of our whole Asian American communities. Those among us who are reluctant to make noise (and that is fine--personalities are different and valued) provide support for the changes we want to accomplish.”

## Asian Pacific American Media Workshop

The Asian Pacific American Media Workshop, organized by the Governor’s Asian Pacific American Advisory Council (GAPAAC) was held at the Front Range Community College in Westminster, Colorado on August 4, 2002. Attended by around 60 participants, the workshop was financially sponsored by the Asian Roundtable of Colorado and

Coors with support from then Philippine/Asian American Times and some GAPAAC members

This workshop was presented as a result of the recommendations of the previous year's Asian Summit. The goal was to develop APA community leaders to work effectively with media representatives and policymakers so that media coverage will be fair, accurate and inclusive. Another goal was to promote dialog and collaboration between mainstream media and APA media in Denver and in local and national network. The workshop, as reflected by the enthusiasm and interest of the participants, made some headway towards realizing these goals. The authors consider this workshop very important as this was the first ever done with APA participation.

After Daniel Oh, GAPAAC Chair, welcomed the members and guests, Nestor Mercado, Media Workshop Chair and GAPAAC Media Relations Chair, acknowledged the sponsors, the contributors, and the members of the Workshop Committee who worked hard to make this event successful.

The five-hour intensive workshop started with warm-up mental and physical exercises led by Gil Asakawa and Erin Yoshimura as facilitators. These two wonderful people not only served as facilitators; they actually designed, created and facilitated the entire workshop.

Mary Lee Chin, Media Trainer, conducted the media training for community leaders to learn how to effectively do a broadcast interview, whether on TV or radio. She did sample interviews with Erin and later with Gil, gave a critique on how well they did, and then asked the participants to do their own interviews with each other. Having gone through 800 different TV and radio interviews so far, she insisted that she had to prepare for each one every time. It is the responsibility of the interviewee to be ready to repeat the message he or she needs to bring out, carefully and tactfully guiding the interviewer back to the main topic.

The second part of the workshop was a panel discussion focused on how Asian Americans should be portrayed in mainstream media. The panel was composed of Tillie Fong (Rocky Mountain News) Helen Hu (Denver Post) Christina Yao (Channel 4News), Victor Panichkul (President, Asian American Journalists Association), Tim Ryan (Channel 9News), Elnora M. Mercado (Philippine/Asian American Times) and Andy Vuong (Denver Post). Each presented their suggestions on how to contact media particularly on APA issues and concerns. The audience asked questions following the panel discussion.

Victor Panichkul's (Baltimore Sun and President of the Asian American Journalists Association) keynote address focused on the importance of APA media practitioners, as he urged young people to take journalism in college for they are the writers of the future.

## Victor Panichkul on Asian American Media Coverage

The following are excerpts from his keynote speech.

Quoting the mission of the Asian American Journalists Association (AAJA), Panichkul urged the future generation of Asian journalists to encourage APAs to enter the ranks of journalism; to work for fair and accurate coverage of APAs; to increase the number of APA journalists and news managers in the industry.

Panichkul said that newspapers and TV newscasts are supposed to reflect the communities that they cover. "When you watch TV news and read the newspaper, do you see news about you and people who look like you?" he asked. "Most often, you don't. What you see quite often is a misrepresentation of who you are – the negative stereotypes of Asian Americans. If you believe most of the media's portrayal of Asian Americans, you'd believe that we're foreigners who can't be trusted. That we're only concerned with making money, that Asian women are sex objects and that we don't make good leaders."

Media portrayal of people of color has a great impact on how those communities are viewed by the majority. By perpetuating stereotypes, the media continues to provide a distorted view of who we are as Asian Americans. With that distortion comes ignorance and ignorance breeds fear. Fear breeds hatred and hatred brings violence.

Panichkul lamented on the internment of thousands of Japanese Americans, many of whom were U.S. citizens during World War II. Very few papers debated the moral rightness of such action with the exception of one paper, the Bainbridge Review in Seattle.

To change things, he suggests: Speak with critical voice when the media uses a negative stereotype or when there are no stories about your community in the paper or newscast; meet with news directors, editors and even publishers and bring your criticism to the table.

## APA PRINT, TELEVISION AND ONLINE NEWS MEDIA IN COLORADO

This section introduces the various print, television and online news media in Colorado, which are owned, operated and staffed by APA journalists or writers. The first one is a brief history of the Asian Pacific American Times.

## ASIAN PACIFIC AMERICAN TIMES

(The Voice of Asian Pacific Americans in the Rockies)

The *Asian Pacific American Times*, a monthly newspaper, started in March, 1996 as Philippine American Times. After two years, the newspaper expanded to include news and activities about APAs in Colorado changing the title to Philippine/Asian American Times. In March 15, 2003, the management made a final change of the title to Asian Pacific American Times. Added was a Board of Advisers of prominent Asian community leaders, who gave expert advice on the contents for the paper.

Joseph "Noli" Lopez, APA Times CEO/Publisher, envisioned highlighting contributions of APAs in Colorado and as a vehicle in sharing APA diverse culture. At the helm was Nestor J. Mercado, the editor-in-chief. El-Dani Aguila, editorial cartoonist, drew cartoons appropriate to the topics of the editorials. Elnora M. Mercado, managing editor, had a myriad of duties, including covering APA organization activities, writing and reporting on them, as well as, actually preparing the paper for printing, while Connie Lopez, chief financial officer, took care of soliciting advertisements from businesses and collecting from advertisers and subscribers. Art/Literary/Lifestyle Editor, Maaria C. Panlilio, provided a variety of entertaining articles, which readers looked forward to every month, while, Rawley G. Soberano, Ph.D., Asian

Business and Economic Analyst, regularly contributed important and timely articles on Asian business developments both in the United States and abroad. George Yoshida, community reporter, faithfully attended APA events and reported on them with photos. Ret. Major Mary Ruth Yardley served as staff reporter during the first few years of the paper. Mary Rose McCourt, graphic artist, did the logos, graphics and overall layout of the paper in the early years, while Amanda Minoza, editorial assistant, helped edit texts before publication. John and Giselle Rushford, of LaRush.com were our website and service providers.

Over the years, APA Times endeavored to share Asian culture and values, including festivals celebrated by member organizations, covered activities of community leaders, featured Asian youth, supported local and worldwide causes, promoted Asian artists, reported triumphs and tragedies. In addition, APA Times regularly published national and Colorado State news briefs as they affected APAs. APA Times recognized the role of local advisory councils like the Denver Mayor's Asian Advisory Council and the Governor's Asian Pacific American Advisory Council.

The APA Times was awarded the 2003 Small Business of the Year Award by the Asian Chamber of Commerce for reporting issues important to emerging Asian communities. The APA Times was given the 2005 Martin Luther King, Jr. Award for Business and Social Responsibility.

Hon.Mark Udall, 2nd District Representative of Colorado, officially congratulated the newspaper's celebration of its 10th anniversary and officially published the event in the Congressional Record, Tuesday, March 7, 2006, vol. 152, no.28.

Nestor and Elnora Mercado retired after more than 10 years of service to the paper and to the community. As editors of APA Times, they are most grateful for the great opportunity to learn about APAs in Colorado and to meet leaders, members, business people, youth, as well as, officials of the State.

Authors with Denver Mayor John Hickenlooper and APA Times CEO/Publisher Joseph "Noli" Lopez

On the 10th anniversary celebration of APA Times, the management recognized the presence and support of the following dignitaries through the years: Denver Mayor John Hickenlooper and wife, Helen Thorpe, Lakewood Mayor and Mrs. Steve Burkholder, Secretary of State Mike Coffman and his mother, Aurora Mayor Ed Tauer, Richard Poole, representing Sen. Wayne Allard. In addition, grateful thanks are given to Mayor Paul and Kate Tauer for their heartfelt support for numerous APA activities through the years.

The following editors/owners of newspapers or online media are have struggled and worked hard to provide the community with local news about their activities, businesses, and news from the homeland in general. Each one of them emphasized the value of hard work in order to succeed at the same time, contributing and attending to the various APA social, humanitarian activities and events. Balancing between family, work and social activities can be very stressful; it is even more so when managing the newspaper business.

## Wendy Chao

**Publisher of Colorado Chinese News**

"It doesn't matter how smart you are, you have to work hard." Those were the words of advice, Wendy Chao constantly used to remind her daughter, Jocelyn, whenever she had the chance. Wendy followed her own advice when she came to to the U.S. in 1978 and definitely, it worked well for her. She is now the President/Owner of Colorado Chinese News. Through hard work and determination, Wendy and her husband, Frank, successfully built up the newspaper from a struggling business to become a thriving enterprise.

Colorado Chinese News, the largest Chinese newspaper in Colorado, is distributed free to businesses in 40 locations in Metro Denver and Colorado Springs. Starting with just Wendy and Frank, they now have several full and part time employees: a CPA, a Bookkeeper, two computer programmers, a news editor, an entertainment editor and a community editor, etc. The COCNews has steady advertisers from well-known corporations and small business enterprises in Colorado. They have also established connections with five sister papers: Ohio Chinese News, Michigan Chinese News, Dallas Chinese News, Arizona Chinese News and Saint Louis Chinese News. Sharing important, current news from various international sources is relevant to their customers.

Colorado Chinese News is the weekly source of information for more than 35,000 Chinese Americans in Colorado. Through more than 14 years, it has always been on time even during big snow storms, Wendy proudly states.

Wendy and Frank came from Taipei, Taiwan in 1978, with a definite goal to start a business in the United States. They first stayed in Canada for one year and later moved to Utah. There they tried the motel business. Unlike other immigrants who either came to look for work in the land of opportunity or as refugees from persecution in their home country, the Chaos brought their own capital ready to start a small business. They decided to buy and manage a motel called Prospector Lodge. Frank had a degree in Math from Taiwan and another business degree from Brigham Young University-Hawaii, which helped with their first start. They also became members of the Moab Lion's Club, where Frank became its vice-president. Social connections with prominent businessmen in this club further helped their business and assimilation to the American society. Furthermore, they did not have any problem since both already spoke English, although with an accent. Wendy had a degree in Chinese literature from National Normal University in Taiwan. She had taught in middle and junior high school. In 1983, Jocelyn was born and Wendy, following her Chinese custom, decided to stay home to take care of the baby. When Wendy's sister and brother-in-law, both professors at the University of Colorado in Boulder, persuaded them to move to Colorado, the Chaos sold their motel business and moved to Colorado.

In Boulder, Wendy and Frank started another life. Wendy's desire to help others led her to organize and establish the Boulder Chinese School, where she was the principal. This was later renamed Rocky Mountain Chinese School (RMCS), a small non-profit educational institution whose mission is teaching and sharing the Chinese language and cultural traditions of the Chinese-speaking world. Since 1985, they have educated more than a thousand children and adults in the Denver/Boulder area. Recently, hosted by the Front Range Community College in Broomfield, Colorado, they hold classes on Sunday afternoons. Wendy also founded the Denver Chinese Cultural Center of Colorado in 1991. Through all her efforts, Wendy Chao has become a bridge, a liaison from her world to the culture of other nations.

Wendy's main aim is to encourage second-generation immigrants from the Asian communities to become more active in politics and business in the U.S.

Her services to community organizations include: vice president Asian Round-table of Colorado, member Denver City Mayor's Asian Advisory Board, member National Chinese Community Newspaper Association, in the U.S., as founder and honorary president, president of the Chinese American Press Institute, member City of Lakewood Cultural Diversity and Human Relationship Committee, Colorado Asian Chamber of Commerce, as first and second term board member, Colorado Chinese Writer Association - founder and president, Denver Chinese Cultural Center, as its founder and president, Boulder Chinese School (Rocky Mountain Chinese school), and founder and principal of Southwest Improvement Council.

Wendy received numerous awards, such as: Excellent Service Award from Denver Baptists Organization (1991), Appreciation Award for outstanding contributions and services to children from Asian Education Advisory Council (1991); Outstanding Service and Contribution Award from Denver Chinese Culture Center (1992); Appreciation Award from Commission On Cultural Diversity and Human Relations, Lakewood; Colorado Small Business Administration's Minority Small Business Advocate of the 1997; Appreciation Award from Denver Chinese Culture Center (1998-1999); Outstanding Service Award from Colorado Chinese News Library (1999); The Denver Business Journal's Outstanding Woman in Business (2003); Wendy Chao Day from the Colorado State Government (2003); American Cancer Society Maida Awards (2002); Appreciation Award from Rocky Mountain Chinese School (2003); Girls Scouts and WB2 Gives Woman of Distinction (2005); Appreciation Award from Denver Chinese School (2005); Parents of Excellence Award from Colorado Parent's Day

Council and United States Congress (2005). As is evident, she has contributed a lot to APA society in Colorado.

## Gil Asakawa
### Editor, nikkeiview.com

Started as a weekly online column in 1998, Nikkeiview.com is the brainchild of Gil Asakawa, Japanese American, author, editor, artist and journalist. This website is the leading online voice representing contemporary Japanese American and trans-national Japanese popular culture and politics from a Japanese American perspectives.

Nikkei, a Japanese financial index based in Tokyo, also means people of Japanese descent residing outside Japan.

Gil is very well-informed and writes on a wide-range of topics from book reviews, technology, occupational hazards, patriotism, civil rights, role models, anime, entertainment, assimilation, separatism, more. Check his website and his archives, which are open to anyone who wants to learn about almost any topic under the sun.

Asakawa is author of the book, Being Japanese American (Stone Bridge Press June 2004), and co-author of The Toy Book, a history of baby-boom era toys (Knopf 1991). He has over 20 years of experience covering popular culture and the arts at-large -- as a music critic, feature writer and editor of a weekly arts and entertainment magazine. He has served as Content Editor for Digital City Denver, TRIP.com, and ServiceMagic.com, and Denver's TamTam.com. His writing has appeared in Denver Rocky Mountain News, Rolling Stone, Pulse, and Creem, among many others. In 2003, Asakawa became Executive Producer for Denver Post.

Also active in the Asian Pacific American Communities both in Colorado and nationally, he has contributed to the Colorado Dragon Boat Festival, served as a board member of the Aurora Asian/Pacific Community Partnership, and as the board chairman for the national newspaper of the Japanese American Citizens League.

*Asian Pacific American Times* published a series of his articles from nikkeiview.com, which had received many good comments from the readers for its universality of themes and appeal.

# Joseph Dinh Nguyen

**Editor-in-Chief**
**AsianXpress.com**

He is Editor-in-chief of an important online source of contemporary news, events and activities of APAs in metro-Denver - asiaXpress.com, is a Colorado-based online publication that covers the Asian-American community. It began in late 1998 when a number of young Asian-American professionals were fed up that the only press the Asian-American community was receiving was negative. At the time, only Asian gangs were being highlighted in the news while positive aspects were overlooked and ignored. AsiaXpress.com was created to tell these other stories. The publisher is Tod Nguyen and the assistant editors are Ashton Do and Monica Ly

When the site was launched in 1999, AsiaXpress.com relied heavily on the contribution of community members in order to showcase news and accomplishments. In 2007, there was a shift in the publication's editorial approach. Rather than relying on the community to produce content, the staff decided to go out and cover these stories themselves. The result was a more balanced style of storytelling. AsiaXpress.com also highlights other aspects such as profiles of various people, entertainment reviews and in-depth reports about cultural, political and social issues. The stories of the APA community are not all negative nor are they all positive. The pieces that are written are meant to show a balanced view of the APA community and not one that is skewed.

APA events are overlooked by the mainstream American media. Often the only stories that are told involve crime or those that emphasize culture. In entertainment, roles for APA actors are largely stereotypical with Asian characters often written to speak broken or no English at all. Men are largely open only to roles of martial artists, computer nerds or doctors, and rarely are they ever seen as a romantic interest. Women are exoticized and continued to be used as sexual objects and eye candy. Rarely are APA women portrayed as strong female characters.

In order to alleviate the drawbacks, we must start from within the community. As a member of the media, Joe feels that it is his responsibility to tell the stories that are ignored by the mainstream media.

The only way the APA community's stories will be told is if there are people to tell them. As for the entertainment industry, there has been a movement of young APA filmmakers who are changing the ways APAs are portrayed. The more support they receive, the more films they will be able to make. And with anything in Hollywood, money speaks. If there is enough support, eventually there will be more Asian faces shown in a wide variety of roles.

Joe Nguyen, a 2007 graduate from Metropolitan State College of Denver, major in journalism with news/editorial emphasis, has been receiving First Place, Society of Professional Journalists (SPJ) Region 9 Mark of Excellence award for Best Nondairy Newspaper from 2005-2007.

Joe was Design-editor, online editor and staff writer for the Metropolitan. He also covered and reported on events for the MetroWest Newspapers as an intern in Brighton, Colorado. He also is the Web and special sections editor for the Aurora Sentinel. With his experience both in writing, editing and website construction and maintenance, Joe is the perfect person to take complete charge of asiaXpress.com. Since 1999 to the present, Joe has been the writer, photographer, copy editor, Web developer and graphics designer. He is everywhere, covering events around the various Asian-American communities in Colorado. He is proficient in numerous software tools for web based publishing.

## Yu Tai "Christina" Guo

Christina came to the United States in 1987 from Taiwan. She graduated from Taiwan's Fu-Jen University, with a major in Mass Communication. She used to be an editor and reporter of an Asian magazine in Taiwan.

Her husband, Chwen-Geng, graduated from the University of Colorado at Denver with a Master's degree in engineering. They have two daughters and a son. Her older daughter, Jenny, 23 was a class valedictorian in high school and a recipient of the Boetcher Foundation scholarship. She graduated at the University of Colorado at Boulder, major in accounting and finished another degree in four years. She also holds an MBA degree in Finance from University of Colorado. Her second daughter, Annie is now 21 and is also a class valedictorian with a Bachelor of Arts degree in advertising and a Master's degree in Journalism from the University of Colorado at Boulder. Her son, Chun, graduated from the University of Colorado at Boulder, with a B.A. in Asian Studies. He is active in Asian social issues.

Christina wants to preserve strong family ties, respect for elders and helping one another. Growing up in Asia, family values are important to her. It is not unusual for three generations living together in one household in Taiwan. "We also take care of our parents," she said.

Aside from being editor and publisher of Asian Avenue Magazine, Christina was also a former president of the Chinese American Council of Colorado (CACC), where she introduced the Chinese Model Mother of the Year. This year, she added another award: Asian Model Mother of the Year, to include other Asians deserving the award. She has founded the Asian Avenue Magazine.

## Asian Avenue Magazine

The mission of *Asian Avenue Magazine* is to bridge Asian cultures with mainstream and other societies in Colorado. The English publication serves the mile-high area as an excellent resource for Asian culture, dining, businesses and community events.

The magazine's ultimate goal is to provide in-depth understanding and insights to the diverse Asian cultures, with sections that include travel to Asia, restaurant reviews, food culture, business features, and better living tips. The staff has been contacted by national companies interested in expanding their branches and relocating to Denver. *Asian Avenue Magazine* provides these companies with a glimpse of Asian lifestyles in Colorado that may influence their decisions to expand to the mile-high market. Christina hopes in the future the magazine will attract more large companies to Denver; thereby increasing job opportunities and improving Colorado's economy.

The magazine's readers are diverse with an even mix of Asians and those from the American mainstream populations. The feedback received from both in- and out-of-state readers, subscribers, and community organizations have been very positive. Readers are impressed with the content, layout and design of the well-structured publication. Many fans ask if the publication will eventually go national. But the magazine is still in its early stages and there is still a long way to go. Christina is excited to see where the magazine takes off in the future. But before thinking too far ahead, the magazine will remain a monthly local publication with a circulation of 10,000 magazines at more than 550 locations, dedicated to adding “a new mix to life” for mile-high readers.

## The Asian Public Media of Colorado and Denver TV channels

Stella Yu tells of her role in the organization of the Asian Public Media of Colorado and why this project is so important: “When Denver Community Television (DCTV) closed its operations in late 2004, I was aware of the different organizations that proposed to continue its operations. Among them was a small nonprofit group called DeProduction. I have worked with DeProduction on various youth education programs and was aware of their integrity and their mission of empowering the community with public access through the power of media. DeProduction subsequently was awarded the contract to manage the public TV Channels 57 and 58, and launched Denver Open Media (DOM) and to offer opportunities for communities to have a public voice in a normally elite, expensive and primarily privately controlled media. I saw DOM as an excellent opportunity for the APA community of Colorado to gain visibility; promote understanding between Asians and non-Asians and among our diverse Asian ethnic groups and an excellent way to involve our younger generation in society affairs. Fran Campbell, Kit Williams, Karen Nakandakare, Jericho Javier and I became the founding members of the Asian Public Media of Colorado.”

Tony Shawcross of Denver Open Media/Deproduction, Frances Campbell and Jerico Javier, then co-chairs of Denver Mayor’s Asian Advisory Council introduced the Asian Public Media of Colorado during the 10th Anniversary celebration of the Asian Pacific American Times on March 25, 2006. It is a goal to establish an effective use of media to increase the visibility, outreach and recognition of the Asian Pacific American communities of Colorado. Today, Asian Public Media of Colorado produces "Colorado Asian Today" - the only local television program featuring the issues important to the APA community in the Metro Area. This program is produced in collaboration with APA print and web publications at the Denver Open Media studio and televised on cable access in both Denver and Aurora. The program is supported in part by the Office of the Mayor of Denver, the Denver Asian Pacific

Advisory Commission, the Agency for Human Rights and Community Relations, and the Asian Roundtable of Colorado. Among the first programs shown were: Aya Medrud and Marge Taniwaki on their experiences during WWII at the internment camp and interviews with Filipino Americans in support FilVets bill pending in Congress.

# Chapter 16

# ASIAN PACIFIC AMERICAN CELEBRATIONS AND FESTIVALS IN COLORADO

Celebrations and festivals provide an important perspective on the lives of Asian and Pacific Americans. They showcase the vibrant, rich, and diverse cultures of APAs and provide them with an opportunity to revel in their heritage. They also provide an excellent opportunity for cultural sharing which helps to promote harmony and understanding with other segments of American society. Most APA celebrations and festivals are based on cultural traditions in Asia with origins going back several centuries that were brought to America by Asian immigrants. On the whole, APA celebrations and festivities are very colorful and quite entertaining. They add much to the vibrant multicultural atmosphere of Colorado.

Every year, two major APA cultural celebrations are held that are attended by representatives from the various APA groups in Colorado and the general public: the Asian Pacific American Heritage Month in May and the Colorado Dragon Boat Festival in July. The Colorado Dragon Boat Festival is featured in the chapter on APA Organizations in Colorado. Each Asian Pacific American community also commemorates their own special events. Thus, almost every month, something special is going on metro Denver.

## The Asian Pacific American Heritage Month

The Congress of the United States, by Public Law 102-450 as amended, has designated the month of May of each year as "Asian Pacific American Heritage Month to honor the achievements of Asian Pacific Americans.

President George W. Bush, in his last proclamation, stated, "I call upon our citizens to learn more about the history of Asian Pacific Americans and how they have contributed so much to our national heritage and culture." Furthermore "we also recognize millions of Asian Pacific Americans whose love of family, hard work and community have helped us as a people and sustain us as a nation."

The Asian Roundtable of Colorado (ARC), the umbrella organization of APA organizations, has taken charge of the Asian heritage month yearly celebration. The event is usually supported by various sponsors such as Asian banks, stakeholders and businesses. In the past few years one such sponsor has been the Wells Fargo Bank N.A. Several ethnic organizations are assigned to present cultural performances while other groups and Asian restaurants donate delicious cuisine for the audience. This is also the occasion to thank the various corporate sponsors who have been supporting the ARC and its partner organizations. ARC also started to give scholarship awards to deserving students, encouraging the awardees and other Asian students to work hard to qualify for the grants.

**The Filipino American Community of Colorado "Mano Po Singers" sang the U.S. National Anthem, the Philippine National Anthem and a medley of Filipino folk songs during one of the Asian Pacific American Heritage Month celebrations in May**.

The ARC honors numerous APA individuals involved in media and journalism during the annual Asian Pacific Heritage Month celebrations. They also invite Asian TV anchors to serve as masters of ceremony for the event, making the occasion more special and lively.

## The Shaolin Hung Mei Kung Fu Association (SHMKF) and Howie Solow – The Man behind the Lion and Dragon Dances

He is always there during Asian cultural events – Chinese New Year celebrations, Dragon Boat Festivals, Asian Film Festivals, etc., but you hardly see him. He is the one beating the drums during the huge Lion dances or when the Giant Dragon slithers during parades. **Howie Solow** is the man during the opening of Asian and Chinese events. He looks very young, but when he told me he has been doing this for the last 35 years. He must have been only five years old when he started.

Howie visits Taiwan or China at least once a year for business or Kung Fu related activities. Although he feels he knows all he can about Kung Fu, he knows there are other systems to learn, new masters to meet, new things to be shared from his colleagues in these two countries.

Actually, Howie brought the Shaolin Hung Mei Kung Fu Association (SHMKF) to Boulder, Colorado. This organization teaches the history, philosophies, theories, culture, and techniques of the traditional martial arts of Shaolin Hung Mei Kung Fu. The Academy of Chinese Martial and Cultural Arts was founded and is managed by the Shaolin Hung Mei Kung Fu Association. The Academy appeals not only to the Chinese community, but to all communities in the Boulder/Denver region in Colorado. Regularly scheduled classes in Shaolin Hung Mei Kung Fu, Dragon and Lion performance training, Tai Chi, Qi Gong, and traditional Chinese folk dance are offered at the Academy. The Academy also sponsors/hosts demonstrations, exhibitions, seminars, and workshops.

Howie teaches four Kung Fu classes a week, two hours each, in addition to special classes for seniors. He also writes grants to continue receiving funding from SCFD and other sources. He counted around 50 performances a year for which they receive fees, but most participants are volunteers. Wow! Just watching Howie beat the drums during Dragon or Lion Dances makes one feel physically exhausted, but his dedication and commitment to this type of livelihood make it all worthwhile, even enjoyable.

## Boulder Asian Cultural Festival (BAPA)

The ever-popular Boulder Asian Cultural Festival attracts 20,000 visitors or more and is held on the Pearl Street Mall every year. This annual event offers multi-ethnic food for purchase, art displays, and performing arts along with other cultural demonstrations for young and old. Participation for various APA organizations is increasing and becoming more enthusiastic. In the past it has attracted reputable performers such as: Ayame Minyo Kai, Rocky Mountain Polynesian group, performers from the Boulder Yullin Korean Church, Yoko Hiraoka Japanese Music Ensemble, Julia Misawa, Boulder Taiko, HIBIKI, Denver Taiko and others.

The Boulder Asian Pacific Alliance (BAPA) is a grassroots coalition of representatives from the diverse Asian Pacific populations, the second largest minority group in the city and county of Boulder. We came together in early 1994 in order to become a more active part of the Boulder community and to impact social change. BAPA represents Hmong, Laotian, Cambodian, Vietnamese, Korean, Chinese, Japanese, Filipino, Malaysian, Indian, Thai, Nepalese and other groups of Asian Pacific background.

## Gateway to the Rockies Parade / Festival International

The Gateway to the Rockies Parade was celebrated annually in Aurora for decades and participants included various Aurora businesses and cultures, including many APA organizations. The Aurora Asian/Pacific Community Partnership entered an Asian-themed float in the parade annually, winning many trophies for its cultural themes and creativity. APAs in colorful costumes on floats or on foot helped make this annual event a festive occasion. The parade would wind its way through downtown Aurora, ending at historic Colfax Avenue, where judges waited to make their decisions. Festival International is now produced in place of the parade, held in mid-September, and APA cultures are featured at this newer expanded event.

## Cherry Blossom Festival

The Tri-state/Denver Buddhist Temple is primarily responsible for organizing the Annual Cherry Blossom Festival in Colorado. This unique festival attracts thousands of people every year in celebration of Japanese American heritage. Next only to the Colorado Dragon Boat Festival, this is one of the highly attended festivals in Metro Denver that has been embraced by the mainstream population in the city.

In 1916, the Tri-State Buddhist Temples' headquarters was formed. The organization was incorporated as the Denver Buddhist Church because of its Denver location, but it serves Buddhists in the tri-state area of Colorado, Nebraska, and Wyoming. The first headquarter, was at 1942 Market Street. Many Japanese immigrants to the United States came from areas where Jodo Shinshu Buddhism was strong.

Held each year since 1972, the festival celebrates the Japanese American (JA) heritage and culture of the Denver residents through live entertainment, music and dance, food and drink, cultural demonstrations and an Asian arts and crafts marketplace. The fun culminates Saturday night with the traditional Obon street dance on Lawrence Street amidst Denver's downtown cityscape.

For a taste of Japanese cuisine, there is a huge hall where people gather to enjoy authentic shushi, teriyaki chicken, and more.

Crowd pleasers include the Denver Taiko's rousing drum performances and the Japanese dances, koto and martial arts, Tri-State/Denver Buddhist Temple house, the ikebana exhibits and bonsai demonstrations, tea ceremony and calligraphy.

Although the Cherry Blossom Festival raises funds for the Tri-State/Denver Buddhist Temple's programs and operations, it relies on help from volunteers and members.

**The Denver Taiko in performance**

## Chinese Lunar New Year

The Chinese Lunar New Year takes place in January or February, depending on the Chinese lunar calendar. Each year is named after an animal: Rat, Ox, Tiger, Rabbit, Dragon, Snake, Horse, Ram, Monkey, Rooster, Dog and Pig. People born in a particular year are believed to share some of the personalities of that particular animal.

Preparations begins a month before the date of the Chinese New Year, when people start buying presents, decoration materials, food and clothing. A huge clean-up gets underway to sweep away any traces of bad luck and doors and windows are decorated with paper cuts with themes such as happiness, wealth and longevity. The eve of the New Year starts with dinner of seafood and dumplings for good luck and prosperity.

It's usual to wear something red to ward off evil spirits. After dinner, the family plays cards, board games or watch TV. At midnight, the sky is lit up by fireworks. On New Year's Day, all Chinese children have new clothes to wear. Parents and elders give their traditional gift of "lucky money" in red and gold envelopes. One of the most popular performances is the lion dance, which is full of energy and movement as the performers skip, march and dance to the beat of the drum and cymbals. Together they frighten away the evil.

Chinese Lunar New Year celebration

## Double Tenth Celebrations in Denver

The Double Ten National Day commemorates the October 10, 1911 revolution, which led to the overthrow of the Qing dynasty and establishment of the Republic of China (ROC) in Taiwan. In Denver, the Chinese American community celebrate the anniversary of this event every year usually in October, thus the double tenth (10-10) and lasts from one to three days.

Proclamations and greetings from various Colorado and Denver government officials are published on the program-book and/or read by their official representatives.

## Filipino Festivals

In the Philippines, considered the "only Christian country in Southeast Asia," predominantly Catholic Filipinos, rejoice in the birth of Jesus Christ, the Prince of Peace during the Christmas season (December 16-25). The celebration starts with early mass (*mesa aguinaldo*) followed by breakfast, ending with the opening of presents on Christmas day. Actually, the Christmas season lasts till January 6, the Feast of the Three Kings. Some Filipino American families carry on the traditional Christmas celebration by attending midnight mass, followed by a "Noche

Buena" or an evening meal of Filipino delicacies.

Other religious festivals celebrated by Filipino Americans in the country include the Feast of the Santo Nino (Infant Jesus) in January and the Santa Cruzan in May. Both festivals have been celebrated by members of the Bayanihan Society of the Queen of Peace Catholic Church in Aurora.

The Feast of the Santo Nino is held usually on the last Saturday of January with a mass, followed by a potluck dinner and a "Sinulog," the dance of petition and thanksgiving. Attendees, mostly from Cebu, bring their statues of the Infant Jesus for the yearly blessing and to participate in the "Sinulog." The Santo Nino is one of the patron saints in the Philippines. Both a religious and a cultural event, it celebrates the Christianization of the Philippines, which started when Magellan landed in Cebu in 1521 and planted the cross to claim the country for the King of Spain.

The Santa Cruzan, another religious festival held yearly by Filipino Americans in the Queen of Peace Church, commemorates the finding of the Holy Cross by St. Helena, mother of Emperor Constantine. The event starts with a mass followed by a procession of "sagalas" (young ladies) dressed in beautiful gowns. The main character is St. Helena with a young boy to represent Emperor Constantine. The procession ends in church, after which, participants and guests gather for a potluck dinner in the church hall.

The Filipino American Community of Colorado celebrates annually the independence of the Philippines from Spain every June 12th (or on the second Saturday of June). Special guest speakers are invited to talk about the importance of the historical event to remind Filipino Americans of the significance of freedom from a foreign rule. Live entertainment, cultural performances, booths of arts and crafts, and Filipino cuisine are the special features of the whole-day celebration. Every year since 1995, attendance gets bigger and merrier.

## Hmong New Year

The Hmong people in Colorado celebrate their New Year during Thanksgiving, in November, because of their busy schedule and lifestyle during the year. They hold their celebrations at the Adams County Fairgrounds and feature cultural shows; fashion show, talent show, live music, food and crafts. There are three important aspects of the Hmong New Year Festival. The first one is the religious ritual, which must be observed. The second is the mating game, which goes on among the young people and the last one is the display of wealth.

Hmong people believe in a wide variety of spirits, both good and bad. These religious rituals include Sweeping the House, Magic Rope Nkaum Taw Qaib, Calling Home the Spirits, Household Spirit, and Honoring the Ancestors.

The mating game includes sports like Kato, soccer, volleyball, topspin, tossing ball, talent and culture shows. This is the time for young people to find their mates as they have been working all year round and have not had time for courtship. Young people usually get married after the New Year. Hmongs are proud of their wealth of culture. During the New Year celebration, the women wear their newest native costume and jewelry. The men usually hold a feast and invite their relatives and friends.

## Diwali --Asian Indian Festival

Of all the festivals celebrated in India, Diwali is the most glamorous and best celebrated. Homes are decorated with lighted lamps to create a magical atmosphere of joy and festivity. And every year, in the fall, the Indian community of Colorado joins together for this grand celebration. Good food, clothes, dances and meeting friends are the highlights of this celebration. Exchanging sweets and presents, lighting candles or oil lamps, are just a few of the salient features of this Indian celebration.

Diwali (pronounced Divalee) known as the "Festival of Lights", is a contraction of the full Sanskrit name Deepvali (Deepa, meaning light and Avali meaning a row of lights). It originally commemorated the homecoming of Lord Rama (an ancient ruler who later was believed to have been divine) after seven years of absence from his home and warfare against his enemies and his subsequent coronation as King.

The first day of Diwali is Dhanteras or Dantraydashi (Dhan means wealth) and is devoted to Lakshmi, the goddess of wealth and prosperity. The second day, Choti Diwali (little Diwali) is devoted to devotion of Kali Chaudash, the dark-skinned goddess. The third day is Diwali itself with gifts and treats for children, visits to family and friends and business people. Workers honor their tools of trade. The fourth day is New Year's Day in the Hindu calendar. In India, Diwali is seen as a time of renewal of life. Old oil lamps are thrown out and new ones are purchased to be lighted. People wear their best clothes or buy new ones and houses are decorated with flowers. Traditionally, Hindus would visit the temple before eating and celebrating, and the children are given presents and fire-crackers. The celebration of Diwali varies throughout India because it has been adapted to regional beliefs.

In Colorado, Diwali is celebrated by the religios places such as the Hindu Temple of the Rockies and Hare Krishna Temple. It is also celebrated by the India Association of Colorado, India Association of Northern Colorado and Indians living in Colorado Springs.

# TET -- Vietnamese Lunar New Year

Tet Nguyen Dan or Tet is the Vietnamese Lunar New Year festival. It began thousands of years ago with joyous feasts and ceremonies celebrating the return of spring. On Tet, people visit pagodas and churches to pray for good fortune and happiness. Officially, lasting only three days, the celebration of Tet can cover more than a week of feasting, parades, dances and games. Children who have been good are rewarded by gifts of money in red envelopes, known as "li-xi". Fireworks are set off to scare away evil spirits and colorful lions and dragon dances can be found in the streets.

People abstain from sweeping the floor during Tet for fear of sweeping away good luck. In the belief that the first day of the New Year will set the course of the next 12 months, people eat large feasts to assure that they will eat as well throughout the year. Since the family is the focal point of Vietnamese life, everyone visits their extended family members and friends.

Tet is also the time to honor and pay homage to their Vietnamese ancestors. They light candles and offer food on altars set up in their homes or in public. Designated members of the community, usually the elders, recite prayers. The Vietnamese honor their dead relatives regularly, especially on the anniversary of their deaths. They believe that the spirit of their ancestors will help them achieve success in life, in school or in business.

# Chapter 17

# JAPANESE AMERICAN DAY OF REMEMBRANCE

During World War II on February 19, 1942, President Franklin Delano Roosevelt signed Executive Order 9066. This gave the U.S. military the authorization to remove, from their homes and communities, nearly 120,000 Japanese Americans living in California, Oregon, Washington, and Arizona. These Japanese Americans were imprisoned in a number of locations including ten concentration camps located in California, Idaho, Arizona, Utah, Wyoming, Arkansas, and Colorado The removal and incarceration of Japanese Americans was done in complete violation of their constitutional rights and is widely regarded to be an act of racism.

These actions against Japanese Americans were supported by the politicians of that era. A notable exception was Colorado Governor Ralph L. Carr who stood virtually alone among public officials in his opposition to the persecution of Japanese Americans and their internment in concentration camps. Carr's actions cost him his political career. In recognition of his political courage, Japanese Americans erected a monument to honor Governor Carr in Denver's Sakura Square. In 1996, the Colorado General Assembly passed a resolution honoring Carr for his efforts to protect Americans of Japanese descent during World War II. Carr's life is described in a new book, *The Principled Politician: The Ralph Carr Story*, by Adam Schrager.

The World War II Japanese American concentration camp in Colorado was located just outside the town of Granada and was known as Amache. Like other concentration camps, Amache was enclosed by barbed wire fences and guarded by armed soldiers. Yamamoto Ichihashi, former history professor at Stanford University who was interned at Amache from 1943-1945, described the place as a "desolate prairie, only sagebrush, cactus and Russian thistle survived the winter snow and the hot summer sun." Amache is the subject of a recent book-length study by Robert Harvey entitled *Amache: The Story of Japanese American Internment in Colorado During World War II.*

In spite of their treatment during World War II, U.S. citizens of Japanese ancestry joined the military and fought with great distinction in Europe and the Pacific. George T. "Joe" Sakato, now living in Colorado, was honored with the Congressional Medal of Honor. Thirty-one young men from Amache died fighting for their country.

Japanese Americans in Colorado remember their World War II experiences through annual community pilgrimages to the site of the former concentration camp at Amache, which has been designated a National Historic Landmark. Also each February, around the day President Roosevelt signed Executive Order 9066, Japanese Americans in Colorado and across the nation hold Day of Remembrance ceremonies. The 2006 Denver Day of Remembrance featured the screening of *Within the Silence,* written by Ken Mochizuki. Alison Hiroto, a professional actress narrated and dramatized a play about a family stressed and traumatized by their wartime experiences. It followed the chronological screened account of life in a concentration camp: arrival at the camp; settling in crowded, cramped spaces; families trying to normalize their lives as much as possible; support for men serving in the military; the closing of the camp. Following this screening, Alison led discussion groups.

Everyone needs to remember and share the lessons of the past so that they will never happen again. Executive Order 9066 changed the lives of Japanese Americans who were imprisoned under primitive and harsh conditions. This act of racial injustice demonstrates the need to be constantly vigilant in protecting basic rights guaranteed under the U.S. Constitution.

This chapter features three prominent Colorado Japanese Americans who were incarcerated during World War II, Bill Hosokawa, Minoru Yasui and Aya Medrud. The stories of Bill Hosokawa and Min Yasui are told through reprinted articles. Aya Medrud was interviewed for this book. Marge Taniwaki and Carolyn Takashita, both young girls during the internment period, tell their stories in their own words.

The following article about Bill Hosokawa, a Japanese internment camp survivor, is provided by Joe Nguyen.

## Bill Hosokawa: Former Denver Post Editor, Internment Camp Survivor Leaves Legacy

Bill Hosokawa was a Japanese internment camp survivor, a pioneer for Asian American journalists, and for 60 years, a member of Denver's community. Hosokawa died of natural causes on Nov. 9, 2007 in Sequim, Wash. where he lived with his daughter. He was 92. "Bill Hosokawa was a giant in the Japanese-American community because of his books and decades of writing in JA publications," said Gil Asakawa, director of content for Examiner.com. "But he was also a giant in the larger Asian Pacific American community. He was the highest-level Asian American in journalism and helped serve as a role model for many of us."

Hosokawa wrote seven books and co-wrote two others. He was Denver's honorary Japanese consul for 25 years. And for 38 years, he worked for The Denver Post as a reporter, editor and columnist. It was a career he said he loved, but it had a rocky start. In an interview with the Maynard Institute, he said he dreamt of becoming a journalist as a boy in Seattle. But while in college, he discovered the harsh reality when his classmates went to newspapers to work during Christmas break. Hosokawa, however, wasn't allowed to go. "It was very obvious that if Bill Hosokawa, the Asian American, and Jack Armstrong, the All-American-Boy, went to apply for the same job – and we had identical qualifications – that I wasn't going to get the job," he said in an interview with the Maynard Institute.

When he graduated in 1937, he had to travel overseas to find a job, working for the *Singapore Herald* and *Shanghai Times.* In October 1941, he returned to the U.S. to be with his wife. It was five weeks before the Japanese attack on Pearl Harbor.

"In the eyes of the government, I was not a native-born American citizen — I was an enemy alien," he said in an interview. "Why? Because my parents were born in Japan, a country with which we were at war."

Seven months later, Hosokawa and his family – and thousands of other Japanese Americans – were sent to Camp Harmony in Puyallup, Wash. before being moved to Heart Mountain, Wyo. There, he began publishing an eight-page weekly called *The Heart Mountain Sentinel.*

After leaving the camp, he found work at *The Des Moines*

*Register* in Iowa on the copy desk. In 1946, Hosokawa returned west and found work with *The Denver Post* where he climbed the ranks to become the editorial page editor, the highest-ranking position of any Asian American journalist during his time.

"Bill Hosokawa was ever the gentleman, and unusually calm for a newspaper editor," said Fred Brown, retired Capitol Bureau chief for *The Denver Post*. "His wit was often sharp, and his language could be quite sharp sometimes, but he never raised his voice or an eyebrow. And he was a multitasker before the word was even invented."

After "retiring" in 1984, he became the readers' representative for the *Rocky Mountain News*. But Hosokawa never truly retired, he just pursued new opportunities.

"If there's any lesson, it's that the opportunity is there if you are prepared to seize it," he said in an interview. "You have to be qualified. You have to have an education. But if you have the stuff to make good with, the opportunity is there."

## Minoru Yasui

**"We are all put into this earth to leave it a better place for our having been here."**

The late Minoru Yasui was a community leader dedicated to improving the quality of life for all people. Educated as an attorney, Minoru Yasui served as the executive director of the Denver Commission on Community Relations for 16 years and was a champion of civil rights. It was during his tenure that he introduced the monthly recognition of volunteers who devoted time to helping others. The vital work of volunteers throughout the Denver metropolitan community is recognized through the Minoru Yasui Community Volunteer Award.

Minoru was born on October 19, 1916, in Hood River, Oregon. His parents, Masuo and Shidzuyo Yasui, were first generation Japanese. He attended school in Hood River and graduated as a valedictorian from high school in 1933. He was the first Japanese American graduate of the University Of Oregon School Of Law and he graduated with honors. After graduation, he was unable to find employment in Oregon. He moved to Chicago and worked as a consular attaché for the Consulate General of Japan. Immediately following the bombing of Pearl Harbor by Japan on December 7, 1941, he resigned his position with the Consulate and returned to Oregon, where he volunteered for the U.S. Army but he was not accepted because of his ancestry. Minoru Yasui was the first person to test in court the constitutionality of the internment of 120,000 Japanese Americans solely because of their ancestry. He later was interned at a concentration camp in Idaho called Minidoka.

After the war, he began his law practice in Colorado with his brother-in-law, Toshio Ando. In 1945, a bill was introduced in the Colorado General Assembly to prohibit aliens from owning land. It was clear that the intent of this bill was to keep Japanese aliens from resettling in Colorado and purchasing land. At a time when anti-Japanese sentiment was strong, Minoru or Min spoke vigorously against this piece of legislation at personal risk to himself. Min also lobbied for passage of the McCarran-Walter Act of 1952, which removed the prohibition on Japanese aliens applying for U.S. citizenship.

Min was active with the JACL Mile-Hi Chapter, and a founding member and board member of the Urban League of Denver, a group dedicated to addressing issues of concern to the African American community. He assisted in founding the Latin American Research and Service Agency (LARASA). In addition, Min helped organize Denver Native Americans United. He vehemently believed that the U.S. government needed to acknowledge the wrong that had been committed against the Japanese Americans during World War II and pay reparations for the economic losses suffered by those forcibly relocated and incarcerated. However, Min died in 1986 before seeing the culmination of his hard work by the enactment of the Civil Liberties Act of 1988, providing redress, reparation, and an official apology from the government.

## Mariagnes Aya Uenishi Medrud

Now a retired schoolteacher, Aya continues her volunteer work with more passion than ever. "She never stops," says husband "Med" Medrud, also now retired. It seems her greatest enjoyment is in helping others. Suffering from arthritis on her knees, causing pain when she walks, Aya still drives all over town to attend meetings, even as far as South Dakota to teach art to students of the Oglala Tribe of the Lakota.

Mariagnes prefers to be called Aya now that she is a practicing Quaker. Aya means love and affection in Japanese. Born on April 9, 1925 in Malden, Washington, 40 miles south of Spokane, Aya is the oldest of three children. She had a younger sister and a brother. Her father and grandfather were Japanese immigrants who worked on the railroad during the late 1900s and early 1920s. When her grandfather suffered a paralyzing stroke, he returned to Japan and Aya's family moved to Seattle where she studied in a Catholic School.

After World War II broke out in December 7, 1941, Aya's life was turned upside-down. Because she is of Japanese descent, she was one of those interned in concentration camps in the U.S. On February 19, 1942 President Franklin D. Roosevelt signed. Executive Order 9066, authorized the U.S. Army to evacuate all persons of Japanese Americans from coastal regions to be "interned" inland. Aya tells her story, how her family suffered during WWII and how this experience started to shape the philosophy of her life. The FBI came in the middle of the night and ransacked their house and arrested her father like a criminal. They would not see him for more than 2 years. Before he left, he charged her to take care of her mother and 2 siblings. An obedient daughter, she followed her father's orders. Her mother did not know how to cope, did not speak English and was hysterical most of the time, so Aya took care of all of them.

They were taken by train to Pullyap fairgrounds where her family and hundreds of other Japanese Americans lived in horse stalls on dirt floors under a grandstand. They slept on straw mats for some time. Later, under military guard, they were off again by train to a place called Minidoka, near Jerome, Idaho. There, they were housed in army-style barracks. All four of them lived in a 20' x 20' room. She said there were about 10,000 of them in that camp, where they ate in a mess hall and took showers in a communal bathroom in another building. That was their life from May 1942 to December, 1944.

Recalling how she felt, Aya said she felt depressed. "Psychologically, it was a difficult time for all of us." There were no books to read, no library to visit, no school for some months.

She does not remember writing letters to the President, to the Attorney General, FBI, to Herbert Edgar Hoover, and to lawyers appealing for the release of her father. However, from the National Archives, she has retrieved some of her letters in her own handwriting as proof that she wrote them. She must have some help and encouragement from a mentor. She tries to recall who could that be? Could it be my grade school teacher, Mr. Victor Vincent McLaughlin? Did he give her stationery and stamps to mail them? How she wishes she could have thanked him.

She also just recently learned that her grandfather, uncle and father had registered in 1918 in the U.S. military service. They were willing to serve in WWI. "Why didn't the FBI look into this and consider my father a loyal American?" Aya answered herself, "Perhaps they did not know that since they did not have good records or online access to information."

All she knew was that her father was moved around during the war. When his letters came, they were postmarked from different states (from North Dakota, Montana, Louisiana, Texas, Arizona, etc.). The last one was from Kooskia, Idaho, where he had volunteered for a road project. During the war, they built the transcontinental U.S. Highway 12 going through that beautiful part of Idaho. Her father was finally released in June 1944 and she remembers how joyful the reunion was! Although they were crowded in their small room, Aya remembers putting up a curtain for her parent's privacy.

In December 1944, her father found a job as an all-purpose man, driver and maintenance person in a Catholic orphanage. As a family, they were allowed to move to Utica, N.Y., where her sister and brother continued their studies. In the meantime, she had completed her high school. She later studied fashion design in Traphagen School of Design in New York. She worked as a medical secretary at Mount Sinai Hospital to support herself. Instead of following her chosen career as a fashion designer, she decided to go to Tokyo where she worked her way up to become an administrative assistant in the U.S. Army in General MacArthur's headquarters. There she met and married "Med", a young flying officer and a meteorologist. As a military wife, Aya followed her husband wherever he was assigned. That explains why she is very well traveled and also why her resume shows many states where she enrolled in colleges (New York, Alaska, Ohio, Maryland). She graduated from the University of Colorado, Boulder, with a Bachelor of fine arts degree. She also took continuing education courses at the University of Denver, University of Northern Colorado, Colorado State University and University of Colorado. She taught fine arts at Broomfield Junior High School and Louisville Middle School, retiring after 20 years.

Her list of professional and community services and her awards recognizing her countless volunteer work will fill several pages, but some of her significant contributions and experiences are recorded here.

Pine Ridge Indian Reservation (South Dakota) was the next part of her life. After Aya retired in 1991, she and her husband "became unpaid co-directors of an American Indian fund devoted to the education of able and motivated American Indian high schoolers." Of the 70 students under their guidance, she says about half of them went to college, some to graduate school, and some went back to their community. She considers the eight years she spent with these students an exciting and fulfilling time. She guided them to improve their lives and to develop their sense of responsibilities towards their tribe.

American Friends Service Committee (AFSC) – Aya became a Quaker where she found expression for her passion for humanitarian volunteerism and her devotion to non-violent and peaceful endeavors. At first concentrating on local activities in the Denver area, she became involved with the Regional Committee and eventually with the National Committee. She was active in the Nationwide Women's Program, the Asian Pacific Program, the Third World Coalition, Affirmative Action, Community Relations and the Youth Task Force.

Boulder Asian Pacific Alliance (BAPA) was an important event for her. Aya, together with Narayan, Ramani Kandan and Shirley Fong (now in San Francisco) co-founded the BAPA in 1994. It is a grassroots coalition of representatives from the diverse Asian Pacific American populations, organized to become a more active part of the Boulder community and to impact social change. BAPA represents Hmong, Laotian, Cambodian, Vietnamese, Korean, Chinese, Japanese, Filipino, Malaysian, Indian, Thai, Nepalese and other groups of Asian Pacific American background. As Aya says, "We are not seen as viable members of the community and are largely invisible. We are often not included in the policy-making decisions that affect our communities." Aya is involved in BAPA activities including the annual Boulder Asian Festival and the Boulder Asian Film Festival.

In order to commemorate the Day of Remembrance, in 2002 Aya was charged with organizing an exhibit of photographs, newspaper clippings, and other materials to remind the people of Colorado of the injustice done to the Japanese Americans during WWII. Due to her resourcefulness, Aya was able to gather 70 different items for display complete with captions. Every year thereafter, this photographic exhibit has been displayed in various venues.

Aya was recently featured on Denver Television Channel 57 when she was interviewed by Gil Asakawa about her World War II experiences. The Asian Public Media wanted topublicize Aya's remarkable journey.

Aya has many words of wisdom and advice not only for Asian Pacific Americans but also for white Americans. Through our interview with her and a DVD of an interview conducted by Erin Yoshimura and

Gil Asakawa, Aya shares many significant experiences and defining moments that struck her and formed her philosophy of life.

The first one was the shock when she saw wounded soldiers in the Utica General Hospital (1945). She was not prepared to see the bandaged soldiers with missing parts of their faces or limbs. On the way home from the hospital, while waiting for the bus, a white woman, a total stranger, screamed at her face, "You d---d Japs!" How can you deal with real anger? How does one go beyond that and do something about it? In that instant, Aya began to understand that no one can determine who she is. It helped her see that anger is within oneself and that we don't know the unintended consequences of what we say or do. Although crying is good because it shows a piece of compassion for other people, it does not help much.

Another defining moment was her experience in Stockholm, Sweden where her family lived for two years. She was impressed by the Swedish benign form of government. She hoped that the U.S. could be more benevolent and can be good to its people. In Sweden, they took especially good care of their women and children.

Later in her life, when she became a Quaker, she became a strong anti-war person. "War," she says, "is a useless way to solve problems. War is legalized killing. War is wrong." As a Quaker, she is more attentive to women's issues and to people of color, human relations. She feels that people are thirsting for opportunities to talk to each other.

At a United Nations Conference on women's issues in Kenya, she experienced another instance that truly touched her. The Kenyan women she met had nothing, but they were singing songs – tribal, cultural songs. She was struck by their joy and realized what reality means and that we are part of it. They sang, whether they were happy or not, but that was what kept them going.

When asked whether Japanese Americans are still angry about the injustice in their incarceration during WWII, she answered, "There are still some remnants of anger among the older Japanese Americans but we need to move on."

"Race is a difficult subject to talk about," Aya said. "When whites say that the U.S. can go anywhere in the world and solve their problems – economic, social, political, that is racist. Sometimes, they feel guilty about what they have done in the past." Aya wisely says, "All of us have a common experience, then when we begin to understand, we don't have to feel guilty. I want to start a conversation through faith communities and talk about how we can get together and understand one another and move on. We must value each person for whoever they are."

On the subject of education, Aya says, "What is missing in education is that kids grow up without understanding their role in the larger world."

With regards to preserving our APA culture, Aya emphasizes that we need to preserve humanity not just one ethnic culture. We must have a way to share our historic culture with the rest of the world, not just within ourselves.

## Marge Taniwaki

Marge Taniwaki is co-producer of La Lucha Sigue, a Latin American-Caribbean news program and sits on the board of community radio station KGNU. She has been active in many civic groups and social movements. In 1969 she was the first woman elected president of the Mile-High Chapter of the Japanese American Citizens League. Marge helped organize the first pilgrimage to Colorado's Amache internment camp. She is active in the struggle to save Manual High School, her alma mater, and is involved in the ongoing struggle for police accountability in Denver.

**A three-generation photo of her family**

**Vicki Taniwaki - Kimiko Yamada - Marge Taniwaki**

# They Are Pointing at Someone Again to Take Them Away

by Marge Taniwaki

On each desert pilgrimage, the grit in my mouth evokes memories of the almost daily sandstorms blowing across our desert prison, the home of my earliest childhood.

Insects crawled up and down the tar-papered walls of the barracks as we shuffled in line, waiting in the desert heat to eat at the mess hall. My mother's voice grew sharp each time she warned me to never touch the barbed-wire surrounding us because other internees had been shot and killed for getting too close to the fence. I often looked up from my play at the guard tower overhead where a US soldier watches me, cradling a rifle with a fixed bayonet.

One hundred twenty-thousand of us were hauled away to isolated inland camps, prisoners because we were demonized as minions of the Japanese war machine. Two-thirds of our number was US-born citizens. Many of the elders would have been citizens, but Japanese nationals were not allowed to apply for US citizenship until 1952.

Before WWII, Japanese in America had turned marginal lands into productive farms. War hysteria and the brief time permitted us to put our affairs in order led to many Japanese selling their homes and property for pennies on the dollar to opportunistic former friends and neighbors.

After four years of imprisonment, the camps closed, we received $25.00 and a bus ticket to go elsewhere and pretend life was normal, pretend we were average.

We'd lost all our material belongings in our eviction from our homes and were traumatized by the shock, denial, and undeniability of the surreal experience of being rounded up and shipped away like cattle to far-away barb-wired outposts.

What we now know as Post Traumatic Stress Disorder was near universal as well as the Stockholm Syndrome in which one identifies with one's captor in a perverse form of assimilation.

Our parents abandoned the Japanese language and encouraged our conformity to Euro-American customs. Our goal was to look into a mirror and see George Washington or Jackie Kennedy.

About 60% of Japanese-American males and up to 70% of Japanese-American women "out-marry" -- almost always to Euro-Americans -- raising questions about what underlying factors are causing such a huge rate of out-marriage. Most ethnicities perpetuate themselves through "in-marriage", but Japanese-American society seems determined to fragment.

Manzanar, the camp in which I was imprisoned, is located 100 miles west of Death Valley in California. Upon our release in late 1945, my family could not return to our home in Los Angeles because my mother was considered a risk to national security.

She was born in San Francisco in 1914, but was educated in Japan from elementary through high school. Even after the war, U.S.-born citizens of Japanese ancestry who had been educated in Japan could not return to their homes on the west coast!

In late 1945, we resettled in the inner-city ghetto of Five Points in Denver, Colorado, where we became part of the Japanese community to which clustered former internees from all around the country, but especially from Amache, just past Lamar on Hwy. 50 near the town of Granada. Amache was one of the ten major US concentration camps. It is located in Prowers County very near the Kansas border.

In 1976, the Denver-based Asian American Community Action Program (AA CARP) helped organize the first pilgrimage to Amache. AA CARP was made up mostly of third generation Japanese, Chinese, Filipino and multi-racial university students as well as older community activists. My mother, Kimiko Yamada, translated for the Japanese elderly whom we served through a hot-lunch program at the Buddhist Temple and a summer food distribution program at the Japanese Association Hall.

We gleaned vegetables and produce from local Japanese farmers, then sacked and delivered the fresh produce to the elderly who lived in single rooms, cooked on hotplates and rarely interacted with anyone.

About fifty persons made the first pilgrimage to Amache. For the third-generation Sansei, it was a quest for the truth about our history and how the United States had unjustly imprisoned our families. For the first-generation Issei, it was the opportunity to go back and see the place where they were forever marked as different, as hateful, and as suspicious. Few second-generation Nissei took part: they seemed generally busy assimilating.

Our eyes welled with tears as our buses turned off the highway onto the dirt road leading to the small Amache cemetery. We strained to imagine hundreds of tar-papered barracks, the latrines, the clotheslines and mess halls amid today's waist-high sagebrush, chaparral, and tumbleweeds. We stepped onto the hot sand and the constant wind blew dust in our faces, grit between our teeth. Trees planted by the internees grew stunted, framing the outlines of the long-gone barracks.

An owl startled us as it swooped out of a tree, disturbed by our scuffing through shards of wartime dishes, broken in the long-gone mess halls. We pulled weeds in the cemetery, swept the rough headstones, propped up flowers in tin cans and said a prayer for the dead.

We promised that we would never forget. But what good does it do to remember if today's news is replete with reports of how it is all happening again? So many today are silent (as if they have forgotten!) while Arabs and Moslems are being targeted for surveillance and proofs abound that new camps are being readied.

## Carolyn Takeshita

Carolyn Takeshita was a child when she was interned at an American concentration camp in Poston, Ariz. While there, her father received permission to move the entire family to Colorado to work as farm hands during the sugar beet harvest season. The family was able to stay in Colorado after the harvest and not be returned to the Camp because of the support for Japanese Americans by Gov. Ralph Carr.

Because of racial housing restrictions, the family settled in the section of Denver, where there were many hotels and apartment houses that were rented to Japanese. When the Amache Camp was closed many Japanese Americans came to Denver, temporarily, to live until it was safe to return to the West Coast. Carolyn remembers, as a child that Denver had a large section along Larimer and Lawrence Street with many Japanese owned businesses, consisting of restaurants, hotels, dry cleaners, grocery and dry good stores. The family moved back to California for a short period of time but returned to Denver. Carolyn spent her teenage years attending Cole Junior High and Manual High School both of which hard a large Japanese student population. She then earned her Bachelor's and Master's degrees in education and speech pathology from the University of Denver. She taught at the University of Denver and Jefferson County Public Schools and often speaks publicly about the Japanese American experience and their confinement behind barbed wire during World War II

Her husband Mickey volunteered to help dismantle two former (barracks) living quarters where the Japanese Americans lived) from the Heart Mountain Internment camp in Wyoming. The barracks were shipped and reassembled at the Japanese American National Museum in Los Angeles for a profoundly moving exhibit on the confinement of American citizens of Japanese ancestry during World War II. Currently, Carolyn is very involved in Chibi No Gako, a Japanese American Heritage school for children, second grade through seventh, the Japanese American Resource Center of Colorado and the Japanese American Community Graduation Program. In the past, she also served on the Asian Roundtable, the Governor's Asian Pacific Advisory Council, and the Denver Public Schools Asian Advisory Council.

# Chapter 18

# SUMMARY, RECOMMENDATIONS AND CONCLUSION

The Asian Pacific Americans interviewed in this book represent a cross-section of the diverse Asian ethnic communities in Colorado. Nestor and Nora Mercado met many of the interviewees during their decade's long experience as editors of the *Asian Pacific American Times,* and after they retired. Likewise Alok Sarwal, working as an APA community service provider, developed indelible relationships with many intervees, creating experiences that have contributed to this book. The people interviewed are community leaders who are catalysts of change that enhance the visibility of APAs in Colorado. Their struggles and successes, and their ideas and opinions, can provide much-desired inspiration for the younger generation - our true hope for the future.

Through the years, APAs have learned that they should no longer think of themselves just as Filipinos, Chinese, Japanese or Koreans, or another group, concerned only with their own issues or concerns. They need to develop a unified multi-ethnic outlook such that they can see beyond their smaller spheres of interest and be able to "seek common ground while respecting differences."

## Summary of Interview Responses

1. A majority of the interviewees desire to blend the better of two cultures, Western and Eastern, for themselves and their children. Some, however, have concluded that culture is not static but dynamic and that changes must be made to adjust to American society. American-born generations of APAs have more readily adjusted, especially in regard to popular culture and the use of new technologies, but they still embrace important elements of Asian culture.

2. APAs would like to be perceived as Americans and not as foreigners. This is especially true for APAs born and raised in America.

3. APAs should strive to have more of a voice in government and decision-making bodies, at all levels: local, state, and national. Some are anxious for the next generation and to begin preparing for such activities as soon as possible.

4. There is an emerging desire to work together toward the growth and development of APA communities and also for humanitarian causes. Some of the interviewees have been doing these activities for quite some time.

5. More APA teachers/professors need to be hired at all levels of education. Materials dealing with APA history, cultural norms and social values are needed in K-12 and college curricula.

6. The main reasons expressed by interviewees for their remarkable successes in their businesses or professions primarily include hard work, the desire to succeed, and their positive outlook on life. APA people are generally hard working and motivated.

7. Successful parents, in general, become good role models who display strong work ethic for their children to emulate, excel academically and develop as successful professionals and good citizens.

8. Many of the successful entrepreneurs have been challenged by the economic opportunities available in the U.S., an aspect that encourages them to take matters in their own hands and take charge of their careers.

9. Many APAs have more conservative orientations toward their attitudes and behaviors, but respect people with other points of view.

10. Racism continues to be an important issue, and at times, quite blatant and emotional. This feeling was expressed by many interviewees, and perhaps, needs resolution at a deeper level by continuous discussion.

11. The APAs who came to the United States to obtain advanced education, and who decided to remain in America, eventually became successful American citizens.

Finally, the featured articles speak for themselves. These individuals are outstanding citizens and important assets to the state and nation. The authors salute all of them for their ideas, hard work, talents and achievements.

## Summary of Recommendations

Based on the answers obtained from the interviews and from other published sources and researchers of Asian studies, the following is a summary of recommendations.

1. **Improve the educational systems**: The educational system should be more responsive to the changing realities of the demographic composition of Colorado and the nation. More material on APAs should be included at all levels of the educational system.

2. **Offer more leadership training for APAs**: APA students should be encouraged to develop their leadership abilities in order to be more effective in their adult lives, professions and socio-political environments.

3. **Build sustainable relationships between APAs and major media organizations**: Mass media needs to improve and increase their coverage of APAs. Also, more APA students should be encouraged to pursue media-related careers, especially in journalism.

4. **Participate in politics**: All stakeholders should encourage APAs to enter the political arena at all levels of government.

5. **Debunk the "model minority myth":** Point out that not all APAs are academically successful or have high-level jobs or incomes. This myth places barriers for APAs, who have educational, economic, health and human services needs, from obtaining appropriate assistance.

## Conclusion

In their ten-year period, as editors of the *Asian Pacific American Times*, the Mercados tried their best to enhance the visibility of Asian

Pacific Americans in Colorado. In this book, all three authors pursue the same goal but with more intensity and fervor.

Asian Pacific Americans should no longer be invisible and voiceless. The three authors have asked themselves the same question many journalists have asked, "How can this happen?" APAs are one of the fastest growing populations in the country. The projected number of U.S. residents in 2050 who will identify themselves as APA is 33.4 million, which will be eight percent of the total U.S. population. Also, how can APAs remain invisible in the U.S. given their increasing social, economic, and cultural contributions and influences?

There are many books published on Asian Pacific Americans in the U.S., but this one is different because it is specifically written about the experiences of and by APAs in Colorado. However, we also have addressed issues that are relevant for Asian and Pacific Americans elsewhere. We believe this book provides information for filling the gaps of existing knowledge about APAs.

The highlights of the book are the interviews with a cross-section of APAs in Colorado. We hope our readers will not only learn about the APAs, but will also find inspiration from them. We also hope that the APAs will unite and work together for addressing all the existing problems.

Finally, as stated in the beginning of the book, we hope we have captured and conveyed the America of Colorado's Asian and Pacific Americans. We further hope that as a consequence our readers now have a better understanding of an important segment of American society and that they will want to continue the journey for learning more on this topic.

# APPENDIX

## Working Together

**An experience of the Aurora Asian/Pacific Community Partnership**

By Frankie Anderson, Partnership Secretary

### Leadership

Leadership is sometimes defined not by a style so much as by those who follow. The Partnership took the position that all communities within the APA communities would be invited to participate in the meetings and activities of the organization. It took time to develop trust, and many 'official' leaders within the APA communities chose to stand by outside of the organization and just watch what might happen. Part of the success of the Partnership actually lies in the fact that, rather than be told who the leaders were in the communities, by keeping an all-inclusive 'open door', leaders were developed as monthly meetings took place. A different Asian Co-Chair and Co-Chair Elect lead the organization annually (along with the City Co-Chair, the Small Business Coordinator), and the Partnership Steering Committee became a conduit for leadership development as an unnamed 'benefit' of membership. Many Co-Chairs went on to become leaders of other APA organizations. Of course, the Partnership can't take the credit for an individual's leadership style, nevertheless, the Partnership did help to identify potential leaders, and became a role model for organizational structure, inclusiveness (insisting upon being Pan-Asian in outreach) and, changing out the leadership through the years.

### Communication

Communication is a key to any relationship, and the Partnership's aim was to communicate by being available to members of the Steering Committee, helpful and impartial. The Partnership as a whole could take credit for ideas and achievements, not just a few members. A small example is that minutes were written, not to single out individuals, but to summarize main points. At the same time, main points were described in enough detail to give those who missed a meeting enough information to make informed decisions. It should be noted that the Partnership agreed to use e-mail as a means of communication to save time and money. The reality is that some leaders were not comfortable with the 'impersonal' e-mail and the Partnership lost valuable contributions from a few as a result. Partnership members are incredibly patient to listen to discussions in thick accents and differing points of view. Consensus is usually achieved on the most practical matters, even if philosophies are at odds. When communications break down, all it generally takes to set things straight is a personal apology, a smile and a genuine gesture of friendship.

## Friendship

The foundation of the Partnership is built on friendships. More than putting on an event, holding a meeting or getting the roster put in order, the Partnership is able to reach out to various APA communities and say, "You're welcome here." The objective has always been to learn, be educated about, Asian/Pacific cultures. The Steering Committee members admit that they don't all identify with one another on identical plains of thought. Issues, language, talents, level of organization within groups, leadership styles, etc., are different for different cultures. But since one of the goals is 'education', members realize we're all learning. One of the most frustrating problems with the Partnership is sitting through a meeting with little input, but hearing the input after the fact. This is partly due to personal conflicts, but also to the excellent attribute of listening first, acting later. It is sometimes difficult to work 'backwards'; nevertheless, the objective is to keep friendships in tact, and conflicts are usually resolved. It seems somewhat trivial, but the inability for many Asian leaders to say a definitive 'No." is exceptionally difficult in knowing whether or not to move forward with ideas. On another point, the Partnership agreed to keep religion and politics out of this particular organization's activities. No wonder we are all friends.

## Organizational skills

In the beginning of the Partnership (early 1990s), Colorado APA leaders who were also members of the Partnership were not strong in organizational skills. This is not a criticism. It could have been because the leaders who were strong in organizational skills were already heavily involved in their own communities' activities and not with the Partnership. Nevertheless, the Partnership Steering Committee seemed to learn from the efficiency and methodical methods of a municipality. Roberts Rules of Order were still being learned by many, the need to speak eloquently yet briefly was no easy assignment, follow-up to meetings required a few reminders and personal contact, etc. The Pan-Asian approach to programs was still fairly unique. Over the years, consistency in leadership has had a positive effect on the APA communities. Many Partnership Steering Committee members are currently effective leaders metro-wide, getting diverse communities to take on "bigger and better" projects. As an example, the Aurora Asian Education Awards Program is aiming towards a metro-wide APA Education Initiative that not only recognizes outstanding APA students in academics and leadership, but that can address educational issues on a broader scale.

## Pursuing Goals

It is not uncommon for Partnership Steering Committee members to 'test' ideas through the Partnership. That's one of the benefits of friendship. What do you think? That's not a bad question. Goals are more easily achieved when there is some momentum behind them. An example is in the production of the Aurora Asian Film Festival for 10 years. Even though all the goals of the film festival were not achieved, such as getting cross-cultural attendance to ALL the films, the lasting results include: understanding the value of film as an art form; recognizing that APA filmmakers have a voice; realizing that all film will not always depict Asian cultures as positive; not everything is about tourism and setting a culture in a good light as though there are no problems to address; feature films and documentaries by APA filmmakers and about APA cultures may not always become 'favorites.' Nevertheless, film can educate, enlighten and enliven conversation, all of which could lead to effective change within communities. It must be noted that, without regular consistent meetings, goals are rarely defined, much less pursued by the majority. The Partnership's success is partly due to consistency in meeting together.

## Constructive Discussion

If I could offer any help, it would be to speak with leaders one-on-one about how their insistence on one point of view is hurting others. Being willing to listen to criticism offered in friendship, or to differing opinions, is a strong leadership quality. I wonder how such strong people as individuals can sit back and allow one point of view sway the opinion of an entire group, even if there is a better way. If leaders can't speak up in a single meeting, how can they speak up about public issues, address the needs of entire APA communities, voice problems on a larger scale that impact the greater community? One can be in disagreement without being disagreeable. However, not voicing objections in a constructive way, could lead to unnecessary setbacks. It seems to me that it's okay to have healthy discussions, even if an event is placed on the 'back burner'. What is the objective, to hold an event, for instance, or to hold an effective event?

As an example, after over 15 years of impactful activities, the Partnership has made the strategic decision to take a one-year 'rest' to concentrate on more effective planning, adding fresh voices to the Steering Committee, and re-evaluating the structure and programs of the organization. This could be viewed as 'death' to the organization, but even if that's the ultimate outcome, which is highly unlikely, the question should always be asked, "Is the organization existing only for the sake of existing?" In other words, what collaborations would be more effective than doing it alone? What leaders, if any, are ready to go forward with the organization? Is it possible to re-organize and become more effective?

## Connecting Communities

It has been my honor to get to know so many leaders within the different APA communities. I'm 'just a secretary', but my goal is to be the best 'staff' and supporter as possible as long as I hold the position with the Partnership. I also work for the city of Aurora in business development, which is how I came to become involved with the Partnership. There are many different activities within the various communities from year-to-year, so in an unofficial way, I represent the city of Aurora at many events or in various committees, mainly because I wanted to be involved and city officials are not always available. Even though I am currently a paid employee of the city, much of my time with the Partnership is a volunteer activity.

By being helpful and 'present' over the years, friendships have grown unawares. By maintaining a good database, I help connect people with people, pointing those interested in culture to different cultural organizations and activities, and suggesting the right leader for the right situation. I field many calls for assistance, and if I can personally help, it is my pleasure to do so. One of my strengths is follow-up, so after meetings or activities, I keep on top of the next steps. I'm rarely the 'idea' person, but once in a while, I manage to add value to ideas in the making. As I'm often told, I'm the "glue" that holds the Partnership together. Nevertheless, I'm not satisfied with that description, because I don't want things to fall apart if I move on - - I'd rather be a quiet supporter that goes unnoticed when my time comes to 'take the next step' in new directions.

On one other point, on a weekly basis, I actively study the music and culture of Bali, Indonesia as a founding member of the music and dance performance group, Gamelan Tunas Mekar.I feel better connected to the Asian/Pacific communities through this in-depth approach to study (since 1988) than I would if I had no involvement with another Asian/Pacific culture on a regular basis. Most importantly, I want to remain a 'Friend' of the Partnership and the APA communities now and in the future. This keeps me motivated to always learn more and participate with enthusiasm.

## U.S. - Philippine Relations – Historical Context

The following articles will reaffirm the close relationship between the United States and the Philippines, especially during World War II when the Filipinos fought side by side with the American Armed Forces in the Pacific under General Douglas MacArthur (1941-1945).

## God Bless America – The Song

In recent times of pain and suffering, God Bless America has become the most beloved song in the United States together with America, the Beautiful.

Interestingly enough, God Bless America is also very popular in the Philippines especially among the older generation. During the Second World War, the Philippines, being a commonwealth under the United States, was drawn into this war. On December 8, 1941, all radio stations in the Philippines played God Bless America as nearby airfields around Manila were bombed incessantly by enemy forces. The Filipinos kept faith in America throughout those dark years. Everyone learned this song by heart.

Yes, indeed, God has blessed America, not only with its culturally diverse people but especially with its natural beauty: the breath-taking views of the snow-capped mountains, the sweeping meadows, the majestic pine trees along clear streams. In fall, the changing colors of the foliage never fail to astound us. In spring and summer, the wildflowers always delight us. In winter, the quiet stillness of the land covered with snow makes us kneel in gratitude for its awesome beauty.

The song, God Bless America has continued to inspire the country and awakened patriotism especially during these recent tragic times. The people have become more united against international terrorism and have risen as one in defense of our democratic way of life. As we face a critical period in our history, we believe the American spirit and compassion of our people will be able to extricate our country from the present economic recession and from other malaise. Besides, our early economic recovery is critical to the world economy.

In our quest for material prosperity and spiritual rebirth, there is an "invisible force" that guides the destinies of men and nations. The songs, God Bless America and America the Beautiful will forever be enshrined in the hearts of our people regardless of faith. They represent the inner feelings of a great nation.

## The "Bataan Death March" Remembered

The Bataan Death March is one of the most tragic World War II events in Philippine history.

On April 9, 1942, General Edward King, Commander of the combined American and Filipino troops in the Bataan peninsula, surrendered with his 78,000 men to the Japanese imperial forces. This triggered the forced hike of sixty-five kilometers from Bataan to San Fernando, Pampanga under scorching summer sun by day, and malaria-infested mosquito bites by night; not to mention massive dysentery from drinking polluted canal waters along the way. Those who suffered from extreme fatigue, hunger and thirst, were beaten up, shot or bayoneted to death.

On May 6, 1942, one month after the march started, General Jonathan Wainwright, Commander of the United States Armed Forces in the Far East (USAFFE) in Corregidor, surrendered the remnants of his entire force to the Japanese. Loyal Filipinos set up a guerilla network and galvanized it to carry on their unfinished fight. It served as an active, effective resistance movement against the Japanese Occupation, which ultimately helped the Liberation of the Philippines in 1945.

To understand why the Philippines gave unwavering support to the United States during the Second Global Conflict and why American military installations became the targets of enemy bombardments is very important. When the war broke out in December 1941, the Philippines was a Commonwealth government under America. Then-President Franklin D. Roosevelt issued an executive order on July 26, 1941 that brought the entire Philippine armed forces under the command of General Douglas MacArthur.

This series of historical events bonded an enduring friendship between the US and the Philippines, even long after July 4, 1946, when the Philippines became an independent country. At present, both countries are committed in fighting international terrorism. US military assistance, notwithstanding a mutual defense agreement with the Philippines, is limited to training of Filipino soldiers and supplying military equipment in the fight against the Abu Sayyaf in Mindanao. However, the Philippines has been supporting the US in humanitarian and peacekeeping activities in many instances. Presently, the Philippines has a close relationship with Japan, which is providing economic assistance to the country.

The recognition and compensation for Filipino veterans who fought with the US during WWII has been stalled for years when the U.S. Congress reneged on the pledge with the passage of the Recission Act of 1946. This Act virtually deprived Filipino WWII veterans of their rights, privileges and benefits accorded European and allied veterans who also served under the US flag.

Sadly, It has been an uphill battle for Filipino veterans. The US should honor its commitments to the Filipino veterans, who fought bravely and loyally under the American flag during WWII.

## Benefits for Filipino Veterans of WWII Long Overdue

When the Filipino veterans of WWII, as well as the Filipino guerillas, fought with the United States Armed Forces in the Far East (USAFFE) against the Japanese, they understood that they would be provided with the same U.S. military benefits as other WWII veterans when the war ended.

In a letter to then Senator Dennis de Concine, dated March 11, 1994, Michael L. Smith, Commander of the U.S. Army, stated, "Our Government in the 1940's was racist. We interned Japanese-Americans, but did not intern German Americans or Italian Americans. We know today that this was wrong. Our country has a history of correcting past wrongs. It is time we correct this one." In its editorial of June 17, 1947, the Washington Post wrote, "We cannot help thinking that if Congress reviews this situation with full realization that those men were members of our own Army and subject to its orders, it will see that a grave injustice has been done." Furthermore, the U.S. Attorney General ruled in 1946, "there is no doubt that a Filipino soldier in active service in the U.S. Army, is a veteran of WWII." Of the estimated 200,000 Filipinos who fought with the U.S. military in WWII, only one small group -- the "old scouts" (officially called Philippine Scouts) who were full-fledged members of the U.S. Army units received full veteran's benefits.

The "vanishing" veterans prefer an Equity Bill sponsored by Senator Daniel K. Inouye (D. Hawaii) that would provide a more comprehensive package, including pensions for disabled and low-income veterans.

With the passage of Senate Bill 1345, known as the Veterans Benefit Act of 2007 under the leadership of U.S. Senator Daniel K. Akaka (D-HI), Chairman of the Veteran’s Affairs Committee, a separate bill in the House of Representatives still has to be voted on. It is hoped that this will close the Filipino Veteran's quest for recognition and benefits. As Rep. Mike Honda (D-CA) said, "This is not a Republican or Democrat issue – This is an American issu."

# Two Asian National Heroes

This chapter is about two Asian national heroes one from India and, one from the Philippines. The authors believe they will serve as shining examples for our youth to pattern their lives.

The national heroes have sacrificed their lives for their beliefs. Their strength and passion during their lifetime demonstrate rare qualities, which are noble and inspiring. They have made the world a better place: Mahatma Gandhi and Jose Rizal.

## Mahatma Gandhi: India's National Hero

## Relevance of Mahatma Gandhi Now!

By Manu Raval

On the168th day after Indian Independence Mahatma Gandhi was felled by three despicable bullets from a diabolical Hindu of extreme fanaticism. That evening Gandhi was late for his daily interfaith prayers, not confined only to the Judeo-Christian religions but all great religions of universal humanity. All his life he was punctual by minutes but that day he was late for the prayer grounds by eleven minutes because he was engaged with Sardar Patel, the Deputy Prime Minister of India, in discussing the complex problems created by the partition of India by a sinister design of the departing British paramountcy. One of the most complex problems discussed was doing full justice to the Muslim minority leaving India and those who stayed back and now constitute the second largest population in a non-Muslim nation. He wanted the minority to be treated likc siblings in spite of the holocaust created by them before Independence and after partition during the exodus beyond borders. His theory of Hindu-Muslim brotherhood was not acceptable to a small Hindu clique which subscribed to the extreme Hindutva which never existed in that religion's long history of seven thousand years.

Conditions in India when Gandhi returned from South Africa after his triumphant victory through his new weapon of non-violence, first time in politics in human conception, conditions in India were deplorable. Eight hundered years of Muslim invasion and 200 years of British rule had impoverished the richest country before 1000 years of the dark age.

Gandhi awakened the hybernating behemoth out of its dark age slumber to a nation pulsating with its past glory, present awareness and future dream of self-rule. There is no field of human activity that he did not touch and there is none that he touched and did not turn into gold. He was primarily a patriot with political zeal, saintly aspirations and a social reformer of rare imagination and courage. From humble beginnings of a British trained barrister-at-law who could not open his mouth before the Bombay High Court in his first appearance, he rose to be the greatest man on earth in his millennium.

But the current fashionable trend in India and elsewhere is to criticize the great Indian Trinity of Gandhi-Nehru- Patel without ever knowing the facts surrounding the momentous events that took place in a short time of a decade which liquidated all the European Empires, which thrust 400 hundred years of slavery on subject nations of Asia and Africa. Out of total ignorance of their contribution to the world events, persons born after independence criticized the trio without any knowledge of their life, mission and their contribution to world peace and personality.

We are aware that their contemporaries killed Socrates and Jesus because they could not bear the stark truth they taught. They did not like the utter reality they brought to their opinionated compatriots and the latter had no other option but to get rid of them by assassination. That's what happened to Gandhi, John Kennedy, Martin Luther King, Anwar Sadat and the Israeli prime minister killed by his own race. The last three were converted to total non-violence by reading what Gandhi had done and said.

When we are facing frightening terrorism, impending nuclear and chemical outbursts by "evil" powers, is it in our interest to blame Gandhi for what he did not do rather than appreciating what he did do for humanity? Misleading, envious and ignorant criticism arises out of personal agenda, lack of self-esteem and the misguided enthusiasm to show oneself, " better than thou". Let's search our souls and read a man whose life and work we are incapable of assessing in one life.

## Jose Rizal Alonso Mercado Rizal:
### Universal Man and Philippine National Hero

On December 30 every year, Filipinos and Filipino Americans commemorate the martyrdom of Dr. Jose Rizal, the national hero of the Philippines. Dr. Jose Rizal was born in Calamba, Laguna, Philippines in June 19, 1861 and was shot in Luneta Park (now Rizal Park) in Manila by the Spaniards on December 30, 1896. A martyr to the cause of freedom, he became the national hero of the Philippines.

On the eve of his execution, he wrote his famous poem, "*Mi ultimo Adios*" (My Last Farewell) dedicated to his family, the Filipino people and his country. He also wrote two novels: *Noli me tangere* and *El Filibusterismo* which kindled nationalist fervor in many of his countrymen.

Ranked with the world's geniuses, he was a physician, poet, linguist, novelist, artist, scientist, historian, educator, nationalist and internationalist, Rizal was the greatest product of the Philippines. He was recognized as the leading Filipino of his time by Ferdinand Blumentritt, an Austrian professor with whom Rizal corresponded for ten years. Not only is Rizal the most prominent man of his own people, but the greatest man the Malayan race has produced. He graduated from the Universidad de Madrid. He later specialized in ophthalmology in Paris and Germany.

Rizal learned 22 foreign languages using five effectively – Tagalog, Spanish, English, French and German. He traveled extensively winning numerous friends of different races, creeds, social classes and vocations. He fraternized with statesmen, scholars, writers and scientists.

Rizal believed in the brotherhood of men, irrespective of creed and nationalities, in universal peace and justice and in the happiness and welfare of humanity. He envisioned a new world order in which men are free of tyranny, bigotry and slavery, where justice reigns and where all nations live together in fraternal harmony. According to Rizal, "Genius has no country, genius bursts forth everywhere, genius is like light and air, the patrimony of all; cosmopolitan as space, as life, as God."

Rizal was the first person in all of Asia to advocate and introduce ideas, which can be called modern democracy and Western liberalism. As early as the eighteen-eighties, years before Gandhi or Sun Yat-Sen began their fight for freedom, Jose Rizal, through his essays, letters and novels, was already espousing such principles as the worth and dignity of the individual, the inviolability of human rights, the innate equality of all men and races, the necessity for constitutional government and due process of law, popular sovereignty as the basis of all political authority, faith in human reason and enlightenment, the right of the masses to public education, and belief in social progress through freedom.

The first champion of racial equality in Asia, Rizal expressed that there was no difference in innate mentality and capacity between Westerners and Asians – that cultural and environmental rather than biological or racial factors played a part in determining the degree and scope of social development. Jose Rizal is recognized not only as a great Filipino but also a great citizen of Asia – an inspiration wherever people cherish freedom and resist oppression in all its forms.

# China's Contributions to the World

By John H. Yee

(Reprinted from APA Times, June 2003, p. 7)

If one looks at an historical world map, circa 100BC-100AD, one would see there were two greatest empires in the world that co-existed during that time. In the West, there was Rome, an empire extending around the Mediterranean, which the Romans called Mare Nostrum, "Our Sea". In the Orient, there was the expansive empire of Han China.

Just as modern Europe is so deeply imbued with Greco-Roman cultural values, language and traditions such as: rule of law, importance of the individual, the arts, languages of Latin origin, to name but a few, Asia, in the same way, has been greatly affected by the early and continuous historical and cultural developments of China and India.

China's contribution to the world has been many. Silk, gunpowder (probably not a good idea), paper and printing are items of common knowledge. The Chinese written language – a completely non-Indo European language, along with Chinese culture, has extended to countries of the Far East as well as some parts of Southeast Asia. It is not difficult to see the significance of this as one realizes that language is not merely a tool for human communication but is also the tool with which we use to think. In the realm of ideas, Confucianism (the philosophy advanced by the sage Confucius, a way to find order and harmony in society) and the Civil Service System (later adopted and modified by Great Britain and America) were developed. But more significantly, was the development of Daoism (Taoism) by the sage Laotzu (Laozi). It is the Chinese philosophical approach to the theory of relativity, seeking harmony and oneness with nature.

While Confucianism emphasizes harmony in society, Daoism (Taoism) stresses man's need to seek unity and harmony with nature. Dao is the eternal force that governs the universe. But Dao is beyond the possibility of human explanation, just as the Void cannot be fully explained. But think of the following Dao concepts: There is beauty because there is ugliness. There is good because there is evil. One cannot lose if one does not possess. Creating but not possessing, working, yet not taking credit, when work is done, and then forgotten. Therefore it lasts forever. Shape clay into a vessel, it is the space within that makes it useful. From the non-being "empty space" of a house, comes the utility of a house. Think about the significance of "emptiness". Sainthood, kindness, and ingenuity are three outward forms. It is more important to see simplicity, realize one's true nature and cast off selfishness and temper desire. Mastering others requires force; mastering one's self needs real power. Dao abides in non-action (non interference) yet nothing is left undone. A truly good man does nothing, yet nothing undone. A foolish man is always doing, yet much remains to be done. The softest thing in the universe overcomes the hardest thing in the universe. That without substance can enter where there is no room. Hence I know the value of non-action. Teaching without words and working without doing are understood by very few.

The great philosophy and religion of Buddhism came from India. It was founded by the great Indian prince Siddhartha Gautama who, in the sixth century BC, renounced his nobility to seek the truth. After finding the truth through many years of searching, he preached his first sermon of the Four Noble Truths at the Deer Park near Benares, India. He was known as the Buddha, the Enlightened One. Buddhism spread throughout India and beyond during the reign of the good king Asoka, (circa 269-232 BC). During the years between 520-527 AD, the Indian monk Bodhidharma came to China. He is the founder of a branch of Buddhism known as Chan, or better known by its Japanese name Zen. Daoism blended very well with Chan Buddhism, which taught that there is no Buddha, save the Buddha that is in one's own nature. Only by meditation and thus coming to know one's own nature can enlightenment be attained. The Absolute is immanent in every man's heart...Only one thing avails – to discover the unreality of the World by contemplating the Absolute which is at the root of one's own heart.

Like the popular song, "What the World Needs Now, Is Love, Sweet Love", we need to take stock of what's happening in the world today. In the West, particularly in America, we have rapidly advanced in technology and science, but in the area of human relations we have regressed to the point where we may have the highest standard of living in the world, but in most cases, a very low quality of life. Some sociologists have described the American way of life as the pursuit of loneliness – with a "flush toilet" approach in dealing with domestic and foreign problems.

Except for Siamese Twins who are born attached to each other, human beings are usually attached to one another in two ways. One is through "role". The task or duty we need to perform based on the role we play in society, such as father, son, auto mechanic, soldier, etc. Each society has certain rules, mores, customs one is advised to follow. The second is through "affect" – which has to do with feelings and emotions derived from various human relations, conditions or circumstance, which one experiences. What effects "Affect" hasn't changed since the days of Confucius or Shakespeare. That is to say, what makes one happy, sad or angry is basically the same for most people now as it was 2,000 years ago. "Role" on the other hand has not only changed but also proliferated, as witnessed by the increase in volume of the Yellow Pages over the last 50 years. The problem lies in that a great many modern roles, as required by many modern technologies, have become so mechanized and impersonal as to be in conducive to good mental health. Human contacts, human relations, social welfare, all have become mechanized and very impersonal. We are forced to be lonely in a crowd. Such conditions create negative "affect".

The late Jawaharlal Nehru, the first Prime Minister of India once said that modern man is a scientific giant but a spiritual infant. This bespeaks the root of our problem today, for "what good is it that a man gains the whole world, but loses his soul?"

The renowned English traveler, writer and poet Rudyard Kipling wrote in the nineteenth century: "East is East, and West is West, but never the twain shall meet." That might be true at a different time and different place. But today, the word "global" is not merely a concept, it is a reality; and as the world advances in science and technology, it is time for us to pause and take stock of our lives. In our pursuit of life, liberty and happiness, there is the need for the search for meaning. Today, East not only meets West, but also they have become interdependent. The human condition and the quality of life may very well be greatly enhanced, if we were to combine the science of the West with the wisdom of the East. Is it not better to seek harmony and oneness with nature rather than trying to conquer it?

A Zen poem reads:

***Sitting silently, Doing nothing,***
***Spring comes, And the grass grows by itself.***

# Table 3-1-08

## Census Counts, Estimates and Projections of Asian American Population in the U.S. and In Colorado (1980-2007)

| | 1980 Census | 1990 Census | 2000 Census (Alone) | 2000 Census (Combined) | % Growth (1990 – 2000) | 7-1-2006 Est. | 7-1-2007 Est. |
|---|---|---|---|---|---|---|---|
| USA-total Pop. | 226,545,805 | 248,709,873 | 281,421,906 | 281,421,906 | 13.15% | 298,754,819 | 301,621,157 |
| APA in USA | 3,726,440 | 7,273,662 | 10,641,833 | 13,176,683 | 81.16% | 15,257,436 | 15,702,275 |
| % | 1.64% | 3.21% | 3.78% | 4.68% | | 5.11% | 5.21% |
| AA in USA | 3,466,421 | 6,908,638 | 10,242,998 | 12,275,972 | 77.69% | 14,731,380 | 15,165,186 |
| % | 1.53% | 2.78% | 3.64% | 4.36% | | 4.93% | 5.03% |
| Colorado - total Pop. | 2,889,735 | 3,294,394 | 4,301,261 | 4,301,261 | 30.56% | 4,766,248 | 4,861,515 |
| APA in Colorado | 34,257 | 59,862 | 97,639 | 134,858 | 125.28% | 169,081 | 175,552 |
| % | 1.19% | 1.82% | 2.27% | 3.14% | | 3.55% | 3.61% |
| AA in Colorado | 32,733 | 57,122 | 93,099 | 124,439 | 117.85% | 156,369 | 162,387 |
| % | 1.13% | 1.73% | 2.16% | 2.89% | | 3.28% | 3.34% |
| Korean | 5,143 | 11,339 | 16,395 | 20,304 | 79.06% | 33,748 | |
| | 0.18% | 0.34% | 0.38% | 0.47% | | 0.71% | |
| Chinese | 3,997 | 8,208 | 14,898 | 19,292 | 135.04% | 35,033 | |
| | 0.14% | 0.25% | 0.35% | 0.45% | | 0.74% | |
| Japanese | 10,841 | 11,402 | 11,571 | 18,676 | 63.80% | 18,182 | |
| | 0.38% | 0.35% | 0.27% | 0.43% | | 0.38% | |
| Vietnamese | 3,247 | 7,210 | 15,457 | 17,108 | 137.28% | 26,514 | |
| | 0.11% | 0.22% | 0.36% | 0.40% | | 0.56% | |
| Filipino | 2,764 | 5,426 | 8,941 | 14,716 | 171.21% | 17,400 | |
| | 0.10% | 0.16% | 0.21% | 0.34% | | 0.37% | |
| Asian Indian | 2,565 | 3,836 | 11,720 | 13,809 | 259.98% | 21,110 | |
| | 0.09% | 0.12% | 0.27% | 0.32% | | 0.44% | |

**Notes:**

Sources: US Census Bureau: Census Counts (1980, 1990, and 2000)

1. Annual National and States Population Estimates-- Characteristics (Age, Sex, Race, and Hispanic Origin), 2000-2007
2. Projected population of the U.S. by Race and Hispanic Origin, 2000-2050, 3-8-2004
3. APA means Asian and Pacific Americans, AA means Asian Americans, and Census data taken alone or Combination of Interracial-Claims

# Asian American Media in Colorado

**Asian Avenue Magazine**
Christina Guo, Publisher
P..O. Box 27502
Denver, CO 80227-0502
303-534-6868
**editor@asianavenuemagazine.com**

**Asian Pacific American Times**
Joseph Noli Lopez, Publisher
14720 E. Navarro Pl.
Aurora C0 80014
303-699-7294
**noli@apatimes.com**
(under reconstruction)

**Asian Public Media of Colorado**
Fran Campbell, Executive Director
720-480-8310
**frandenver@yahoo.com**

**AsiaXpress.com**
Joe Nguyen, Editor
303-587-3569
**joe@asixpress.com**

**Chinese American Post**
Mimi Feng, Editor
11 Federal Blvd., Suite 1-2
Denver, CO 80219
303-934-1773
**chinesepost@aol.com**

**Colorado Chinese News**
Wendy Chao, President/Editor
1548 W. Alameda Ave. #A
303-722-8268
**wychao@hotmail.com**

**Colorado Times Newspaper**
Yuen Shin, Editor/Publisher
1450 So. Havana St. #336
Aurora, CO 80012
303-337-7797
**coloradotimes@gmail.com**

**Himalayan News**
Mohan Ashtakala, Publisher/Editor
1305 Krameria St., #H-166
Denver, CO 80220
303-393-1893
**himalayan_news@yahoo.com**

**Korea Times Denver**
Hyun Joo Kim, Editor
3001 So. Jamaica Ct. #210
Aurora, CO 80014
303-750-9500
**ktdenver@koreatimes.com**

**Korean News**
Ki Sun Cho, Editor
3053 So. Steele St.
Denver, CO 80210
303-757-5300

**Nikkeiview.com**
Gil Asakawa, Editor
**http://nikkeiview.com**

**Shin Ho Dung Weekly**
2000 So. Havana St., Suite A
Aurora, CO 80014
303-695-8696

**The Korea Daily**
Sang-Yong Park, Editor
2222 So. Havana St., Suite D
Aurora, CO 80014
303-338-1234
**koreadailyco@gmail.com**

**Thoi Bao**
Hau Ngo, Publisher
1091 So. Federal Blvd.
Denver, CO 80219
303-742-0101
**ngogiahau@gmail.com**

**Viet Business News Magazine**
Dung Doan, Publisher
P.O. Box 19553
Demver. CO 80219
720-297-2816
**vietbizw004@yahoo.com**

**Vietnamese Public Radio of Colorado**
Hung Vu, Director
2200 W. Alameda Ave., #3
Denver, CO 80223
**vnus@vnus.net**

**Vietnamese Television Network**
Que Nguyen, Director
1091 so. Jasper St.
Aurora, CO 80017
303-752-0228
**qunnguyen109@msn.com**

**Vox Koreana**
Thomas Park, Editor
10020 E. Girard Ave. #270
Denver, CO 80231
**voxkoreana@gmail.Com**

**Weekly Focus**
Hyun-Joo Kim, Chief Editor
11000 E. Yale Ave. #119
Aurora, CO 80014
303-751-2567
**weeklyfocus@gmail.com**

**Y-Dan Vietnamese Newspaper**
Thang Nguyen
2306 So. Benton Ct.
Lakewood, CO 80227
303-374-3865
**huytvn@yahoo.com**

## List of Contact Information to Organizations

- **asiaxpress.com** Joe Nguyen, editor-in-chief
- **Asian American Student Services, University of Colorado, Denver**
  Campus Box 132, North Classroom 2014 303-556-2578
  Peggy Lore, Director; plore@cudenver.edu
- **Asian Pacific Development Center (APDC)**
  1544 Elmira St. Aurora, Co 80010 303-365-2959
  1825 York St., Denver, CO80206 303-393-0304
- **Asian/Pacific American Student Services**
  Colorado State University, 212 Lory Student Center
  Fort Collins, CO 80523
  Phone: (970) 491-6154; Fax: (970) 491-2574
  Reagan.Le@ColoState.EDU http://apass.colostate.edu/
- **Boulder Asian Pacific Alliance – Boulder Asian Festival**
  P O Box 21406 Boulder, Colorado 80308-4406
  303.499.0108
- **Boulder Asian Film Festival**
  Alan O'Hashi is the Festival Director (303-910-5782)
- **Census Counts and estimates:** Richard Lin at (303) 866-4989
  or at Colorado State Demography Office.
- **Christina Yeh Dance Studio**
  Studio South: 3871 E. Erwin Place, Centennial, CO
  80122 Studio North 1060 Bannock St., Denver CO
  80204. 303 596-6168' 303-770-8011. or, visit:
  christinayehdance@yahoo.com
- **Colorado Asian Health and Promotion (CAHEP)**
  6795 E. Tennessee Ave. #427,433 Denver CO 80224
  303-300-5263/5269 www.cahep.org
- **Colorado Kannada Koota**
  Prabhakara Rao, Founder/Senior Distinguished Member
  303-979-4193, 303-979-7812, PrabRao@comcast.net
- **Denver Asian Pacific American Commission (DAPAC)**
  201 W. Colfax Ave. Dept. 2102, Denver, CO 80002
  720-913-8450 www.denvergov.org
- **Empowerful Changes™** Erin Yoshimura, Trainer/Coach
  Emotional & Cultural Intelligence
  303-200-0031 empowerful.com

- **Filipino American Community of Colorado (FACC)**
  1800 Harlan St., Edgewater, CO 80214
  303-233-6817, 2008-2009 President: Jay LaVigne
- **Friendship Bridge**
  3560 Highway 74, Suite B-2 Evergreen, CO 80439
  303-674-0717
- **The Hindu Temple and Cultural Center of the Rockies (HTCC)**
  8375 S. Wadsworth Blvd. Littleton, CO 80128
  303-948-9693, www.hindutempleofcolorado.org
- **Hmong-American Association of Colorado (HMAAC)**
  President: Chue Feng Lee; Past President: Somxai Vue
  303-430-0680, info@hmongcolorado.org
- **Iglesia ni Cristo (INC)** 2605 W Mosier Pl, Denver, CO 80219
  (303) 922-6960
- **India Association of Colorado (IAOCO)**
  2008 President: Deepak Kaithakhapuzha
  720-290-5874, iaocdenver@yahoo.com
- **Lao-Hmong American Coalition (LHAC)** yang.chee@comcast.net
  President-Emeritus/Founder Yang Chee
- **Nathan Yap Foundation**
  8400 E. Prentice Ave. #808 303-817-8400
  info@nathanyipfoundation.org
- **nikkeiview.com** by Gil Asakawa
- **Pacific Mercantile Co.** 1925 Lawrence St., Denver, CO 80202
  303-285-0293; FAX: 303-295-2753
- **Pacific Pride and Island Hearts**
  sandra.bodnar@schriever.af.mil
- **Philippine American Society of Colorado (PASCO)**
  Current President: Elbert Eloriaga 720-810-2780
  www.**coloradopasco**.org
- **Polynesia-Pacifica Foundation of Colorado**
  Current President: Helen Simms
  elenasimms@cs.com or
  www.geocities.com/polynesia-pacifica/
- **Queen of Vietnamese Martyrs' Catholic Church (Wheat Ridge)**
  4655 Harlan, Wheat Ridge, CO 80033
  (303) 431-0382
- **Saint Lawrence Korean Catholic Church**
  4310 South Pitkin St., Aurora, CO 80015
  303-617-8265

- **Sikh Temples in Colorado**
  Guru Amar Das Niwas, 303-494-6806
  Guru Ram Das Ashram, 970-243-545
  Colorado Singh Sabha, 303-697-6374
- **Simpson United Methodist Church**
  6001 Wolff St. Arvada, CO 80003 303- 428-7963
- **Tri-State/Buddhist Temple (Japanese)**
  1947 Lawrence Street, Denver, CO, 80202
  (303) 380-8972
- **Uplift Internationale --**President: **Jaime Yrastoza,** DMD
  www.upliftinternationale.org, mndyrz@yahoo.com
- **Unified Nationalist Vietnamese Committee of Colorado (UNVCC)**
  1st President**:** Sum C. Nguyen scn1693@netzero.com
- **University of the Philippines Alumni Association of America (UPAAA) Colorado Chapter:** 303-298-0498
  Erlinda Rojas-Santos, Ph.D., Founding President
- **Vietnamese Elderly Association of Colorado (VEAC)**
  615 S. Federal Blvd., suite 103, 105 (303) 922-3033

# BIBLIOGRAPHY

Agoncillo, Teodoro. *A History of the Filipino people.* Quezon City, Philippines: Garotech Publishing, 1990.

Bulosan, Carlos. *America is in the heart.* New York, NY: Harcourt Brace and World, 1946. Republished by the University of Washington Press, 1973.

Cao, Lan and Novas, Himilic. *Everything you need to know about Asian American history.* New York, NY: Penguin Books, 1996.

Chao, Jessica. "Asian American philanthropy: Acculturation and charitable vehicle." Pp. 57-79 in Pier C. Rogers (ed.), *Philanthropy in communities of color.* Indianapolis, IN: Association for Research on Nonprofit Organizations and Voluntary Action, 2001.

Carnes, Tony and Yang, Fenggang. *Asian American religions: The making and remaking of borders and boundaries.* New York, NY: New York University Press, 2004.

Chandrasekar, S. (ed.). *From India to America: A brief history of immigration, problems of discrimination, admission, and assimilation.* La Jolla, CA: Population Review Publications, 1982.

Choy, Bong Youn. *Koreans in America.* Chicago, IL: Nelson-Hall, 1979.

Colorado Department of Public Health and Environment. *Racial and ethnic health disparities in Colorado.* Denver, CO: author, 2005.

Ebihara, May, Mortland, Carol, and Ledgerwood, Judy (eds.). *Cambodian culture since 1975: Homeland and exile.* Ithaca, NY: Cornell University Press, 1994.

Endo, Russell. "Japanese of Colorado: A sociohistorical portrait." *Journal of Social and Behavioral Sciences*, v. 31 (Fall 1985), pp. 100-110.

Endo Russell, Sue Stanley, and Wagner, Nathaniel (eds.). *Asian Americans: Social and psychological perspectives.* Palo Alto, CA: Science and Behavior Books, 1980.

Espina, Marina E. *Filipinos in Louisiana.* New Orleans, LA: A.F. Laborde & Sons, 1988.

Galang, Evelina M. (ed.). *Screaming monkeys: Critique of Asian American images.* Minneapolis, MN: Coffee House Press, 2003.

Glodava, Mila (ed.). *In search of a dream.* Denver: Filipino-American Community of Denver, CO: 1974.
Gupta, Roxanne Kamayani. *A yoga of Indian classical dance: The yogini's mirror.* Rochester, VT: Inner Traditions, 2000.
Hallmark, Kara (ed.). *Encyclopedia of Asian American arts.* Westport, CT: Greenwood Press, 2007.
Harvey, Robert. *Amache: The story of Japanese internment in Colorado during World War II.* Lanham, MD: Taylor Trade, 2004.
Hosokawa, Bill. *Colorado's Japanese Americans: From 1886 to the present.* Boulder, CO: University Press of Colorado, 2005.
Huang, Guiyou (ed.). *Asian American poets.* Westport, CT: Greenwood Press, 2002.
Japanese American Citizens League. *A lesson in American history: The Japanese American experience.* San Francisco, CA: Japanese American Citizens League, 1996.
Kim, Hyung-chan (ed.). *Korean diaspora: Historical and sociological studies of Korean immigration and assimilation in North America.* Santa Barbara, CA: ABC-CLIO, 1978.
Korean Embassy. "Korean religious dances." Retrieved May 2008 from http://www.asianinfo.org/asianinfo/korea/perform/religious_dances.htm.
Lee, Esther Kim. *A history of Asian American theater.* New York, NY: Cambridge University Press, 2006.
Lee, Gus. *China Boy: A novel.* New York, NY: Dutton, 1991.
Lee, Gus. *Honor and duty.* New York, NY: Knopf, 1994.
Lee, Gus. *Courage: The backbone of leadership.* San Francisco, CA: Jossey-Bass, 2006.
Lee, Josephine. *Performing Asian America: Race and ethnicity on the contemporary stage.* Philadelphia, PA: Temple University Press, 1997.
Lee, Robert. *Orientals: Asian Americans in popular culture.* Philadelphia, PA: Temple University Press, 1999.
Leonard, George (ed.). *The Asian Pacific American heritage: A companion to literature and arts.* New York, NY: Garland Publishing Company, 1999.
Ling, Amy (ed.). *Yellow light: The flowering of Asian American arts.* Philadelphia, PA: Temple University Press, 1999.

Mercado, Nestor J. *God bless America: A discussion of family values*. With a special chapter by Elnora M. Mercado. Denver, CO: Kimco, 1995.

Oh, Seiwoong. *Encyclopedia of Asian American literature*. New York, NY: Facts on File, 2007/

Ourada, Patricia K. "The Chinese in Colorado." *Colorado Magazine*, v. 29 (Oct. 1952), pp. 274-284.

Panlilio, Maria Concepcion. Art, literary, lifestyle columns in various issues of the *Asian Pacific American Times,* 1996-2006.

Rudolph, Gerald E. *Chinese in Colorado, 1869-1911*. Thesis presented to the faculty of the Graduate College, University of Denver, 1964.

Scharager, Adam. *The principled politician: The Ralph Carr story*. Golden, CO: Fulcrum, 2008.

Soberano, Rawley G. "The Diversity that is Asia." *Philippine/Asian American Times*, February, March, April 2003.

Takaki, Ronald. *Strangers from a different shore: A history of Asian Americans*. Updated and revised edition. New York, NY: Little, Brown and Co., 1998.

Um, Hae-kyung (ed.). *Diasporas and interculturalism in Asian performing arts: Translating traditions*. New York, NY: RoutledgeCurzon, 2005.

Villangca, Caridad Concepcion. *The second wave: Pinay, pinoy (1945-1960)*. San Francisco, CA: Strawberry Hill Press, 1987.

Wei, William. "The Anti-Chinese movement in Colorado: interethnic competition and conflict on the eve of exclusion." *Chinese America: History and perspectives*, 1995, pp. 179-193.

Whitman, John W. *Bataan our last ditch: The Bataan campaign, 1942*. New York, NY: Hippocrene Books, 1990. 754 p.

Wong, Deborah. *Speak it louder: Asian Americans making music*. New York, NY: Routledge, 2004.

Younhap New Agency. *Korea-U.S.A. centennial, 1882-1982*. Seoul, Korea: Yonhap News Agency, 1982.

Zia, Helen. *Asian American dreams: the emergence of an American people*. New York, NY: Farrar, Straus and Giroux, 2000.

Zonkel, Phillip. "Naples woman researches Long Beach's first Filipino.." Long Beach Press Telegram, May 23, 2005

# INDEX